FIGHT TO THE FINISH

www.penguin.co.uk

Fight to the Finish

The First World War –
Month by Month

Allan Mallinson

BANTAM PRESS

LONDON · NEW YORK · TORONTO · SYDNEY · AUCKLAND

TRANSWORLD PUBLISHERS
61–63 Uxbridge Road, London W5 5SA
www.transworldbooks.co.uk

Transworld is part of the Penguin Random House group of companies
whose addresses can be found at global.penguinrandomhouse.com

Penguin
Random House
UK

First published in Great Britain in 2018 by Bantam Press
an imprint of Transworld Publishers

Maps by Lovell Johns

A CIP catalogue record for this book is available from the British Library.

ISBN 9780593079140

Typeset in 10/14.5pt ITC Stone Serif by Jouve (UK), Milton Keynes
Printed and bound in Great Britain by Clays Ltd, Elcograf S.p.A.

Penguin Random House is committed to a sustainable
future for our business, our readers and our planet. This book
is made from Forest Stewardship Council® certified paper.

MIX
Paper from
responsible sources
FSC
www.fsc.org   FSC® C018179

1 3 5 7 9 10 8 6 4 2

*Endpapers: cartoon map of Europe at the beginning
of WWI by J. Amschewitz, 1914.*

'Germany elected to make it a finish fight with England.
Now we intend to see that Germany has her way.
The fight must be to the finish.'

David Lloyd George, secretary of state for war
(later prime minister), September 1916

'The only wonder to the compiler of these records is that any sure
fact whatever should be retrieved out of the whirlpools of war.'

Rudyard Kipling, *The Irish Guards in the Great War*

CONTENTS

List of Maps   xi

Preface   xiii

Introduction: In the Time of the Breaking of Empires   1

Prologue: The Alliances   3

PART ONE: 1914 – 'OVER BY CHRISTMAS'   5

1   August: To Arms!   7

2   September: 'Miracle on the Marne'   15

3   October: The Wars of the World   21

4   November: The Sea Dog   25

5   December: 'Wipers'   32

PART TWO: 1915 – DEADLOCK   41

6   January: Eastern Approaches   43

7   February: Cruiser Rules   48

8   March: Drum-fire   54

9   April: Gallipoli   59

10   May: 'Gas!'   68

11   June: Those Magnificent Men   76

12   July: Askaris   82

13   August: Suvla Bay   89

14   September: Loos   95

15   October: The Gardeners of Salonika   102

CONTENTS

16   November: 'Mespot'   109
17   December: Casualties   115

PART THREE: 1916 – 'PURE MURDER'   121

18   January: Enter Haig   123
19   February: The Blood Pump   131
20   March: Q vs U   139
21   April: A 'Stab in the Back'   147
22   May: The Victory that Looked Like Defeat   157
23   June: Pillars of Wisdom   167
24   July: Sixty Thousand Casualties before Breakfast   175
25   August: Exit Falkenhayn   183
26   September: The Rude Mechanical   193
27   October: 'Preparedness'   200
28   November: Attrition   207
29   December: The Welsh Wizard   214

PART FOUR: 1917 – DEFEAT; AND DELIVERANCE   221

30   January: The Turnip Winter   223
31   February: Biblical Terms   230
32   March: Alberich   234
33   April: The Cruellest Month   241
34   May: All Goes Quiet on the Western Front   248
35   June: Messines   252
36   July: 'Passchendaele'   259
37   August: 'O for a beaker full of the warm South'   266
38   September: 'Boom'   272
39   October: Caporetto   278
40   November: Cambrai   285
41   December: 'How the devil can we finish this war?'   291

CONTENTS

PART FIVE: 1918 – *FINIS GERMANIAE*   299

42 January: Peace without Victory?   301
43 February: Doughboys   307
44 March: *Kaiserschlacht*   314
45 April: 'Backs to the Wall'   325
46 May: The Cruel Sea   332
47 June: The Bread Offensive   340
48 July: *Friedensturm*   348
49 August: The Black Day of the German Army   355
50 September: The Return Push   362
51 October: *Tout le monde à la bataille!*   369
52 November: The Eleventh Hour   375

Conclusion: The War to End All War?   385

Annex A: The Armistice Terms   389
Annex B: The War for Civilization – The Reckoning   391
Further Reading   393
Picture Acknowledgements   397
Index   399

MAPS

The Schlieffen concept   8–9
Coronel and the Falklands, 1914   26
The Dardanelles   60–1
Colonial Africa in 1914   83
The Balkans: offensives and counter-moves, 1914–17   103
Eastern Front   124
Area of operations for U-boats in northern coastal waters   140
The 'Easter Rising', Dublin, 1916   148
Battle of Jutland, 30 May–1 June 1916   158
Suez and Sinai   168
The first day of the Somme, 1 July 1916   176
Battle fronts in mid-1916   184–5
Palestine   292
Kaiserschlacht: the German offensives of 1918   315
Western Front   376

Preface

The genesis of this book goes back many years, but to four years ago in particular, when, just before the centenary of the outbreak of the First World War, Simon Pearson of *The Times* asked me to write a monthly commentary of a thousand words or so on the course of the conflict. I am most grateful for Simon's advice and encouragement during that project, which in many ways has shaped this book. I have of course expanded on those monthly pieces, and – although each retains a certain unity – they have been edited with a view to reading as a continuous narrative rather than as discrete articles. This latter task has been the assured work of my copy-editor, Gillian Somerscales, who as ever (she has edited all my non-fiction save the first) has been the most diligent assayer of the text. I am, of course, indebted to Simon Taylor, my editor at Penguin Random House, who over very many years has steered my writing with the deftest of touches. I am most grateful once again to Auriol Griffith-Jones for her indexing, Liane Payne for the picture research, Lovell Johns Ltd for the clarity of the maps, Phil Lord for his design, Steve Mulcahey for another most striking cover, and Katrina Whone, managing editor, for pulling it all together as if it were no effort at all.

The text is not referenced or footnoted – very deliberately. This is not a polemical work or an academic treatise, whose propositions must be backed by scrupulous citations. It is a narrative designed to flow. Although some books are mentioned in the text itself, if every statement, quotation and allusion were to be catalogued, the multi-tude of primary and secondary sources would change not just the book's weight but its complexion.

At the end of the book, however, I offer – principally for the British reader – a short list of further reading.

Introduction

In the Time of the Breaking of Empires

From the opening shots to the signing of the Armistice, the First World War lasted some fifty-two months. It was fought on, or in the waters of, six of the seven continents, and in all of the seven seas. For the first time, the fighting was on land, at sea and in the air. It became industrial, and unrestricted: poison gas, aerial bombing of cities, and the sinking without warning of merchantmen and passenger ships by submarines. Military and civilian casualties probably exceeded forty million. During its course, four empires collapsed – the German, Austro-Hungarian, Russian and Ottoman. In all its military, political, geographical, economic, scientific, technological and above all human complexity, the First World War is almost impossible to comprehend.

Day-by-day narratives – excellent reference books – can be dizzying for the reader trying to make sense of the whole. Freer-flowing accounts help to convey the broader trends and factors, but offer less of a sense of the human dimension of time. The month is a digestible gauge. We remember months, because months have names, because they are linked to the seasons, and because they have their own characters. Looking at the First World War month by month reveals its complexity while preserving the sense of time.

Fight to the Finish is not intended to be a comprehensive account of the fighting, nor of all the other factors in the war. It does not examine the conflict's causes or its consequences. It aims simply to give a picture of each of those fifty-two months: what was the predominant action, how and why it came about, and how it looked. The narrative, while not Anglocentric, is told in the main from a British perspective.

It is called *Fight to the Finish* because that is what David Lloyd George, the British prime minister for twenty-four of those fifty-two months, and minister for munitions and then secretary of state for war for the preceding eighteen, said that it must be. Such a demand – in effect, the Germans' unconditional surrender – required a national effort of unprecedented proportions. It was this that gave the war its unique and terrible face, which *Fight to the Finish* seeks to portray.

Prologue

The Alliances

1839: Britain, France, Prussia, Austria and Russia sign the Treaty of London, which requires Belgium to remain perpetually neutral, and by implication commits the signatory powers to guard that neutrality in the event of invasion.

1879: Germany and Austria-Hungary enter into a treaty: the Dual Alliance.

1882: Italy joins Germany and Austria-Hungary in the Triple Alliance. (In 1914 she would remain neutral, stating that the Triple Alliance was defensive and that both Austria and Germany had acted aggressively.)

1892: France and Russia enter into a treaty: the Dual Entente.

1902: Britain signs a treaty of mutual naval assistance with Japan to safeguard British interests in the Far East.

1907: After *rapprochement* with France (the Entente Cordiale), which settles years of colonial disputes, Britain joins Russia and France to form the Triple Entente. While France and Russia conclude treaties of mutual assistance, however, Britain has no formal treaty commitments.

3

PROLOGUE

1908: Austria-Hungary annexes Bosnia – formally still a province of the Ottoman Empire – which contains many Serbs. Serbia and her ally Russia protest strongly. An enlarged Bulgaria declares independence from the Ottomans.

1912: Britain signs a treaty of mutual naval assistance with France. In the event of war with a third party or parties, France will take responsibility for the security of the Mediterranean, while Britain will take care of the North Sea.

1912–13: A series of wars in the Balkans. Serbia emerges as the main beneficiary and a perceived threat to Austria-Hungary.

PART ONE

1914

'Over by Christmas'

28 June: Archduke Franz Ferdinand, heir to the Austrian throne, and his wife, visit Sarajevo in Bosnia, a province of the Austro-Hungarian Empire. A lone assassin, Gavrilo Princip, shoots and kills them both. Austria believes the killer is linked to the Serbian nationalist movement.

23 July: Austria-Hungary, with the backing of Germany, delivers an ultimatum to Serbia. The Serbs offer to submit to arbitration, but also begin to mobilize their army.

25 July: Austria-Hungary cuts diplomatic ties with Serbia and begins to mobilize.

26 July: Britain tries to convene a conference of the major European powers to resolve the situation. France, Italy and Russia agree to take part. Germany refuses.

28 July: Austria-Hungary declares war on Serbia.

29 July: Britain calls for international mediation. Russia urges German restraint, but then begins partial troop mobilization as a precaution. The Germans warn Russia, and then begin to mobilize.

30 July: Austria shells Belgrade, the Serbian capital.

31 July: Russia begins full mobilization.

1 August: Germany declares war on Russia. France and Belgium begin full mobilization.

3 August: Germany declares war on France and invades neutral Belgium. Britain delivers an ultimatum to Berlin demanding withdrawal from Belgium. Germany ignores it.

4 August: Britain declares war on Germany. The declaration is binding on the British Empire, including Canada, Australia, New Zealand, India and South Africa.

6 August: Austria-Hungary declares war on Russia.

19 August: President Woodrow Wilson announces that United States will remain neutral.

23 August: Battle of Mons.

26 August: Battle of Tannenberg (East Prussia) begins.

5 September: Battle of the Marne begins.

19 October: Battle of Ypres ('First Ypres') begins.

29 October: Turkish fleet bombards Russian Black Sea coast.

1 November: Russia declares war on the Ottoman Empire.

5 November: France and Britain declare war on the Ottoman Empire.

1

AUGUST

To Arms!

Churchill makes a decisive move seven days before the war

Soon after 11 p.m. on 4 August the Admiralty flashed the signal to His Majesty's ships: 'Commence hostilities against Germany.' Earlier the War Office had sent telegrams to army headquarters bearing the single word 'Mobilize'.

The Foreign Office issued a statement explaining why:

> Owing to the summary rejection by the German Government of the request made by his Majesty's Government for assurances that the neutrality of Belgium will be respected, his Majesty's Ambassador to Berlin has received his passports, and his Majesty's Government declared to the German Government that a state of war exists between Great Britain and Germany as from 11 p.m. on August 4, 1914.

Invading Belgium was merely a means to an end. General Alfred von Schlieffen (1833–1913), the former chief of the *Grosser Generalstab*, the great general staff, had devised a strategy for war on two fronts, which the Franco-Russian alliance made inevitable if Berlin

7

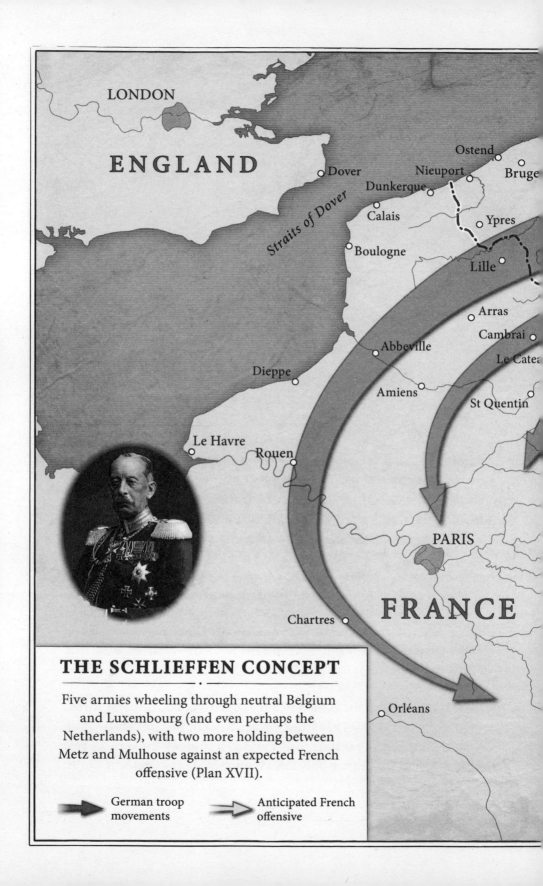

LONDON

ENGLAND

Straits of Dover

Dover

Dunkerque

Calais

Boulogne

Ostend

Nieuport

Bruge

Ypres

Lille

Arras

Cambrai

Le Catea

Abbeville

Dieppe

Amiens

St Quentin

Le Havre

Rouen

PARIS

FRANCE

Chartres

Orléans

THE SCHLIEFFEN CONCEPT

Five armies wheeling through neutral Belgium
and Luxembourg (and even perhaps the
Netherlands), with two more holding between
Metz and Mulhouse against an expected French
offensive (Plan XVII).

German troop
movements

Anticipated French
offensive

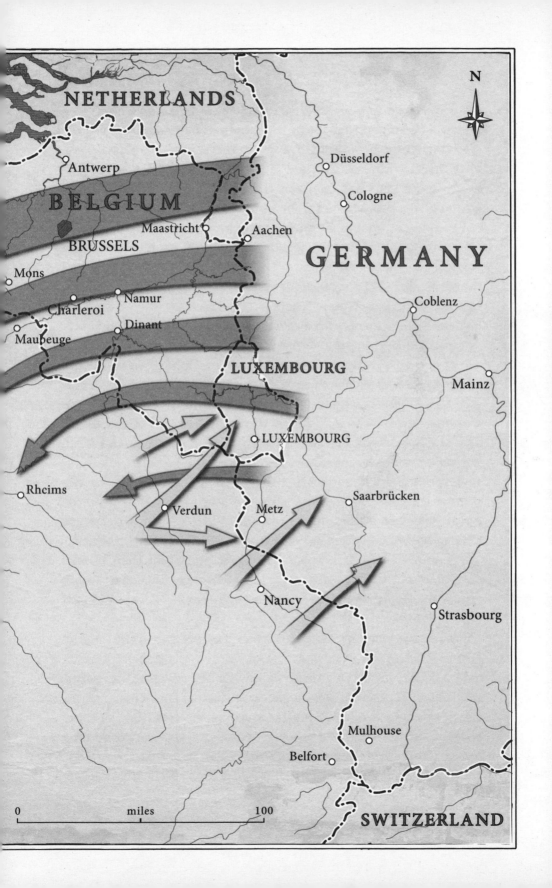

were to declare war on either country. The Schlieffen Plan entailed a huge wheeling movement through neutral Belgium to bypass the strong defences in Alsace-Lorraine on the Franco-German border. Only in this way, he had told the Kaiser, could Germany defeat France quickly enough to be able then to send her victorious troops east to defeat the slower-mobilizing Russians.

By midnight on 4 August every branch of the British government was putting into action its chapter of the 'Red Book', a document without precedent that set out the instructions for transition to war drawn up over the preceding four years by the Committee of Imperial Defence. The first offensive action was taken by the Postmaster-General's department, whose cable ship *Alert* dredged up and cut, or else patched into the British network, the German communication cables in the Dover Straits, severing Berlin's telephone and telegraph connections with much of the world beyond the Central Powers, crucially the Americas. However, one of the most decisive acts of the war had been taken seven days earlier when the first lord of the Admiralty, the 39-year-old Winston Churchill, ordered the Grand Fleet, with all its reservists aboard after a practice mobilization, to steam 'at high speed and without lights' through the Channel to its war stations at the lonely Orkney anchorage of Scapa Flow. At a stroke the Royal Navy had gained mastery of the North Sea and the English Channel, without which no British army could be sent to France. While cruiser patrols from the east coast ports kept the Channel clear of nuisance raids, Admiral Sir John Jellicoe's Grand Fleet would ensure the *Hochseeflotte,* the German High Seas Fleet, stayed in port at Wilhelmshaven.

On the afternoon of 5 August a council of war met in the Cabinet Room. After much discussion the decision was taken to send an expeditionary force to France. Following the meeting the prime minister, H. H. Asquith, appointed Field Marshal Lord Kitchener secretary of state for war. Kitchener, doubting the prevailing military wisdom that the war would be over quickly, at once set out to raise a huge citizen army. Britain, unlike the other major European powers, did not operate conscription; it had a relatively small – though extremely well trained – long-service army, and consequently fewer reservists (former regulars who still retained a reserve liability) it could call up. Nevertheless, of the 100,000 men of the British Expeditionary Force (BEF) – four infantry divisions and a cavalry division – who would go to France as soon as mobilization was complete, some 60 per cent would be reservists. The Territorial Force comprised fourteen divisions, but these were primarily for home defence and could not be compelled to serve overseas. Some units volunteered almost to a man, but it would not be until November that territorials would go to France in significant numbers, and not until 1915 in formed divisions.

Mobilization and the subsequent move of the BEF to the principal embarkation ports of Southampton, Queenstown (Ireland) and Glasgow went like clockwork, thanks to the War Office's well-laid plans – which had come as a surprise to many of the cabinet, who had not been informed of the Anglo-French staff talks authorized by Sir Edward Grey, the foreign secretary, in 1906, by which they had been hatched.

The first British casualties of the war occurred early in the morning of 6 August when HMS *Amphion*, leader of the 3rd Destroyer Flotilla at Harwich, lost 150 of her crew after striking a mine laid by the *Königen Luise*, which the flotilla had sunk the day before off the Thames estuary. Nevertheless, advance parties of the BEF sailed for France the next day without mishap, the main bodies following a week later. The only military force ever to have left Britain other than by sea – Nos 2, 3, 4 and 5 Squadrons (sixty aircraft) of the Royal Flying Corps (RFC) – took off from Dover and crossed the Straits to Boulogne, followed the coast to the mouth of the Somme, and then flew upstream to Amiens. Not every aircraft made it, however: on 12 August, as the squadrons were leaving their stations for the staging field at Dover, a Blériot flown by Lieutenant Robert Skene, with Air Mechanic Raymond Barlow aboard, crashed on take-off from Netheravon airfield in Wiltshire, killing both men.

Thanks to the detailed railway movement plans drawn up by the British and French staffs under the supervision of the War Office's director of military operations, Major-General Henry Wilson, the BEF was more or less complete in its concentration area at Maubeuge, near the Franco-Belgian border on the left flank of the French armies, by 20 August. That same day, however, 90 miles to the north-east, the great fortress of Liège, literally pulverized by the huge siege guns produced in the Krupp and Skoda factories, fell to the German 2nd Army, signalling the beginning of the end of the Belgians' heroic defence of the River Meuse. Next day the BEF began its march north across the border towards Mons to close up with General Charles Lanrezac's 5th French Army and attack the Germans' right flank as they turned south, for the French commander-in-chief, General Joseph Joffre, persisted in his belief that the German main effort was in Alsace-Lorraine, and that their advance through Belgium would therefore be confined to the south-east towards Sedan and Verdun. This belief suited the French military doctrine of *offensive à outrance* – attack to the utmost, to excess even: Joffre had already launched his counter-offensive in Alsace-Lorraine (the famous 'Plan XVII'), where he believed he could disrupt the entire German campaign plan. His 1st and 2nd Armies hurled themselves into the former French *départements* (incorporated in the *Kaiserreich* since 1871), where the German 5th and 6th Armies were in fact preparing not to advance but to repulse the expected French attack. The German right wing, in Belgium, was far stronger than appreciated by Joffre – though not, strangely, by *The Times*'s military correspondent Colonel Charles à Court Repington, who on 12 August published a map showing detailed German deployments, concluding that 'the bulk of the German Armies about to operate against France is to the northward of Lorraine'.

The commander-in-chief of the BEF, Sir John French, though not entirely convinced by Joffre's appreciation, relied nevertheless on the assessments from the *Grand Quartier Général*, the French general staff, and was tardy in getting the RFC into the air to obtain his own strategic intelligence. At Mons on 23 August the BEF ran straight into General Alexander von Kluck's 1st Army, which had – to Joffre's astonishment – crossed the Meuse and turned south.

Fortunately, French, having learned the night before of the great numbers of enemy actually before him, had ordered his troops to dig in along the line of the Condé Canal amid the slag heaps and mining villages of the Borinage. The British army was about to fight a major battle in a built-up area for the first time. 'I took one look at it and thought what a bloody place to live,' said Private Jim Cannon of the 2nd Suffolks: 'I took a second look and thought what a bloody place to fight.'

The desperate encounter at Mons would also be the first test of the revolution in the army's rifle-shooting, prompted by its drubbing at the hands of the Boers a dozen years before. Fifteen aimed rounds a minute with the new magazine-fed Lee–Enfield convinced the Germans that the BEF had many more machine guns than hitherto supposed, though in fact each battalion (of 1,000 men) had just two. Wave after wave of German infantry was brought to a bloody halt by the rapid fire of two divisions of Sir Horace Smith-Dorrien's II Corps (Sir Douglas Haig's I Corps, guarding the right flank in the gap between the BEF and Lanrezac's 5th Army, saw little action that day).

Four Victoria Crosses were won at Mons, two of them by Lieutenant Maurice Dease (posthumously) and Private Sidney Godley (wounded, presumed dead, though taken prisoner) of the machine-gun section of the 4th Battalion Royal Fusiliers, for defending the canal bridge at Nimy, and two by sappers (Royal Engineers), Captain Theodore Wright (killed three weeks later) and Lance-Corporal Charles Jarvis, for laying demolition charges on the bridges under fire. Jarvis had left the colours in 1907 and was within months of the expiry of his reserve liability when he received his recall telegram.

Outnumbered and pummelled by heavier artillery, II Corps was forced off the canal towards evening. On learning that Lanrezac's army had also suffered a major reverse, and from the RFC that the Germans were manoeuvring to outflank the BEF on the left, that night Sir John French ordered a general withdrawal.

So began the retreat from Mons, which would continue for ten gruelling days until the Germans could be checked at the Marne. Smith-Dorrien would make a controversial stand at Le Cateau three days later when, having lost contact with Haig's corps the other side of the Forest of Mormal and the River Sambre, he stood his ground for a morning with three divisions (the 4th Division having just arrived from England) and the cavalry division, in the British army's largest battle since Waterloo. Though with some loss, II Corps imposed such a check on Kluck's 1st Army that the BEF was able to continue the retreat in reasonable order.

Schlieffen's Plan seemed to be going well, and not only on the Western Front. In the east, the German army, which expected to have to hold off Russian spoiling attacks as the bulk of the Tsar's forces – the reservists – slowly mobilized, not only held the attacks but mounted a spectacularly successful counter-offensive.

As soon as Berlin had declared war, two Russian armies, only partially mobilized, had at once marched into East Prussia – as vividly described in Aleksandr Solzhenitsyn's novel *August 1914*. Things began well for the Russians, whose 1st Army under General Paul von Rennenkampf defeated eight divisions of the German General Friedrich von Prittwitz's 8th Army at Gumbinnen on 20 August. Simultaneously Aleksandr Samsonov's 2nd Army moved to threaten the German rear.

Prittwitz panicked and announced that he intended withdrawing to the Vistula river, which would have meant abandoning most of East Prussia including the capital-fortress, Königsberg. He was at once replaced by Field Marshal Paul von Hindenburg who, with his new chief of staff Erich Ludendorff – names that would later become famous on the Western Front – immediately launched a counter-offensive. By 27 August Samsonov's 2nd Army had been surrounded in a double envelopment at Tannenberg; by 30 August his entire command had disintegrated, the Germans taking 92,000 prisoners and Samsonov committing suicide. A week later, Rennenkampf's 1st Army would lose another 100,000 at the Battle of the Masurian Lakes.

2

SEPTEMBER
'Miracle on the Marne'

The Schlieffen Plan is thwarted within sight of Paris

On Sunday, 30 August, exactly a week after the BEF's first, bruising battle at Mons, followed by six days of fighting retreat, the commander-in-chief, Sir John French, wrote in his diary: 'I have decided to retire behind the Seine to the west of Paris, if possible in the neighbourhood of St. Germain. The march will occupy at least 10 days.'

The massive German hook through Belgium, in execution of the 'Schlieffen Plan', had taken the allies by surprise, and the three French armies on the Franco-Belgian and Luxembourg borders were in full retreat. On their left the BEF had taken over 10,000 casualties; withdrawing from the fight would leave the French left flank in a perilous position.

When French's telegram announcing his intentions reached the War Office the next day, an alarmed prime minister, Asquith, told the secretary of state for war, Lord Kitchener, to go at once to France to 'put the fear of God into them'. Just after midnight on 1 September, Kitchener set off in uniform by special train from Charing Cross and fast cruiser from Dover to see his fellow field marshal.

As he crossed the Channel in the grey dawn, one of the BEF's most heroic actions was being fought at Néry, a farming village in the valley of the Oise. The 1st Cavalry Brigade had bivouacked for the night and were waiting for the early-morning mist to clear before continuing the retreat, the six 13-pounder guns of L Battery Royal Horse Artillery drawn up as if on parade, ready to move. When the mist lifted, however, the brigade found themselves over-looked by high ground 600 yards to the east, which the German 4th Cavalry Division had occupied during the night. The Germans at once opened a furious fire, cutting down L Battery's men and horses and destroying three of the guns. Led by the battery captain, Edward Bradbury, the survivors scrambled to unhook the other three and bring them into action, then fought an unequal duel for an hour in which two of the guns were destroyed, the ammunition ran out and Bradbury was killed. He and the last two gunners in action, Battery Sergeant-Major George Dorrell, at thirty-four a vet-eran of the Boer War, and 28-year-old Sergeant David Nelson from County Monaghan, were awarded the VC. After recovering from wounds both returned to service and were commissioned, Dorrell rising to lieutenant-colonel, and Nelson – killed in action in 1918 – to major. The VCs and No. 6 Gun, the last to remain in action, are on permanent display at the Imperial War Museum.

Later that morning Kitchener met French at the British embassy in Paris. The meeting was frosty, not least because the commander-in-chief thought it improper for the secretary of state to be in uniform. As a minister, Kitchener could not give him orders; as a field mar-shal, he could. In the event, persuasion was enough. French agreed to stay in the line and conform to the movements of General Lanrezac's 5th Army, remaining, in effect, under the operational control of General Joffre, the French commander-in-chief. Joffre, belatedly realizing that the German main effort was being focused not on Alsace-Lorraine but on Belgium, had at last begun to move troops by rail west from the Franco-German border, but had advised the government to quit Paris for Bordeaux.

Fortune now favoured him. The RFC, shepherding the BEF from

the air, together with their French counterparts operating from Paris, reported that the movement of German troops was shifting south-eastwards, away from the capital. And then a blood-stained map was found on a dead German staff officer, marked with pencil lines indicating that the German axis of advance was indeed south-east.

Not only did this perfect gift of intelligence indicate that Paris would not be invested, as it had been in 1870; it suggested the opportunity for a decisive counter-attack. By marching south-east, the Germans were presenting their right flank to the Paris garrison, now reinforced by the newly created French 6th Army under General Michel-Joseph Manoury, and commanded overall by the incomparable veteran 'colonial' General Joseph Gallieni, Joffre's mentor.

On 3 September, nevertheless, the BEF crossed the River Marne, the last obstacle on what Sir John French still regarded as a march to haven west of Paris. Sergeant David Brunton of the 19th Hussars, French's old regiment, recorded in his diary that he and his troop 'had a swim . . . washed underclothes, and dryed them in sun'. In thirteen days the BEF had marched nearly 200 miles – the infantry on their feet, the cavalry half in the saddle and half afoot. Which was the better off is debatable: an infantryman got an average of four hours' sleep in twenty-four during the retreat, a mounted man – cavalry or gunner – an hour less, for he had his horse to attend to before he could lie down, and before he could march again. Brunton's troop had had an eventful and bloody time, including the action at Néry, but, like most of the BEF, they just wanted to turn and fight rather than keep retreating. Some battalions of Haig's I Corps had yet to fire a shot.

Two days later, however, Joffre would literally have to beg Sir John French to join in the counter-attack. Having driven to the BEF's new headquarters, at Melun on the banks of the Seine in the south-east suburbs of Paris, the massive, usually imperturbable 'Papa' Joffre, having explained his plans, clasped his hands together and beseeched his ally: 'Monsieur le maréchal, c'est la France qui vous supplie.' French, reduced to tears, tried to reply but language

17

failed him. Turning to his interpreter, he said: 'Dammit, I can't explain. Tell him all that men can do, our fellows will do.'

At first light on 6 September, therefore, 100,000 British troops (reinforced since Mons by two divisions) joined close on a million French to begin the great counter-offensive against the 750,000-strong German right wing on a front of 150 miles between Paris and Verdun. Gallieni even requisitioned 700 Parisian taxicabs to rush forward two regiments, including Zouaves (colourfully clothed light infantry) just arrived from North Africa. 'Eh bien, voilà au moins qui n'est pas banal!' he remarked ('Well, here at least is something out of the ordinary!').

The main weight of the counter-attack was in the valley of the Marne, and the turning back of what had looked like an unstoppable advance on Paris would be dubbed 'the Miracle on the Marne'. By 13 September the Germans had fallen back 60 miles to the River Aisne, leaving evidence of the sort of atrocities which the newspapers were reporting from Belgium: 'One town we passed through today was a pitiful sight,' wrote Sergeant Brunton. 'The Huns had played hell with it and many young girls violated.'

The swelteringly hot weather now broke and torrential rain swelled the streams lying in the path of the allies, gaining the Germans time to dig in on the high ground north of the Aisne, finally checking any further advance. Nevertheless the BEF would suffer 12,000 casualties in the next fortnight attempting to dislodge them, bitter losses when in the advance from the Marne they had taken fewer than 2,000.

Those 12,000 were indeed a heavy toll, but a week later 1,459 men and cadets would be lost in the space of an hour when a German U-boat torpedoed three British cruisers, *Aboukir*, *Cressy* and *Hogue*, prompting Asquith, in a curious anachronism, to tell the first lord of the Admiralty, Churchill, to mine the North Sea 'on a Napoleonic scale'.

Meanwhile, on 13 September the German commander-in-chief, Colonel-General Helmuth Johann von Moltke (the 'Younger Moltke'), in a state of nervous collapse, had told the Kaiser: 'Your Majesty, we have lost the war.' Next day he was replaced by the Prussian war minister, General Erich von Falkenhayn.

The allied counter-offensive was running out of steam, however, and the nature of the battle beginning to change, as Sir John French noted in a letter to the King: 'From now on the spade will be as great a necessity as the rifle, and the heaviest types and calibres of artillery will be brought up on either side.'

But for the moment the flanks still hung tantalizingly in the air, with 200 miles of open country to the west, and each side now desperately tried to outflank the other. With each attempt the lines would be prolonged west and north, in what would become known as 'the Race for the Sea', though the object was not so much reaching the coast as re-establishing a war of manoeuvre.

*

The defeat of two Russian armies at Tannenberg and the Masurian Lakes at the end of August and early September had been a major setback for the Triple Entente of Russia, France and Britain, but the Russian invasion of East Prussia had drawn off two German army corps from France and Belgium, to the advantage of the counter-attack on the Marne.

In the south of Poland, too, at that time the territory of the Tsar, the Russians got the better of their other enemy when Austria-Hungary, hitherto preoccupied with Serbia, launched its belated offensive towards Warsaw. Waiting for this very move were four fully mobilized and well-supplied armies. On 30 August, under Generals Nikolai Ivanov and Aleksei Brusilov, these mounted a counter-offensive which by the end of September had inflicted 130,000 casualties and forced the Austrians out of Galicia.

For their part the Germans, having checked the threat to East Prussia, could now switch troops to south-western Poland, where the Austro-Hungarian offensive had failed. Little progress would be made, though, for Russian mobilization was at last complete, and sheer numbers began to tell.

To the south, Austria-Hungary had made no better progress against Serbia, its first invasion brought to a rapid end on the Cer Mountain (15–20 August) and at Šabac (21–4 August) by the experienced Serbian General Radomir Putnik. In early September, however, Putnik's counter-offensive on the Sava river, in the north, had to be broken off when the Austrians began a second attack, against the Serbs' western front on the Drina river. Weeks of deadlock followed, tying down many Austrian troops on whom the Germans had been counting for operations against Russia.

The Schlieffen Plan was beginning to come undone on both the Western and the Eastern Fronts.

3

OCTOBER

The Wars of the World

The fighting spreads beyond Europe as imperial troops rally to the cause

By the middle of September, after the great allied counter-attack at the River Marne, almost at the gates of Paris, some believed the war on the Western Front was as good as won – that it would indeed be over by Christmas. Major-General Henry Wilson, the most influential officer in Britain's pre-war planning and now the BEF's deputy chief of staff, told his French counterpart that 'unless we make some serious blunder we ought to be at Elsenborn [across the German border] in four weeks'. The French general thought three.

They would make a serious blunder, however: under-estimating the Germans' power of recovery. All further allied advance was checked on the River Aisne; and it was during the ensuing 'Race for the Sea' that the BEF would fight its most desperate action to date, at the place that would become synonymous with British arms on the Western Front: Ypres.

General Joseph Joffre had formed a new army, the 6th, north of Paris, and was bringing his 2nd Army from the Franco-German border, where the fighting was less intense, to prolong his line

21

north-west. The BEF now found itself sandwiched between French armies, rather than on the western flank as planned. Sir John French therefore asked Joffre to allow him to resume his position on the left of the French line. He was expecting the arrival of significant reinforcements, including the newly formed 7th and 8th Divisions (both regular) and the leading elements of the Indian Corps and the Indian Cavalry Corps, telling Joffre: 'My present force of six Divisions and two Cavalry Divisions will, within three or four weeks from now, be increased by four Divisions and two Cavalry Divisions, making a total British force of ten Divisions (five Corps) and four Cavalry Divisions' – in all, some 250,000 men.

The BEF also needed to shorten its lines of communication, and to that end shift its supply base from Le Havre to Calais or one of the other more northerly Channel ports.

Joffre acceded to French's request, and on 3 October the BEF began the move, towards Ypres in Belgian Flanders. However, the Belgian government, now in Antwerp with the remnants of the field army, Brussels having fallen, asked the allies for troops to prolong the defence of the city (which would also allow the BEF to reach the coast). The 7th Division was therefore diverted to Ostend and Zeebrugge, and Winston Churchill, as first lord of the Admiralty, was sent to Antwerp to assess the situation. 'I don't know how fluent he [Churchill] is in French,' wrote Asquith to his confidante Venetia Stanley, 'but if he was able to do himself justice in a foreign tongue, the Belgians will be listening to a discourse the like of which they have never heard before. I cannot but think that he will stiffen them up to the sticking point.'

At Churchill's urging a Royal Marines brigade and two more of the Royal Naval Division – reservist sailors not required for ships' crews, half-retrained as infantry (among them, hastily commissioned, Rupert Brooke) – were sent at once to Antwerp. The French then withheld their reinforcements, and with the city's defences disintegrating, the 7th Division, transported in London buses, some still bearing their metropolitan destinations and advertisements for soap, was ordered to cover the withdrawal of the Antwerp garrison. The city surrendered on 10 October, with Albert, King of the

Belgians, reputedly firing the last shot. Many Royal Marines and sailors were taken prisoner, or interned when they crossed into neutral Holland, but the bulk of the Belgian army managed to slip south to take up positions along the River Yser between Ostend and Dunkirk. Albert ordered the sea-locks at Nieuport to be opened to flood the countryside and thereby stem the German advance.

The allies had won the 'Race for the Sea'.

At Ypres, however – 'Wipers' in Tommy parlance – the duke of Württemberg's 4th Army, brought by rail from south-east Belgium, reinforced by fresh troops from Germany and from the siege of Antwerp, was making a determined effort to break through. The BEF halted the attacks, and on 21 October Sir John French, urged on by General Ferdinand Foch, whom Joffre had placed in local command of his left flank, ordered a counter-offensive.

It soon ran into trouble, hampered by a shortage of artillery shells and over-optimistic estimates of German strength. A month's desperate fighting would follow as the Germans made their own counter-attacks on the 'Ypres salient', 8 miles at its widest. The first regiments of the Territorial Force (those who had volunteered for service overseas) would be blooded in this 'First Battle of Ypres', notably the London Scottish, who lost half their strength in the fighting. The Germans also had their first sight of the turbans, pugarees and Gurkha pillboxes of the Indian Corps. At Hollebeke on 31 October Sepoy (Private) Khudadad Khan of the Duke of Connaught's Own Baluchi Regiment won the first ever Indian VC in an action almost identical to that in which Lieutenant Dease and Private Godley of the Royal Fusiliers had won theirs at Mons: 'The British Officer in charge of the [machine-gun] detachment having been wounded,' ran the citation, 'and the other gun put out of action by a shell, Sepoy Khudadad, though himself wounded, remained working his gun until all the other five men of the gun detachment had been killed.'

The situation looked so bad that Sir John French told Foch: 'There is nothing left for me to do but go up and be killed with I Corps.' Foch replied simply: 'You must not talk of dying but of winning.'

*

While the BEF was fighting for its life in Flanders, the war was spreading world-wide. British and German troops clashed in both East and West Africa, and South African forces invaded German South-West Africa (Namibia). Louis Botha, the South African prime minister, and his defence minister Jan Smuts, who as Boer commanders had been fighting Britain only twelve years before, had been quick to declare the dominion's support, despite armed opposition by German-sympathizers.

In the Pacific, cruiser warfare and operations against German colonies had begun at once with Australian, New Zealand and Japanese help, Japan having declared war on Germany on 23 August in accordance with the Anglo-Japanese naval treaty of 1902. The German cruiser *Karlsruhe* sank merchant ships in the Caribbean, while the *Emden* raided shipping in the Indian Ocean and bombarded the oil storage tanks at Madras.

On 29 October, the war took a critical turn with the entry of the Ottoman Empire on the side of the Central Powers. A secret Turco-German treaty had been signed on 2 August, but Constantinople had at first been hesitant to act. Berlin therefore decided to force the issue. The German battle-cruiser *Goeben* and light cruiser *Breslau* of Admiral Wilhelm Souchon's Mediterranean squadron had managed to give the Royal Navy the slip and reach the Dardanelles, and Souchon now took both vessels – under Ottoman colours – plus a Turkish squadron into the Black Sea, from where they shelled Odessa and Sevastopol.

With the allies' subsequent declaration of war on the Ottoman Empire, fighting would now spread to the Middle East, at huge opportunity cost in manpower and resources, not least those of India, Australia and New Zealand. The Russians too now faced a new front, in the Caucasus, in addition to those in East Prussia, Poland and the Carpathians, while the closure of the Dardanelles to shipping meant that armaments could not be sent to them via the Mediterranean. The road to the Russian Revolution was beginning to open up.

No two warships have ever had more decisive strategic effect than the *Goeben* and the *Breslau*.

4

NOVEMBER
The Sea Dog

A defeat for the Royal Navy in the South Pacific,
and then an emphatic victory in the South Atlantic

At 6.18 p.m. on 1 November, off the coast of central Chile near the port of Coronel, Rear-Admiral Sir Christopher Cradock, a bachelor Yorkshireman with a passion for foxhunting, signalled to the distant HMS *Canopus*, a pre-dreadnought battleship sent by the Admiralty to reinforce his South Atlantic cruiser squadron: 'I am now going to attack enemy.'

So began, wrote Winston Churchill, first lord of the Admiralty, 'the saddest naval action in the war. Of the officers and men in both the squadrons that faced each other . . . nine out of ten were doomed to perish. The British were to die that night: the Germans a month later' (*The World Crisis*, vol. 1, 1923).

The Battle of Coronel, still the subject of controversy, was the result of faulty intelligence, misunderstanding and miscommunication. After commerce raiding in the Indian and Pacific Oceans, Vice-Admiral Maximilian Graf (Count) von Spee's East Asia squadron had turned its attention to southerly waters. The squadron

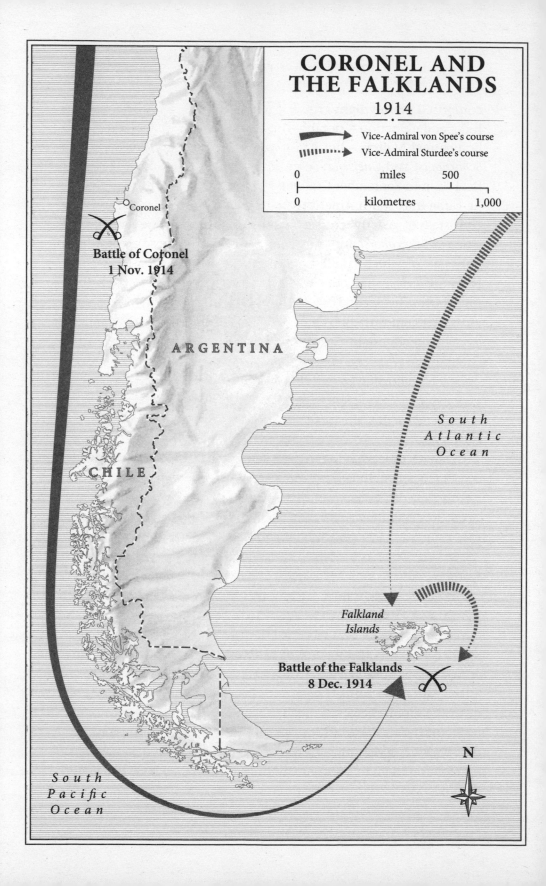

CORONEL AND
THE FALKLANDS
1914

→ Vice-Admiral von Spee's course
⇢ Vice-Admiral Sturdee's course

miles
0   500

kilometres
0   1,000

Coronel

Battle of Coronel
1 Nov. 1914

ARGENTINA

CHILE

South
Atlantic
Ocean

Falkland
Islands

Battle of the Falklands
8 Dec. 1914

South
Pacific
Ocean

N

comprised mainly light cruisers, some of which were detached for independent action – notably the *Emden*, which in September had bombarded Madras – but had two modern armoured cruisers, the *Scharnhorst* and *Gneisenau*, crewed by the best men of the German fleet. In mid-September Cradock was told to prepare to meet Spee if he came into South American waters. However, his own squadron consisted of elderly cruisers manned largely by reservists, and whereas *Scharnhorst* and *Gneisenau* could each dispose eight 8-inch guns, six of which could fire on either beam, Cradock's flagship, HMS *Good Hope*, had but two 9.2-inch guns that could match their range, while his second cruiser, *Monmouth*, carried only nine 6-inch guns that could fire on the beam. The Admiralty, judging that not a single dreadnought-class battle-cruiser could be spared from the Grand Fleet, which was keeping the German High Seas Fleet penned up in Wilhelmshaven, sent south instead the elderly battleship *Canopus*. Her four 12-inch guns could easily deal with *Scharnhorst* and *Gneisenau*, but she lacked speed – 15 knots compared with *Good Hope*'s 23.

In late October, having intercepted signals from the cruiser *Leipzig*, Cradock concluded that she was the only one of Spee's ships to have reached Chilean waters, and so took the armoured cruisers *Good Hope* and *Monmouth*, the light cruiser *Glasgow* and the armed merchant ship *Otranto* round Cape Horn to intercept her, leaving the slower *Canopus* to escort his colliers. *Glasgow* scouted ahead to Coronel, where on 1 November, instead of just *Leipzig*, she found Spee's entire squadron.

In the coming darkness Cradock could have withdrawn to the cover of *Canopus*'s 12-inch guns 300 miles to the south, but he decided to stand and fight. Not the least of his reasons was that a fellow rear-admiral, Ernest Troubridge, was facing court martial for letting slip the cruisers *Goeben* and *Breslau* in the eastern Mediterranean the month before.

According to *Glasgow*'s log, 'the British Squadron turned to port four points together towards the enemy with a view to closing them and forcing them to action before sunset, which if successful would have put them at a great disadvantage owing to the British Squadron being between the enemy and the sun'. However, Spee used his superior speed to overcome the dazzle, putting his ships on a parallel course south. Within an hour Cradock's ships were silhouetted against the afterglow of the sun, which had now dipped below the horizon, while his own were scarcely visible against the dark background of the coast. At seven o'clock he opened fire.

The sea was high, adding to the difficulties the *Good Hope*'s and the *Monmouth*'s gunners faced, for their 6-inch guns were on the main deck, while the Germans' were on the upper. *Scharnhorst*'s third salvo put one of *Good Hope*'s 9.2-inch guns out of action, and shortly afterwards she exploded with the loss of all hands, including Cradock and his beloved terrier Jack. *Monmouth*, though holed and listing badly, refused to surrender and was shelled at close quarters by the cruiser *Nürnberg* until she too sank without survivors. *Otranto*, unarmoured and having only 4.7-inch guns, was incapable of taking part in the action, and managed to use her 18 knots to get away. *Glasgow* remained pluckily in action until darkness overcame her, when she too managed to escape. In all, the British had lost 1,654 sailors in less than an hour, the Germans none.

Coronel threw the Admiralty into a rage, for not only was it the Royal Navy's first defeat at sea in more than a century, it left Spee in command of South American waters and with a wide choice of alternatives. But Spee himself had doubts. When the German community in Valparaiso, where he had put in after the battle, pressed congratulatory bouquets on him, he replied: 'They will do for my funeral.'

This time the Admiralty spared no measures. While Churchill arranged for the Japanese navy to cover the South Pacific, the 73-year-old first sea lord, Admiral of the Fleet Lord (Jacky) Fisher, who had been brought out of retirement days earlier following the enforced resignation of the German-born Prince Louis of Battenberg, detached the dreadnought battle-cruisers *Inflexible* and *Invincible* from the Grand Fleet. After hasty refit at Devonport, these raced south under command of the square-jawed Vice-Admiral Sir Doveton Sturdee and, having rendezvoused with Rear-Admiral Archibald Stoddart's mid-Atlantic cruiser squadron at the Abrolhos Archipelago off Brazil, reached Port Stanley in the Falkland Islands on 7 December. Here they found *Canopus* undergoing repair to her boilers, but her guns ready for action, and began at once to coal.

It was not a moment too soon, for the day before Spee had sailed through the Straits of Magellan intending to destroy the signal station at Stanley. At about eight o'clock on 8 December his leading armoured cruiser, *Gneisenau*, with his younger son Heinrich on board, came in sight of Sturdee's guardship. 'A few minutes later a terrible apparition broke upon German eyes,' wrote Churchill. 'Rising from behind the promontory, sharply visible in the clear air, were a pair of tripod masts. One glance was enough. They meant certain death.' For only dreadnoughts had tripods – and eight 12-inch guns apiece.

But Sturdee's battle-cruisers, still coaling, could not immediately raise steam, and it was *Canopus*, beached on the mudbanks, that opened fire first as *Gneisenau* turned away to rejoin the main body of the squadron. Soon all five of Spee's ships were making full steam east then south, pursued by the cruisers *Glasgow*, *Kent* and *Carnarvon*, but it was not until nearly ten o'clock that *Invincible* and *Inflexible* could give chase. However, both ships, fresh out of dry dock, had a 5-knot advantage over Spee's, and in three hours closed to within 17,500 yards of *Leipzig* and opened fire. Spee now ordered his light cruisers to turn south-west, while *Scharnhorst* and *Gneisenau* turned north-east to cover their retreat. They opened fire half an hour later and scored a hit on *Invincible*, though the shell burst harmlessly on the belt armour.

British gunnery was poor at first, scoring only four hits out of more than 200 rounds fired, largely owing to the copious quantities of smoke generated. Sturdee therefore decided to put distance between the opposing squadrons and, as in Nelson's day, to seek the weather gauge, though not for steerage but to get upwind of the smoke. But Spee closed again to 12,500 yards to enable him to use his 5.9-inch guns, and firing continued for some hours, both sides now troubled by poor visibility. Damage to both *Scharnhorst* and *Gneisenau* mounted, however, while that to *Inflexible* and *Invincible* was negligible. *Scharnhorst* ceased firing at four o'clock and capsized a quarter of an hour later with not a single survivor, Spee going down with his flagship. *Gneisenau* was pounded for another hour and a half by both battle-cruisers, which had closed to just 4,000 yards, until her captain opened the sea-cocks and she too capsized, the British ships picking up 176 men from the freezing sea. Lieutenant Heinrich von Spee was not among them.

Sturdee's cruisers, which had given chase to the lighter ships, overtook and sank the *Leipzig* later that evening, pulling just eighteen sailors from the water. HMS *Kent* had earlier caught and sunk the *Nürnberg*, having exceeded even her design speed. *Nürnberg* had refused to surrender, and as she foundered by the head, a huddle of her remaining crew on the rising stern could be seen waving the German flag. All but seven of her complement of over 300 perished, including Lieutenant Otto von Spee, the admiral's elder son.

Only the *Dresden* escaped, but she was cornered three months later in Chilean waters, where she too was scuttled and her crew interned; they included Lieutenant Wilhelm Carnaris, the future chief of Hitler's military intelligence service, the *Abwehr*. In December 1939 the German pocket battleship *Admiral Graf Spee*, named in honour of the victor of Coronel, would herself be scuttled in South American waters after a brilliant affair of gunnery and deception by Commodore Henry Harwood's cruiser squadron at the Battle of the River Plate, off Montevideo, when once again Churchill was first lord of the Admiralty.

With the fortuitous wreck of the *Karlsruhe* off the West Indies in November, the cornering of the *Königsberg* in German East Africa and the destruction of the *Emden* by HMAS *Sydney* in the Indian Ocean, by the middle of March 1915, as Churchill wrote, 'no German ships of war remained on any of the oceans of the world'. The consequences of their exclusion, he noted, 'were far-reaching, and affected simultaneously our position in every part of the globe'.

From now on the Germans' war against merchant shipping would have to be waged by submarine – activity which would do so much to bring the United States into the conflict – or else the High Seas Fleet would have to break out of Wilhelmshaven. This they would not try until the middle of 1916, when at the Battle of Jutland the Royal Navy forced them back into their North Sea haven for the rest of the war.

While the Royal Navy's distant drama of tragedy and revenge was being played out, the fighting at Ypres on the Western Front had become very bloody indeed as the Germans made desperate attempts to break through to capture the Channel ports. Reservists of every type, as well as dismounted cavalrymen and Indian troops, many still in their tropical uniforms, were thrown in to hold the line. On 6 November, Captain Arthur O'Neill of the 2nd Life Guards became the first MP (for Mid Antrim) to be killed – the first of nineteen. His youngest son would be prime minister of Northern Ireland in the 1960s. Casualties at 'First Ypres' to 22 November, the close of the qualifying period for the medal known colloquially as the Mons Star, were some 60,000.

Fighting on the Eastern Front, though, remained fluid. Having managed to defeat an Austro-Hungarian offensive in Galicia and a German attempt to take Warsaw, in early November Russian forces began a counter-offensive into Silesia. After heavy losses, however, both sides accepted they had gone as far as they could, and in early December the Russians withdrew to a new and stronger line closer to the Polish capital.

Meanwhile, in Mesopotamia, the British were striking the first blow against the Turkish army. On 7 November the 6th (Poona) Division of the Indian army landed at the mouth of the Shatt al-Arab water-way to secure the Persian oilfields, taking Basra a fortnight later. It would be another three and a half years, however, before the Turks were finally ejected from what is now Iraq.

31

5

DECEMBER
'Wipers'

Heroic resistance in Flanders as the home front comes under fire

December began exceptionally wet for the BEF on the Western Front. The incessant rain turned the stone-less soil of Flanders into 'a sort of liquid mud of the consistency of thick porridge', wrote the commander-in-chief, Sir John French, 'without the valuable sustaining quality of that excellent Scots mixture. To walk off the roads meant sinking in at once.'

The BEF of December 1914 was not, however, the same force that had crossed to France three and half months earlier. Reinforced by regulars from around the world, by troops of the Indian army and territorials, it was now nearly three times its original strength. But the casualties in the retreat from Mons, the counter-attack on the River Marne and the subsequent fighting on the Aisne, and above all in the Ypres salient, had borne heavily on the 'Old Contemptibles', as the pre-war regulars called themselves after the Kaiser had supposedly remarked that they were a 'contemptible little army' (he would later admit only that he might have said that Britain's army was 'contemptibly little' – which by continental standards it was).

The BEF had arrived in France with around 80,000 infantry, and by 22 November, the official end of the First Battle of Ypres, casualties of all kinds since the beginning of hostilities numbered 86,237. Most of these were in the infantry, and disproportionately high among the officers. The 1915 edition of *Debrett's Peerage* would be delayed for many months until the editors could revise the entries for almost every blue-blooded family in the kingdom.

Of First Ypres, that usually stern critic of British arms, and the most influential military theorist of the inter-war years, Captain Sir Basil Liddell Hart, wrote:

> No battle in Britain's annals has given clearer proof of fighting quality. It was a battle in the natural line of British tradition – a defensive attitude combined with timely ripostes. Thus it suited the nature of the troops who conducted it. If it did not directly fit their pre-war tactical training, predominantly offensive in imitation of the continental fashion, it appealed to their native instincts, which count for more than a fashionable dogma under the test of battle.

There were times when that fighting quality had faltered, but only momentarily, a reality the duke of Wellington himself would have recognized. Once, in the Peninsula, one of his staff pointed to some troops abandoning their position, to which he replied: 'Oh, they all do that at some time: the question is, will they rally?' Despite the mounting losses at Ypres, the regiments of the BEF always rallied. Their morale and superlative weapon skills – fifteen accurate rounds a minute with the Lee–Enfield magazine-fed rifle – were the decisive factors in the battle, said Liddell Hart: 'The little British Army had a corporate sense that was unique . . . "First Ypres", on the British side, was not just a soldiers' battle but a "family battle" – against outsiders . . . After the battle was over, little survived, save the memory of its spirit.'

But although First Ypres officially ended on 22 November, fighting did not, each side trying to gain local advantage. The Indian Corps won two VCs the very next day, and a third the day after.

Commanders, all too conscious of the loss of so many experienced officers and NCOs, as well as the worsening physical conditions, were determined to keep up the pressure.

Opportunity for offensive action now seemed to beckon when intelligence revealed that the Germans were transferring troops to the Eastern Front (the secretary of state for war, Lord Kitchener, told the cabinet there was 'nothing in front of them [the BEF] but men and boys'). The French commander-in-chief, Joseph Joffre, ordered his armies to renew the offensive, and asked the BEF to renew their partial attacks at Ypres without delay. Unfortunately, the Germans who had gone east had not taken their barbed wire with them. On 12 December Sir John French gave orders for a series of divisional actions, and to achieve surprise no artillery preparations were to be made, the infantry being issued instead with wire-cutters and mattresses with which to cross the obstacle belt.

The results were bloody and fruitless. Nor were they unpredictable, as Captain Billy Congreve of the Rifle Brigade (who would later win the VC, as his father had, before being killed on the Somme) with the staff of the 3rd Division, wrote in his diary: 'Yesterday we made an attack and, as we only put two battalions into it, the attack naturally failed. We had about 400 casualties. It is very depressing. I should have thought that we had learnt our lesson at Neuve Chapelle [in October] about unsupported attacks, but it seems not.'

Notwithstanding the weather and mounting casualties, attacks continued in this vein throughout December, and while the Germans were no less active at times, by the end of the month General Joffre could declare that there was now no possibility of their breaking through the allied line. However, while Berlin and London were coming to terms with fighting a long war, August's boast of 'over by Christmas' now a distant dream, Joffre remained convinced he could achieve an early and decisive victory in France. This disparity of views would lie at the root of the allies' problems in 1915.

From Churchill's perspective as first lord of the Admiralty the situation looked equally promising, if for a different reason. With German cruisers swept from the oceans after the battles of Coronel and the Falkland Islands, the *Hochseeflotte* for the moment skulking in its anchorage at Wilhelmshaven in fear of Jellicoe's Grand Fleet at Scapa Flow, and the submarine threat still relatively small, trade routes were now safe. But the commander of the *Hochseeflotte*, Friedrich von Ingenohl, now tried to lure Jellicoe into a skirmish, aiming to wear down his numbers and thereby even the odds for the great fleet action that he knew must come at some point. On 16 December he sent Franz von Hipper's scouting group, comprising five battle-cruisers (*Seydlitz*, *Moltke*, *von der Tann*, *Derrflinger* and *Blücher*) with a screen of light cruisers and destroyers, to bombard the North Sea ports of Scarborough, Whitby and the Hartlepools, in the hope that this would bring out a part of the Grand Fleet, which his own battleships, following up Hipper's group, would then ambush.

The Admiralty's signal intercept service, 'Room 40', had intercepted *Hochseeflotte* signals, however, and knew there was a sortie, if not its object. Jellicoe despatched Vice-Admiral Sir George Warrender's 2nd Battle Squadron, comprising six dreadnoughts, four battle-cruisers, four heavy cruisers, six light cruisers and eight submarines, to intercept Hipper's group. In the pre-dawn murk these ran into the *Hochseeflotte* itself, however, and Warrender's destroyers opened fire. Ingenohl, fearing torpedo attack and mindful of the Kaiser's injunction to avoid heavy losses, turned away and ran for port. Meanwhile Hipper's battle-cruisers had crossed the North Sea, and at 8.10 a.m. began bombarding the largely undefended ports, firing 1,150 shells in an hour and twenty minutes before escaping in the mist. They inflicted some 650 casualties, mainly civilian, including 137 killed of whom 78 were women and children. Scarborough in particular suffered much damage.

Public opinion and the press held the Royal Navy to blame for failing to prevent the raid, but the bombardment reinforced the image of German 'frightfulness' gained from the earlier atrocities in Belgium. 'Remember Scarborough' became a rallying cry for recruiting officers, as well as provoking outrage in the United States. The Kaiser's orders to the *Hochseeflotte* became even more restraining.

'As December passed,' wrote Churchill, 'a sense of indescribable relief stole over the Admiralty . . . The mighty enemy, with all the advantages of preparation and design, had delivered his onslaught and had everywhere [on land and sea] been brought to a standstill. It was our turn now. The initiative had passed to Britain – the Great Amphibian . . . It was for us to say where we would strike and when.'

*

The Pope called for it. The high command gave orders to prevent it. The Christmas truce of 1914 is perhaps the best known but least understood episode of the First World War.

What is incontrovertible is that on that Christmas Day British and German troops climbed out of their trenches along several stretches of the Western Front and met in no-man's-land on sociable terms. Why, and what this moment signified, are questions more complex than suggestions of incipient pacifism or warweariness allow. Pope Benedict XV, elected in early September and appalled by what he called 'the suicide of civilized Europe', had from the outset urged a general ceasefire. 'The greatest and wealthiest nations,' he said, were 'well-provided with the most awful weapons modern military science has devised . . . day by day the earth is drenched with newly shed blood and is covered with the bodies of the wounded and of the slain.' In early December he asked specifically that 'the guns may fall silent at least upon the night the angels sang' to allow negotiations for an honourable peace.

The belligerent powers dismissed the plea more or less peremptorily. For a decade the French government had been fervidly anti-clerical. Germany, despite Catholic Bavaria, was also unreceptive: the *Kulturkampf*, the aggressive secularization policy of the former chancellor, Bismarck, was of recent memory. Austria-Hungary, though 80 per cent Catholic, was deeply suspicious of Rome – which was not just the seat of the Pope but the capital of Italy, its erstwhile ally, now veering towards the Entente powers. Russia, being Orthodox, had always rejected claims to papal authority, and in any case, adhering to the old Julian calendar rather than the Gregorian, celebrated the Nativity on 7 January. Britain, for its part, retained the distrust embodied in the Book of Common Prayer: 'The Bishop of Rome hath no jurisdiction in this realm of England.' Indeed, despite the heroism of Irish troops (the first VC of the war was an Irish-born Catholic), the British army's leadership could be suspicious of the commitment of Catholic officers. As late as November 1917 the BEF's chief of intelligence, Brigadier-General John Charteris, would write to his wife: 'My chief opponents are the Roman Catholic people, who are really very half-hearted about the whole war.'

The western allies, France, Britain and Belgium, had fought the Germans to a standstill and were in no mood for peace negotiations. The French alone had lost 300,000 killed, and twice that number wounded, captured or missing. The front now consisted of continuous parallel lines of trenches from the North Sea to the Swiss border, and Joffre was determined to evict the invader from French soil before the German defences were strengthened. Senior officers of the BEF were therefore anxious to keep up the offensive spirit, and on 5 December, the General Officer Commanding (GOC) II Corps, Sir Horace Smith-Dorrien, issued instructions to his divisional commanders:

> It is during this period that the greatest danger to the morale of troops exists. Experience of this and of every other war proves undoubtedly that troops in trenches in close proximity to the enemy slide very easily, if permitted to do so, into a 'live and let live' theory of life . . . officers and men sink into a military lethargy from which it is difficult to arouse them when the moment for great sacrifices again arises . . . the attitude of our troops can be readily understood and to a certain extent commands sympathy . . . Such an attitude is however most dangerous for it discourages initiative in commanders and destroys the offensive spirit in all ranks . . . friendly intercourse with the enemy, unofficial armistices, however tempting and amusing they may be, are absolutely prohibited.

Joffre asked Sir John French to renew his attacks south of Ypres as quickly as possible to distract the Germans while he himself made preparations for the French army's counter-offensive. In mid-December, therefore, the British army made some of its most flawed and costly assaults of the war, notably at Messines and Ploegsteert (known inevitably to the troops as 'Plug Street'), and as a result by Christmas large numbers of dead of both sides lay unburied in no-man's-land.

Despite the orders against 'friendly intercourse', the static and routine nature of trench warfare and the proximity of the enemy – in some cases as close as 50 yards, which meant that they could be heard talking, and even their breakfast cooking smelled – made for curiosity. Because, too, the weather was particularly cold and wet, a degree of mutual respect developed among those enduring it on both sides. On 20 December there was a local truce on 22 Brigade's front when the Germans began taking in British wounded from no-man's-land, though there was no fraternization.

Meanwhile the festive spirit was being fuelled by the respective armies' postal services, with huge volumes of mail and gifts arriving for the troops from home. King George V sent a Christmas card to every soldier, sailor and nurse, and the Princess Mary Fund despatched a gift box to every soldier at the front, one for smokers and another for non-smokers. In her letter launching the scheme, the 17-year-old daughter of the King and Queen wrote: 'Could there be anything more likely to hearten them in their struggle than a present received straight from home on Christmas Day?'

The Kaiser likewise sent tobacco, and cigars for the officers and NCOs, and ordered 100,000 Christmas trees for the front, much to the dismay of his staff officers, who were appalled at the appropriation of transport for non-warlike supplies.

For both sides, therefore, Christmas approached with some degree of festal promise. For the British regulars in particular, 25 December had always been a holiday, with reduced duties and relaxed discipline whether in barracks or on active service. Traditionally the men were served tea in the morning by the sergeant-majors and dinner by the officers. Why should 1914 be any different?

At this stage of the war, too, the ground had not been churned-up into the moonscapes of the later years, and many parts of the line had a familiar pastoral look. On Christmas Eve the temperature plummeted, a peculiarly welcome event, for the liquid mud now froze solid. Getting out of the trenches was therefore easier and more inviting.

Many of the immediate accounts of what actually happened that night and on Christmas morning were rushed, confused or contradictory, while others, written long after the event, were overlaid with hindsight. To begin with there was no particular pattern beyond the shouted exchanges, or the signs – initially probably ironic – hoisted above the trenches wishing those opposite respectively a Merry Christmas or *Frohe Weihnachten*, and in places carol-singing and counter-singing. But on the whole it was the Germans who left the trenches first and advanced without their weapons to the wire in the middle of no-man's-land. The British seem to have responded out of inquisitiveness, and the sheer absurdity of milling around between the lines of trenches shows on the faces of those photographed (both sides prohibited cameras in the trenches, which accounts for the paucity of such photographs). Once footballs were produced, as happened here and there, the soldier's natural inclination to fun took over. In other sectors, however, the grim business of recovering the dead made for a more sombre encounter, with occasional exchanges of mementos, an attempt perhaps on the part of each side to proclaim its humanity.

Some British troops made full use of the opportunity to spy out the enemy's defences, as Brigadier-General Walter Congreve, commanding 18 Brigade near Neuve Chapelle, related in a letter home that day:

> My informant, one of the men, said he had had a fine day of it & had 'smoked a cigar with the best shot in the German army, then not more than 18. They say he's killed more of our men than any other 12 together but I know now where he shoots from & I hope we down him tomorrow.' I hope devoutly they will.

There were instances of temporary, localized ceasefires between the French and Germans, and even the Russians and Germans (and

Austrians), but the Christmas truce of 1914 appears to have been a phenomenon principally of the British and German sector, probably for the simple reason that to the regulars of the BEF the war was not as 'personal' as it was for the French and Belgians, whose homelands had been violated and whose domestic life had been up-ended by mobilization. Indeed, when civilians in the rear areas heard of it the reaction could be hostile. Frank Richards, a former regular recalled to the colours, and author of *Old Soldiers Never Die*, recalls how his battalion, marching back to billets through Armentières on 27 December, were spat at by Frenchwomen shouting: 'You no bon, you English soldiers, you boko [*beaucoup*] kamerade Allemenge.'

Nor was there any consistency in the pattern of truces: General Congreve relates that while '1st [battalion] Rifle Brigade were playing football with the Germans opposite them, the next-door regiments fired all day.' The 2nd Grenadier Guards, for example, took many casualties in heavy fighting. The Commonwealth War Graves Commission's records show that two officers and sixty-eight other ranks were killed on 25 December (there is no record of those wounded or posted missing that day).

Disciplinary action against a number of officers was initiated, though it largely fizzled out with the renewal of attacks in the weeks following. There would be no repeat of the Christmas truce, in part because of the firm hand of authority on both sides, in part because of the growing bitterness of the fighting.

In reality, the Christmas truce was less romantic than it is frequently portrayed. In retrospect it was but a passing episode, a relic of pre-war soldiering which, while it appears to have left a profound impact on some of those who took part, in the majority of regiments of the BEF hardly registered a mention.

PART TWO

1915

Deadlock

19 February: Dardanelles campaign begins.

22 April: Second Battle of Ypres begins.

25 April: Gallipoli landings begin.

7 May: RMS *Lusitania* sunk by U-20.

23 May: Italy joins the war on the side of the Entente.

25 September: Battle of Loos begins.

14 October: Bulgaria declares war on Serbia.

6

JANUARY

Eastern Approaches

As the soldiers dig in on the Western Front,
the politicians look elsewhere to fight

The new year brought new thinking about how to prosecute the war. Winston Churchill, first lord of the Admiralty, wrote in a memorandum to the prime minister, H. H. Asquith:

> I think it is quite possible that neither side will have the strength to penetrate the other's line in the Western theatre . . . My impression is that the position of both armies is not likely to undergo any decisive change – although no doubt several hundred thousand men will be spent to satisfy the military mind on the point . . . On the assumption that these views are correct, the question arises, how ought we to apply our growing military power. Are there not other alternatives than sending our armies to chew barbed wire in Flanders?

'The military mind' of which Churchill was rightly suspicious was principally that of the French high command, which though understandably determined to evict the invader from French soil had no

43

means of doing so except frontal assaults against the strengthening German defences. As the junior partner on the Western Front, the BEF would have little option but to support them. Indeed, this would be the story of the war until mid-1918, when British military strength at last reached rough parity with that of France, not least because the French high command had squandered so much of their own.

In the short term Britain's 'growing military power' consisted of those few regular troops still in overseas garrisons, together with territorials who volunteered for overseas service and 'colonial' troops, principally Indian, Canadian and Australian (the Canadian division, assembling in England, would cross to France in early February). In the longer term, the strength would be in the 'new armies' that Kitchener was raising through voluntary recruitment in Britain and Ireland. Formed in successive tranches of 100,000, known unofficially as K1, K2 etc., each was to mirror the original BEF. However, K1 would not be ready to take to the field for at least six months, K2 and K3 not for a year, there being neither the equipment nor the instructors to train them any more rapidly. But the question of where to send them was already exercising David Lloyd George, the chancellor of the exchequer. These new armies would be, he argued – correctly –

a force of a totally different character from any which has hitherto left these shores . . . drawn almost exclusively from the better class of artisan, the upper and the lower middle classes. In intelligence, education and character it is vastly superior to any army ever raised in this country, and it has been drawn not from the ranks of those who have generally cut themselves off from home . . . So that if this superb army is thrown away upon futile enterprises, such as those we have witnessed during the last few weeks, the country will be uncontrollably indignant at the lack of provision and intelligence shown in our plans.

Lieutenant-Colonel Maurice Hankey (a Royal Marines officer), secretary of the Committee of Imperial Defence and of the new 'war council', a slimmed-down cabinet attended by the first sea lord and the chief of the imperial general staff (CIGS), had recently circulated a paper along the lines of Churchill's memorandum of 14 December, 'The Apparent Deadlock on the Western Front', in which he argued that Britain should use the Royal Navy to project her power. On 1 January, therefore, Kitchener wrote to Sir John French:

> The feeling here is gaining ground that, although it is essential to defend the line we now hold, troops over and above what is necessary for that service could better be employed elsewhere. The question where anything effective could be accomplished opens a large field and requires a good deal of study. What are the views of your staff?

Sir John was alarmed. He and his French counterpart, General Joseph Joffre, estimated that although the Germans had suffered one and a half million casualties on both the Western and Eastern Fronts, they had a further 800,000 men in training. By March or April they would be able to 'wipe out their existing inferiority and even once again make themselves superior to us . . . It seems, therefore, of the utmost importance that we should take the offensive and strike at the earliest possible moment with all our available strength.'

Kitchener was not persuaded. December's losses, on both sides, demonstrated all too clearly the price and outcome of frontal attacks. He told the war council: 'An advance could only be made by means of developing a tremendous volume of artillery fire, and the ammunition for this is simply not available.'

The Russians, under pressure from the Ottoman Turks in the Caucasus, were calling for a diversionary effort to be made against Constantinople. Churchill, confident that Jellicoe's fleet could maintain its blockade of Germany and keep the *Hochseeflotte* penned up in its anchorage at Wilhelmshaven, having already eliminated the cruiser threat to the trade routes, believed that the Admiralty could spare some obsolescent warships to force the Dardanelles Straits and open up communications with the Russians in the Black Sea. This would also encourage Italy, Greece and Bulgaria, who were still sitting on the fence, to come in on the allied side.

Only a fortnight earlier the first naval VC of the war to be gazetted had been won by 26-year-old Lieutenant Norman Holbrook, who had taken his elderly submarine B11 under five rows of mines to sink the armoured frigate *Mesudiye*. The Dardanelles looked ripe for the taking; all it needed was equally bold action on the surface. Although the first sea lord, Admiral Jacky Fisher, was sceptical, on 13 January the war council instructed the Admiralty to make preparations for an expedition against the straits the following month. So began the ill-fated Gallipoli campaign.

Meanwhile the war was spreading with an apparent impetus of its own. Although it was not until 1918 that *The Times*'s war correspondent Colonel Charles Repington coined what would become the official expression 'First World War', as early as September 1914 the German biologist and philosopher Ernst Haeckel had written prophetically in the *Indianapolis Star*: 'There is no doubt that the course and character of the feared "European War" . . . will become the first world war in the full sense of the word.'

In January 1915, not only was the conflict drawing in troops from around the world – French colonials to the Western Front; imperial British forces to the Middle East for defence of the Suez Canal against the Turks, and to secure the oil fields of present-day Kuwait and Iraq – but the actual fighting was becoming global too. In his novel *All Our Yesterdays*, published in 1930, the former war correspondent H. M. Tomlinson describes in vivid prose the almost surreal extension of the conflict that had begun in a street in Sarajevo:

Russians were hurling Kurds from the slopes of Mount Ararat. And at Basra, that port of the Persian Gulf for which Sinbad set sail, Sikhs had arrived from the Punjab, and Gurkhas from the Himalayas . . . to dislodge Ottomans who were entrenched in the Garden of Eden. The coconut groves of New Guinea were stormed by Australians . . . Far to the north of Singapore, by the Yellow sea, the Japanese landed in Shantung, and attacked Tsingtau, a Chinese city, though occupied by Germans, who were ordered by the Kaiser never to surrender that symbol of Germanic honour.

Yet while the allies were trying to contain the Germans, looking for a distant, strategic flank to turn, Berlin was only too keen to see the fighting spread in the hope that it would divert allied resources from the decisive European theatre. Although her cruisers in the South Atlantic, the Indian and Pacific Oceans had all met their end, there was still the dark continent in which to make war on land. From her colonies in West, East and South-West Africa, with native troops and a cadre of German professionals, Germany made war – notably in what are now Burundi, Rwanda and mainland Tanzania, under Colonel Paul von Lettow-Vorbeck – on British, French and Belgian colonies. In doing so she drew in, among others, South African troops under the leadership of two of Britain's former Boer adversaries, Louis Botha and Jan Smuts, whose readiness to rally to the British cause prompted armed rebellion by pro-German Afrikaner settlers.

'In the twilight aisles of the Congo,' wrote Tomlinson,

the pygmies knew of an ominous stirring among the leaves, by a terror unknown in their simple law. Negroes fought each other because of it on Lake Tanganyika. White men died on the red hot iron of burning ships sequestered in the mangrove swamps near Zanzibar; they pursued each other, with black levies, through East African jungles, and across the waterless sands of Namaqualand. African tribes, that had forgotten raw head and bloody bones through the gentle persuasion of the followers of Jesus of Nazareth, were dislodged from their mealie fields and hunting grounds because the Emperor of Germany had invaded Belgium.

7

FEBRUARY

Cruiser Rules

The U-boat campaign begins

No month of the war was to prove more fateful than February 1915. With stalemate on the Western Front, eyes were turning to other theatres – the Germans to the Eastern Front, the Ottomans and their German advisers towards the Suez Canal, and the British to the Dardanelles and beyond to the Black Sea.

A naval stalemate had also developed. The Grand Fleet at Scapa Flow in the Orkneys, and her standing cruiser patrols along the east coast, had neutralized the German High Seas Fleet, keeping the fruit of the Kaiser's great pre-war naval building programme, the 'Dreadnought Race', bottled up the other side of the North Sea at Wilhelmshaven. The attempt in December to even the odds by luring the Royal Navy into ambush with the bombardment of Scarborough and other ports on the north-east coast had ended in failure, and Admiral Jellicoe, conscious of being, in Churchill's memorable words, 'the only man who could lose the war in an afternoon', was consistently able to out-manoeuvre the Germans thanks to superior signals intelligence. On 24 January another cruiser raid was intercepted in what became known as the Battle of Dogger Bank, and although the Royal Navy was slow to follow up its success, the armoured cruiser *Blücher*, one of the villains of the Scarborough raid, was sunk with heavy loss of life. Her capsizing was filmed at close quarters by British destroyers, one of the earliest moving-picture records of the death of a warship. Ingenohl was promptly replaced as commander of the *Hochseeflotte* by Admiral Hugo von Pohl, a notably cautious officer.

While the Admiralty pondered how to tempt the *Hochseeflotte* into decisive battle, the Germans were determined to take the war underwater. U-boats had already sunk a number of allied merchantmen as well as warships, but had observed the so-called 'cruiser rules'. Under these rules, laid down by the Hague Conventions of 1899 and 1907, a submarine intending to attack an unarmed vessel was first meant to surface and allow the crew into lifeboats. Nevertheless, on 26 October U-24 had become the first submarine to attack an unarmed merchantman without warning when she torpedoed the French *Admiral Ganteaume* with 2,500 Belgian refugees aboard, her commander, Kapitänleutnant Rudolf Schneider, claiming that he had mistaken the Channel steamer for a troop transport. Then, on 30 January 1915, U-20, commanded by Kapitänleutnant Walther Schwieger, torpedoed and sank the *Ikaria*, *Tokomaru* and *Oriole* in the English Channel without warning, and on 2 February the German chancellor agreed to the request of the navy minister, Grand Admiral Alfred von Tirpitz, to launch unrestricted submarine warfare against all ships, including neutrals, bringing food or supplies to the Entente powers. That day an American diplomat at the embassy in Paris, John Coolidge, wrote in his diary: 'Another little merchant ship has just been sunk by the Germans, just at the mouth of the Mersey, which gives us all a horrid feeling. The Germans are so angry at not getting ahead that they leave nothing undone.'

American distaste at increasing German 'frightfulness' solidified into something stronger when on 4 February Berlin declared that the torpedoing of neutral ships 'cannot always be avoided', and that 'cruiser rules' would not always apply. This brought a sharp response from Washington, President Woodrow Wilson declaring that it was an 'indefensible violation of neutral rights' and that the United States would take the 'necessary steps' to safeguard American lives and property.

There was some logic in Tirpitz's thinking, which was reinforced by Germany's own experience of the effects of the British naval blockade. For before the war there had been a widespread belief that Britain was wholly dependent on food imports from North America, the influential newspaper editor W. T. Stead declaring as early as 1901 that without them 'we should be face to face with famine'. But compared with the cruiser, the U-boat was not well adapted to commerce raiding or blockade. Its speed both on the surface and underwater was no greater than that of many a merchant ship, and its light gun was inadequate against larger vessels, some of which were now armed. For the new strategy of blockade to have any chance of success, therefore, now that all Germany's cruisers bar auxiliaries had been swept from the seas, the U-boat would have to exploit its trump card, the attack without warning using torpedoes, abandoning the stop-and-search rules that had hitherto safeguarded neutrals. On 19 February the Norwegian tanker *Belridge* was torpedoed by U-8 in the Dover Straits, the first neutral to be attacked without warning. Berlin again claimed that it had been fired on in error.

From 1 February, therefore, Berlin was almost inexorably set on a course of conflict with Washington. So too were Kapitänleutnant Schwieger and U-20: on 7 May they would sink the Cunard liner *Lusitania* off the south-east coast of Ireland with the loss of 1,200 passengers and crew, including 128 American citizens. And although President Wilson would be measured in his response, stating that 'there is such a thing as a nation being so right that it does not need to convince others by force that it is right,' his new secretary of state, Robert Lansing, would write in his memoirs that although it was another two years before the United States entered the war, after the sinking of the *Lusitania* he had had no doubt 'that we would ultimately become the ally of Britain'.

Meanwhile, at the urging of Churchill at the Admiralty, plans were under way to force the Dardanelles (the old Hellespont), the narrow (in places less than a mile) 40-mile waterway linking the Aegean with the Sea of Marmora and thence Constantinople, thereby opening up communications with Russia. Pre-war studies had concluded that this operation would be extremely hazardous, and both the Admiralty and the War Office had discounted it as an option, but stalemate in the west and increasingly urgent calls from the Tsar to take action to relieve the Turkish pressure on his southern flank had led to a reappraisal. The war cabinet, not least the war minister, Lord Kitchener, now had high hopes that seizing Constantinople would also have profound diplomatic advantages, encouraging Bulgaria and Romania to join the allies. However, the first sea lord, Admiral Fisher, remained sceptical, which did nothing to energize Vice-Admiral Sackville Carden, the commander charged with forcing the Dardanelles with a flotilla of elderly battleships. In fact, Carden himself had begun to doubt his original assessment that the straits might be taken by a methodical advance and systematic bombardment of the shore batteries, which Churchill had used to urge the war cabinet to approve the operation. On 16 February, therefore, the war cabinet decided to mount in addition a land operation to clear the shore batteries, and a substantial force under General Sir Ian Hamilton, one of the most highly regarded officers in the army, began assembling in Egypt for the task. It included both British regulars and reservists, two French brigades, Indian Army troops, and those of Australia and New Zealand on their way to France.

On 19 February Carden began the naval operation with the bombardment of the defences at Sedd-el-Bahr on the Gallipoli peninsula and Kum Kale on the Asiatic side of the straits. This was not successful, in part because of bad weather, and was quickly broken off before being resumed on 25 February at closer range. A party of Royal Marines landed the next day, along with a naval demolition party led by Lieutenant Eric Robinson. Turkish troops put up stiff opposition, but Robinson, alone and in his tropical whites, strolled up the Achilles Mound, the supposed tomb of the Greek hero of the

Trojan war, and under heavy fire proceeded calmly to blow up the two guns. For this and later acts of courage he was awarded the VC, the first of the Gallipoli campaign. Bad weather returned, however, and little progress was made subsequently, despite a more concerted effort in mid-March.

Worse still, surprise had now been lost, and the initiative no longer lay with the allies. A further month would elapse before Hamilton's Mediterranean Expeditionary Force landed at Gallipoli, with great loss of life and to no effect but to draw Turkish troops from the Caucasus, though by that time the Russians had been able to stabilize their southern front. The campaign would be one of the great lost opportunities of the war, and would have serious political and diplomatic repercussions.

Success was to come the allies' way in Egypt, however, doubly welcome after near-catastrophic losses by the Russians in Polish Masuria. The Suez Canal was the lifeline through which troops from the Empire passed to France, and in late January an Ottoman force of some 23,000, in large part Syrians but including a regular Turkish division, under the direction of Colonel Friedrich Kress von Kressenstein, mounted an offensive to block it. They crossed 130 miles of the Sinai desert with 5,000 camels as water carriers, using wells dug in advance by German engineers, but aircraft of the RFC and Royal Naval Air Service (RNAS) observed their advance throughout. On 3 February determined attempts to cross the canal at Kantara and Ismailia were decisively repulsed by Indian and Egyptian troops with the aid of naval gunfire.

Reassuringly, contrary to the hopes of the Ottoman high command and German efforts at incitement, the Muslim troops of the Egyptian and Indian armies showed no inclination to rise up against the British in support of a Turkish 'holy war'. Indeed, one officer of the 5th Battery Egyptian Artillery, Mulazzim Awaal Effendi Helmi, was killed in a particularly gallant stand at his gun during hand-to-hand fighting, and according to the despatch in the *London Gazette* would have been recommended for an award had he lived.

The repulse was not immediately followed up because the GOC of the Canal Defence Forces, Major-General Alexander Wilson, believed his troops were ill-trained for the task; but although it would be nearly three years before imperial forces cleared Gaza and entered Jerusalem, the defeat on the Suez Canal was the beginning of the end for Ottoman power in Palestine.

8

MARCH
Drum-fire

Neuve Chapelle: a taste of the battles to come

With the better weather and drier ground in early spring 1915 came renewed thoughts of an allied (Anglo-French) offensive on the Western Front. The moment appeared auspicious – 'particularly', in the words of Sir John French, in view of 'the marked success of the Russian Army in repelling the violent onslaughts of Marshal von Hindenburg, the apparent weakening of the enemy in my front, and the necessity for assisting our Russian Allies to the utmost by holding as many hostile troops as possible in the Western Theatre'.

This too was the opinion of his French counterpart General Joffre, who although having no official authority over the BEF carried the moral authority of the stronger ally. Joffre planned to reduce the great German bulge to the north-west made in the first months' fighting by attacking its extreme points in Artois and Champagne. If the lateral railways in the plain of Douai could be recaptured, he reasoned, the Germans, deprived of the means of supply and rapid reinforcement, would have to withdraw. And there was always the chance of breakthrough and the restoration of mobile warfare, the holy grail of the allied command.

There was for the British another reason too: in the words again of Sir John French's later despatch 'perhaps the most weighty consideration of all, the need of fostering the offensive spirit in the troops under my command after the trying and possibly enervating experiences which they had gone through of a severe winter in the trenches'. Certainly the Indian Corps, comprising the Lahore and Meerut Divisions, wanted to prove themselves. The courage displayed by the newly arrived sepoys in the fighting at Ypres in October and November was undoubted, but their commanders' tactical skill had been less convincing.

By March 1915, although it was still but a fraction of the size of the French forces holding the 400-mile line of trenches from the Belgian coast to the Swiss border, the BEF had grown to such a strength that it had been reorganized into two armies: 1st Army, commanded by the newly promoted General Sir Douglas Haig, and 2nd Army under General Sir Horace Smith-Dorrien. French delegated the planning of the British element of the Artois offensive – the attack at the village of Neuve Chapelle – to Haig and 1st Army, which consisted of IV Corps and the Indian Corps, while the exploitation was to be the business of Smith-Dorrien and 2nd Army. Logic would have suggested the roles be reversed – Smith-Dorrien, the infantryman, planning the set-piece attack, with Haig, the cavalryman, ready to exploit – but besides the actual positions of the armies in the line, Haig's stock stood particularly high after holding the line at Ypres in November, whereas Smith-Dorrien's decision to stand and fight at Le Cateau in August had become such a bone of contention with Sir John French that the peppery infantry general was to be increasingly marginalized.

Neuve Chapelle lay on the road between Bethune and Armentières, the ground flat and cut by drainage ditches. A mile beyond the British lines lay Aubers Ridge, which though barely 20 feet higher than the surrounding country gave a significant advantage in artillery observation, while some 15 miles to the south lay the far greater heights of Vimy Ridge. In consequence, perhaps, the German lines were relatively lightly held, the defenders being able to place greater reliance on their artillery to defeat any attack.

The French assault was to be at Vimy Ridge to threaten the road, rail and canal junctions at La Bassée from the south, while the British attack would menace them from the north. However, the attack on Vimy Ridge would be cancelled when Sir John French said he was not able to relieve the French IX Corps in the line north of Ypres to release them for the assault. Instead Joffre promised the BEF heavy artillery support.

Haig's preparation was thorough. Despite poor weather in late February the RFC had carried out much aerial photography. The Royal Engineers Survey Branch was therefore able to map the area over which the attack was to take place to a depth of nearly a mile, each corps receiving 1,500 copies of 1:5,000-scale (1 cm to 50 m) sheets. Neuve Chapelle was the first deliberately planned British offensive, and would provide something of a template for the BEF's future attacks on the Western Front: a scheduled artillery bombardment followed by infantry advancing at a fixed time, conforming as best they could to the fire plan.

Haig was able to concentrate 340 guns – as many as the BEF had taken to France the previous August – against the German salient at Neuve Chapelle, a ratio of one gun to every 6 yards of front attacked. But guns were one thing, ammunition another. The expenditure rate on the Western Front in 1914 had come as a surprise to everyone. At the end of September Sir John French had written to the War Office calling urgently for more shells, especially high explosive (HE), as the field batteries hitherto had fired only shrapnel. The master-general of the ordnance, Major-General Sir Stanley von Donop, a Royal Artillery officer who steadfastly refused to anglicize his name (his family had come to England when Bonaparte invaded Lippe-Detmold), replied: 'I am commanded by the Army Council to point out that they have provided in the first instance, and have also sent out, replenishments in almost every case fully up to the quantities of gun ammunition which were laid down before the war.' And a subsequent request elicited the reminder from the war minister, Kitchener: 'You will of course see that economy is practised.'

If this sounded bureaucratic, the War Office was in fact faced with a serious problem: even if it accepted the need for far higher scales of ammunition, where was it to find the shells? The ordnance factories did not have significant spare capacity, and building more or outsourcing to industry was not an overnight affair. Von Donop was worried about quality control, not least safety in both production and use. In September the French General St Claire Deville, co-designer of the famous *soixante-quinze*, the 75 mm field gun, had come to London with a new design for an HE shell that could be manufactured quickly from readily available components. Everyone was impressed except von Donop. After the conference Kitchener, asking why he had been so 'stuffy' about the design, received the reply: 'Because in my opinion it is unsafe.' In 1915, when perhaps as many as 800 French guns would suffer barrel explosions, deranging many of Joffre's plans, Kitchener told Asquith that had it not been for the restraining hand of von Donop they would have been 'hanged on the gallows of public opinion'. But what soon developed in the newspapers as 'the great shell scandal' would bring David Lloyd George to the fore at a newly created Ministry of Munitions, and would be one of the factors (the principal being the Dardanelles fiasco) that forced Asquith to form a coalition ministry in May.

Haig's artillery preparation at Neuve Chapelle was therefore limited to thirty minutes. Initially it proved effective enough. Though the night before the attack was wet and snowy, turning to damp mist on the morning of 10 March, the shock of the hurricane bombardment – what the Germans afterwards described as 'the first true drum-fire [*Trommelfeuer*] yet heard' – kept the defenders' heads down just long enough for the assaulting infantry to gain their first objectives. In Artois, too, the water table was so high that the German trenches were dug relatively shallow and built up with earthworks, making them more susceptible to HE. However, after the first set-piece attack the tempo faltered, command impaired by poor communications (there was no tactical radio) and the gunners unable to respond quickly to the infantry's needs owing to shellfire having cut the field-telephone cables. Haig sought to renew the advance by attacking where the original assault had failed, repeating the detailed preparation of the first day, which cost precious time. The casualties mounted. A German divisional counter-attack early on 12 March was beaten back but at heavy cost, and soon afterwards Haig cancelled further attacks and ordered the gains to be consolidated prior to a new attack further north. The shell shortage was now so acute, however, that this attack was soon abandoned but for a local effort by the 7th Division, which also failed, again with high casualties.

Indeed, the losses in many battalions were catastrophic. Of the 750 men of the 2nd Scottish Rifles (2nd Battalion the Cameronians) who went into battle on 10 March – many of the officers with swords drawn – three days later only 143 came out, led by the surviving officer, a second lieutenant, and the regimental sergeant-major. Their dead, wounded and missing included twenty-nine sergeants, a devastating loss of experienced NCOs. Their story is told in one of the finest studies of men in battle, *Morale* (1967) by the late Sir John Baynes, himself a former Cameronian.

In all, the fighting cost some 7,000 British and 4,200 Indian casualties out of the 40,000 who took part, and almost as many Germans. Heroism was common currency: one of the ten resulting VCs was awarded to Gabar Singh Negi of the Gharwal Rifles, a brigade whose tenacity in the attack had been particularly marked. His citation reads: 'During our attack on the German position he was one of a bayonet party with bombs who entered their main trench, and was the first man to go round each traverse, driving back the enemy until they were eventually forced to surrender. He was killed during this engagement.'

Yet if the battle showed no appreciable gain, the French at least were to become cautiously optimistic that the BEF might be reliable in offensive operations. Given the French obsession with the offensive, however, this would prove a distinctly mixed blessing.

9

APRIL
Gallipoli

The greatest stratagem of the war that ended in the greatest failure

As calls increased for conscription to be introduced, a popular song of 1915 mocked Charlie Chaplin, a British citizen, for refusing to enlist. It ended:

And his little baggy trousers
They want mending
Before they send him
To the Dardanelles.

Why the Dardanelles? Because no hardships on the Western Front could compare with those of the Gallipoli peninsula, which commanded the Dardanelles Straits and thereby maritime access to the Black Sea. The extremes of heat and cold, the lack of water, the rocky, inhospitable terrain with its deep gullies and ravines, the close fighting which left the dead unburied, and the flies and other vermin which spread epidemic sickness – Gallipoli was just the very worst place to do battle. John Masefield, later poet laureate, would

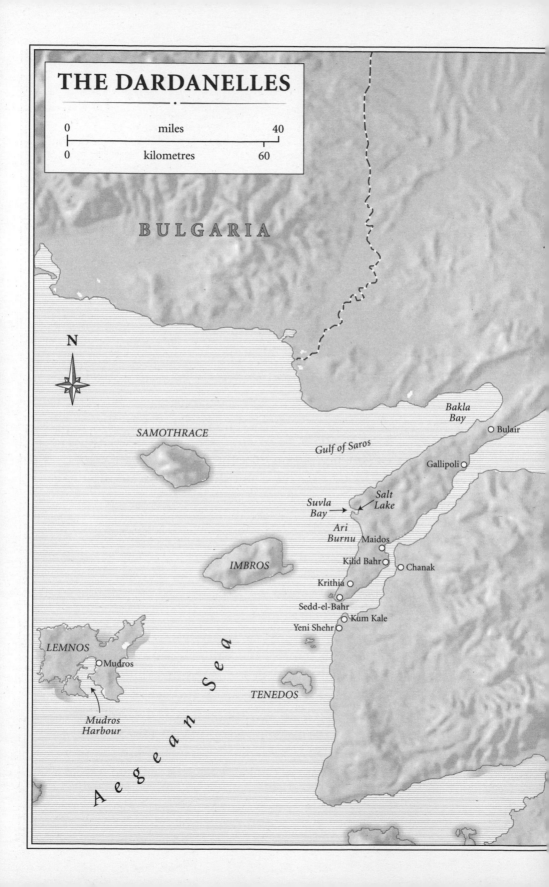

THE DARDANELLES

0	miles	40
0	kilometres	60

BULGARIA

N

SAMOTHRACE

Bakla Bay

Bulair○

Gulf of Saros

Gallipoli○

Salt Lake

Suvla Bay →

Ari Burnu

Maidos ○

IMBROS

Kilid Bahr ○

○ Chanak

Krithia ○

Sedd-el-Bahr ○

○ Kum Kale

Yeni Shehr ○

LEMNOS

○ Mudros

Aegean Sea

TENEDOS

Mudros Harbour

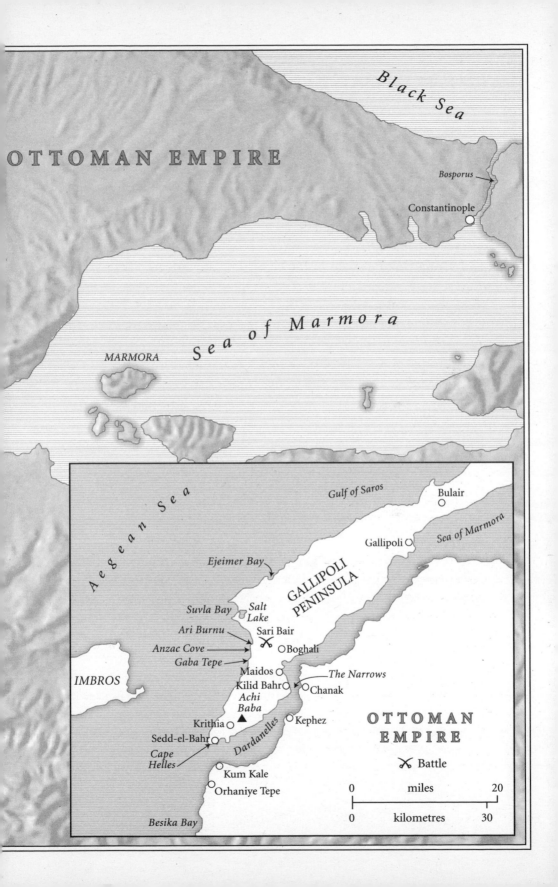

Black Sea

OTTOMAN EMPIRE

Bosporus

Constantinople

S e a   o f   M a r m o r a

MARMORA

A e g e a n   S e a

Gulf of Saros

Bulair

Gallipoli

Sea of Marmora

Ejeimer Bay

GALLIPOLI
PENINSULA

Suvla Bay

*Salt
Lake*

Ari Burnu

Sari Bair

Anzac Cove

Boghali

Gaba Tepe

Maidos

The Narrows

Kilid Bahr

Chanak

*Achi
Baba*

IMBROS

Krithia

Kephez

OTTOMAN
EMPIRE

Sedd-el-Bahr

Dardanelles

*Cape
Helles*

⚔ Battle

Kum Kale

Orhaniye Tepe

0   miles   20

0   kilometres   30

Besika Bay

write of it: 'Men in Gallipoli in the summer of 1915 learned to curse the sun as an enemy more cruel than the Turk.'

From the start it had gone badly, although the margin of failure was much narrower than is sometimes supposed: success would have been possible with a few more resources, a little more skill, and a good deal more resolution at high level. The seaborne assault on 25 April by British, French, Australian and New Zealand troops quickly proved to be an over-improvised and bloody muddle, and everything that followed in the eight-month campaign little more than a series of desperate and costly, if heroic, attempts to overcome the initial failure.

Yet it had begun as one of the boldest and potentially most decisive strategic ploys of the First World War – indeed, the only allied stratagem worthy of the name.

On 2 August 1914 the Ottoman Empire had concluded a secret treaty with the Central Powers against Russia, and had taken the offensive in the Black Sea in late October. Britain and France had declared war the following month. With the situation in France and Flanders still fluid, however, little attention could be given to the new enemy except to strengthen the defences of the Suez Canal and to secure the oil fields of Mesopotamia. But as the Western Front turned to stalemate, the strategic gaze turned to the eastern theatre of war.

Winston Churchill, first lord of the Admiralty, vigorously championed a scheme proposed by Lieutenant-Colonel Maurice Hankey, secretary of the Committee of Imperial Defence, to turn the Central Powers' strategic flank. As he explained in volume 1 of *The World Crisis* (1923):

> As long as France was treated as a self-contained theatre, a complete deadlock existed, and the front of the German invader could neither be pierced nor turned . . . [but] once the view was extended to the whole scene of the war, and that vast war conceived as if it were a single battle, and once the sea power of Britain was brought into play, turning movements of a most

far-reaching character were open to the Allies . . . the Teutonic Empires were in fact vulnerable in an extreme degree on either flank.

The Tsar had already appealed for an offensive against the Turks to take the pressure off his forces in the Caucasus, which would also, it was argued, encourage the neutrals, notably Bulgaria, to enter the war on the allies' side, as well as opening up an ice-free supply route to Russia, which was in desperate need of war materiel.

The war council accepted the Hankey proposal but, shy of providing resources at the expense of the Western Front, initially authorized only a naval operation to force the narrow straits. In mid-February, however, just before the naval operation began, they also authorized preparations for a landing lest bombardment of the shore batteries alone prove insufficient. This was the first grievous mistake: a joint operation, with surprise on the allies' side, might have succeeded, for at that stage the peninsula was not garrisoned very strongly; a naval and only then, in the event of failure, a sequential military operation with surprise gone risked disaster.

By mid-March the naval operation had indeed stalled, and the war council now sanctioned the landing.

General Sir Ian Hamilton, a clever, brave but diffident man, was appointed to command the Mediterranean Expeditionary Force (MEF). He had little time to prepare for what would be the first machine-gun-opposed amphibious assault in history. Nor had much preliminary planning been carried out at the War Office, for the General Staff had been sent to France with the BEF in August, and their replacements had not yet found their feet or gained the confidence of the secretary of state, Field Marshal Lord Kitchener. The first problem was that the MEF was scattered around the eastern Mediterranean and its equipment and supplies embarked haphazardly. Hamilton saw no alternative but to recall them to Egypt to reorganize and regroup before sailing for his advance base on the Greek island of Lemnos.

The Turks were by now thoroughly on the alert. By the end of

March they had reinforced Gallipoli to a strength of four divisions, with another two on the Asiatic shore, and the war minister, Enver Pasha, had appointed Lieutenant-General Otto Liman von Sanders, head of the German military mission, to command them. Sanders was supremely confident of his ability to repel invasion, 'if the English will only leave me alone for eight days'.

'The English' would in fact leave him alone for a whole month.

Against these six divisions Sir Ian Hamilton had only five. By far the best was the virtually all-regular 29th Division, Britain's strategic reserve. The Royal Naval Division, comprising Royal Marines and surplus naval ratings, had seen action at Antwerp but was ill-equipped and ill-trained. The magnificent Australian and New Zealand Army Corps ('Anzac'), consisting of one Australian and one mixed Australian and New Zealand division, under the outstanding Indian army Lieutenant-General William Birdwood, was as yet unblooded. The single, weak division of the French Corps Expéditionnaire d'Orient, formed of colonial troops, was also largely untried.

Hamilton had hoped for the 28th Division too, another regular formation, but Kitchener had promised it to Sir John French for one more offensive on the Western Front. He told Hamilton that in the coming months he could expect 'New Army' divisions – men who had flocked to the recruiting offices in August and September – and perhaps some territorials and Indian army, but these would be raw troops, fit initially only for defensive tasks and labouring.

Hamilton's choice of landing places was limited. The Gallipoli peninsula is only 10 miles across at the widest point and about 45 miles long. Cape Helles lies at the southernmost tip, overlooked by the heights of Achi Baba (709 feet), with Sari Bair ridge (971 feet) some 12 miles north overlooking both sides of the straits at the narrowest point (5 miles). There were a number of small sandy beaches at Cape Helles, as on the western side, but none on the eastern, which in any case was covered by fire from across the straits. There were no towns, just a few settlements, of which Krithia in the south and Bulair in the north were the most important. The roads were unmade tracks.

Given that his options were limited, not least by the inexperience of many of his troops, and given that the months of naval bombardment had forfeited strategic surprise, Hamilton tried to achieve tactical surprise by deceiving the Turks as to the actual main effort. While the 29th Division were to make the main landings at Cape Helles to capture the forts at Kilid Bahr, with the Anzacs landing some 15 miles up the west coast at Gaba Tepe to advance across the peninsula and cut off any Turkish retreat or prevent reinforcement, the French would make a diversionary landing on the Asiatic shore. The Royal Naval Division would also make a demonstration in the Gulf of Saros, which was, indeed, where Sanders expected the main effort to come.

The plan was sound, if pedestrian, but so much dispersal multiplied the chances of things going wrong.

The Anzacs did indeed gain tactical surprise by landing before dawn on 25 April without preliminary bombardment. But while they made some progress inland, casualties and the inexperience of commanders began to tell, and soon, in crude terms, their luck simply ran out, not least in finding themselves opposed by the Turkish 19th Division under command of the brilliant 34-year-old Mustafa Kemal Bey ('Atatürk' – first president of the post-war Turkish republic), one of the original 'Young Turks' who in 1908 restored the country's constitutional monarchy.

The experiences of 'Anzac Cove' would forge a strong national consciousness in the Australian and New Zealand troops, in turn carrying back to the home countries and, later, to the Western Front. The sense of 'mateship' was profound, as exemplified by the story of Private Jack Simpson, who had enlisted in Perth as a stretcher-bearer when war broke out. He had spent his boyhood holidays as a donkey-lad on the beach at South Shields, County Durham, and while bringing in casualties over his shoulder on the second day of the landings he saw an abandoned Turkish donkey and at once pressed it into service. In the next four weeks he would bring in over 300 casualties on its back. Colonel (later General Sir) John Monash wrote that 'Private Simpson and his little beast earned the

admiration of everyone . . . They worked all day and night throughout the whole period since the landing, and the help rendered to
the wounded was invaluable. Simpson knew no fear and moved
unconcernedly amid shrapnel and rifle fire, steadily carrying out his
self-imposed task day by day' – until on 19 May he was killed by a
machine-gun bullet.

At Cape Helles the landings went badly from the outset. The 29th
Division, under Major-General Aylmer Hunter-Weston, a Royal
Engineers officer who though fearless had limited experience of
handling infantry, impaled themselves on the cliffs and machine
guns in broad daylight after a preliminary naval bombardment that
left the defenders in no doubt as to what was happening. Only sui-
cidal gallantry on the part of his regulars – the Lancashire Fusiliers
would win six VCs 'before breakfast' – carried the day. One of the
Fusiliers' VCs, Captain Harold Clayton, killed six weeks later,
described the desperate scene at 'Lancashire Landing', as it was later
dubbed:

> There was tremendously strong barbed wire where my boat was landed.
> Men were being hit in the boats as they splashed ashore. I got up to my
> waist in water, tripped over a rock and went under, got up and made for
> the shore and lay down by the barbed wire. There was a man there
> before me shouting for wirecutters. I got mine out, but could not make
> the slightest impression. The front of the wire was by now a thick mass
> of men, the majority of whom never moved again. The noise was ghastly
> and the sights horrible.

The battalion had started the day with 27 officers and 1,002 other
ranks. Twenty-four hours later, just 16 officers and 304 men answered
roll-call.

Yet despite the heroic efforts, 29th Division could gain only very
limited beachheads. Indeed, at no stage of the campaign could
Hamilton's forces drive further inland than a few miles. Planning
had concentrated on the landings, with insufficient thought about
what would happen subsequently, especially in the event of high

casualties. By 5 May the division had lost half its initial strength, including two-thirds of its officers.

The Gallipoli peninsula would become a salient every bit as lethal as Ypres, with the added complications of supply across open beaches, water shortage, intense heat and insanitary conditions. As on the Western Front, barbed wire, machine guns and artillery put paid to tactical manoeuvre. The only alternatives would be head-on attacks or evacuation, the latter eventually conceded in January 1916. The bold move to break the stalemate of the Western Front had ended merely in its extension into the eastern Mediterranean. The campaign for mastery of the Dardanelles Straits cost the allies some 250,000 casualties, of which nearly half were from sickness, with over 40,000 dead. Turkish losses were roughly the same.

'That the effort failed is not against it,' wrote Masefield in his fine apologia *Gallipoli* shortly after the evacuation; 'many great things and noble men have failed.' But besides the strategic failure and the appalling losses, which in turn exacerbated the situation in France and Flanders, the Dardanelles campaign would have far-reaching political consequences. It spelled the end for Churchill as a voice in the direction of the war, and severely damaged the reputation and confidence of Kitchener. It forced Asquith to form a coalition government and set Lloyd George on course for the premiership. Above all, it reinforced the view that the Western Front was the only place in which the war could be decided. And with that would come the abysmal strategy of attrition, the wearing down of the enemy in bloody offensives that would prove equally costly to the allies themselves.

10

MAY

'Gas!'

The Germans tear up the rule book at the Second Battle of Ypres

Before the Somme became a byword for insensate slaughter, and the defining image of the First World War, it was Ypres that was the British army's centre of gravity on the Western Front.

Hard fighting there in October and November 1914 had cost the BEF some 58,000 casualties, most of them the irreplaceable regulars who could march all day, use cover artfully and fire fifteen aimed rounds a minute. By Christmas in many battalions there remained but a single officer and a few dozen soldiers who had heard the opening shots at Mons.

In the early months of 1915 the BEF had become a harlequin affair, reinforced by men of the Indian army, by territorials, by the few remaining regulars drawn from distant garrisons, and by Canadian regulars and militiamen, the first of the 600,000 of the Canadian Expeditionary Force who would serve on the Western Front. And aside from the futile blood-letting in March of the BEF's first independent offensive, at Neuve Chapelle, they had been able to rest, reorganize and train, so that in mid-April they could begin relieving the French in the Ypres salient.

The timing was unfortunate, however. General Erich von Falkenhayn, chief of the *Grosser Generalstab* – in effect, commander-in-chief – had authorized an attack on the Ypres salient as a strategic diversion from the German army's main offensive on the Eastern Front. With a limited objective, however – to 'pinch out' the salient rather than capture the important road junction of Ypres itself – and not wanting to commit too many troops, Falkenhayn decided, in flagrant breach of the Hague Conventions of 1907, to use chlorine gas. This had been developed and advocated for use as a weapon by the German Franz Haber, who would win the Nobel Prize in Chemistry in 1918 for his work on synthesizing ammonia for use in fertilizers and explosives – an innovation that helped prolong the war.

Though intelligence sources had suggested that gas might be used, the warnings were unspecific and therefore not paid much heed by the French general staff. In consequence, the strange mist that drifted across no-man's-land from the German line on the evening of 22 April towards the left (north-west) of the Ypres salient, where the trenches were still occupied by the French, took the defenders by surprise. Those who could, fled; those who could not, suffocated. Private Anthony Hossack of the Queen Victoria's Rifles, a territorial regiment, described the panic:

> Over the fields streamed mobs of infantry, the dusky warriors of French Africa; away went their rifles, equipment, even their tunics, that they might run the faster. One man came stumbling through our lines. An officer of ours held him up with levelled revolver. 'What's the matter, you bloody lot of cowards?' says he. The Zouave was frothing at the mouth, his eyes started from their sockets, and he fell writhing at the officer's feet.

A gap 4 miles wide had opened in the allied line, into which the Germans advanced, but hesitantly, for their high command seemingly had as little confidence in the new weapon as the French had belief in its existence, and had not conjured enough reserves to exploit the success. Fortunately, too, the Canadian division, on the French right – their first time in action – held their positions just long enough for British and Indian reinforcements to be brought up to check the advance.

Nothing could be done for the gas casualties, however, though Private Bert Newman of the Royal Army Medical Corps recalled his sergeant-major's desperate attempts to force Vaseline into the throats of men gasping for breath to ease the burning.

A German soldier who took part in the attack, Pioneer Willi Siebert, wrote:

> What we saw was total death. Nothing was alive. All of the animals had come out of their holes to die. Dead rabbits, moles, and rats and mice were everywhere. The smell of the gas was still in the air. It hung on the few bushes which were left. When we got to the French lines the trenches were empty but in a half mile the bodies of French soldiers were everywhere. It was unbelievable. Then we saw there were some English. You could see where men had clawed at their faces, and throats, trying to get breath. Some had shot themselves. The horses, still in the stables, cows, chickens, everything, all were dead. Everything, even the insects were dead.

Two days later the Germans released more gas, which struck the Canadian 8th Brigade near St Julien. With only the most primitive of anti-gas masks – towelling or handkerchiefs soaked in urine – the Canadian division paid dearly in the heavy fighting, with some 1,700 dead, 2,000 wounded and almost as many taken prisoner. One of the first of the Canadians' VCs was awarded posthumously to Company Sergeant-Major Frederick Hall of the Winnipeg Rifles, for repeatedly bringing in the wounded under fire. He and two other VC winners all came from homes on Pine Street in Winnipeg, subsequently renamed 'Valour Road'.

The gas attacks shocked public opinion on both sides of the Atlantic, as well as the authorities. Kitchener wrote to Sir John French:

The use of asphyxiating gases is, as you are aware, contrary to the rules and usages of war. Before, therefore, we fall to the level of the degraded Germans [in retaliating] I must submit the matter to the Government . . . These methods show to what depth of infamy our enemies will go in order to supplement their want of courage in facing our troops.

This sentiment did not, however, prevent the British from developing their own – and better – chemical weapons.

Meanwhile the BEF were also facing the conventional logic of defence: if ground is worth holding in the first place, it is worth counter-attacking to regain if lost. And the greatest apostle of offensive action, General Ferdinand Foch, commanding French troops in the north-west and therefore with moral authority over the BEF, now ordered just this.

The counter-attacks began in earnest on 26 April. That day the Lahore Division suffered 1,700 casualties – over 10 per cent – without even reaching the German front line. The story was much the same everywhere, and General Sir Horace Smith-Dorrien, commanding the BEF's 1st Army, voiced his concern at the high cost of so little gain, suggesting instead that the line of defence be straightened and therefore shortened by withdrawing from the now even more constricted salient. Sir John French refused, though after another costly and futile attack by the Lahore Division, on 1 May, he authorized a limited withdrawal from its apex. Five days later, resenting this reversal, he took the opportunity to dismiss Smith-Dorrien and appoint in his place the less volcanic commander of V Corps, Lieutenant-General Sir Herbert Plumer.

The German attacks had dampened neither French's nor Joffre's ardour for the long-intended allied offensive. The two commanders-in-chief would stick to the plans made months before to attack in Artois, south of Ypres, notwithstanding the manifest shortage of artillery shells. 'Sir John, undeterred by the drain on his resources during his recent struggle,' wrote Kitchener's private secretary and biographer, 'was determined to adhere, on its broad lines, to his main plan. "The ammunition will be all right," he had told

Kitchener on May 2; he knew his men to be in as high fettle as ever.'

Kitchener was far from convinced but gave the go-ahead nevertheless, largely at Joffre's urging. Early on the morning of 9 May, therefore, the BEF attacked towards Aubers Ridge, while the French attacked towards Vimy Ridge – ground familiar from the Neuve Chapelle battle. Joffre said it was 'the beginning of the end'; the war would be over in three weeks, because Foch was employing a new tactic of prolonged and heavy bombardment instead of surprise. Six days' hard pounding by 1,250 guns along a 12-mile front held by four German divisions, and then eighteen French divisions would attack, with the BEF in support on the flank.

But the attack soon broke down, as all previous attacks had, except in the centre, where the corps commanded by General Philippe Pétain, later the hero of Verdun (and in the Second World War the 'arch-collaborator', president of Vichy France), broke through to a depth of 2 miles. However, the Germans managed to close the gap before reserves could be brought up to exploit the success, a pattern that would be repeated in every allied offensive for the next three years.

Progress in the British sector was just as disappointing. As Kitchener's private secretary noted: 'It was quickly and unhappily evident that Sir John [French] would be unable to make good the substantial support he had so manfully intended to lend. He could do little but to employ and destroy a considerable number of Germans, and capture – at sad cost to himself – some not very important trenches.'

Foch's troops suffered 102,000 casualties, but the BEF's were proportionately more: over 11,000 killed or wounded on 9 May alone, the great majority within yards of their own front-line trenches. Mile for mile, division for division, the Artois offensive saw some of the highest losses of the entire war.

But Sir John French knew where the blame lay – with the inadequate supply of shells, the result of the war council's giving priority to the Dardanelles campaign. And when he returned to his headquarters on the first day of the battle, in despondent mood having watched the stalling of the attack from atop a church tower, what should he find but a telegram from Kitchener asking him to 'hold in readiness for despatch to the Dardanelles via Marseilles by quickest route 20,000 rounds 18-pounder ammunition and 2,000 rounds 4.5-inch howitzer ammunition'.

In dismay he replied: 'This morning I commenced an important attack, and the battle is likely to last several days. I am warding off a heavy attack East of Ypres at the same time. In these circumstances I cannot possibly accept the responsibility of reducing the stock of ammunition unless it be immediately replaced from home.'

Kitchener was adamant: 'I will see that it is replaced [but] the state of affairs in the Dardanelles renders it absolutely essential that the ammunition which has been ordered should be sent off at once.'

The consignment was indeed replaced within twenty-four hours, but French was still dismayed, in part because he genuinely could not understand why industry could not supply more shells, or why the Dardanelles – a 'sideshow' – should have priority over his 'decisive theatre', but principally because he had a failed offensive to explain and consequently his neck to save. He therefore enlisted the support of the press, in the shape of Charles Repington, *The Times*'s influential military correspondent (dubbed 'the Playboy of the Western Front' because his promising career had been cut short a decade before as a result of a liaison with another officer's wife).

On 14 May Repington wrote an excoriating piece on the shell shortage under the headline 'Need for shells: British attacks checked: Limited supply the cause: A Lesson From France', and for good measure French also sent two of his personal staff to London to brief politicians, including Lloyd George and Arthur Balfour, leader of the Conservative opposition, in what Kitchener's private secretary called 'a minor coup d'état'.

Although it would redound to his discredit and, later, contribute to his dismissal, for the time being the 'shell scandal', on top of the Dardanelles setback, advanced French's cause: on 25 May Asquith reluctantly formed a coalition government, with Lloyd George leading a newly created Ministry of Munitions and the Tory cabinet ministers increasingly arguing for priority to be accorded to the Western Front.

Meanwhile the wearying attacks and counter-attacks at Ypres continued, with the largest discharge of gas on 24 May preceding a huge German push across a front of 4½ miles. Plumer's men, now with rudimentary but effective gas masks, were able to halt the enemy well short of the British line, and that evening Falkenhayn issued the order to cease all further attacks on the salient.

When Sir John French was relieved of command in December he would take the consolatory title 'Earl of Ypres'; but there was to be a Third Battle of Ypres, even bloodier and more futile, in 1917, known thereafter as 'Passchendaele'.

On 3 May 1915 Italy, having the previous August declared her neutrality on the grounds that the Triple Alliance was a defensive treaty and that Germany and Austria had waged offensive war, officially revoked the treaty. On 23 May she declared war on Austria-Hungary, though the declaration of war on Germany would not come until August 1916.

The acquisition of Italy as an ally, a considerable diplomatic coup, would add significantly to the Entente's naval strength in the Mediterranean, act as a beacon (for a time at least) to the wavering Balkan states, and divert Austro-Hungarian troops from the Galician and Serbian fronts. The Austro-Italian border was 400 miles long, stretching from the Stelvio Pass to the Adriatic Sea. Italian forces outnumbered the Austrian, which had to remain on the defensive while Russia resisted strongly, but the difficult terrain was in the defender's favour. The Italian commander-in-chief, Luigi Cadorna, a proponent of the frontal assault, planned to attack at once on the Isonzo river with the intention of sweeping across the Karst plateau into Slovenia, in turn threatening Vienna.

It was a grandiose concept, which, like similar plans hatched on the Western Front, took insufficient account of the defensive power of the machine gun and heavy artillery, and the variable quality of the available troops. The *Alpini* were tough mountain fighters, and the *Bersaglieri*, light infantry, experienced in recent wars against the Turks in Libya, but many of the conscripts from the south were ill-suited to the conditions.

Cadorna had some initial successes in his preliminary operations in late May and June, but as on the Western Front the fighting soon developed into trench warfare, though here the trenches had to be dug in Alpine rock and glaciers, and often at altitudes of 10,000 feet. It would become known as the 'White War'. In the first six months of his campaign Cadorna would launch four separate offensives on the Isonzo, each without appreciable success and costing in all some 60,000 dead and more than 150,000 wounded, a quarter of his mobilized forces.

11

JUNE
Those Magnificent Men

War in the air sees fiction turn into reality

No aspect of warfare saw greater advances between 1914 and 1918 than aviation, though progress before the war had been cautious. In H. G. Wells's futuristic novel *The War in the Air*, published in 1908, just five years after the Wright brothers' pioneering heavier-than-air flight, airships and flying machines did battle over New York, with the wholesale destruction of buildings, bridges and ultimately each other. In reality, the major powers were slower to exploit the Wrights' success than Wells prophesied. At the beginning of the war the British had fewer than 113 aircraft in naval and military service, the French 160 and the Germans 250 – and only Germany had a strategic airship capability.

By June 1915, however, Wells's original vision was beginning to take real form. In January the Kaiser had sanctioned an air campaign against military targets in Britain, including naval bases, fuel and ammunitions dumps but excluding royal palaces and residential areas. On 19 January, two 'Zeppelins', as they were invariably known, whatever their manufacture (Count Ferdinand von

Zeppelin's airships were aluminium-framed, while others, notably the Schütte-Lanz, were of wood), had attacked the Norfolk coastal towns of Great Yarmouth and King's Lynn, killing four civilians, and while the raids did little significant damage they caused much alarm. The Kaiser afterwards expressed the hope that 'the air war against England will be carried out with the greatest energy', and in May, therefore, the German high command took the decision to mount a sustained bombing offensive on the British mainland, especially the London docklands.

One of the reasons they were able to do so was the unexpected availability of most of the airships. The Zeppelins were not needed for scouting by the largely inactive German High Seas Fleet, and had already proved too vulnerable to anti-aircraft fire for use to support the army. Airships now began appearing regularly in the skies over the eastern counties, and on the night of 31 May the first attack on London was made, Zeppelin LZ38 dropping eighty-nine incendiary bombs and thirty grenades. Number 16 Alkham Road, Stoke Newington, had the distinction of being the first house in the capital to be destroyed, though without casualties; LZ38 then turned south over Hackney and Stratford, where its bombs killed seven people and injured thirty-five. Nine RFC aircraft attempted to intercept it, but flying above 10,000 feet the airship was beyond their reach. Though this first attack was almost certainly a navigational error (the docks were the riper target), the bombing of civilian targets now became routine, like the sinking of passenger ships by submarine.

On the Western Front, too, aerial warfare was developing apace. Before 1914 aircraft were regarded as an ancillary element at best, sometimes merely as an irrelevance. Tethered observation balloons and experimental dirigibles had been operated by the Royal Engineers since the Boer War, and their use in siege operations acknowledged, but the limited payloads of heavier-than-air machines and their dependence on good weather made them unreliable when it came to reconnaissance. On 27 September 1913 Charles Repington of *The Times* quoted the opinion of Field Marshal Sir John

French, at that time CIGS, at the autumn manoeuvres, in which for the first time a relatively large number of aircraft took part: 'Aeroplane reconnaissance cannot always be depended upon . . . it may be mentioned that, owing to fog and mist on the morning of the 23rd [September], they were unable to leave their camp, although information as bearing upon the strategic problem was perhaps more urgently needed on that morning than on any other.' Cavalry would therefore remain the primary means of reconnaissance.

From 1912, however, both the War Office and the Admiralty had been trying to make up for lost time, with the active backing of their new ministers, Jack Seely and Winston Churchill respectively, who themselves took to the air at the controls of primitive aircraft (in Churchill's case with near-fatal results). In May that year the Royal Flying Corps was formed, comprising a naval as well as a military wing, and in August 1914, after conversion of the naval wing into the Royal Naval Air Service the previous month, four RFC squadrons with some sixty aircraft – BE2 (Blériot Experimental) biplanes, Blériot monoplanes, Farmans and Avro 504s – flew to France with the BEF. No 1 (balloon) Squadron joined them in 1915 when the war of movement had ended and the Western Front become entrenched.

The 'workhorse' BE2, a two-seater designed by Geoffrey de Havilland and built at the Royal Aircraft (formerly Balloon) Factory at Farnborough, had a maximum speed of 63 knots (116 km/h) at 6,500 feet, an operational ceiling of 10,000 feet and endurance of around three hours. Until the swivel-mounted Lewis gun was introduced in 1915 the observer was armed with a rifle, which was effective enough at the BE2's low speed, though equally at 63 knots the aircraft was vulnerable to ground fire. On 21 August, three days before the BEF's first battle at Mons, Sergeant-Major David Jillings, an observer with No. 2 Squadron RFC, brought down a German Albatros with a single shot near Lessines in Belgium. Next day he became the BEF's first casualty to enemy fire when small-arms fire from the cavalry division he was flying over wounded him in the leg. (He recovered, won the Military Cross (MC) the following year, and was later commissioned, rising after the war to the rank of group captain.)

Realizing almost immediately when fighting began that his cavalry could not penetrate the Germans' own cavalry screen to bring him information, Sir John French, now commanding the BEF, rapidly modified his earlier views, turning increasingly to Brigadier-General David Henderson's RFC squadrons to pinpoint the enemy. On 22 August, urged by Joffre to mount an attack to ease the pressure on the French army to his right at Charleroi, he replied that he could not commit to an attack before discovering what lay to his front – that is, 'until he got reports from his aeroplanes', as his deputy chief of staff recorded. French's trust in the RFC during the long retreat to the Marne over the next ten days saved the BEF from being outflanked or overwhelmed.

Bad weather had for the most part kept the German airships on the ground in the first days of the war, but on the night of 25 August Zeppelin Z9 dropped nine bombs on Antwerp, killing or wounding twenty-six people and damaging the palace in which the Belgian royal family had taken up residence. The RNAS detachment on fleet support in nearby Zeebrugge at once began sorties to try to destroy the airships at their moorings. On 8 October Z9 was wrecked in its hangar at Düsseldorf by two 20 lb bombs dropped from 600 feet by Lieutenant (later Air Vice-Marshal) Reginald Marix in a single-seater Sopwith Tabloid, one of the fastest aircraft of the time, having flown a zig-zag course from Antwerp, a straight-line distance of just over 100 miles – a magnificent early strategic use of air power.

When the war began, by and large only airships had radio. The aircraft of the *Deutsche Luftstreitkräfte* (German air force), as it became known, the French *Aéronautique Militaire*, and the RFC and RNAS communicated with the ground by signalling lamp. On 24 September, however, during the allied counter-offensive on the River Aisne, Lieutenants D. S. Lewis and B. T. James used airborne telegraphy (Morse Code) for the first time to direct artillery fire, their radio log beginning 'A very little short. Fire! Fire!', and ending forty minutes later with 'I am coming home now.'

The end soon afterwards of the war of movement at once increased the value of photographic reconnaissance. An experimental air photographic section was set up in January 1915, and this bore fruit in the BEF's first independent offensive, in March at Neuve Chapelle, when as a result of the RFC's extensive aerial photography the Royal Engineers Survey Branch was able to map the German trench system in considerable detail.

Aerial combat was also developing fast, and in June 1915 the so-called 'Fokker scourge' began. A monoplane (*Eindecker*) built by Fokker Flugzeugwerke GmbH in Schwerin, Prussia, designed by the Dutch-born Anton Fokker, incorporated an interrupter gear allowing a machine gun to fire forward through the propeller. This gave a pronounced advantage to the attacking aircraft, and losses to the Fokker *Eindecker* mounted alarmingly, the press referring to the lumbering BE2 in particular as 'Fokker fodder', until in April 1916 the allies produced comparable fighters, the British Airco DH2 and the French Nieuport II.

Meanwhile Zeppelin raids on London were increasing, almost with impunity. On the night of 13 October 1916 five airships would drop bombs killing seventy-one people. More and more RFC aircraft would be diverted from the Western Front and elsewhere to cover the capital and east coast ports.

But the Zeppelin was a large, slow target, and improved anti-aircraft artillery and searchlights, as well as aircraft able to fly higher, at night, to intercept them, began steadily to take a toll. As early as June 1915, Sub-Lieutenant Rex Warneford of the RNAS destroyed one with a bomb over the Belgian city of Ghent, for which he was awarded the VC. From the spring of 1917, therefore, the Germans would turn their attention to long-range bombers such as the twin-engined Gotha, which, flying at greater speed, could risk attacks in daylight. On 13 June that year a raid by twenty Gothas killed 162, and a similar raid less than a month later 57. By the standards of the Blitz in the 1940s these figures were small – in all, there were some 1,400 civilian deaths and 3,500 injuries during the war – but the effect on public morale was considerable, 300,000

Londoners routinely using the Underground for shelter overnight. Public opinion turned even more bitter towards Germany, demanding reprisal raids, and frustration with the RFC's inability to intercept or subsequently destroy the raiders grew. Both factors contributed to the decision the following year to form the Royal Air Force, thereby reintegrating the RFC and RNAS – which had begun the war as 'Cinderella' branches of the army and navy respectively – under unified command, but in an entirely independent service. When fighting ceased in November 1918 the RAF was operating 22,000 aircraft, most of them incomparably faster and longer-range than those that had left for France in 1914. In 1909 Louis Blériot had just managed to cross the English Channel in an aircraft little more powerful than a motorized kite. Only ten years later, in June 1919, two former RNAS and RFC pilots, Captain John Alcock and Lieutenant Arthur Whitten Brown, would fly a Vickers Vimy bomber across the Atlantic.

12

JULY
Askaris

War in Africa: a sideshow that inspired Hollywood

Africa had seen the first shots of the Great War between British and German troops, and in November 1918 it would see some of the last. Indeed, the small German force in East Africa would claim the unique distinction of not having been defeated in the field, returning to the Fatherland in 1919 like triumphal Roman legionaries from a distant campaign.

After the setbacks suffered by the allies in the spring offensives in France in 1915, July brought a welcome victory when the last German forces in German South-West Africa (Namibia), a territory six times the size of England and Germany's second-largest colony after German East Africa, surrendered to South African troops under the personal command of Louis Botha, the prime minister and former Boer commander.

Africa, though a military sideshow, had been dragged into the war because it was almost completely controlled by European powers. Berlin, expecting attacks on her colonies, also saw an opportunity to divert Anglo-French troops and resources from the Western

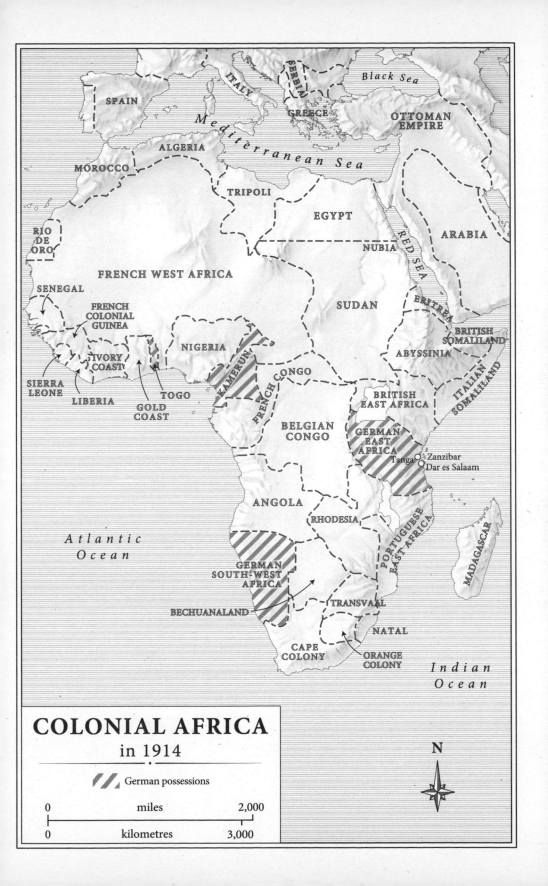

SPAIN

ITALY

SERBIA

Black Sea

GREECE

OTTOMAN
EMPIRE

Mediterranean Sea

ALGERIA

MOROCCO

TRIPOLI

EGYPT

ARABIA

RIO
DE
ORO

NUBIA

RED SEA

FRENCH WEST AFRICA

SENEGAL

FRENCH
COLONIAL
GUINEA

NIGERIA

SUDAN

ERITREA

BRITISH
SOMALILAND

ABYSSINIA

IVORY
COAST

SIERRA
LEONE

LIBERIA

GOLD
COAST

TOGO

KAMERUN

FRENCH CONGO

ITALIAN SOMALILAND

BRITISH
EAST
AFRICA

BELGIAN
CONGO

GERMAN
EAST
AFRICA

Tanga ○ ○ Zanzibar
Dar es Salaam ○

ANGOLA

RHODESIA

*Atlantic
Ocean*

PORTUGUESE EAST AFRICA

MADAGASCAR

GERMAN
SOUTH-WEST
AFRICA

BECHUANALAND

TRANSVAAL

NATAL

CAPE
COLONY

ORANGE
COLONY

*Indian
Ocean*

COLONIAL AFRICA
in 1914

//// German possessions

| 0 | miles | 2,000 |
| 0 | kilometres | 3,000 |

N

Front. Distances were vast, and a small force could tie down far greater numbers of troops here than in Europe.

However, the Royal Navy's rapid destruction of German cruisers, and the bottling-up of the *Hochseeflotte* in the North Sea by the British Grand Fleet, made communication and supply almost impossible for the German colonies, which increasingly had to rely on primitive local resources.

The campaign against German South-West Africa had begun in September 1914, with London's request to destroy the wireless stations crucial for the control of German vessels in the South Atlantic. Botha said that he could do it with South African troops alone, leaving imperial troops free for service elsewhere.

South African troops mobilized along the border under the command of Major-General Henry Lukin, a British officer seconded as inspector-general of the Union [of South Africa] Defence Force, and Lieutenant-Colonel Manie Maritz, leader of the commando (mounted irregular) forces. There was, however, much sympathy for the Germans among the Boers. Only twelve years had passed since the end of the Second Boer War, in which Germany had offered the two Boer republics both moral and material support. Now Maritz turned against the British, issuing a declaration that

> the former South African Republic and Orange Free State as well as the Cape Province and Natal are proclaimed free from British control and independent, and all white inhabitants of the mentioned areas, of whatever nationality, are hereby called upon to take their weapons in their hands and realise the long-cherished ideal of a Free and Independent South Africa.

Botha declared martial law, suppressing the 'Boer revolt' with considerable bloodshed, and in November with a force of some 50,000 was able to launch an offensive against the Germans across the Orange River from Walvis Bay. The defenders consisted of 3,000 locally raised *Schutztruppe* (the officers and NCOs were mainly German nationals, with a core of professionals) and 7,000 armed settlers,

84

but Botha's methodical tactics quickly gained him the wireless stations, and in May the capital, Windhoek, surrendered without a fight. South African casualties were remarkably light, indeed fewer than in the revolt. It was to be the only campaign of the war planned and executed entirely by colonial forces. As a result, Deutsche-Südwestafrika would in 1919 become a South African possession.

Windhoek had in any case been isolated in August 1914 with the destruction of the powerful wireless station at Kamina in Togoland, Germany's smallest African colony, severing all radio communications with Berlin. Defended by fewer than 1,000 local police, the colony was invaded immediately after the outbreak of hostilities by British troops from the Gold Coast and French troops from Dahomey to the east. On 7 August an advance patrol of the Gold Coast Regiment ran into fire near the capital, Lomé, at which point Private Alhaji Grunshi became the first soldier in British service to fire a shot in the war. Resistance ended within a fortnight, though not without casualties on both sides. Grunshi was later mentioned in despatches, and in East Africa would win both the Distinguished Conduct Medal and the Military Medal.

He was among two million Africans who were to serve in the First World War, on three continents, either as soldiers or in labour corps. The French in particular used their colonial troops on the Western Front, but despite calls from Churchill and others, the War Office would not raise African battalions for service in Europe. In part this was because of the practical problems of language, training and command, but it also undoubtedly reflected a belief that African troops would not be able to bear the rigours of the Western Front in either the moral or the physical sense. Nevertheless, an estimated 300,000 Africans were to die, or be killed in action, over the course of the war.

Progress in the other German West African colony, Kamerun (Cameroon), was trickier. The British commander, Major-General Charles Dobell, had arrived off the coast in late September with a force of 13,000 largely local recruits, the majority French. Although the port of Duala fell without a shot, German troops withdrew inland to begin a sharp resistance in the forested interior. The local German commander urged Dobell to call a ceasefire to avoid the 'unsightly spectacle' of European troops killing each other in front of Africans. He refused.

More Entente troops entered the country from Nigeria and French Equatorial Africa, but by March 1915 Dobell's numbers had been so greatly reduced by sickness that for many months he was able to act only on the defensive. Operations dragged on until 1916, when the remaining German troops finally surrendered after last-ditch fighting in the Spanish-controlled province of Muni. Nevertheless, as commander of a successful independent campaign, Dobell would be one of those celebrated in John Singer Sargent's large group portrait *General Officers of World War I* (1920–2), now in the National Portrait Gallery.

The main – and least successful – allied campaign in Africa was in German East Africa (now Rwanda, Burundi and mainland Tanzania). Here, distances, climate, terrain and the resourcefulness of the German commander, Colonel Paul von Lettow-Vorbeck, combined to thwart the efforts of the Indian army, the King's African Rifles, and South African forces under Jan Smuts, one of the most famous commanders of the Boer War, and in 1914 also serving as his country's defence minister.

With scant artillery, a few hundred Europeans and 3,000 askaris – local black troops, commanded by German officers and NCOs – Lettow-Vorbeck conducted a masterly defence, defeating an Indian army expeditionary force in November 1914 at Tanga and, from 1916, waging a campaign of manoeuvre against a largely South African imperial force many times its size. Smuts's reputation might well have been tarnished by the setbacks had he not been recalled early and sent to London as South Africa's representative on the newly formed war council.

Lettow-Vorbeck was not, as is sometimes asserted, a convinced practitioner of guerrilla warfare. On the contrary, he was a Prussian officer in the orthodox mould who, having seen service with the international force suppressing the Boxer rebellion in China in

1900, and in putting down the tribal uprisings in South-West Africa in 1904, had developed a strong aversion to guerrilla tactics, which he saw as inimical to discipline. He favoured instead the classical German military doctrine of envelopment to try to bring about the decisive encounter, though he was always careful to avoid major pitched battles. In the end, the sheer disparity of numbers forced him to adopt hit-and-run tactics.

Karen Blixen, the Danish author of *Out of Africa*, with whom Lettow-Vorbeck formed a lifelong friendship after meeting her on a voyage to East Africa, later recalled: 'He belonged to the olden days, and I have never met another German who has given me so strong an impression of what Imperial Germany was and stood for.'

If the scale of fighting in Africa on land was small, that on water was smaller still, but not without drama. The Germans had controlled Lake Tanganyika since the outbreak of the war with three armed steamers and two unarmed motorboats. In June 1915 two British gunboats, HMS *Mimi* and HMS *Toutou*, each armed with a 3-pounder and a Maxim machine gun, were transported 3,000 miles overland to the British shore and, on 26 December, captured the 45-ton German steamboat *Kingani*, renaming it HMS *Fifi*. Soon afterwards, *Fifi*, with two Belgian boats, under Commander Geoffrey Spicer-Simson, sank the *Hedwig von Wissmann*, leaving only three German vessels on the lake, which in their turn were run aground or sunk by mid-1916. The war on the lake was the inspiration for C. S. Forester's 1935 novel *The African Queen*, memorably brought to the screen in 1951 by John Huston with Humphrey Bogart and Katharine Hepburn in the leading roles.

Lettow-Vorbeck also mounted spoiling attacks into the neighbouring British colonies of Northern Rhodesia (Zambia) and Nyasaland (Malawi), and Portuguese Mozambique. His only reinforcements during this time were men and guns from the cruiser *Königsberg*, which had taken refuge in the Rufigi river in October 1914. Indeed, for four years, with a force that never exceeded 14,000, and over an area of 750,000 square miles, he held in check some 300,000 imperial, Belgian and Portuguese troops, and was the only

German commander to invade British colonial soil with any claim to success. Never in the field of human conflict was so much tramped by so many after so few.

At the Armistice the *Schutztruppe* were still fighting, the only German troops to end the war undefeated, and in March 1919 Lettow-Vorbeck would be accorded the honour of leading 120 officers and NCOs in their tattered tropical uniforms on a victory parade through the Brandenburg Gate, which was decorated in their honour.

13

AUGUST
Suvla Bay

Another bold stratagem at Gallipoli fails through poor generalship

By the summer of 1915 not only was there stalemate on the Western Front and an unpromising situation on the Eastern, the campaign at Gallipoli was well and truly stalled. What had begun in the spring as a bold idea to use Britain's naval power to outflank the Western Front, forcing open the Dardanelles Straits to gain better communications with Russia, was becoming a byword across the Empire for incompetence and futility, an affair of trenches and barbed wire every bit as murderous as France and Flanders.

In part the blame could be laid with the commander-in-chief of the Mediterranean Expeditionary Force, Sir Ian Hamilton, a highly regarded if reticent man who had played poorly the bad hand dealt to him by the Admiralty and the War Office. But only in part: for when initial success eluded his force, London began starving him of the resources needed to recover the initiative. Despite the decisions of the war council in January and February, in part emanating from Lloyd George's particular demand that the 'New Armies' being raised should be used in a way that befitted the 'better class of man from which they are drawn' – in other words, elsewhere than the Western Front – by August no fewer than sixteen divisions had been sent to France, but only five to Gallipoli.

Nevertheless, Hamilton was determined to break the stalemate, using the same principle that had generated the Dardanelles campaign in the first place: turning the flank by amphibious means. He chose as his landing place Suvla Bay, 8 miles north of 'Anzac Cove', the bridgehead held by the Australian and New Zealand Army Corps commanded by the British Lieutenant-General William Birdwood. Suvla Bay was tricky to approach because of its shoals, but had plenty of room for boats to beach and, beyond that, a plateau mostly of salt marsh, so that the initial beachhead would not be as confined as at Anzac Cove, or at Cape Helles where the British landings had taken place.

Suvla was watched by just a regiment's worth of infantry – around a thousand men, lightly armed. Hamilton's plan was to reinforce Birdwood's corps for a renewed offensive to tie down the Turks around the heights of Sari Bair, and then land two fresh divisions – IX Corps – at Suvla: these, in conjunction with the Anzacs, would advance quickly across the peninsula and take the high ground dominating the Dardanelles 'Narrows'. The naval operation to force the straits could then begin anew.

Hamilton also wanted some younger generals fresh from the fight in France to command IX Corps and its two New Army divisions, the 10th (Irish) and 11th (Northern), and the 53rd (Welsh) Territorial, which would spearhead the landings. The first six months of the war had seen the rapid promotion of talent, and he asked specifically for Lieutenant-Generals Julian Byng and Henry Rawlinson. The War Office, however, was unresponsive. Because both Byng and Rawlinson were junior to the divisional commanders (who were already in place) on the peacetime gradation list, they appointed instead Lieutenant-General Sir Frederick Stopford, Lieutenant of the Tower of London. Aged sixty-one, Stopford had seen little actual fighting and had never commanded men in battle. It was a risky appointment at best, and at worse a reckless one.

Hamilton's intention was to open the operation with a diversionary attack by the British in the Cape Helles sector, then begin the offensive from Anzac Cove in early evening, with the landing at Suvla following in darkness, by which time the Australians and New Zealanders were to have broken out towards the Sari Bair heights. Because of the shoals in Suvla Bay, however, the plan for IX Corps had to be modified: 11th (Northern) Division would land in darkness south of Nibrunesi Point, the bay's southern headland, and 10th (Irish) Division within the bay the following morning, followed by the 53rd, with the immediate objective of seizing the ring of hills dominating the Suvla plain.

When Stopford was first shown Hamilton's plan in late July he thought it a good one: 'I am sure it will succeed and I congratulate whoever has been responsible for framing it.' However, there was now the most perverse, if well-meaning, of counsels. Stopford's chief of staff, the newly promoted Brigadier-General Hamilton Reed, a Gunner who had won the VC in South Africa, and come fresh from the Western Front, believed they lacked sufficient artillery: 'The whole teaching of the campaign in France proves that troops cannot be expected to attack an organized system of trenches without the assistance of a large number of howitzers,' he minuted.

For once, it seemed, lessons were being learned. But at Suvla, aerial reconnaissance had established that there were no entrenched positions. While this intelligence demanded wariness, especially if the Turks were to get wind of the landings in time to dig in, the wariness should not have dominated the planning. It did. Compton Mackenzie, author of the 1947 comic novel *Whisky Galore!*, was a counter-espionage officer with the Secret Service Bureau in the eastern Mediterranean, and recalled meeting Stopford and Reed on the island of Imbros during the planning:

Next to me was Sir Frederick Stopford, a man of great kindliness and personal charm, whose conversation at lunch left me at the end of the meal completely without hope of victory at Suvla. The reason for this apprehension was his inability to squash the new General opposite . . .

91

This Brigadier was holding forth almost truculently about the folly of the plan of operations drawn up by the General Staff, while Sir Frederick Stopford appeared to be trying to reassure him in a fatherly way. I looked along the table to where Aspinall and Dawnay [junior staff officers] were sitting near General Braithwaite [Hamilton's chief of staff]; but they were out of earshot, and the dogmatic Brigadier continued unchallenged to enumerate the various military axioms which were being ignored by the Suvla plan of operations. For one thing, he vowed, most certainly he was not going to advance a single yard until all the Divisional Artillery was ashore. I longed for Sir Frederick to rebuke his disagreeable and discouraging junior; but he was deprecating, courteous, fatherly, anything except the Commander of an Army Corps which had been entrusted with a major operation that might change the whole course of the war in twenty-four hours.

Slowly but surely Stopford began limiting the objectives of the landing. His final orders were imprecise, requiring only that the high ground be taken 'if possible', whereas in fact this was essential if the whole purpose of the Suvla offensive – cutting the Gallipoli peninsula and taking the heights above the Dardanelles Narrows – was to be achieved. Those who had to execute the orders now began to doubt how important the objective really was, and the necessary sense of urgency was lost.

Unsurprisingly the whole operation, launched on 6 August, miscarried. At Anzac Cove the attack had taken the Turks by surprise but then run out of steam, the commanders over-cautious, the troops over-burdened. At Suvla Bay the steam was never got up. Twenty thousand men were put ashore safely enough, if in places mixed up in the pitch dark, and for thirty-six hours there was nothing barring their way across the peninsula but at most 2,000 Turks with no machine guns, very little artillery and no reserves within 30 miles. The steep climbs beyond the plain were daunting but largely unopposed. Stopford, sleeping aboard the sloop HMS *Jonquil* during the landings, failed to recognize that his divisional commanders were more concerned to consolidate the beachhead than to push on, and when Hamilton himself at last realized what was happening he found that the naval arrangements had broken down and he could not leave his headquarters at Imbros.

In the confusion and hesitation casualties at Suvla began to mount – 1,700 in the first twenty-four hours, nearly as many as there were Turk defenders. On the second evening, the German adviser at Suvla reported to the head of the German military mission to the Turkish army, Liman von Sanders, in effect its commander-in-chief: 'No energetic attacks on the enemy's part have taken place. On the contrary, the enemy is advancing timidly.'

Sanders rushed reinforcements to Suvla, sacking the local Turkish divisional commander for failing to use his reserves and replacing him with Mustafa Kemal, the young general who would become Turkey's first president. When on 9 August, at Hamilton's urging, Stopford at last pressed forward his attack, the odds had almost evened.

Casualties began to mount, the fighting savage, the Turks giving no quarter with the bayonet. Three days later the 'Sandringham Company' of the 5th (Territorial) Battalion of the Norfolk Regiment, formed predominantly of estate workers from the royal residence and led by the King's land agent, the 54-year-old Frank Beck, were wiped out along with others of the battalion. It has long been believed that many of them were killed after capture. Their story was movingly told in the 1999 BBC dramatization *All the King's Men*, starring David Jason as Captain Beck.

There were moments of chivalry, though. Lieutenant John Still of the 6th East Yorkshires, a New Army battalion, recalled how, after he had been taken prisoner, a Turkish officer drew his pistol to shoot him and three others, when 'an Imam with a turban on . . . wrestled with him [the officer] and took his pistol away.'

It was soon apparent that all that had been achieved at Suvla was another beachhead that was going nowhere. Stopford and several of the divisional commanders were replaced, but the failure signalled the beginning of the end for the Dardanelles campaign. London now began to think of withdrawal altogether from Gallipoli, especially after Bulgaria entered the war in September on the side of the

Central Powers, ending any realistic chance of forcing a way into the Black Sea. Although Hamilton's staff came up with an estimate of 50,000 casualties to evacuate the peninsula, it was clear that the number would be higher if they stayed.

In October Hamilton himself was relieved of command. The Dardanelles Committee, as the war council had become (and from November simply 'war committee'), had wearied of the eastern adventure and now plumped for withdrawal at whatever cost. Yet on the night of 18 December, in a remarkable display of originality, field discipline and meticulous staffwork, the withdrawal from Suvla and Anzac would be carried out practically without loss, the final evacuation from Cape Helles following on 8 January, again without casualties. The penultimate officer to leave the beach at Suvla was the future Labour prime minister Clement Attlee, commanding a company of the 6th South Lancashires, another New Army battalion. The last was the divisional commander himself, Major-General Frederick Maude, who would command the expeditionary force in Mesopotamia with considerable success until succumbing to cholera in November 1917.

'Thus ended a sound and farsighted venture [the Dardanelles campaign] which had been wrecked by a chain of errors hardly to be rivalled even in British history,' wrote Captain Basil Liddell Hart, the pre-eminent military commentator of the post-war years. Erich von Falkenhayn, former chief of the *Grosser Generalstab*, testified in his memoirs to just what a strategic prize opening the Dardanelles would have delivered: 'If the Straits between the Mediterranean and the Black Sea were not permanently closed to Entente traffic, all hopes of a successful course of the war would be very considerably diminished. Russia would have been freed from her significant isolation.'

And in that case the events of 1917, culminating in the Russian Revolution, might have been quite different.

14

SEPTEMBER
Loos

An ill-starred offensive by Kitchener's 'New Army'

John Buchan's classic novel *Greenmantle* (1916), sequel to *The Thirty-Nine Steps*, opens with its hero Richard Hannay and his friend Sandy Arbuthnot convalescing from wounds received at the battle of Loos, two of the 50,000 casualties (twice those of the Germans) in one of the British army's bloodiest ever defeats.

Among the dead in the real battle was 2nd Lieutenant John ('Jack') Kipling of the Irish Guards, Rudyard Kipling's only son, who was just eighteen and had been in France for but a month.

The long-planned allied offensive of autumn 1915 was meant to snip out the great salient formed by the German line in northern France. It consisted of simultaneous attacks against both sides of the bulge, General Noël de Castelnau's group of armies making the main effort with thirty-four divisions in Champagne, while General Ferdinand Foch's were to strike near Arras, with the BEF carrying out a supporting attack on his left towards the mining town of Loos. At his final conference before the offensive, General Joseph Joffre, the French commander-in-chief, said they had 'a certain guarantee of success'. He was 'confident of a great and possibly complete victory'. The cavalry were to move up ready to pour through the breaches and 'make a relentless pursuit without waiting for the infantry, and with the frontier as their objective'. A four-day bombardment would suppress or destroy the defences.

The German commander-in-chief, Erich von Falkenhayn, did not believe an offensive was possible, and refused to reinforce either the Champagne or the Artois sector. Although for months there had been talk in the streets of Paris and London of a 'big push', and despite aerial reconnaissance and increased signal traffic indicating a build-up of troops, the *Grosser Generalstab* calculated that after their setbacks earlier in the year the French were in no condition to attack. This was not unreasonable, since it was the view of most French generals other than Joffre.

As the intensive shelling began on 21 September the local German commanders pulled back their forward troops to secondary positions, avoiding its worst effects. When the French attacked four days later, Castelnau's army group quickly over-ran the first line but then ran into serious opposition from the laid-back positions. For three days the French battered away at the German second line, giving Falkenhayn time to rush in reserves, until General Pétain, commanding the French 2nd Army, called off his attack in defiance of orders.

Not only did Castelnau's offensive in Champagne fail, its initial success had the perverse effect of hastening the failure of that in Artois, and therefore the BEF's. Seeing the spectacular progress on the first day, with its delusive promise of breakthrough and the victory he himself had been predicting, Joffre told Foch to halt his attacks temporarily but to 'take care to avoid giving the British the impression that we are leaving them to attack alone'.

The attack at Loos was the biggest the BEF had yet carried out: six infantry divisions and one of cavalry – more than had gone to France in August 1914 – with a further two divisions of the Indian Corps in support, under General Sir Douglas Haig commanding 1st Army, and three more divisions in reserve under control of the commander-in-chief, Sir John French.

Of the nine British infantry divisions, though, only five were regular. Three were 'New Army' divisions, two of which had not yet been in the trenches, and one was from the Territorial Force. This meant that although there was no want of courage and eagerness for the fight – the 'New Army' men had been the first to answer Lord Kitchener's call for volunteers in 1914 – too many of the troops were green. A year was hardly time in which to train an individual soldier, let alone battalions, brigades and divisions.

The Loos battlefield was uniformly flat and dominated by slagheaps. Joffre insisted it was 'particularly favourable'. Haig agreed, but in so far as it was particularly favourable for the defenders, not the attackers. His misgivings were to some extent allayed by the availability of a new and secret weapon: gas, the use of which had been approved by the cabinet in the wake of the German chlorine attacks at Ypres in April.

Haig's high hopes for his gas attack were to be cruelly dashed. Artillery gas shells had not yet been developed, so the chlorine had to be released from cylinders, and needed a breeze strong enough to carry it to the enemy's trenches but not so strong as to disperse it. The weather in the days before the attack, scheduled for 25 September, had been foul, with heavy rain. On the morning of the twenty-fifth, as Haig's intelligence officer Colonel John Charteris noted, 'There was not a breath of wind until 5 a.m.'; but the reports from the meteorological officer, Gold, 'had become pretty confident that the wind would be favourable'.

I went to D.H. [Douglas Haig] at 2 a.m., when we had just received a report from a distant station that made Gold reasonably hopeful. Our own report from the line was that it was dead still. At 3, when the decision had to be made, I took Gold . . . to D.H. Gold was then more confident and D.H. ordered zero hour for 5.50 . . . At 5 he came to our office with Fletcher [ADC]. There was quite a faint breath of wind then, and Fletcher's cigarette smoke moved quite perceptibly towards the Germans. But it died away again in a few minutes, and a little later D.H. sent down a message from the tower to 1st Corps to enquire if the attack could still be held up. Gough [corps commander] replied that it was too late to change. I was with D.H. when the reply was brought in. He was very upset.

Major-General Henry (later General Lord) Horne, commanding 2nd Division, ignored the advice of his gas officer not to release the cloud because of insufficient breeze: 'The programme must be carried out whatever the conditions,' he insisted. As a result his division, with their rudimentary gas hoods, suffered over 2,000 gas casualties, though mercifully only a handful were fatal.

In all, 140 tons of chlorine were released from 5,000 containers. Some of it did indeed serve its purpose. On the extreme right, where the 15th (Scottish) Division attacked, the gas carried well into the German lines, and the Scots nearly broke through, causing considerable consternation in the German command. The 47th (London) Division, territorials, despite heavy casualties also made good progress, in one case with unauthorized tactics. Disobeying orders, just before zero hour Rifleman Frank Edwards, one of the London Irish Rifles' football team, pulled a leather football from his knapsack and started to inflate it. 'Just imagine, as I did,' he later recalled, 'a party of London Irishmen, with our war cry of "Hurroo" charging across No Man's Land passing the ball forward to finish up the mad rush by leaping into their trench with the rifle and bayonet.' The ball got stuck in wire, but enough of the riflemen didn't, though Edwards himself was wounded.

Haig had no reserves to exploit these partial successes, however, having put all his forces into the attack, trusting to the early release of the extra three divisions by GHQ. These, however, had on Sir John French's insistence been kept 16 miles to the rear, which now meant an approach march throughout the night of 25–6 September. By dawn the men were already tired, with several miles still to go to the German front line. Congestion on the roads further slowed their progress. As the *Official History* put it, 'It was like trying to push the Lord Mayor's procession through the streets of London without clearing the route and holding up the traffic.' And two-thirds of the 'procession' (the New Army divisions) had never been in the 'streets of London' before – or, indeed, in a procession of any kind.

When the reserves eventually reached the front, again in heavy rain, they would make their attacks with inadequate artillery support against defences which the Germans had worked all night to strengthen. In the words of Sir Basil Liddell Hart, 'The attack broke down and the survivors broke back.'

Joffre, French and now Haig were determined to continue, for too many lives had been lost in what would otherwise be seen as a worthless sacrifice, and they were certain that the Germans had suffered at least as badly (in fact the total German casualties at Loos were around half the number of British lives lost). Over the coming days troops were brought to Loos from the Ypres sector, but unexpectedly strong German counter-attacks and more heavy rain checked all progress. Haig ordered the last attack on 13 October; fighting continued until 18 October when the offensive was formally closed down.

The *Official History* would conclude that the renewed attacks 'had not improved the general situation in any way and had brought nothing but useless slaughter of infantry'.

It was not only the number of dead that was significant, but also who they were. A large percentage were officers, many of them experienced regulars. Three divisional commanders (major-generals) were killed, three brigade commanders, and a staggering twenty-nine commanding officers – one in four of those taking part. Not surprisingly, the great majority of the latter were of New Army battalions: the less experienced the unit, the more visible its leadership had to be. While in the short term senior officers and battalion commanders could be replaced relatively easily, the junior leadership, the company officers, could not. The weakening of the battalions numerically was but a temporary setback, for battle-casualty replacements had been earmarked and in many cases were already in France at the base depots, but the loss of junior officers weakened the battalions far more in the long term. The typical 'bayonet' (attacking) strength of a battalion at this time was 650–750 men and 30–35 officers. In thirty-two battalions the loss of officers was over 50 per cent. The 8th Seaforth Highlanders and 12th Highland Light Infantry each lost twenty-three officers, and the 8th Royal West Kents and 8th Royal East Kents (The Buffs) – all New Army battalions – twenty-four. Six battalions lost over 600 men each, of which two lost almost 700. So grimly satisfied were the Germans with their machine guns that they called the battle *Der Leichenfeld von Loos*, 'The Field of Corpses of Loos'.

*

The subsequent failure to locate his son's remains would haunt Kipling for the rest of his life. His poem 'My Boy Jack', written in memory of his 'dear old boy', is one of his best-loved works. The eventual identification of his remains by the Commonwealth War Graves Commission in 1992 is still disputed.

Captain the Honourable Fergus Bowes-Lyon of the 8th Black Watch, the late Queen Mother's brother, also has no precisely known grave. Nor does Captain Charles Sorley of the Suffolks, who had left Marlborough College only two years before aged eighteen, already a published poet and in the opinion of John Masefield, later poet laureate, the greatest loss of all the poets killed during the war. His name is among the sixteen poets of the Great War commemorated on a slate stone in Westminster Abbey.

MY BOY JACK

Rudyard Kipling

'Have you news of my boy Jack?'
Not this tide.
'When d'you think that he'll come back?'
Not with this wind blowing, and this tide.

'Has any one else had word of him?'
Not this tide.
For what is sunk will hardly swim,
Not with this wind blowing, and this tide.

'Oh, dear, what comfort can I find?'
None this tide,
Nor any tide,
Except he did not shame his kind—
Not even with that wind blowing, and that tide.

Then hold your head up all the more,
This tide,
And every tide;
Because he was the son you bore,
And gave to that wind blowing and that tide!

15

OCTOBER
The Gardeners of Salonika

A new front opens in the southern Balkans

In a malaria-infested backwater, which at times both the allies and their enemies were wont to deride, two of the leading figures in British music and art found themselves among the ranks of a largely forgotten army.

Ralph Vaughan Williams, one of the greatest English composers of the twentieth century, and the celebrated painter Stanley (later Sir Stanley) Spencer were serving as medical orderlies on the Macedonian front, which would one day witness a spectacular allied counter-offensive precipitating a nervous breakdown in the German commander-in-chief, Erich Ludendorff.

In October 1915, however, such a feat could scarcely be imagined. For a year and more the doughty Serbs had held off a succession of Austrian attacks, but Berlin was keen for a knockout blow that would then allow the Austro-Hungarian army to put its full weight into defeating the more dangerous foe, the Russians, while fending off the Italians, who had entered the war on the Entente's side in May.

Italy's move, a considerable boost for the allies, was however

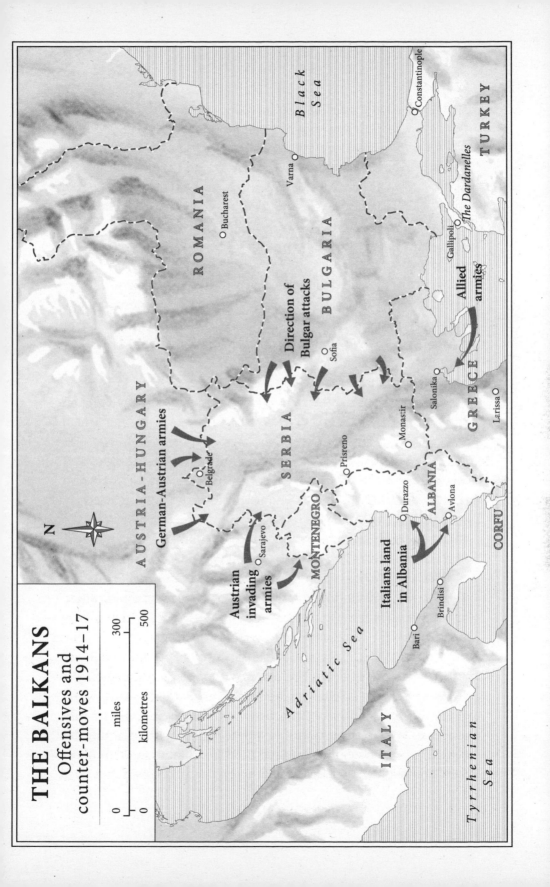

THE BALKANS
Offensives and counter-moves 1914–17

miles
0   300

kilometres
0   500

N

AUSTRIA-HUNGARY

German-Austrian armies

Austrian invading armies

ROMANIA

Bucharest

BULGARIA

Sofia

Varna

Black Sea

Direction of Bulgar attacks

SERBIA

Belgrade

Sarajevo

MONTENEGRO

Prisreno

Monastir

ALBANIA

Durazzo

Avlona

Italians land in Albania

Brindisi

Bari

ITALY

Adriatic Sea

Tyrrhenian Sea

CORFU

GREECE

Salonika

Larissa

Allied armies

Gallipoli

The Dardanelles

Constantinople

TURKEY

offset by Bulgaria's declaration for the Central Powers five months later. The chief of the German general staff, Erich von Falkenhayn, had long planned a concerted German–Austrian offensive against Serbia, and on 2 October Sofia told Berlin that the Bulgarian army would join the offensive. Two days later the Germans and Austrians struck, Belgrade quickly falling, and on 14 October the Bulgarians launched a strong attack from the east. Against such a heavy, three-pronged offensive the Serbian army could do little but fall back towards the south and west.

The British and French had been promising direct aid to the Serbs for some time, but it had never been forthcoming because of the per-ceived greater need of the Western Front. Nor could they be certain that Athens, still officially neutral, would allow them lines of com-munication through Greek territory. Greece, in fact, seemed to be heading for civil war over the issue. The Serb commander-in-chief, the redoubtable Marshal Radomir Putnik, had suggested that the allies intervene via Albania, covered in the north by the army of Montenegro, a Serb ally, but this too seemed fraught with difficulties. Besides, the Entente had been trying to woo Bulgaria, and had there-fore hesitated to do anything to drive her into the German camp. One of the justifications of the attempt to take the Dardanelles had been that it would draw in the Bulgarians on the side of the allies; the failure of that campaign was one of the major factors in Sofia's deci-sion to throw in its lot with the Central Powers.

When the Bulgarians struck, however, Britain and France were quick to act, at once declaring war on Berlin's newest ally and warn-ing troops at Gallipoli to be ready to go to Serbia's aid. But Greece was still divided. The king, Constantine, was pro-German (his queen was the Kaiser's sister), while the prime minister, Eleutherios Venizelos, was strongly pro-Entente. The country itself had expanded territori-ally in the recent Balkan wars, and stood to lose these gains if it now chose the wrong side. With Serbia now looking as if she would be over-run, and with no certainty where the Bulgarians would halt, Venizelos boldly but unilaterally invited the allies to send troops into southern Serbia (now Macedonia) through north-east Greece.

104

A force of two divisions, one British (the 10th Irish) and one French, under command of the French General Maurice Sarrail, was rushed across the Aegean from Gallipoli to the Greek port of Salonika. By the time they arrived, however, the mood in Athens had swung back against Venizelos, and the 10th Division found themselves under threat of internment, observed by German spies and hostile Greek officials.

In the event they were able to land unhindered, and found the port an altogether pleasant change from the beachheads of Gallipoli. Inland, however, the conditions soon proved just as bad. 'When you step out of Salonika you step into a virtual desert, roadless, treeless, uncultivated, populated only by scattered villages of the most primitive kind, inhabited by a low-grade peasantry,' wrote the divisional commander, Major-General Bryan Mahon.

> Two roads, in a condition quite inadequate to support heavy traffic, and three single lines of railway ran, at the most divergent angles possible, from Salonika towards the enemy's territory. Apart from these there was hardly even a track which in winter was possible for wheeled traffic. So that from the very beginning the Allied Forces have had to build up slowly, laboriously, the whole of the system of locomotion necessary for themselves and their supplies – piers, roads, bridges, railways – all have had to be created where nothing of the kind previously existed.

The 10th Division, soon followed by four more divisions from the BEF in France, much to the dismay of Sir John French, had arrived poorly equipped for the worsening weather. They had been sent to Gallipoli in August in cotton drill uniform to take part in what was expected to be the short and decisive operation at Suvla Bay, and had no greatcoats. As they struck into the mountainous interior, General Mahon found the weather 'most unpropitious for soldiering, cold and wet in winter, hot and feverish in summer . . . Winter, right up to the beginning of April, is a season of snow, rain, and, above all, mud.'

Indeed, during the next three years, casualties from disease and climate would be twenty times those from enemy action in this theatre. Salonika was one of the malarial black spots of Europe, and with the soldier's customary sardonic humour the Salonika veterans would name their newspaper *The Mosquito*.

The arrival of the Anglo-French force came too late to save the Serbs. Marshal Putnik ordered a general retreat through Montenegro into neutral Albania; of the 200,000 who began that arduous march, only some 125,000 would reach the Adriatic coast. Here, in a Dunkirk-like operation, they were embarked on allied ships, chiefly Italian, and taken via Corfu to join the Anglo-French force in Salonika. Over the next two years the 'Allied Armies of the Orient', as the polyglot force on the Macedonian front was known, would be joined by Russians, Italians, Czechs and troops from French Indo-China, and eventually by the Greeks themselves.

In December 1915, the Bulgarians having driven a wedge between the retreating Serbs and the allies, General Sarrail's force fell back from southern Serbia towards Salonika. There was a particularly sharp engagement with Bulgarian troops in the Kosturino Pass north of Lake Doiran, and for a while the situation looked dangerous, the chief of the Greek general staff warning Sarrail: 'You will be driven into the sea, and you will not have time even to cry for mercy.'

Despite the confusion and the worsening weather, however, the allies were able to establish a line of defence along the Greek border. Crucially, Berlin, anxious not to over-extend the effort and bring in the Greek army, told the Bulgarians that their troops must not violate Greek territory. The fighting subsided, and the Macedonian front settled into the uncomfortable tedium of watching and waiting, to the increasing frustration both of allied statesmen, who wanted to see more action there, and of the generals, who wanted to see the troops brought back to the Western Front. The soldiers themselves, like those in Italy in 1944 who were incensed at being called 'D-Day Dodgers', bridled at a jibe by Georges Clemenceau, the future prime minister of France, that they were 'the gardeners of Salonika' because instead of attacking all they did was dig. The Germans were just as contemptuous: with eventually half a million allied troops on the Macedonian front, Berlin would call Salonika the Entente's largest internment camp.

There were occasional bursts of small-scale fighting, however, some of it intense, as witnessed by the award of the VC in 1916 to twenty-year-old Private 'Stokey' Lewis of the Welsh Regiment, one of Kitchener's first volunteers, for his part in a savage trench raid. But with so little hard fighting until the autumn of 1918, Macedonia became the forgotten front. Certainly both Ralph Vaughan Williams and Stanley Spencer thought it so, and a none too congenial place either.

Although in his forties and a figure of national stature, Vaughan Williams had volunteered for the Royal Army Medical Corps almost as soon as the war began. After serving as a stretcher-bearer on the Western Front, he was transferred with his field ambulance to Salonika in November 1916. A fellow orderly, Private Harry Steggles, described sharing a two-man tent 'little less than the area of a double bed' with the editor of the *English Hymnal* and composer of *Fantasia on a Theme by Thomas Tallis* – known in the field ambulance simply as 'Bob':

We had a groundsheet and blanket a piece and all our worldly goods included razor, comb, lather brush, also Isaiah and Jeremiah [which were] two empty pineapple tins in which we lit charcoal and after whirling them round and round like the old fashioned winter warmer we rushed them into the 'bivvy' and sealed up any air intakes we could find. I think we slept more from our rum ration plus carbon monoxide from Isaiah and Jeremiah than fatigue. One lost everything in these confined spaces, but Bob always gave up the chase with a grunt saying, 'Find it in the morning', and the great man slept.

One particularly filthy night however, Steggles recorded:

We both sat with our knees drawn up in the 'bivvy' looking at a guttering candle, water creeping in, plus snakes, scorpions and centipedes. A few shells were sailing over which thrilled Bob, a typical Bairnsfather

'Better' 'ole' scene; when Bob suddenly said: 'Harry, when this war ends we will (a) dine at Simpson's on saddle of mutton, (b) see *Carmen*.'

They would indeed dine at Simpson's after the war, but *Carmen* eluded them.

Stanley Spencer, already an acclaimed painter of landscapes and allegorical subjects though still in his twenties, was serving with another field ambulance. Deeply if unconventionally religious, he was strongly affected by the experience of Salonika, which would have a profound and disturbing effect on his art. During his early months there, however, the landscape and colour thrilled him. 'I do wish I had my paints out here,' he wrote home. 'The pearly sky at sunrise (in winter), the deep blue sea, and the shadows of big ships along the surface, and the bronze hills beyond. The regular ridges of foam all gleaming in the sun like a Claude.'

His brush would find its real expression three years later in one of the most singular images of the conflict. In 1919 the War Memorials Committee commissioned him to paint a large work for their planned Hall of Remembrance. Though the hall was never built, the resulting work, *Travoys Arriving with Wounded at a Dressing Station at Smol, Macedonia, September 1916*, is now on permanent display at the Imperial War Museum. It recalls his time, he explained, in 'the middle of September 1916 [when] the 22nd Division made an attack on Machine Gun Hill on the Doiran Vardar Sector and held it for a few nights. During these nights the wounded passed through the dressing stations in a never-ending stream'.

Not until September 1918, however, would the Macedonian front show any return on the allies' huge investment of troops, when at last a spectacular counter-offensive would drive the Austro-Bulgarian forces out of Serbia, precipitating Ludendorff's breakdown and the weakening of the Western Front.

'It was upon this much-abused front that the final collapse of the Central Empires first began,' wrote Winston Churchill, an assessment confirmed by Ludendorff himself in his memoirs.

16

NOVEMBER
'Mespot'

The 500-mile British advance on Baghdad is turned back almost within sight of the city, leading to the most humiliating surrender of the war

'Winston is getting more and more absorbed in boilers,' the chancellor of the exchequer, David Lloyd George, had complained in 1913. The new first lord of the Admiralty's demands for an increase in the navy's budget to convert the fleet to oil propulsion thoroughly dismayed a Treasury struggling to fund the Liberal government's welfare programme. Besides, some argued, coal was to be had in abundance throughout Britain; oil propulsion would make the Royal Navy dependent on foreign supplies. Nevertheless Churchill got his way, and in July 1914, with just days to the declaration of war, he managed to secure for the Crown a 51 per cent controlling interest in the Anglo-Persian Oil Company, which itself had a 50 per cent interest in the Turkish Petroleum Company exploring resources in the Ottoman Empire, of which Mesopotamia was a part.

The British campaign in Mesopotamia – roughly, present-day Iraq – was first therefore about oil, lately discovered in large quantities around Basra and Mosul. However, the necessity of protecting the navy's oil supplies after Constantinople declared war on the Entente in early November was not the only factor: London and Delhi were concerned that Turkish agents would stir up trouble among India's Muslims, inciting them to *jihad*, 'holy war'. A campaign in Mesopotamia would demonstrate to Indian Muslims that the British were still in control, and also encourage an Arab revolt against Ottoman rule which would spread throughout the Middle East, easing the Turkish threat to the Suez Canal and hastening the defeat of the Ottoman Empire.

Mesopotamia derived its Greek name from its position between the two rivers Tigris and Euphrates, which meet at El Qurnah, 40 miles north of Basra, to form the Shatt al-Arab waterway which flows into the Persian Gulf at a complex delta. Baghdad, then the Ottoman administrative capital, lies on the Tigris some 550 miles upstream. For the most part the land is desert and very flat, the rivers flooding the immediate plains when the winter snows in the northern mountains thaw. In 1914 there were no roads to speak of, nor railways south of Baghdad, so strategic movement depended on the rivers.

The operation to secure the oil fields and pipelines around Basra and what would become present-day Kuwait was mounted by the army of India and directed from Delhi, rather than from London, the British army and its colonial reinforcements being already hard pressed in France and Egypt. 'Our Indian ewe-lamb,' the viceroy, Lord Crewe, called it. However, the mixed motives of the intervention had not made for clear strategic focus, and the operation began to over-reach itself. The best of the Indian troops and British regiments in India had anyway been sent to the Western Front, and many of the most experienced officers who remained, especially those on home leave when the war began, were redeployed to train Lord Kitchener's 'New Army' battalions. Nor was the Indian army equipped for intensive fighting, its divisions having for example only half the artillery of those in the BEF.

Early success had seemed promising. Basra, which the Turks evacuated, had been taken on 22 November by the 6th (Poona)

110

Division, and El Qurnah a fortnight later. Over the next few months the 'Indian Expeditionary Force D', as it was officially known, was therefore reinforced by a division and corps troops, and in March Delhi told its new commander-in-chief, the highly experienced Lieutenant-General Sir John Nixon, who in 1906 had succeeded Douglas Haig as Inspector-General of Cavalry in India, to 'retain complete control of the lower portion of Mesopotamia' and submit plans for an advance on Baghdad.

It made sense to expand what was little more than a toehold at the end of two strategic waterways along which the enemy would otherwise have been free to move, but 'the lower portion of Mesopotamia' was far from secured. In April the Turks had made a determined attempt to retake Basra, in which Major George Massy Wheeler of the 7th Hariana Lancers had won, posthumously, the first VC of the campaign. His medal, previously thought lost, was found in 2017 in the archives of the Brighton Museum, to which his widow had left it on her death in the 1950s.

In May 1915, despite the advice of the commander of the 6th Division, Major-General Charles Townshend, hero of the defence of Chitral on the North-West Frontier twenty years earlier, Nixon despatched two divisional columns upstream: while Townshend's moved along the Tigris towards Baghdad, Major-General George Gorringe's 12th Indian Division worked up the Euphrates, taking Nasiriyah on 25 July.

The ease of advance quickly proved deceptive, however, for it became increasingly difficult to supply the two divisions. And while Nixon's supply line grew longer, that of the Turks shortened accordingly, though he remained convinced that he could take Baghdad. Townshend continued to disagree. The 6th Division was tired, and its casualties to the enemy and the heat had not yet been made up.

The advance continued nevertheless, and at first Nixon looked vindicated. The Turks evacuated the bulk of their 10,000-strong garrison at Kut al-Amara, just 120 miles from Baghdad, leaving Townshend to take possession on 28 September, though not without some sharp fighting. As the division ploughed up the Tigris, the leading gunboat, *Comet*, commanded by Lieutenant-Commander Edgar Cookson, found the river blocked by dhows linked by wire hawsers and covered by heavy rifle and machine-gun fire from both banks. Having failed to sink the centre dhow by gunfire and then by ramming, Cookson, who only a fortnight before had won the Distinguished Service Order in an ambush, placed the *Comet* alongside and jumped aboard to set about the hawsers with an axe. Hit several times, for his courage and determination he would be awarded a posthumous VC.

The Admiralty and the War Office were now getting anxious. In a joint memorandum they warned against the diversion of troops to a campaign 'which cannot appreciably influence the decision as between the armies of the allies and those of the Central Powers'. The cabinet concluded nevertheless that success in Mesopotamia would offset the recent failure in Gallipoli, telling Nixon: 'Unless you consider that the possibility of eventual withdrawal is against the advance . . . we are prepared to order it.'

Although he had received intelligence that Baghdad was being reinforced by troops sent from Gallipoli, Nixon told Townshend to press on.

After waiting six weeks for resupply, Townshend resumed his advance and by 22 November had reached Ctesiphon, capital of the old Parthian empire, just 25 miles from Baghdad. But here his luck ran out. The Ottoman war minister, Enver Pasha, had appointed Baron Colmar von der Goltz to command the Turkish 5th Army in Mesopotamia. Goltz was a Prussian of the most determined kind, brought out of retirement in 1914 to serve as military governor of Belgium, where he had ordered reprisals against civilians to deter sabotage. When the 6th (Poona) Division attacked, they found a strong and well-sited defensive line awaiting them, and Townshend lost over 4,000 men, more than a quarter of his force. Without reserves, and with fresh Turkish troops arriving by the hour, all he could do now was begin a fighting withdrawal back to Kut.

This he did, and with some skill, reaching the town on 3 December;

but the remnants of his division were at once besieged by Goltz's now very superior forces, Townshend only just managing to get his cavalry and flying corps away before the old fortress-town was encircled.

Over the next four months three attempts to relieve Kut would be bloodily repulsed, including one in which the future Labour prime minister, and Churchill's deputy in the Second World War, Clement Attlee, who had earlier fought at Gallipoli, was badly wounded.

Attempts to buy off the Turks with upwards of £2 million came to nothing, but led to confused reports that their compatriots at Gallipoli had been paid to let the allied troops finally slip away in January. Indeed, General Nixon himself had earlier bribed his way past pro-Ottoman Arabs when his paddle steamer had become grounded.

Conditions at Kut in the winter of 1915–16 proved particularly severe. With casualties from disease and exposure mounting, and food about to run out despite resupply by aircraft for the first time in the history of war, on 29 April Townshend would be forced to surrender, at which point his last hope, General Nikolai Baratov's largely Cossack force of 20,000 advancing from Persia, turned back.

This defeat was a major blow to British prestige in both the Middle East and India. Kitchener tried to salvage some honour in a statement in the House of Lords by saying it had been only 'the imminent starvation itself [that] compelled the capitulation of this gallant garrison, which consisted of 2,970 British and some 6,000 Indian troops [and] followers,' commending them in their 'honourable captivity' and insisting that their surrender 'reflects no discredit on themselves or on the record of the British and Indian armies'.

The outcome would, however, reflect ill on British generalship. In the parliamentary inquiry that followed, Nixon was roundly blamed, as were the authorities in Delhi, and control of the campaign was taken over by London. Townshend was at first lauded for his skill in the withdrawal and for repelling all attacks on Kut, but when news began to emerge of the treatment of his troops in captivity – of the 11,800 men who left Kut with their captors on 6 May, 4,250 died either on their way to internment or in the camps that awaited them (many of them when released at the end of the war were as badly emaciated as those liberated from Japanese PoW camps in 1945) – compared to his own palatial captivity on the small island of Heybeliada near Constantinople, there was a storm of indignation. Kipling, in his poem *Mesopotamia* published in 1917, railed against the evasion of responsibility by many of the senior commanders and officials involved, and the subsequent closing of ranks:

> Shall we only threaten and be angry for an hour?
> When the storm is ended shall we find
> How softly but how swiftly they have sidled back to power
> By the favour and contrivance of their kind?

Though the army in Mesopotamia was eventually reinforced to nine divisions, with Kut recaptured in February 1917 and Baghdad falling the following month, the campaign would drag on until October 1918. Former US President Theodore Roosevelt's second son, Kermit, was awarded the Military Cross while serving with the (British) Machine Gun Corps, before transferring to the US army once America entered the war in April 1917. His father had repeatedly denounced President Woodrow Wilson's non-interventionism and the stance of Irish-Americans and German-Americans who put the interests of Ireland and Germany before those of America. A US citizen had to be 100 per cent American, he insisted, not a 'hyphenated American' juggling multiple loyalties. 'Teddy' Roosevelt would eventually be given permission to raise four divisions of 'Rough Riders', like those he had led in the Spanish–American war of 1898, though the scheme was dropped when Wilson decided instead to send an American Expeditionary Force to France.

Left 'Churchill makes a decisive move seven days before the war.' Asquith had sent the 36-year-old Winston Churchill to the Admiralty as first lord in 1911 to overhaul its war plans. Churchill's unilateral decision on 28 July 1914 to send the Grand Fleet to its war stations at Scapa Flow gained crucial command of the North Sea. He is pictured here in a contemporary print discussing the options with Admiral Sir John Jellicoe, commander-in-chief of the Grand Fleet.

Bottom 'By 27 August Samsonov's 2nd Army had been surrounded in a double envelopment at Tannenberg; by 30 August his entire command had disintegrated, the Germans taking 92,000 prisoners.'

French cavalry on the move, with a dirigible of the *Aéronautique Militaire* keeping watch, during the 'battle of the frontiers', August 1914.

Above 129th (Duke of Connaught's Own) Baluchis near Hollebeke, Ypres, where on 31 October 1914 Sepoy (Private) Khudadad Khan of the regiment won the first ever Indian VC.

Above Churchill called the twin battles of Coronel (1 November) and the Falklands (8 December 1914) 'the saddest naval action in the war. Of the officers and men in both the squadrons that faced each other . . . nine out of ten were doomed to perish. The British were to die that night: the Germans a month later.' SMS *Scharnhorst* sinking (foreground) and her sister ship *Gneisenau* at the end of the Battle of the Falklands, as imagined in this sketch for a painting by marine artist Lionel Wyllie.

Left On 16 December 1914, in an attempt to draw out the Grand Fleet into ambush, German battle-cruisers bombarded the North Sea towns of Scarborough, Whitby and the Hartlepools, inflicting over 650 casualties, mainly civilian, including 137 killed of whom 78 were women and children. 'Remember Scarborough' became a rallying cry for recruiting officers, as well as provoking outrage in the United States.

Above Men of the BEF's hastily formed 7th Division, transported in London buses, some still bearing their metropolitan destinations and advertisements for soap, covering the withdrawal of the Antwerp garrison, 10 October 1914. The Belgian army, under the personal command of King Albert, would thereafter hold a tiny corner of sovereign territory north-west of Ypres, the last link in 'the race for the sea'.

Above 'Never in the field of human conflict was so much tramped by so many after so few': patrol of the 4th Battalion, King's African Rifles, British East Africa. For four years, with scant artillery, a few hundred Europeans and 3,000 askaris (local black troops, commanded by German officers and NCOs) plus bearers – a force that never exceeded 14,000 – Colonel Paul von Lettow-Vorbeck would hold in check some 300,000 imperial, Belgian and Portuguese troops.

Right 'Our Indian ewe-lamb', the viceroy, Lord Crewe, called it: the Indian Expeditionary Force D, sent in mid-November 1914 to secure the oil fields and pipelines of Mesopotamia. The campaign culminated in the capture of Baghdad in March 1917, though at much cost.

Left Artillery of the French *Corps Expéditionnaire d'Orient* in action at Kum Kale on the southern side of the Dardanelles Straits. The attempt to force the strait by naval action alone having failed, allied landings took place in April 1915 at the tip of the Gallipoli peninsula and on the Anatolian shore.

Below The 'White War': mountain gunners of the *Alpini*. Italy joined the Entente in May 1915 and immediately began offensive operations against the Austrians.

Below 'The use of asphyxiating gases is, as you are aware, contrary to the rules and usages of war,' wrote Kitchener in April 1915. 'Before, therefore, we fall to the level of the degraded Germans [in retaliating] I must submit the matter to the Government.' Men of (probably) the Cameronians wearing goggles and gauze masks, primitive defences against the chlorine gas released during the Second Battle of Ypres.

Left The Kaiser authorizes air raids on Britain (and unrestricted submarine warfare): King's Lynn, 19 January 1915. A Zeppelin dropped explosive and incendiary bombs on the Norfolk town, killing two – a boy of fourteen and a woman whose husband had recently been killed in France – and injuring fifteen.

Left Mass burials at the Old Church Cemetery, Queenstown (now Cobh). On 7 May 1915 a German submarine sank without warning the Cunard liner *Lusitania* off the south coast of Ireland with the loss of 1,200 passengers and crew, including 128 American citizens. The US secretary of state, Robert Lansing, would later write that although it was another two years before his country entered the war, after the sinking of the *Lusitania* he had had no doubt 'that we would ultimately become the ally of Britain'. As a consequence of the outcry, the Kaiser later rescinded his orders for unrestricted submarine warfare.

Right The forgotten ally. After a year of fighting the Austrians unaided, the remnants of the Serbian army would be evacuated from the Adriatic coast by allied ships and taken to the new front in Salonika (the Macedonian front). King Peter of Serbia – in bullock cart – on the march to the sea through the mountains of Albania before the combined Austro-German–Bulgarian offensive of October 1915.

German troops attacking at Verdun in February 1916 (**above**), and (**below**) French artillery, the famous *soixante-quinze* quick-firing 75 mm field gun, the mainstay of the heroic but tragic defence of the fortress-town. Falkenhayn's ploy to 'bleed the French army white' in defence of the emblematic national citadel would cost the German army dearly and lead to his own dismissal.

Left Tsar Nicholas II inspects his troops before the 'Brusilov offensive' in the summer of 1916. His decision to take personal command of the armies, contrary to advice, would contribute to his overthrow, and later murder (or, as the Bolshevists had it, execution) along with the rest of his family.

Left Jutland, 31 May 1916: the long-expected test of the Grand Fleet and Admiral Jellicoe – as Churchill said, 'the only man on either side who could lose the war in an afternoon'. The Grand Fleet outnumbered the enemy in dreadnoughts, so Admiral Scheer decided to take his six pre-dreadnought battleships too, less well armoured and three knots slower, reducing the *Hochseeflotte*'s overall speed, critical to both manoeuvre and fire-control. Here, the pre-dreadnought *Schleswig-Holstein* fires a salvo during the battle, showing the problem of observing the fall of shot.

Right 'Then I rode up-country to Feisal, and found in him the leader with the necessary fire, and yet with reason to give effect to our science.' So wrote T. E. Lawrence (of Arabia) of Feisal bin Hussein al-Hashimi, the future king of Iraq, here with his tribal bodyguard. The Arab Revolt in 1916 would play an important part in the Middle East campaign, particularly the continual harassing of the Hejaz railway.

Below The first day of the Somme, I July 1916: a rare photograph of men (probably the 34th Division) advancing with full equipment and rifles at the slope (on the shoulder) as per orders. They were not expected to have to fight to take the German trenches but merely 'walk-over' to occupy them, the greatest artillery bombardment to date having done the work. The reality was different: the artillery had failed to subdue the defences, or cut the barbed wire in no-man's-land. There would be some 60,000 casualties that first day, a third of them fatal.

Right The Somme. General (later Field Marshal) Sir Douglas Haig, commander-in-chief of the British armies in France and Flanders, tries to impress a point on the new war minister, Lloyd George, during the battle (probably September), with Joffre's support. The French munitions minister, Albert Thomas, looks on somewhat blankly. By this time 'LG' was changing his mind about the new C-in-C: 'Haig is brilliant,' he said later – 'to the top of his boots.'

A tale of two soup kitchens.

Left Hot food on the Somme: good logistics kept up the troops' morale even as losses mounted.

Below Hot food on the streets of Berlin: in 1916 the Royal Navy's blockade began to cause significant food shortages, which by 1918 were materially undermining the war effort.

17

DECEMBER
Casualties

After a year of dismal defeats, new men and old ideas are the future

As 1915 came to its melancholy close, the German auxiliary cruiser *Möwe* (Gull) slipped out of Wilhelmshaven on her first mission, to lay a minefield in the Pentland Firth near the Grand Fleet's anchorage at Scapa Flow. A few days later the battleship *King Edward VII* struck one of the mines and sank.

It was a dramatic lesson in the asymmetry of the new sea warfare: a capital ship of the Royal Navy, named after the late king, sunk by a converted banana boat lately named the *Pungo*, while the two great fleets in their havens eyed each other warily across the North Sea. 'We shall dig the rats out of their holes,' Churchill, first lord of the Admiralty, had said in September the year before; but it would be a full six months before the *Hochseeflotte* would accept battle with the Grand Fleet at Jutland. Meanwhile, with every other German surface warship sunk or incapacitated, Berlin's war at sea would be waged increasingly by auxiliary vessels like the *Möwe*, and more worryingly by the U-boats. It was a mine laid by a U-boat off Scapa Flow that in June 1916 would claim the highest-ranking casualty of the war, Field Marshal Lord Kitchener himself, when the cruiser *Hampshire* taking him on a mission to Russia sank with virtually all hands.

In December 1915 the curtain was also coming down on the Dardanelles campaign, the attempt to use sea power to turn the strategic flank, take Constantinople, open warm-water lines of communication with Russia, and encourage Bulgaria and Romania to join the allies. After a personal reconnaissance by Kitchener the previous month, the war cabinet had taken the decision to withdraw from Gallipoli completely.

In all, the attempt to force an entry to the Black Sea had cost the allies – British, Indian, Commonwealth and French – a quarter of a million casualties (over 40,000 dead), and the Turks the same.

The Dardanelles campaign had been deeply flawed, revealing defects in the direction of strategy and operations in Whitehall, as well as in the capabilities of Kitchener's newly raised battalions and some Commonwealth units and their commanders, who had been thrown into battle prematurely. Nor had it been the Royal Navy's finest hour, notwithstanding the individual skill and bravery of many ships' companies during the nearly twelve months of the campaign – and certainly not that of the first sea lord, Admiral Lord Fisher, who had first applauded the plans and then schemed against them, eventually just walking away from the Admiralty, prompting the prime minister to say that if he didn't return he would send a policeman to arrest him.

The navy's shining accomplishment, however, had been the achievement of its submarines. Having penetrated the Dardanelles Straits, with all the minefields, and the narrow, tricky waters of the Bosporus, even sinking Turkish warships in the harbour at Constantinople, for months British, French and Australian boats ranged widely in the Black Sea. By the time they were recalled in early January 1916, they had sunk some 50 per cent of Turkish merchant shipping.

The most spectacular casualty of the campaign was the navy minister himself, Churchill. When the original landings miscarried, and

Asquith was forced to bring the Tories into a coalition government, Churchill was deprived of the Admiralty and given instead a non-departmental position to keep him in the cabinet. Despite the initial setbacks at Gallipoli he continued to press for an offensive there, championing the landings at Suvla Bay in August to break the deadlock, and even after these failed he advocated holding on and reinforcing. When General Sir Charles Monro, who in October replaced Sir Ian Hamilton, recommended complete evacuation, Churchill remarked bitterly: 'He came, he saw, he capitulated.' And once the war cabinet had made its decision, Churchill, who held the rank of major in the Oxfordshire Hussars (Territorial Force), saw no further place for himself in government and instead put on uniform and reported for duty in France.

Yet Clement Attlee, whose younger brother Laurence also served at Gallipoli, remained convinced that Churchill had been right. In his memoirs he declared: 'I always held that the strategic concept was sound. The trouble was that it was not adequately supported. Unfortunately the military authorities were Western Front-minded.'

With the withdrawal from Gallipoli, attention would indeed turn back to the Western Front. Although the allies had taken the decision early in December to reinforce the Salonika front, Bulgaria having joined the Central Powers in a concerted effort against Serbia, and Italy had entered the war on the side of the Entente in May, opening up yet another theatre of operations, London and Paris regarded the Western Front as the only one on which the Germans could be decisively defeated. General Joseph Joffre, recently appointed commander-in-chief of all French armies in the field, intended keeping just enough troops in Salonika to prevent Greece from being over-run, and drawing troops of the Central Powers south and away from the Russian front, while mounting an early and decisive offensive in France. At the second inter-allied conference, held at Joffre's headquarters at Chantilly, north of Paris, from 6 to 9 December, the British and French agreed on a major combined offensive on the Somme, while Italy and Russia would mount their own offensives to coincide, and all agreed that whenever one ally came under clear threat, the others would immediately launch diversionary attacks.

Herein lay the seeds of some of the worst blood-letting of the war, for the most expeditious way of mounting a diversion was simply to bring forward the start date of the next planned offensive. As the Germans were bound to attack somewhere in 1916, there was a good chance that they would do so first, in which case the counter-offensives would to varying degrees be premature, therefore less well prepared and in turn less likely to succeed.

The British offensive on the Somme would, however, be under new leadership. For many months it had been plain to Kitchener and the war cabinet that Sir John French could not continue as commander-in-chief of the BEF. The Loos offensive in October had been badly conceived and executed, failures for which he had tried to shift the blame. His official despatch, published in *The Times* on 2 November, contained many errors, especially touching on the part played in the battle by General Sir Douglas Haig, commanding one of the BEF's three armies, and had seriously undermined his authority. French had also primed *The Times*'s military correspond-ent, Colonel Charles Repington, to write a supporting article suggesting that the battle might have gone better had French him-self taken personal command rather than leaving things to Haig, whose 1st Army had taken the lead at Loos. Haig at once wrote to French asking for the despatch to be publicly corrected, which French refused to do. Thereafter Haig lost no opportunity to convey his view that French was not fit for command to anyone with influence – including the King through 'back channels', notably Lady Haig, a former lady-in-waiting to the Queen. '[French] is not only very ignorant of the principles of the higher leading of a large Army but is also lacking in the necessary temperament!' he wrote to Leopold de Rothschild on 9 December. 'He is so hot tempered and excitable – like a bottle of soda water in suddenness of explosion – that he is quite incapable of thinking over a serious situation and coming to a reasoned decision.'

The letter crossed with one from Asquith marked 'Secret', enclosed in three envelopes, which Haig received the following day at his headquarters at Hinges in the Pas de Calais: 'Sir J. French has placed in my hands his resignation of the Office of Commander in Chief of the Forces in France. Subject to the King's approval, I have the pleasure of proposing to you that you should be his successor.'

Kitchener had already told Haig what was afoot when he had been in London the week before, ostensibly taking a few days' leave. 'K' had also told him that he was recalling Lieutenant-General Sir William 'Wully' Robertson, the BEF's chief of staff, to be CIGS. This would provide Haig with a powerful ally in the War Office when the disastrous offensives of 1916 and 1917 began to give the cabinet second thoughts.

Kitchener also told Haig that Brigadier-General George Macdonogh, who until August 1914 had been head of the War Office intelligence division concerned with internal security (today's MI5), and thereafter the BEF's chief of intelligence, was to return to London as director of military intelligence. Macdonogh was brilliant. He and a fellow sapper – James Edmonds, who would become the official historian of the war – had gained such high marks in the staff college entrance exam in 1896 that the results, it was said, were adjusted to conceal the margin between them and their classmates (who included Robertson and Allenby). Macdonogh was a Catholic, however, Jesuit-educated, and deeply mistrusted by Haig and others. Although he would turn the intelligence directorate into a first-rate organization, his assessments would never be entirely accepted by GHQ in France. Haig preferred those of the man he appointed in Macdonogh's place as BEF chief of intelligence, Brigadier-General John Charteris – 'Haig's evil counsellor', as he became known – who increasingly fashioned his assessments to support his chief's decisions rather than challenge the assumptions on which they were made (perhaps the original 'dodgy dossiers').

To make matters worse, 'Wully' Robertson's replacement as the BEF's chief of staff, Major-General Launcelot Kiggell, was, it seems, wholly unable to make any impression on Haig and thereby gained the nickname 'the invisible man'.

119

The BEF was therefore to see in the new year with a most perilous team at its head, for while Haig himself lacked the imperfections he had complained of in Sir John French, he also lacked the qualities of humanity that had made French – at least until Loos – a well-regarded leader. After the war, Robertson would write of French, 'the little field marshal', that he doubted 'if any other general in the army could have sustained in [the BEF] to the same extent the courage and resolution which they displayed during the trying circumstances of the first six months of the war'.

On 18 December, French and Haig had a frosty handover meeting, 'in which Haig never for one moment unbent', said one who witnessed it. The outgoing C-in-C asked that Churchill be given a brigade to command.

That evening 'the little field marshal' dined at the Ritz in Paris with his military secretary, and next day at Boulogne was cheered all the way up the gang-plank by his old regiment, the 19th Hussars. Once back across the Channel he was created Viscount French of Ypres and of High Lake in the County of Roscommon, and made Commander-in-Chief, Home Forces.

There would be one more momentous act before the month, and the year, were out. On 28 December the cabinet agreed to lay before parliament the Military Service Bill. Every male British subject who on 15 August 1915 was ordinarily resident in Great Britain (the bill did not extend to Ireland), who had attained the age of 19 but was not yet 41, and who was unmarried or a widower without dependent children, unless he met certain exceptions was deemed to have enlisted for general service.

The bill would be passed with little opposition on 27 January: the first time in history that there was to be general conscription in Britain. The manpower thus assured, the stage was now set for the terrible battles of attrition that would characterize the rest of the war.

PART THREE

1916

'Pure Murder'

9 January: Final evacuation of Gallipoli.

21 February: Battle of Verdun begins.

31 May: Battle of Jutland.

4 June: Brusilov offensive begins (Eastern Front).

1 July: Battle of the Somme begins (with, on 15 September, the first use of tanks).

4 August: Sixth Battle of the Isonzo (Italian Front) begins.

27 August: Romania declares war on the Central Powers.

18

JANUARY
Enter Haig

After a year of failed offensives, the allies decided that the only way to victory was more offensives – but this time successful ones

On Christmas Day 1915 at his headquarters in St Omer in the Pas de Calais, General Sir Douglas Haig read a memorandum in the confidential papers left by Field Marshal Sir John French, from whom he had just taken over command of the BEF. It referred to armoured 'machine-gun destroyers' on 'caterpillars', which apparently had been the pet project of the then first lord of the Admiralty, Winston Churchill, who had recently left government and reported for duty with the army in France.

'Is anything known about the caterpillar referred to in Para 4, page 3?' he wrote in the margin.

A sapper on the staff of GHQ, Major Hugh Elles, was sent to England to find out.

For the time being, however, the new commander-in-chief had greater concerns than the Admiralty's experiments with 'land-ships', as they and the trench warfare branch of David Lloyd

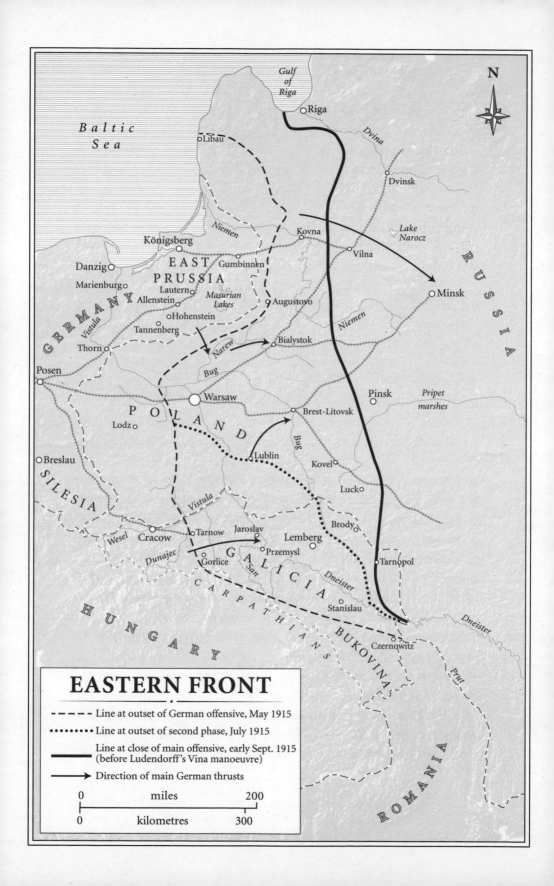

EASTERN FRONT

- – – – Line at outset of German offensive, May 1915
- • • • • • Line at outset of second phase, July 1915
- ——— Line at close of main offensive, early Sept. 1915 (before Ludendorff's Vina manoeuvre)
- ——▶ Direction of main German thrusts

| 0 | miles | 200 |
| 0 | kilometres | 300 |

Baltic Sea

Gulf of Riga

Riga

Dvina

Libau

Dvinsk

Niemen

Kovna

Lake Narocz

Königsberg

Vilna

RUSSIA

Danzig

EAST PRUSSIA

Gumbinnen

Marienburg

Lautern

Allenstein

Masurian Lakes

Augustovo

Minsk

Hohenstein

Niemen

GERMANY

Vistula

Tannenberg

Narew

Bialystok

Thorn

Bug

Posen

Warsaw

Brest-Litovsk

Pinsk

Pripet marshes

POLAND

Lodz

Bug

Lublin

Kovel

Breslau

Lucko

SILESIA

Vistula

Brody

Wesel

Tarnow

Jaroslav

Lemberg

Cracow

Przemysl

Tarnopol

Gorlice

GALICIA

Dunajec

San

Dneister

CARPATHIANS

Stanislau

BUKOVINA

HUNGARY

Czernowitz

Dneister

Prut

ROMANIA

N

George's new Ministry of Munitions called them. At the Chantilly conference in December, the Entente allies had committed themselves to mounting major offensives in the coming year, and to hasten these offensives if one or other of them were attacked beforehand. Yet to 'wear down the Enemy and cause him to use up his reserves,' Haig noted in his diary on 18 January, 'all the Allies must start at once. But Russia may not be ready till later, say July. In that case Germany may turn on her and defeat her – she (Russia) may then make peace!'

The previous summer's offensives by the German and Austrian armies had pushed the Russians back to a line from Riga on the Baltic to Czernowitz on the Romanian border, which besides aught else had done nothing to encourage the Romanians, who were still sitting on the fence, to declare for the Entente. In this 'Great Retreat', which though well conducted was a severe blow to morale, the Russians had surrendered practically the whole of Poland (Warsaw had fallen on 5 August) and the Germans had taken three-quarters of a million prisoners. Indeed, by the close of the year, the Russian army since August 1914 had lost in all some four million men, with another million in that baleful category 'missing'. All thoughts in Paris and London of the 'Russian steamroller' slowly but surely destroying the German army on the Eastern Front were now gone. Worse still, although in September 1914 the Triple Entente powers had signed a pact 'not to conclude peace separately during the present war' in which they pledged that, 'when terms of peace come to be discussed, no one of the Allies will demand conditions of peace without the previous agreement of each of the other Allies', a separate Russian negotiated peace was now, as Haig noted, a distinct possibility.

After the failure of the Dardanelles campaign to open warmwater communications with Russia, the danger of a separate peace should certainly have been the predominant strategic concern. Yet the French commander-in-chief, Joseph Joffre, insisted

125

there was no likelihood of Russian collapse, although he did see a need to draw off German troops from the east by mounting offensives in the west. In theory this was sound enough, except that the Germans understood the game and were not prepared to play it. Throughout 1915, because none of the offensives in the west had had the remotest chance of achieving break-through, given the Germans' agility in switching local reserves to seal any breaches in the line, the German chief of staff, Erich von Falkenhayn, had transferred only two divisions from the Eastern Front to the Western. Why should the allied offen-sives of 1916 be any more successful in diverting German divisions?

And yet there were voices in Vienna which argued that Russia, for all the setbacks she had suffered, was simply too powerful to overcome. At the beginning of January the Austrian chief of staff, Franz Conrad von Hötzendorf, confided to the Hungarian prime minister, Count István Tisza: 'There can be no question of destroying the Russian war machine; England cannot be defeated; peace must be made in not too long a space, or we shall be fatally weakened, if not destroyed.' For the German and Austro-Hungarian armies had suffered a million casualties on the Russian front in 1915, and despite the Austrians' recent suc-cess, finally, in over-running Serbia, the increasing alienation between the German and Austrian high commands was leading to cynicism on both sides, with some German officers complain-ing that 'We are shackled to a corpse.'

Conrad appreciated that the problem for the Russians was not, in fact, the absolute number of Austrian and German troops facing them – there were huge reserves, still, of Russian manpower – but the lack of arms and munitions with which to fight. This, as Conrad perceived, was not a problem beyond solution.

For a year it had seemed so, nevertheless. As early as Decem-ber 1914 the chief of the *Stavka*, the Russian high command, Nikolai Yanushkevich, had written to the war minister, General

Vladimir Sukhomlinov, that the shortage of ammunition was 'a nightmare', as was that of war materiel in general. 'Why should we perish of hunger and cold, without boots,' his men were asking; 'the artillery is silent, and we are killed like partridges.'

On average the Russian army had one surgeon for every 10,000 men, and with medical staff stretched thinly across a 500-mile front, many soldiers were dying from wounds that on the Western Front would have been successfully treated. In June 1915 Yanushkevich wrote that because of the lack of shells 'the enemy can inflict loss unpunished' and that the fighting was 'pure murder'.

If the western allies couldn't or wouldn't help Russia directly, neither could she help herself. The closure of the Dardanelles in October 1914 had been calamitous – essential imports dried up, and her exports, largely grain from southern Russia and Ukraine, declined by over two-thirds – but it was not beyond the wit of a resourceful bureaucracy to cope with. The Russian bureaucracy was made for another age, however, and court intrigue was pernicious. In September the clique that dominated the Winter Palace persuaded the Tsar to dismiss the commander-in-chief, his cousin, the Grand Duke Nicholas, and to take command of the armies himself. This was unfortunate on three counts. First, although the grand duke was no strategist, his judgement of men was on the whole quite sound, which was not a quality that his cousin shared. Second, the Tsar's absence in the field left the Tsarina and her reactionary coterie to block all attempts at political reform. And third, as the cabinet, which had unanimously opposed the change, pointed out, any further reversals would inevitably be blamed on the Tsar himself.

Tsar Nicholas took no notice. (He never did.)

Social and industrial unrest then spread quickly, with food even in the capital becoming scarce. By the end of 1915 Russia was virtually ungovernable. The country desperately needed some military success to put heart into both the army and the civil population. Fortunately – in the short term at least, for in time it would highlight the hopelessness of the *ancien régime* and feed the appetite for revolution – the self-help system of *zemstva*, the semi-official councils which sorted out all manner of affairs in a local, pragmatic fashion, began to make the running. By the spring of 1916 they would bring about a significant improvement in the supply of armaments and munitions, and their welfare work began stiffening military morale.

There would also be some restorative military success, under the innovative cavalryman General Aleksei Brusilov, who in March was given command of the south-western front. His preparations for the offensive in the east promised at Chantilly would be far superior to those of previous commanders, envisaging the use of 'shock troops' to attack and infiltrate in small parties rather than, as before, en masse – tactics that the Germans themselves would later copy and perfect.

Meanwhile, Haig continued to work on a number of plans to fulfil the Chantilly pledge, notably to capture Ostend and Zeebrugge, which had become troublesome U-boat nests, as well as Joffre's favoured combined offensive on the Somme. All the plans were dogged by the same problem, however: how to overcome the deadly combination of barbed wire, machine guns and artillery which had created the stalemate of the Western Front. For the present, there seemed to be only one solution: more and heavier artillery. Indeed, a year later Haig would be no closer to finding a solution, prompting the commander of the Australian 3rd Division, the Gallipoli veteran Major-General John Monash (not a soldier by profession but a civil engineer), to state that 'the Western Front is first and foremost an engineering problem'.

There was, however, a glimmer of hope in Haig's Christmas-day marginal query about the 'caterpillar'. Major Elles would return from his research trip to England with encouraging news of a tracked device that could crush barbed wire, cross trenches and bring fire to bear on the enemy from behind steel protection. Churchill's 'Admiralty Landships Committee', set up in February 1915, had finally borne fruit, thanks to the engineering skill of William Foster and Co. Ltd of Lincoln, specialists in agricultural machinery. Fosters had tested a first design, little more than an armoured box on American tractor caterpillar tracks, in September, but it could not cross a gap of 5 feet – the average trench width – the tracks being prone to shed. Known as 'Little Willie', after either Fosters' chief engineer and managing director, William Tritton, or the British press's derisive nickname for the Kaiser's son, Crown Prince Wilhelm, the trial nevertheless suggested the solution to the tracking problem. A few weeks later Tritton sent a telegram in veiled speech to the Admiralty: 'New arrival by tritton out of pressed plate STOP. Light in weight but very strong STOP. All doing well Thank you STOP. Proud parents END.'

With Lieutenant Walter Wilson of the Royal Naval Armoured Car Division, Tritton had produced a completely new design with bigger tracks wrapped round a hull with forward-sloping 'prows' projecting beyond the crew compartment, a rhomboid giving the machine huge reach. Weighing 28 tons and variously known as 'Centipede', 'Mother' or 'Big Willie', the prototype was ready just three months later. On the night of 19 January, sheathed in tarpaulins and referred to as a 'tank', a deliberately vague term alluding to its boxy shape, it was taken to Burton Park outside Lincoln and the following day was put through its paces, crossing a trench 8 feet wide, climbing a 5-foot parapet and crushing barbed wire entanglements.

A week later the 'tank' was on its way by rail to Hatfield Park in Hertfordshire, seat of the Marquess of Salisbury – whose cousin, Arthur Balfour, had succeeded Churchill at the Admiralty – for demonstrations to the War Office out of public view. Yet although the tank would do all that was asked of it at Hatfield, Kitchener, as secretary of state for war, had his doubts, calling it 'a pretty mechanical toy but without serious military value'.

Fortunately, Major-General Richard Butler, an infantryman and Haig's trusted deputy chief of staff, whom Elles had primed beforehand, saw its potential straight away. Though the tank would be many more months in development, the Tank Corps itself had in effect been conceived that day on Lord Salisbury's golf course. Major (later Lieutenant-General Sir) Hugh Elles would become its first commander.

19

FEBRUARY
The Blood Pump

The Germans gain the initiative with a strategic ambush at Verdun

In March 1916 the proprietor of *The Times*, Alfred Harmsworth, 1st Viscount Northcliffe, went to see the fighting at Verdun. 'This vast battle might have been arranged for the benefit of interested spectators,' he wrote,

> were it not that the whole zone for miles is as tightly closed to the outer world as a lodge of freemasons. Furnished with every possible kind of pass, accompanied by a member of the French headquarters staff in a military car, I was nevertheless held up by intractable gendarmes at a point 25 miles away from the great scene. Even at that distance the mournful reverberation of the guns was insistent. As the gentry examined our papers and waited for telephonic instructions, I counted more than 200 of the distant voices of *Kultur*.

Verdun was not the longest siege in history, but it was the longest battle: ten months of intensive fighting. 'Verdun was a whole war, inserted into the Great War, rather than a battle in the ordinary sense of the word,' said the distinguished academician Paul Valéry in a speech at the Académie Française in 1931 to honour Marshal Pétain, the man who had saved Verdun; 'It was also a kind of duel before the universe, a singular and almost symbolic tourney.'

Verdun was supposedly a trap laid by the Germans, but it turned out to be one in which they themselves were caught and maimed. Falkenhayn planned to use massed artillery as a mincing-machine rather than as a battering ram to break through the French defences. By attacking a place of national prestige, he hoped to draw the French reserves on to his guns like driven birds. In his memoirs he claimed that he sent the Kaiser a memorandum in December concluding:

> The string [of French defences] in France has reached breaking point. A mass breakthrough – which in any case is beyond our means – is unnecessary. Within our reach there are objectives for the retention of which the French General Staff would be compelled to throw in every man they have. If they do so the forces of France will bleed to death.

At first Falkenhayn had considered attacking Belfort, towards the Swiss border, but chose Verdun because it was a (French) salient and therefore cramped the defenders, and because it was close to one of the main German railway arteries, which meant he would be able to keep his troops well supplied. Verdun in 1916 was a town of some 20,000 astride the River Meuse on the old high road from Luxembourg and the Mosel to Paris, and one whose Roman name – Verodunum, 'strong fort' – suggested a long acquaintance with siege warfare. The place had been massively refortified after the débâcles of the Franco-Prussian war, and its prominence in the French national consciousness was such that Falkenhayn reasoned its loss would have so powerful a moral effect that it would have to be held 'at all costs'. A limited offensive would, he hoped, lead to the destruction of the French strategic reserve in fruitless counter-attacks, and the defeat of British reserves in an equally futile relief offensive, which, he told the Kaiser, would lead to the French accepting a separate peace.

Bad weather delayed the start of the offensive for a fortnight, but at 7.12 a.m. on 21 February, two 38 cm railway guns, known as 'Long Max' – naval pieces served by men of the *Kaiserliche Marine* – signalled the opening of *Unternehmen Gericht* (Operation Judgement): a bombardment by over 1,200 guns on a front of 12 miles astride the Meuse in the north of the salient. The intelligence branch at French GHQ had been warning of the buildup of troops – the Germans had concentrated more than 150 aeroplanes over the Verdun sector to prevent French aerial reconnaissance, itself an indicator that something was afoot – but Joffre, preoccupied with plans for his own offensive on the Somme, took no notice of the warnings. Besides, where was the prolonged preparatory artillery bombardment?

The German tactical plan was subtler than Joffre had imagined. It envisaged a continuous series of limited advances, each preceded by a brief (hours rather than days) but intense bombardment which would allow the infantry to take and consolidate their objectives before the French reserves could move up to counter-attack. When eventually they did counter-attack – as their doctrine required – the German infantry would be secure in the trenches and bunkers taken from the French, and their artillery could do its worst. But to minimize casualties in the attack, German patrols would first probe the defences to gauge the effectiveness of their artillery preparation before the main mass of infantry was launched, a tactic not seen before. On 21 February this revealed that the effect of the nine hours' bombardment varied, and so the main attack was launched on only a narrow sector, successfully but with limited gains. The following day the bombardment was repeated to greater effect and the French line buckled in several places.

Joffre was unperturbed. His operations branch assured him the offensive was a feint, perhaps to disrupt preparations for his own. In a sense they were right. The attacks *were* a feint: it would be the artillery strike on the French reserves that would be the real blow.

Joffre could not afford for this assault to be other than a feint, for he had earlier degraded the fortress by taking away many of its heavy guns. There had been representations in Paris that Verdun

133

was no longer impregnable, which he had indignantly repudiated: 'I cannot be a party to soldiers under my command bringing before the Government by channels other than the hierarchical channel, complaints or protests about the execution of my orders.'

On the evening of the fourth day of fighting, General Noël de Castelnau, Joffre's chief of staff, became alarmed by the reports and asked permission to go and judge for himself. Joffre agreed and, as Castelnau set off to drive the 150 miles to Verdun, sent a telegram saying that any commander giving an order to retreat would be tried by court martial – exactly as Falkenhayn had calculated.

Soon after Castelnau arrived, Fort Douaumont, the largest and most elevated in the ring of nineteen forts that protected the town, now denuded of its heavy guns, fell with hardly a fight. Castelnau at once pulled the right flank back but ordered that the remaining line of forts be held, and transferred responsibility for the whole sector to General Pétain, commanding 2nd Army.

The story goes that Pétain, a sixty-year-old bachelor, had to be brought to the battle from the bed of a favourite Parisienne mistress by one of his staff. In any event, he was a good choice, if not Joffre's favourite; for, as an infantryman teaching at the staff college before the war, Pétain had rejected the mantra of *offensive à outrance* – mounting all-out offensives under any circumstances – urging instead the power of the defensive with the axiom *Le feu tue* (fire-power kills). As Pétain's deputy Castelnau appointed General Robert Nivelle, an artilleryman with a strong belief in the moral superiority of the infantry in the attack.

The tardiness of Pétain's promotion, owing to his unorthodoxy, now came to the army's aid. In August 1914 he had been a mere colonel commanding a brigade; he had therefore seen the new warfare from the ground up rather than from a headquarters where the temptation was to make the situation fit pre-conceived doctrine. After the failures of the autumn battles in Champagne, he had written a memorandum saying it was 'impossible to carry in one bound the successive positions of the enemy', and that offensives should be limited to the reach of artillery. He would now use this appreciation in reverse to defeat the German attacks.

His immediate problem, however, was supply, for the German guns had closed all but two routes into the salient – a light railway and the Chemin Bar-le-Duc. While ordering limited counter-attacks to slow the Germans on what was still a narrow front, Pétain set every available pick and shovel to work on widening and maintaining this one road. Motor lorries were soon bringing forward ammunition virtually nose-to-tail – by June, some 6,000 vehicles a day. Auguste-Maurice Barrès, politician and man of letters, dubbed it 'La Voie Sacrée', the sacred way, a name which defiantly stuck.

Falkenhayn in turn widened the frontage, on 6 March extending the attacks to the west bank of the Meuse. During the assault on Fort Vaux, Captain Charles de Gaulle, the future president of France, was wounded and taken prisoner. But the defence was now solidifying, not least through Pétain's own massing of artillery and relieving the infantry divisions before casualties and exhaustion had too great an effect. This called for ever greater numbers of replacements from elsewhere in the line, and as the weeks passed Joffre became increasingly anxious that it was disrupting his own plans. At the end of April he had to change his intended frontage of attack on the Somme from 25 to 15 miles, with thirty not thirty-nine divisions, and 300 rather than 1,700 heavy guns. In consequence the BEF would have to assume more of the burden on the Somme, because of the undertaking given at the Chantilly conference in December that whenever one ally came under clear threat, the others would launch counter-offensives.

On 26 May, Joffre went to Haig's headquarters to ask him to advance the date of the Somme offensive to 1 July to relieve pressure on Verdun. For three months the French had supported the whole weight of the German attacks there, he said, and 'if this went on, the French Army would be ruined'.

Haig had been planning on a start date of 15 August, by which time he would have 200 additional heavy guns and possibly some tanks, as well as more time to train his green 'New Army' divisions.

The Germans had not been having it all their own way, however. At the end of March, Crown Prince Wilhelm, commanding the 5th Army entrusted with the offensive, told Falkenhayn that the bulk of the French reserves had been exhausted and that it was now time to complete their destruction by the conventional methods of attack, using 'men, not merely . . . machines and munitions'. Falkenhayn agreed. But German casualties soon began to mount in the face of sacrificial resistance.

Joffre then came unwittingly to Wilhelm's aid by insisting that, for reasons of prestige, Fort Douaumont – though it had played no part in the initial defence, being stripped of armament – should be retaken. Against Pétain's better judgement, on 3 April Nivelle's corps tried to do so, with a predictably bloody lack of success.

The Germans renewed their attacks, capturing Fleury-devant-Douaumont on 23 June and threatening to break through. Nivelle, by this time commanding the whole Verdun sector, Pétain having been promoted to command the army group, issued an order of the day: 'Ils ne passeront pas!' ('They shall not pass!'). In the Second World War the motto would be worn on the uniforms of troops manning the 'Maginot Line', named after André Maginot, the defence minister, who had lost a leg at Verdun.

By now French casualties had reached 200,000, but German losses were almost as great. Still the 'blood-pump', as Falkenhayn called it, continued – attack after attack, counter-attack after counter-attack. The village of Fleury alone changed hands sixteen times between 23 June and 17 August. A *poilu* of the 65ème Division d'Infanterie wrote home:

Anyone who has not seen these fields of carnage will never be able to imagine it. When one arrives here the shells are raining down everywhere with each step one takes but in spite of this it is necessary for everyone to go forward. One has to go out of one's way not to pass over a corpse lying at the bottom of the communication trench. Farther on, there are many wounded to tend, others who are carried back on stretchers to the rear. Some are screaming, others are pleading. One sees some who don't have legs, others without any heads, who have been left for several weeks on the ground.

Despite Pétain's system of troop rotation, disobedience and desertion in the French army began to increase alarmingly.

The Germans, too, were becoming demoralized at their lack of progress; and not just in the west. Faced with a Russian resurgence – albeit an illusory one – in Galicia, under General Aleksei Brusilov, the fall of Gorizia to the Italians, and Romania's belated declaration of war on Austria-Hungary, the Kaiser replaced Falkenhayn at the end of August with the even more ruthless Paul von Hindenburg.

The fighting at Verdun would continue until 19 December, when a deceptively easy French counter-offensive devised by Nivelle regained much lost ground and forced the Germans to close down Operation Judgement. Unfortunately for both the French army and the BEF, Joffre having been elegantly relieved of command by the device of promotion to marshal of France, Nivelle would now emerge as the man purporting to hold the key to victory on the Western Front. His attempts to turn that key the following year would lead only to more huge losses, widespread mutinies in French units, and his own dismissal. It would then take all the humane skill of Pétain, recalled from the sidelines, to nurse the demoralized French army back to health.

In all, some 40 million shells would plough the ground at Verdun. Flying over the battlefield, the American pilot Edwin Parsons of the famous 'Lafayette Squadron' – volunteers flying for the French army before America's formal declaration of war – saw below him how

> Nature had been ruthlessly murdered. Every sign of humanity had been swept away. Roads had vanished, and forests were fire-blackened stumps. Villages were gray smears where stone walls were tumbled together. Only the faintest outlines of the great forts of Douaumont and Vaux could be traced against the churned up background ... only broken, half obliterated links of the trenches were visible.

Some historians argue that Falkenhayn's 'trap' was a retrospective invention, his true intention always being breakthrough. In terms of attrition, however, he could claim some success: the French suffered well over half a million casualties in the two battles of 1916, and Haig was forced to attack on the Somme six weeks prematurely, with calamitous results. However, German casualties were so great that there would be no further major offensives on the Western Front until 1918. Indeed, it is probably only the collapse of the Russians the following year that enabled Hindenburg to hold on with any practical hope of victory.

20

MARCH

Q vs U

A 'Mystery VC' becomes the scourge of German submarines

At about seven in the morning of 22 March 1916, off Dingle in south-west Ireland, the German submarine U-68 fired a torpedo at what her captain probably took to be a British merchantman, the collier *Loderer*, 3,207 gross tons. The torpedo narrowly missed *Loderer*'s bow, and she continued her same speed and course. Twenty minutes later U-68 surfaced 1,000 yards astern, moved to her port quarter and fired a shot across her bow. The 'collier' stopped, blew off steam, and launched a boat taking off some of the crew. The U-boat closed to 800 yards, whereupon *Loderer* – or rather HMS *Farnborough*, the 'Q-ship' into which she had recently been converted – raised the white ensign of the Royal Navy, uncovered her guns and opened fire with her 12-pounders, scoring several hits. U-68 began to dive. *Farnborough*'s captain, Lieutenant-Commander Gordon Campbell, restarted her engines, steered straight for where the U-boat had submerged and dropped a depth charge, blowing the submarine's bow out of the water. *Farnborough*'s gunners opened fire again, and U-68 sank by the stern with all thirty-eight of her

139

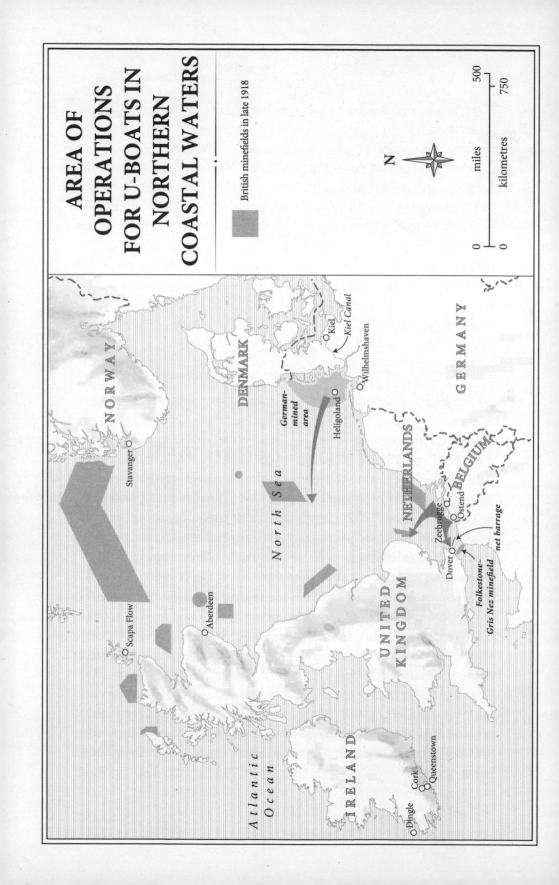

AREA OF OPERATIONS FOR U-BOATS IN NORTHERN COASTAL WATERS

British minefields in late 1918

N

miles   500
kilometres   750

0
0

NORWAY

Stavanger

Scapa Flow

Aberdeen

Atlantic
Ocean

North Sea

DENMARK

German-
mined
area

Kiel
Kiel Canal
Wilhelmshaven

Heligoland

GERMANY

NETHERLANDS

BELGIUM

Zeebrugge
Ostend

Dover
net barrage

Folkestone–
Gris Nez minefield

UNITED
KINGDOM

IRELAND

Dingle

Cork
Queenstown

crew. It was not the first loss of a U-boat to a decoy ship – *U-boot Falle* (U-boat trap), as the Germans called it – but it was the first to the newly developed depth charge, or 'dropping mine'.

No aspect of German 'frightfulness', whether reprisals against Belgian civilians, the shelling of seaside towns such as Scarborough, or the bombing of cities by Zeppelin – came as such a shock and posed so serious a threat as the U-boat campaign against merchant shipping. Before the war, Admiral Sir Jacky Fisher, the first sea lord, had warned that German submarines would flout the so-called 'cruiser', or 'prize', rules and sink merchantmen without warning, but the prime minister, Asquith, had refused to consider that a civilized nation would embark on such a 'barbarous practice in violation of international law'. The rules even prohibited leaving men adrift in open boats, though in practice, because submarines hadn't the room to take them aboard and couldn't spare men for prize crews (to take command of the ship and sail her to a friendly port), and because in the early months the U-boat's range was limited to coastal waters, where there was a reasonable chance of crews being picked up quickly, the convention was that the U-boat surfaced to warn the crew to take to the boats, before sinking the ship by torpedo or gunfire. In the early days some U-boat captains even displayed a degree of chivalry. On 20 October 1914, U-17, commanded by Oberleutnant zur See Johannes Feldkirchner, stopped the British steamship *Glitra* bound for Stavanger with a mixed cargo some 14 miles off the Norwegian coast. Feldkirchner ordered the crew to take to the boats and then, having scuttled the ship, towed them towards the coast, before a Norwegian patrol boat took over.

At the beginning of the war the *Kaiserliche Marine* had only twenty-four operational *Unterseeboote*, the Royal Navy about a hundred. Submarines relying on electric propulsion when submerged were still a recent development. Their first operational use had been with the Imperial Russian Navy in the Russo-Japanese war of 1904–5. Diesel engines gave them a surface speed of around 9 knots and charged the electric-motor batteries. Underwater they could make 15 knots for about two hours. In 1914 submarines on both sides were only around 150 feet in length and displaced about 400 tons. Armed initially with self-propelled torpedoes, once war began they were fitted with deck guns to force merchant ships to stop for searching, and to sink smaller ships that did not warrant a torpedo. The Germans also constructed specialized submarines with vertical mine tubes through their hulls to lay mines covertly.

Both sides saw submarines as adjuncts to the main battle fleet for patrolling, screening and offensive action against warships. On 22 September 1914 German U-boats sank three pre-dreadnought cruisers, *Cressy*, *Aboukir* and *Hogue*, in the North Sea with the loss of 1,400 men. A month later HMS *Audacious* was sunk off the north coast of Ireland by a surface-laid mine, at first thought to have been a torpedo, the only dreadnought to be lost to enemy action during the entire war. The Royal Navy's Grand Fleet at Scapa Flow in Orkney quickly became 'U-boat conscious', wary of torpedoes and mines, and its battle plans were increasingly characterized by caution.

The *Kaiserliche Marine* had never expected its U-boat service to make war on British commerce, even under the 'cruiser rules'. The prevailing view before 1914, at least among the Kaiser and his circle, was that if war came it would be over quickly. France would be rapidly defeated by the surprise offensive through Belgium, leaving the German army free then to deal with the slower-mobilizing Russians – the so-called Schlieffen Plan. Britain's 'contemptible little army' was too small to make any difference, and the Royal Navy could not affect the war on land. Besides, reckoned Berlin, the Grand Fleet would be held in check by the Imperial Navy's High Seas Fleet, the *Hochseeflotte*. War at sea, if it came to it, would therefore be a clash of titans – the dreadnought battleships – not a long-running affair of blockades and counter-blockades.

Germany's naval minister, Grand Admiral Alfred von Tirpitz, who saw a naval war with Britain as somehow inevitable and not necessarily connected with any continental clash, had always advocated submarine warfare against British merchantmen, in addition to trying to outbuild the Royal Navy in dreadnoughts. The Kaiser's qualms over sinking unarmed ships had nevertheless prevailed. In any case, the naval staff had estimated that some 220 U-boats would be needed to carry out such a campaign according to international law, far too many for the naval budget, whose first priority was the 'dreadnought race'. Soon after the war began, however, the commander of the submarine service, Korvettenkapitän Hermann Bauer, urged that his boats be allowed to attack British commerce without restriction on the grounds that Britain had already violated international law by its blockade. Not until 1915 would the Kaiser agree; and then, following the sinking of the Cunard liner *Lusitania* in May that year, with the death of many American passengers, he rescinded the order. Tirpitz continued to press for the restoration of unrestricted submarine warfare, until, frustrated by the Kaiser's vacillations, he resigned in March 1916.

The war on merchant shipping, including neutrals, therefore continued to be a perilous business for the German submarine service. A U-boat on the surface, even with its gun in action, was highly vulnerable to an armed merchantman, and even more so to the Q-ship, so called because they operated largely out of Queenstown (Cobh) in south-east Ireland. The idea of the Q-ship, like so many another in both world wars, can in part be credited to Winston Churchill. In November 1914, ignoring the niceties of the formal chain of command, the first lord of the Admiralty had telegrammed Admiral Sir Hedworth Meux, C-in-C Portsmouth, responsible for the English Channel:

It is desired to trap the German submarine which sinks vessels by gunfire off Havre. A small or moderate sized steamer should be taken up and fitted very secretly with two twelve-pounder guns in such a way that they can be concealed with deck cargo or in some way in which they will not be suspected. She should be sent when ready to run from Havre to England and should have an intelligence officer and a few seamen and two picked gunlayers who should all be disguised. If the submarine stops her she should endeavour to sink her by gunfire. The greatest secrecy is necessary to prevent spies becoming acquainted with the arrangements.

The Le Havre submarine wasn't caught, but soon afterwards the Admiralty ordered its first dedicated decoy vessels, converted merchantmen. The possibilities of decoying were soon demonstrated by the Aberdeen fishing fleet, whose boats were being regularly harassed. On 5 June 1915 a dozen of them were fishing off Peterhead, among them the armed trawlers *Oceanic II* and *Hawk*, when U-14 surfaced in their midst. Days before she had sunk two Danish and Swedish freighters, both neutrals, and not noticing that any of the trawlers were armed she fired warning shots. Both *Oceanic* and *Hawk* returned fire, and U-14 began to sink; the trawlermen managed to pick up the crew of twenty-seven, though not the captain, Oberleutnant zur See Max Hammerle, who was killed when a shell hit the conning tower.

Despite the dangers, the U-boats had to wage war as best they could, for the *Hochseeflotte*'s surface warships were increasingly confined to tip-and-run raiding from their base at Wilhelmshaven, and Germany's armed cruisers elsewhere had long been sent to the bottom or else confined to the Black Sea. All that Tirpitz had otherwise were auxiliary cruisers – converted merchant ships – which were good at laying mines but not in a fight. U-boats would therefore be the mainstay of his *Kleinkrieg* ('small war') campaign to wear down the Royal Navy's numerical advantage or to divert warships from the Grand Fleet for trade protection. As the war went on, the *Kaiserliche Marine* poured resources into building more and more U-boats – 350 in all – increasingly sophisticated technically, ever larger and with greater range. Operating from their main base at Heligoland in the German Bight, from Ostend and Zeebrugge in Belgian Flanders, and in the Mediterranean, by 1916 U-boats were becoming not just an irritation but a menace.

Losses in merchant shipping mounted – a million and a quarter tons between October 1916 and January the following year. From February 1917, after the Kaiser had given in to the resumption of unrestricted submarine warfare, to April that year, U-boats sank more than 500 merchant ships, with latterly an average of thirteen each day. One ship out of every four that left the British Isles never returned.

Still the Admiralty would not adopt the convoy system. The first sea lord, by this point Admiral Jellicoe, would not divert the necessary escort vessels, judging that his destroyers had to remain with the Grand Fleet to screen the dreadnoughts if the *Hochseeflotte* tried to sortie in strength. Just as adamantly opposed were the merchant captains themselves, who did not want to be massed into an array of targets limited to the speed of the slowest ship. Only in May 1917, at the insistence of Lloyd George, now prime minister, were convoys formed, after which the losses began slowly to decline. Nevertheless, a month later, Jellicoe, in a mood of abject gloom, warned the cabinet that nothing could be done to defeat the U-boats at sea, and that unless the army could capture their bases on the Flanders coast he considered it 'improbable that we could go on with the war next year for lack of shipping'.

The Q-ships continued to operate even after the reintroduction of unrestricted submarine warfare, and by December 1917 the losses had significantly reduced; moreover, a new mine barrier in the Channel effectively closed this route for U-boats and inflicted heavy losses on the *U-Flotilla Flandern*. Over the course of the whole war, the German submarine service lost 178 U-boats in combat – 50 per cent – and 39 (11 per cent) to misadventure. How cost-effective the Q-ships were is uncertain. Twice as many were lost as submarines they sank, but this does not take account of their deterrent value. A U-boat commander was sparing of his torpedoes, and it is likely that many allowed smaller prizes to escape rather than risk surfacing to use the deck armament, only to find his submarine on the receiving end of concealed fire. Q-ship ruses grew ever more resourceful. One such was the trawler that towed a submerged submarine, connected by telephone. If a U-boat surfaced, the trawler engaged its attention while the submarine was released for attack. This ploy scored its first success in June 1915 when the Aberdeen trawler *Taranaki*, with Royal Navy submarine C24, sank U-40 off the east coast of Scotland.

Q-ships were also built with especially shallow draughts, so that torpedoes would pass underneath, or else their holds were filled with buoyancy aids and fire-suppressants to limit the damage if struck. After sinking U-68 by depth charge in March 1916, Commander Gordon Campbell became an ever more aggressive exponent of decoy tactics, believing that Q-ships must actually invite torpedo attacks in order to tempt U-boats to the surface to 'finish off' a stricken vessel. On 17 February 1917, off Cork, his audacity was rewarded when *Farnborough* was struck by a torpedo fired by U-83 at extreme range. Campbell had intentionally failed to evade the torpedo, and *Farnborough* took the blow in the hold, causing only minor injuries to some crewmen but serious damage to the ship. As U-83 surfaced, the well-rehearsed 'panic party' took to the boats with a great show of alarm and disorder while the gun crews manned the hidden weapons. When four lifeboats had been released and the ship was low in the water, the U-boat closed alongside. *Farnborough*'s remaining crew now sprang the ambush, opening fire at point-blank range with her 6-pounder and machine guns, killing the commanding officer, Kapitänleutnant Bruno Hoppe (who had sixteen sinkings to his credit). U-83 went down with just one survivor.

Only then did Campbell radio for help: 'Q5 slowly sinking respectfully wishes you goodbye.' In fact, with help she was able to beach at Mill Cove without loss. Campbell, who had joined the navy in 1900 from Dulwich College as a cadet of fourteen, was awarded the VC. The citation was deliberately vague: 'In recognition of his conspicuous gallantry, consummate coolness, and skill in command of one of HM ships in action.' The vagueness backfired, however, with the press referring to him as 'The Mystery VC', which led to reports that German agents had put a price on his head. He would survive the war nevertheless, with the DSO and two bars in addition to the VC, and afterwards rose to vice-admiral. His VC is held by his old school.

21

APRIL

A 'Stab in the Back'

The Easter Rising: the war comes to the streets of Dublin

In the early hours of 21 April 1916, Good Friday, the German submarine U-19 surfaced in Tralee Bay in the south-west of Ireland. Her captain, Raimund Weissbach, was familiar with Irish waters: the year before, in U-20, he had fired the torpedo that sank the *Lusitania*.

As daylight approached, U-19 lowered a boat, into which clambered Sir Roger Casement, a former member of the British consular service, and two men of the 'Irish Brigade' (a failed venture to recruit Irish PoWs to fight the British). Three months later, awaiting execution for high treason in Pentonville Prison, Casement, who had been knighted in 1911 for his humanitarian work in Africa and South America, but who had become disenchanted with colonialism and turned instead to Irish nationalism, would write to his sister:

> The sand hills were full of skylarks rising in the dawn, the first I had heard in years – the first sound I heard through the surf was their song as I waded through the breakers and they kept rising all the time up to the old rath [enclosure] at Currshone where I stayed and sent the others

147

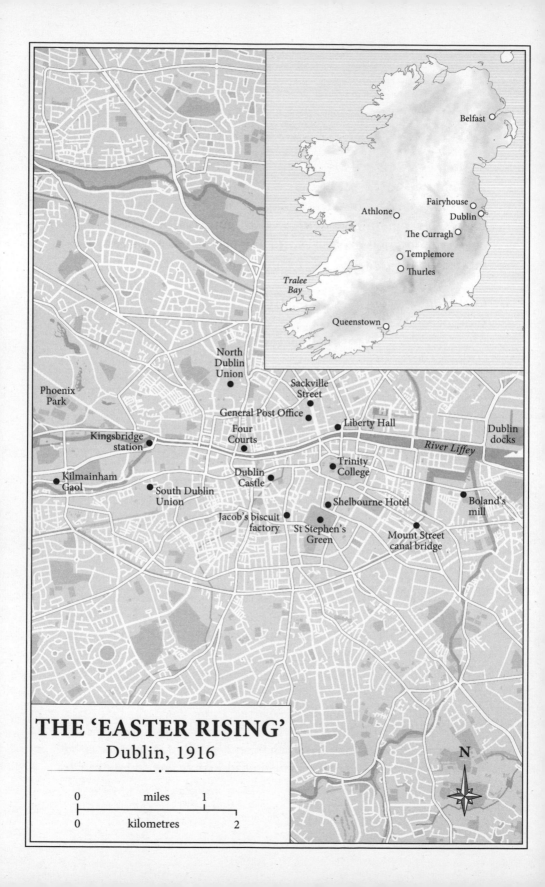

Belfast

Fairyhouse
Athlone
Dublin
The Curragh
Templemore
Thurles

Tralee Bay

Queenstown

North Dublin Union

Sackville Street

Phoenix Park

General Post Office

Liberty Hall

Four Courts

Dublin docks

Kingsbridge station

River Liffey

Kilmainham Gaol

Dublin Castle

Trinity College

South Dublin Union

Shelbourne Hotel

Boland's mill

Jacob's biscuit factory

St Stephen's Green

Mount Street canal bridge

THE 'EASTER RISING'
Dublin, 1916

| 0 | miles | 1 |
| 0 | kilometres | 2 |

N

on, and all round were primroses and wild violets and the singing of the skylarks in the air and I was back in Ireland again.

After encouraging discussions with the German embassy in Washington, Casement had been in Berlin to arrange support for the coming nationalist rebellion – 20,000 rifles and 10 million rounds of ammunition, ten machine guns, each with 100,000 belted rounds, plus explosives and hand grenades. It was less than he had hoped for, and, even more disappointing, would not be accompanied by any troops. With his encouragement, the German foreign ministry had issued an ominous statement, but it stopped short of action:

> Should the fortunes of this great war, that was not of Germany's seeking, ever bring in its course German troops to the shores of Ireland, they would land there, not as an army of invaders to pillage and destroy, but as the forces of a government that is inspired by good-will towards a country and a people for whom Germany desires only national prosperity and national freedom.

Were they having second thoughts about how ripe Ireland was for the 'stab in the back' to Britain? After all, there were 200,000 Irishmen fighting under the Union flag in France and Flanders, Salonika and the Middle East, many of them Catholics from the south. A Leinster man, Maurice Dease, had won the first VC of the war. Was England's difficulty really Ireland's opportunity, as the old nationalist saying went?

Casement had therefore tried to get word to Dublin to postpone the rebellion and disperse the weapons when they arrived. He had no idea if the message had reached the rebel leadership, however. Wracked by a bout of recurrent malaria, all he could do now was lie up in the ancient ring fort at Currshone, hope to evade capture – and dream of a united republic of Ireland.

In 1912 the Liberal government had introduced an Irish home rule bill. The Ulster Unionists, bitterly opposed to rule from Dublin, had raised a paramilitary body, the Ulster Volunteer Force. As a counter-force, the nationalists had raised their own, the Irish Volunteers. The Germans had supplied both sides with weapons. In August 1914, however, mainstream Unionists and Nationalists alike agreed to set aside the home rule question until after the war. Indeed, John Redmond, leader of the Irish Parliamentary Party, urged the Irish Volunteers to enlist in the British army 'in defence of right, of freedom and of religion', and to disprove the Unionist claim that, if given home rule, Ireland would inevitably stab England in the back in her hour of danger.

In April 1916, though, the war on the Western Front was not going well for the allies. Casualties were mounting, and the French were calling for a major British offensive to relieve pressure on Verdun. The effect of trouble at home on Irishmen serving in the army would have been incalculable, as would that of U-boats able to operate from bases in Ireland. Britain had had similar concerns about the 'stab in the back' during the Napoleonic wars, which had led to the 1800 Acts of Union.

Although 90 per cent of the Irish Volunteers – some 170,000 men – had heeded Redmond's call to enlist, others had allied themselves increasingly with hard-line groups such as the Irish Republican Brotherhood, Sinn Féin ('We ourselves') and the small but assertive Irish Citizen Army (ICA). By 1916, with conscription introduced in Britain and fears that it would soon follow in Ireland, these hardliners had decided the time had come for decisive armed action to gain not just home rule but independence. Their plan was to seize the centres of administrative power in Dublin and proclaim a republic and provisional government, hoping that popular support would help them defeat the authorities' inevitable reaction. Their leader and 'provisional president' would be the 36-year-old Patrick Pearse – barrister, teacher, and editor of the Gaelic League's newspaper *The Sword of Light*. Though a fervent Catholic, Pearse's interest in Celtic culture verged on the mystical, with a marked predilection for sacrifice. In 1915 he wrote of the war: 'The old heart of the earth needed to be warmed with the red wine of the battlefields. Such august homage was never before offered to God as this, the homage of millions of lives given gladly for love of country.'

But he had no military experience whatsoever. As one prominent Irish statesman wrote, 'Pearse saw the Rising as a Passion Play with real blood.'

Casement's 20,000 rifles left Lübeck on 9 April in the German freighter *Libau* masquerading as the Norwegian steamship *Aud*. Under command of Kapitänleutnant Karl Spindler with crew from the Imperial German Navy, *Libau* successfully evaded the Royal Navy's patrols in the North Sea and the western approaches to enter Tralee Bay on 20 April, Maundy Thursday. There was no one to meet them, however. Casement had left Wilhelmshaven in U-20 but the boat had developed steering trouble, and he had had to transfer to U-19, delaying his arrival. Worse, the Volunteers' high command, suddenly concerned about security, postponed the rendezvous by three days, to Easter Sunday, but had not been able to get the message to the *Libau*, which carried no radio. Spindler decided to leave, but the sloop HMS *Bluebell* intercepted *Libau* the next day, Good Friday, and took her to Queenstown near Cork. As they approached harbour, Spindler scuttled his ship.

Casement was arrested later that morning by the Royal Irish Constabulary (RIC). The Kerry Brigade of the Irish Volunteers set out to rescue him, but the leadership ordered them to 'do nothing': not a shot was to be fired before the rising was under way.

Meanwhile in Dublin confusion reigned. The rising had originally been planned for Easter Sunday, but last-minute disagreements between the groups led to order and counter-order, and it was postponed until Monday. The loss of the arms shipment greatly reduced the Volunteers' capability; the rising would now be confined almost exclusively to Dublin.

Just how much of a surprise the rising was to the authorities in London and Dublin is still uncertain. The Admiralty's signal intercept service, 'Room 40', was reading radio telegrams from the German embassy in Washington, where Berlin had opened an office to promote an Irish insurgency, and had warned the cabinet of the likelihood of the rising. Neither the civil nor the military authorities in Dublin received orders to increase security, however. The two police forces – the RIC and the Dublin Metropolitan Police – had their own intelligence divisions, but these were focused on crime rather than on insurgency. The military authorities had no intelligence network worthy of the name. The commander-in-chief, Major-General Sir Lovick Friend, even after learning of Casement's capture, saw no reason to cancel his Easter leave, and sailed for England the same day. Augustine Birrell, the chief secretary for Ireland, would tell the commission of inquiry afterwards: 'I always thought that I was very ignorant of what was going on in the minds, and in the cellars if you like, of the Dublin population.'

When, therefore, just before noon on Easter Monday, with the weather unseasonably warm and Dubliners in festive mood, the Volunteers and the ICA began assembling in the city, there were no troops on the streets. Some 900 rebels, in a mixture of grey-green uniform and 'mufti', moved openly towards their objectives, the key buildings dominating the routes into the centre – the Four Courts, Jacob's biscuit factory, the South Dublin Union, Boland's flour mills covering the approaches from the docks and railway station, and, most importantly, the General Post Office in Sackville Street, through which most telephone and telegraph communications in and out of the city passed. Pearse read out the proclamation of an Irish republic from its step.

'Captain' George Plunkett, who as a boy had been at the Catholic public school Stonyhurst with Maurice Dease, the first VC of the war, waved down a tram with his revolver, ordered on his Volunteers, took out his wallet and said 'Fifty-two tuppenny tickets to the city centre, please.' But the rebels were in deadly earnest. When a detachment of the ICA tried to march through the gates of Dublin Castle, seat of the country's administration, and Constable James O'Brien of the Dublin Metropolitan Police tried to bar their way, 'Captain' Sean Connolly shot him dead. Elsewhere a man trying to reclaim his lorry, commandeered by the rebels for a barricade, was shot and killed.

The police, unarmed, were in the main forced to quit the streets, but gave an accurate report of the situation to military headquarters in Phoenix Park. In the absence of the GOC, Colonel Henry Cowan began standing-to the Dublin garrison – with difficulty, for although the military guard had repulsed the attack on the castle, the rebels controlled most of the telephone lines, isolating the civil power. He then managed to get through to the Curragh, just outside Dublin, where there were two brigades, one of cavalry and one of infantry. Brigadier-General William Lowe, commanding the 3rd Reserve Cavalry Brigade, ordered three regiments less their horses (a fourth was already in Dublin for ceremonial and escort duty) to prepare to move. Cowan was also able to telephone the garrisons in Belfast and Templemore, and – crucially – the 5th Reserve Artillery Brigade at Athlone, 75 miles to the west, ordering reinforcements to the city.

The Great Southern and Western Railway rose to the occasion with impressive efficiency. Notwithstanding the diversion of trains for the races at Fairyhouse, the Dublin Society spring cattle show and a hurling match in Thurles, an official was able to report afterwards that

> at 12.25 pm on Easter Monday 24th April the military authorities telephoned the Superintendent of the Line to stop all traffic and to prepare military specials for the Curragh immediately. Empty specials left Kingsbridge [station] at 1.17pm, 1.45pm, 2.0pm and 2.6pm returning at once with troops, the last arriving at 5.30pm. Three thousand men were thus conveyed to the city.

None of these 3,000 were regulars in the true sense. The regular British army in Ireland had left for France in August 1914. What remained were the 'Special Reserve' battalions, whose primary role was to train battle casualty replacements for the eight Irish infantry regiments. These were based at regimental depots around the country, four of which were in Dublin and the Curragh. The cavalry brigade consisted of recruits undergoing training and men waiting to return to their regiments from courses of instruction or other postings, as did the artillery brigade, with its eight 18-pounder field guns. In Dublin there was a 'Kitchener battalion', the 10th Royal Dublin Fusiliers, in whose ranks were former Irish Volunteers who had heeded John Redmond's call to enlist. But in Ireland, unlike Britain, there was no Territorial Force. Cowan sent an officer in plain clothes to the naval base at Kingstown to get a wireless message to London calling for reinforcements. The War Office lost no time in ordering the 59th (2nd Midland) Division, territorials, to Dublin.

The Volunteers at the GPO drew first military blood when they ambushed a patrol of the 6th Reserve Cavalry Regiment sent to reconnoitre Sackville Street. Four troopers were killed and several wounded, but the rebels had opened fire prematurely and the patrol was able to withdraw. Lack of military experience would indeed be the rebels' undoing: besides poor tactics and field discipline, by occupying buildings and waiting for the army to assault, they surrendered the initiative. At St Stephen's Green the ICA's commander ordered his men to dig trenches, all of which were overlooked by buildings surrounding the square, ideal for the army's marksmen.

Brigadier-General Lowe arrived in the city centre in the early hours of Tuesday morning to assume overall command. He at once set about securing a line connecting the main station, the castle and Trinity College to divide the rebel positions north and south of the river. Many Dubliners were eager to help, pointing to where the 'shinners' (a blanket term for Sinn Féin and other republicans) were waiting. By midnight at the end of the first day, the dead numbered twenty-six soldiers, three policemen, eleven rebels – and fifteen civilians. Lord Wimborne, the lord lieutenant, declared martial law.

The noose began to tighten next day as men of the Royal Irish Regiment, the Dublin Fusiliers and the Leinster Regiment, with the dismounted troopers of the cavalry brigade, started to surround the various rebel positions. Overnight the cavalrymen had brought Vickers machine guns into the Shelbourne Hotel on St Stephen's Green, and quickly drove the ICA from their trenches. Mid-afternoon, the Royal Navy's gunboat *Helga*, which had sailed up the Liffey, opened fire on the flour mills with her two 12-pounders.

Four field guns from Athlone arrived soon afterwards and began engaging the barricades.

Lowe knew that it was only a matter of time before his artillery destroyed the strongpoints, but the 18-pounders had only shrapnel ammunition, not high explosive, and the process would therefore be slow and especially dangerous to civilians. By midnight of the second day, a further twenty-two of them, including several children, had been killed. Meanwhile, Lowe needed more troops to contain the rebels.

Public anger with the 'shinners' was growing, for many Dubliners had family fighting in France, and soldiers' wives found they were unable to draw their remittance money because the post offices remained closed. When the advance elements of the 59th Division, the 178th (Sherwood Foresters) Brigade, began arriving at the Dublin docks next morning, Wednesday, they were cheered by the crowds.

The Foresters had no practice in fighting in built-up areas, however, and quickly paid the price. Striking out for the castle, the leading troops ran into heavy and accurate fire on the approaches to Mount Street canal bridge from Volunteers under command of Eamon de Valera, the future president of Ireland. A firefight developed that lasted until early evening, when the Foresters were at last able to drive the rebels from their positions with grenades, which set several buildings alight. As night fell, thirty more soldiers were dead, and almost as many civilians.

A thick pall of smoke hung over the city centre next morning, the fires spreading. The *Helga* had been in action again, moving upriver to shell Liberty Hall. At about ten o'clock the 18-pounders began an indirect bombardment of Sackville Street, igniting the domestic gas supply and setting alight more buildings, forcing the rebels to abandon several barricades. Throughout the day more troops from the 59th Division arrived, and as darkness fell again much of Dublin's main thoroughfare was ablaze, with fires starting on the roof of the GPO.

Shortly after midnight, the absent GOC having been relieved, Lieutenant-General Sir John Maxwell, who a few months before had moved resolutely to counter the threat posed by the Senussi (an Arab Sufi sect) to Egypt from the eastern Sahara, arrived by warship to take command. He quickly confirmed Lowe's strategy, adding that he would accept nothing but the rebels' unconditional surrender.

Increasingly bitter fighting, with summary executions, continued all day and throughout Friday night. On Saturday morning, with the GPO now on fire, recognizing his men were surrounded and outnumbered, and 'to prevent the further slaughter of Dublin citizens', Patrick Pearse surrendered unconditionally. The city centre lay in ruins and 250 civilians were dead. As the rebels were marched off under escort some bystanders applauded them, but many more pelted them with stones and refuse, and shouts of 'Hang the bastards!'

Maxwell lost no time in exacting condign punishment. Over 3,000 men and women were arrested, although most were quickly released. Nearly 1,500 men would be interned in England and Wales. In courts martial a week later, ninety rebels were sentenced to death. Fifteen of them, including all seven signatories of the proclamation, had their sentences confirmed by Maxwell and were executed at Kilmainham Gaol by firing squad between 3 and 12 May, among them James Connolly, leader of the ICA, tied to a chair because of a shattered ankle. As Asquith told Parliament, 'A desperate plot was hatched for the disruption of the British Empire by means of an insurrection in Ireland. It was put into execution at a moment when England and Ireland were fighting for life against a foreign enemy. That enemy fomented and helped it with arms, money and promises.'

There was no doubting the offences – not least the killing of unarmed policemen – but the secret military courts (at least Casement was tried by due process, his case heard ultimately in the court of criminal appeal), the executions over a protracted period, and the heavy-handed, sometimes brutish, follow-up turned popular opinion increasingly in favour of the rebels. In January 1916 the war cabinet had concluded that thirteen divisions must be kept back from France and elsewhere for home defence and to keep the peace in Ireland. The Easter Rising only reinforced that costly diversionary decision.

22

MAY

The Victory that Looked Like Defeat

The long-anticipated clash of dreadnoughts in the
North Sea ends not as England expects

May 1916 would bring the long-expected clash of naval titans in a
contest that the British public expected to be another Trafalgar – a
decisive, strategic British victory. For the Royal Navy was incomparably the most powerful in the world; hundreds of millions of
pounds had been spent in its pre-war modernization programme.

The issue was straightforward – control of the sea, a precept laid
down three centuries earlier by the Elizabethan admiral and strate-
gian Sir Walter Raleigh: 'Whosoever commands the sea, commands
the trade of the world, commands the riches of the world, commands the world itself.' In 1916 control of the sea meant keeping
Britain secure from invasion, allowing her warships freedom of
action worldwide, and keeping open the trade routes to the British
Isles for food and war materiel, while closing off those of the Germans. It underpinned the whole allied war strategy of building
military strength on the Western Front and starving Germany. Loss
of sea control – indeed, supremacy – would have meant national

157

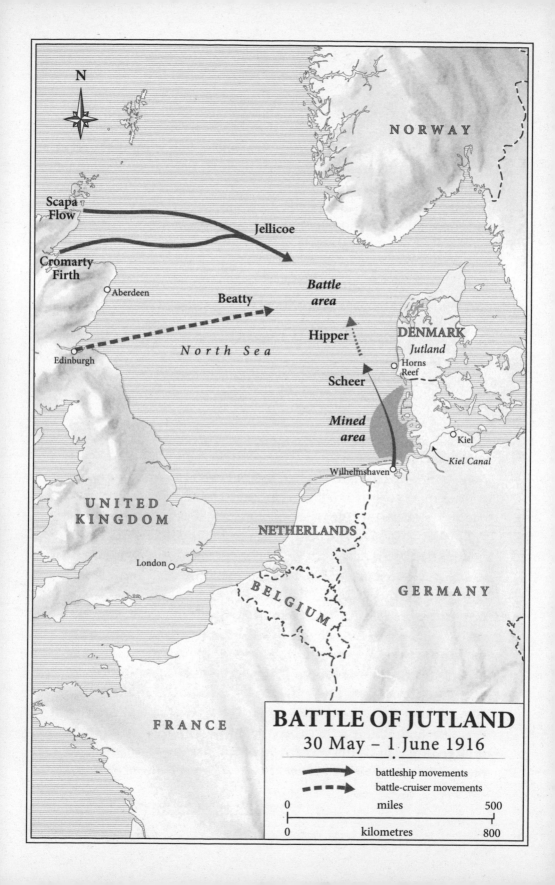

N

NORWAY

Scapa
Flow

Jellicoe

Cromarty
Firth

Aberdeen

Beatty

*Battle
area*

DENMARK

Hipper

Jutland

Horns
Reef

Edinburgh

North Sea

Scheer

*Mined
area*

Kiel

Kiel Canal

UNITED
KINGDOM

Wilhelmshaven

London

NETHERLANDS

BELGIUM

GERMANY

FRANCE

BATTLE OF JUTLAND
30 May – 1 June 1916

battleship movements

battle-cruiser movements

0   miles   500

0   kilometres   800

defeat. Winston Churchill, until mid-1915 first lord of the Admiralty, summed it up succinctly: Admiral Sir John Jellicoe, C-in-C of the Grand Fleet, was 'the only man on either side who could lose the war in an afternoon'.

Germany had tried to outbuild Britain in dreadnoughts, the revolutionary heavily armoured battleships, armed exclusively with big guns (initially 12-inch, increasing to 15-inch), named after the first of their class, HMS *Dreadnought*. Since her launch in 1906, however, Britain had managed to keep ahead in the 'dreadnought race' by almost two to one. Grand Admiral Tirpitz, Germany's long-time naval minister, knew that the *Hochseeflotte*, the High Seas Fleet, had no chance of victory in a straight fight with Jellicoe, and so his strategy was to wear down the Royal Navy's advantage by mines, torpedoes, opportunity skirmishes and ambushes, drawing in the dreadnoughts by deceit or provocation, of which the raid on Scarborough in December 1914 was the first and most infamous attempt. Two months earlier a mine laid by an auxiliary cruiser had sent HMS *Audacious* to the bottom. Since then, however, the *Hochseeflotte* had been unable to make much impression on the Grand Fleet's fighting strength, and both had settled into a routine of watching and waiting.

Like Nelson before Trafalgar, for nearly two years Jellicoe had confined the enemy's fleet to its home port – Wilhelmshaven and its connected bases. But unlike Nelson's blockade of Toulon, Jellicoe's had been a distant one. While his light cruisers, submarines, aircraft and dirigibles patrolled the North Sea, the main battle fleet kept largely to its base at Scapa Flow in the Orkneys, with a force of battle-cruisers (which had guns of similar calibre to the dreadnoughts but were not as heavily armoured, relying more on speed for protection) in the Firth of Forth under Vice-Admiral David Beatty.

Tirpitz had always wanted to use submarines as his prime strategic weapon. Pre-war calculations suggested that Britain would be brought to her knees in months, perhaps only weeks, if her food imports were intercepted. A good deal of these were carried by

1916 – 'PURE MURDER'

neutral shipping, however, and while surface ships of the Royal Navy could intercept neutrals bound for Germany, the *Kaiserliche Marine*, with the main fleet confined to Wilhelmshaven and all her other armed cruisers sunk in the opening months of the war, could not. Only U-boats could get into Britain's trade approaches – but their activities were restricted by the so-called 'cruiser rules', according to which a submarine intending to attack a merchant vessel was meant to surface, issue a warning and allow the crew to take to the lifeboats before sinking her. This was a dangerous procedure, for the U-boat was highly vulnerable on the surface, and Tirpitz was therefore a keen advocate of unrestricted submarine warfare – sinking without warning. In early 1915 the Kaiser had sanctioned this, but the international outcry, not least after the sinking of the *Lusitania* in May that year, had induced him to change his mind. In March 1916, frustrated by what he saw as the Kaiser's passivity, Tirpitz resigned.

The *Hochseeflotte*'s new commander-in-chief, Reinhard Scheer, while also an advocate of unrestricted submarine warfare, was now determined to take aggressive fleet action to whittle down the Royal Navy's superiority. By making a sortie in strength he knew he would bring Beatty's battle-cruisers, the Grand Fleet's reaction force, into the North Sea, and perhaps even some of Jellicoe's dreadnoughts as well. If Franz von Hipper, commanding the *Hochseeflotte*'s battle-cruisers, could tempt Beatty into a fight, he might be able to draw them and perhaps some of Jellicoe's main battle fleet, unsuspecting, on to the guns of his own dreadnoughts, reducing the odds for the next encounter. On 31 May, therefore, Scheer would personally lead the *Hochseeflotte* into the German Bight to bring on what would be the first (and, as it turned out, the last) dreadnought fleet action in history.

The relative strengths were certainly not propitious for Germany. Scheer had sixteen dreadnoughts to the twenty-eight that Jellicoe could bring out, together with Hipper's five battle-cruisers (against Beatty's nine), plus six light cruisers for scouting and thirty-one torpedo boats, as well as various supporting craft. He decided therefore to take his six pre-dreadnought battleships too, less well armoured and three knots slower, reducing the *Hochseeflotte*'s overall speed, critical to both manoeuvre and fire-control.

Scheer had a psychological advantage, however, for he had less to lose. The *Hochseeflotte*'s very existence fixed the Grand Fleet at Scapa Flow. But even if Jellicoe gained a Trafalgar-like victory, allowing the Admiralty to send ships elsewhere, it would not change the essential strategic situation: the economic blockade was already so effective that Germany was beginning to famish. On the other hand, Jellicoe could not risk losing superiority. While Scheer therefore could be bold, Jellicoe *had* to be cautious. And while Jellicoe could take calculated risks based on what he could see and reasonably anticipate were the actions of Scheer's surface ships, he could have no certain knowledge of where and in what strength lay his submarines. Gunnery did not trouble him, although Scheer's would prove unnervingly good; the mine (especially after the loss of *Audacious* in October 1914) and the torpedo did, factors that Nelson never had to consider.

One priceless advantage that Jellicoe possessed, however, was signals intelligence. When without warning the French fleet broke out of Toulon in March 1805, Nelson having withdrawn all but a few frigates to Sardinia for resupply, contact was lost for six weeks. In contrast, Jellicoe knew Scheer's precise sailing plans forty-eight hours before they were put into action, for the famed 'Room 40' at the Admiralty had intercepted and decrypted the *Hochseeflotte*'s radio traffic, revealing the operational plan and the sailing date. Jellicoe therefore left Scapa Flow, and Beatty the Firth of Forth, at last light the evening before, making for the German Bight to cut off and destroy as many of Scheer's ships as possible, but with the imperative of retaining overall superiority come what may. High winds made aerial reconnaissance all but impossible, so both fleets were relatively 'blind' once out of port.

At four in the afternoon of 31 May, Beatty's battle-cruisers, reinforced by the 5th Battle Squadron of dreadnoughts, ran into Hipper's battle-cruisers west of the northern tip of Jutland, beginning a running fight as Hipper turned south to draw them on to Scheer's battle fleet, with Jellicoe's squadrons closing fast but undetected from the north-west. The light cruiser *Chester*, scouting ahead of Rear-Admiral Horace Hood's 3rd Battle-cruiser Squadron, came under heavy fire from four of Hipper's light cruisers which killed or mortally wounded the crew of the forward 5.5-inch gun, leaving only the 16-year-old Boy 1st Class Jack Cornwell on his feet. Though gravely wounded, Cornwell remained standing by the gun through-out until the crippled *Chester* was ordered to break off the action and make for Immingham; he was taken to nearby Grimsby hos-pital, where he died. He was posthumously awarded the VC, the youngest recipient since 1860. His medal is on permanent display at the Imperial War Museum, as is the gun.

Beatty's battle-cruisers were also taking a beating. *Queen Mary* was soon hit by salvoes from the *Seydlitz* and *Derfflinger*. *Seydlitz*'s gunnery officer, Georg von Hase, noted:

> The enemy was shooting superbly. Twice the *Derfflinger* came under their infernal hail and each time she was hit. But the *Queen Mary* was having a bad time; engaged by the *Seydlitz* as well as the *Derfflinger*, she met her doom at 1626. A vivid red flame shot up from her fore-part; then came an explosion forward, followed by a much heavier explosion amidships. Immediately afterwards, she blew up with a ter-rific explosion, the masts collapsing inwards and the smoke hiding everything.

Both forward magazines had exploded, and she sank with all but nine of her 1,275 crew. Short cuts in ammunition handling owing to over-confidence were almost certainly the cause (too much cordite in the turret, and the anti-flash hatches kept open to speed resup-ply). HMS *Indefatigable* had blown up only minutes before, prompting Beatty to snap: 'There seems to be something wrong with our bloody ships today,' though what precisely he said and when, and what exactly he meant, are still disputed. However, as planned, Beatty now turned back north to try to lure Scheer towards Jellicoe's rapidly approaching dreadnoughts, a manoeuvre that Scheer could reasonably conclude was the result of the punishment that Hipper had inflicted.

During this 'run north', as it became known, Rear-Admiral Sir Robert Arbuthnot's 1st (Armoured) Cruiser Squadron plunged into the fight. Rear-Admiral Hood's 3rd Battle-cruiser Squadron had briefly engaged the light cruisers of the German 2nd Scouting Group, damaging several; now, with Nelsonian intrepidity, but unfortunately not the 'Nelson touch', Arbuthnot led his four pre-dreadnought cruisers straight at the damaged scouts. In doing so, he steamed into the middle of the fight between Hood's and Hipper's battle-cruisers, with Beatty's also closing fast and engaging. It was becoming what Nelson said he wanted before Trafalgar – a 'pell-mell battle' in which the Royal Navy's innately superior seamanship and gunnery would carry the day. However, armour-piercing explosive shells were infinitely more destructive than solid roundshot against oak. Arbuthnot's flagship, *Defence*, was caught in a deluge of shells from Hipper's battle-cruisers, detonating her magazines in a spectacular explosion. She sank with all hands – 903 officers and men. Of his three other cruisers, only one – *Duke of Edinburgh* – would survive the battle. *Warrior* managed to limp away, with most of her crew taken off before she sank, but *Black Prince* was lost with all hands too – 857 officers and men. Admiral of the Fleet Lord Fisher, the former first sea lord and architect of the dreadnought concept, called Arbuthnot's 'a glorious but not a justifiable death'.

Soon afterwards, Scheer's leading dreadnoughts began engaging Beatty's 'Barhams', as the Queen Elizabeth class ships were known after the fourth of the class – the fastest, most heavily armed of the dreadnoughts, also dubbed 'super-dreadnoughts'. Scheer believed he had caught an isolated portion of the Grand Fleet, and that he had his long-awaited opportunity for attrition. His hopes were shattered not long afterwards, however, when Jellicoe's ships, in one of which, HMS *Collingwood*, the twenty-year-old Prince Albert, the future King George VI, was serving, steamed into view. Sub-Lieutenant Prince Albert recorded:

We went to 'Action Stations' at 4.30 p.m. and saw the Battle Cruisers in action ahead of us on the starboard bow. Some of the other cruisers were firing on the port bow. As we came up the 'Lion' [Beatty's flagship] leading our Battle Cruisers, appeared to be on fire the port side of the forecastle, but it was not serious . . . The 'Colossus' leading the 6th division with the 'Collingwood' her next astern were nearest the enemy. The whole Fleet deployed at 5.0 and opened out. We opened fire at 5.37 p.m. on some German light cruisers. The 'Collingwood's' second salvo hit one of them which set her on fire, and sank after two more salvoes were fired into her . . . I was in 'A' turret and watched most of the action through one of the trainers telescopes, as we were firing by Director, when the turret is trained in the working chamber and not in the gun house. At the commencement I was sitting on the top of 'A' turret and had a very good view of the proceedings. I was up there during a lull, when a German ship started firing at us, and one salvo straddled us. We at once returned the fire. I was distinctly startled and jumped down the hole in the top of the turret like a shot rabbit!! I didn't try the experience again . . .

It seems that he was being characteristically modest: Sub-Lieutenant Prince Albert would be gazetted with a King's Commendation for his action during the battle.

But while the dreadnoughts on both sides were both taking and inflicting non-capital punishment, Jellicoe's battle-cruisers now suffered another catastrophic loss. Not long after the future King had jumped down the hatch, Rear-Admiral Hood's flagship, *Invincible*, famous for her part in the Falkland Islands victory of 1914, succumbed to *Derfflinger*'s gunnery, a shell penetrating her 'Q' turret (amidships) – the same mortal wound that had destroyed *Queen Mary* a few hours before. Of *Invincible*'s 1,021 crew, there were just six survivors, pulled from the water by attendant destroyers. Hood, great-great-grandson of Admiral Lord Hood, whom Nelson revered, was not among them.

Unlike life at sea, death at sea knew no privilege of rank.

Jellicoe's dreadnoughts were fast bearing down, however, and to extricate the *Hochseeflotte* from its perilous situation, Scheer now ordered a turn to the south-west, but twenty minutes later turned back towards Jellicoe's main force. Finding himself overmatched, he turned once more to break off contact, gallantly supported by Hipper's badly mauled battle-cruisers which charged the British line to cover the retreat. With darkness approaching, and Jellicoe's destroyers – he had seventy-eight in all – keeping up a ferocious if unequal harrying fight, Scheer's dreadnoughts eventually managed to break clean and make for Horns Reef, the shallows 10 miles off the westernmost point of Denmark. Jellicoe, sensing danger from a concerted torpedo attack by submarines if he pursued, broke off the battle – as he had agreed beforehand with the Admiralty he would do in such an event – and turned for home.

Scheer reached Wilhelmshaven in the early afternoon of 1 June. The *Hochseeflotte* had sunk more British ships than the Grand Fleet had sunk German (including six of the Grand Fleet's major ships to two of the *Hochseeflotte*'s, though neither side lost any dreadnoughts), and at once claimed victory, while Jellicoe was slower to return to Scapa and slower still to make capital of the fact that the Germans had been forced back to their anchorages. To the public it looked as if he lacked the 'Nelson touch', failing to win the complete victory that was in his grasp, and at a cost of 6,000 men. For although 'the fleet in being' – a naval force that extends a controlling influence without ever leaving port – had since Pepys's day been accepted strategy, the Royal Navy still maintained that in war its purpose was to seek out the enemy's ships and destroy them. And that was what England had expected.

The Kaiser declared that 'the spell of Trafalgar is broken.'

Yet Scheer's leading battleships had taken a terrible hammering, and over the weeks ahead the foreign section of the Secret Service Bureau (forerunner of the Secret Intelligence Service, MI6) was able to discover the extent to which the Grand Fleet's gunnery had disabled the *Hochseeflotte*. On 2 June the Grand Fleet had twenty-four capital ships in fighting condition, compared to only ten German.

Moreover, Berlin knew that Britain's shipbuilding capacity was much greater than its own, and that as the months passed the relative strengths would only increase in Britain's favour. After Jutland the *Hochseeflotte* would never again put to sea in real strength. Instead, the *Kaiserliche Marine* would increasingly place its faith and resources in the U-boat campaign, thereby hastening America's entry into the war.

23

JUNE

Pillars of Wisdom

The Army of Egypt stirs, and the seeds of the Arab Revolt are sown

'Is the army of Egypt guarding the Suez Canal, or is the Suez Canal guarding the army of Egypt?' asked the wags. For nearly two years British and imperial troops had been unable to do other than sit tight and repel desultory Turkish attacks across the Sinai, and by the Senussi Arabs, a Sufi political–religious order, in the eastern Sahara and Sudan.

The canal was a crucial artery of the Empire. Through this waterway passed men and equipment from Australia, New Zealand and India for the Western Front, and millions of tons of food and raw materials. There had been British troops in Egypt, nominally a province of the Ottoman Empire, since 1882 in what was known as the 'veiled protectorate', but after the Ottomans' defeats in Libya in the Italo-Turkish war of 1911–12, and in the Balkan wars of 1912–13, Constantinople had brought in German advisers to reform the Turkish army, as well as to modernize trade, commerce and communications, strengthening the Sultan's writ throughout the Levant, not least in Palestine.

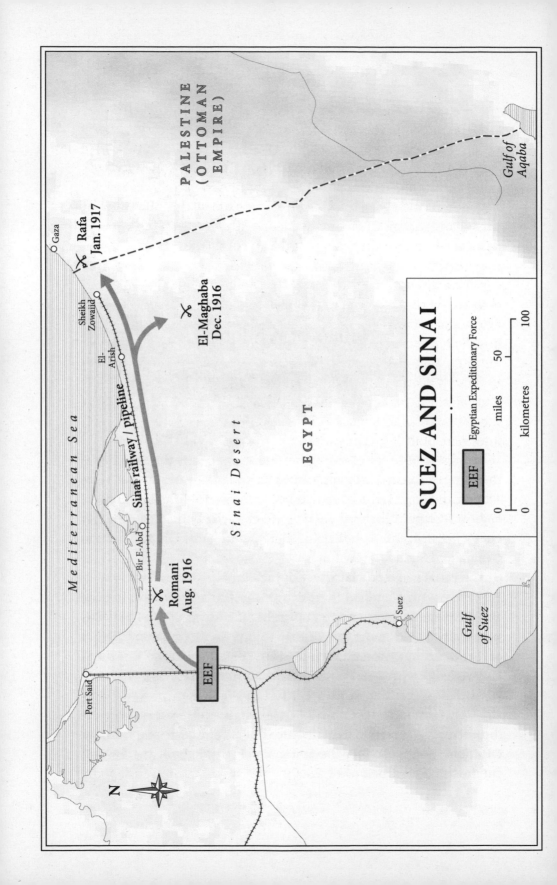

SUEZ AND SINAI

PALESTINE
(OTTOMAN
EMPIRE)

Gulf of
Aqaba

Gaza

Rafa
Jan. 1917

Sheikh
Zowaiid

El-
Arish

Sinai railway / pipeline

El-Maghaba
Dec. 1916

EGYPT

Sinai Desert

Mediterranean Sea

Bir E-Abd

Romani
Aug. 1916

Port Said

Suez

Gulf
of Suez

EEF

EEF   Egyptian Expeditionary Force

miles   0   50   100

kilometres   0

N

The elder Moltke had urged Bismarck to 'build railways, not forts', and this too was the Kaiser's strategy in his *Drang nach Osten* – his drive towards the east in search of new markets, oil and influence in Asia Minor, and for *Lebensraum*, 'room to live'. After Wilhelm's state visit to Constantinople in 1898, the Sultan had approved construction of the Berlin–Baghdad line, an extension of the German Anatolian Railway Company's system, with a further extension to Basra at the mouth of the Tigris, the head of the deep-water navigation of the Shatt al-Arab, and thence to the Persian Gulf. For commercial and strategic reasons Britain, France and Russia had objected – Britain, especially, seeing it as a threat to her position in Egypt and India. The Foreign Office succeeded in preventing the line's extension from Basra to the Gulf by persuading the Sheikh of Kuwait to repudiate Ottoman suzerainty and thereby the obligation to cede rights for building the line, in exchange for British protection; but in 1910, after a personal meeting between the Kaiser and the Tsar, Russia accepted the project on condition that no branch lines were built into Armenia and Kurdistan.

In August 1914, work on the railway had been well advanced, though large sections remained incomplete, especially between Aleppo and Baghdad, and the extension to Basra had not even been begun. A branch line to the port of Alexandretta on the Mediterranean had been built, however, which would prove useful to the German and Austrian submarines operating from there, as had connections with the metre-gauge line from Damascus to southern Palestine, which opened the way for an attack on Suez by routes that British warships could not dominate, and with the Hejaz railway, running 800 miles from Damascus through Arabia to Medina on the Red Sea, the canal route to and from India. Besides this challenge to British power, not only did the Berlin–Baghdad railway and its branches serve the *Drang nach Osten*, the project also bound Constantinople to the Central Powers, while the Sultan was only too pleased to strengthen the sinews of the increasingly rickety Ottoman Empire. Railways were therefore to play a part in the calculations and operations of the Entente which, if not on the scale of the Germans' great *Westaufmarsch* – the mobilization and deployment on the Western Front in 1914, the 'war by railway timetable' – was nevertheless just as crucial, and even more dramatic.

The Turks and Arabs of the Ottoman Empire were coreligionists but, like the constituents of the Austro-Hungarian Empire, were increasingly at odds with each other culturally. With an admixture of their advisers' Teutonic lack of subtlety, Ottoman rule became more and more repressive. Much-publicized executions of Arab nationalist leaders in Damascus played to London's advantage, and in January 1916, on the recommendation of Sir Mark Sykes, the amateur soldier and orientalist who with the French diplomat François Georges-Picot was to negotiate the eponymous agreement on post-war spheres of influence in the Middle East, the Arab Bureau was set up in Cairo to harmonize British political activity and keep Whitehall informed of 'the general tendency of Germano-Turkish Policy'. Among its political officers would be the remarkable desert traveller and archaeologist Gertrude Bell, and the eccentric orientalist and temporary soldier T. E. Lawrence – 'Lawrence of Arabia'.

The bureau's first success came in June when Grand Sharif Hussein ibn Ali al-Hashimi, guardian of the holy city of Mecca, entered into an alliance with Britain and France in return for military aid and a share in the dismemberment of the Ottoman Empire – which was no little diplomatic achievement for London, the Sultan having been trying for a year and more to inspire *jihad*, Islamic 'holy war', against the infidel, with its obvious threat to British India and her Muslim troops.

Sharif Hussein had about 50,000 men at his command, but only some 10,000 rifles. Supplying additional arms might therefore give the bureau considerable leverage, but the civil and military authorities in Egypt were slow to recognize the potential of such a move. The 'Great Arab Revolt' got off to a shaky start on 5 June when two of Sharif Hussein's sons, Ali and Feisal, attacked the Ottoman garrison at Medina, but then had to break off the attacks after three days for want of arms and ammunition. Nevertheless, on 10 June in Mecca, Sharif Hussein publicly proclaimed the revolt, seizing the city and driving the Ottoman garrison into the local fortress, while another of his sons, Abdullah, laid siege to the town of Ta'if 40 miles to the east.

Clans allied to Hussein now attacked Jeddah and other Red Sea ports. The Royal Navy sent a flotilla in support, including a seaplane carrier, the former Isle of Man steamer *Ben-My-Chree*, and landed the first units of the Arab regular army – Ottoman army troops captured at Gallipoli, Mesopotamia or in the Sinai, who had subsequently volunteered to fight for the nationalist cause. T. E. Lawrence, still officially a staff captain in the intelligence section at army headquarters but now attached to the Arab Bureau, would join them in October, and the Hejaz railway, down which the Turks would send many thousands of reinforcements to try to recapture lost ground, became the focus of the Arab offensive, inspiring some memorable cinematography in David Lean's 1962 film *Lawrence of Arabia*.

Railways were also a preoccupation of Lieutenant-General Sir Archibald Murray, the new C-in-C Mediterranean Force (MF), responsible for defence of the Suez Canal. Towards the end of 1915 the Turks had begun extending the Palestine line into Sinai, while his own lines east of the canal were practically non-existent. In January 1915 Murray had been sacked as chief of staff of the BEF in France, and later appointed CIGS in London, only to be replaced in December by Sir William Robertson. Murray was a cerebral officer prone to breakdown under pressure, but evidently the secretary of state for war, Lord Kitchener, who until August 1914 had been the British agent (de facto viceroy) in Egypt, recognized his worth as a methodical planner and so reassigned him to Cairo with instructions to arrange the canal defences more economically and send as many as possible of the 300,000 men in Egypt, who included Gallipoli evacuees and newly arrived Anzacs, to France.

By June 1916 Murray had shipped out 240,000 of them, leaving largely territorial and Indian divisions and some mounted troops – in the main, Yeomanry and Anzac light horse. He had made a thorough appreciation of Ottoman railway capacity in Palestine and water supply in the Sinai, and concluded that he could adopt a more forward defence of the canal – at the choke points along the Palestine border – to shorten his line. In March he had set about preparations for an advance on El-Arish, including much track laying as well as greater use of camels. In January, to deal with the Senussi tribesmen in the Western Desert, camel-mounted troops had been raised, initially from Australian light horsemen recuperating after Gallipoli. Four battalions of what would be known as the Imperial Camel Corps were eventually formed, the 1st and 3rd entirely Australian, the 2nd British, the 4th a mix of Australians and New Zealanders, commanded throughout by the 38-year-old Brigadier-General Clement Smith of the Duke of Cornwall's Light Infantry, who had won the VC in Somaliland in 1904 and for several years afterwards served in the Egyptian army. In July, with the Senussi in retreat, Smith was able to turn east. Without the need of a cumbersome logistic tail, and much less reliant on wells and oases than horsed units, his cameliers were able to range deep in the Sinai desert.

Murray, however, like the other professionals in Egypt, was initially sceptical of the value of the Arab Revolt. In *Seven Pillars of Wisdom* Lawrence described him as of 'a very nervous mind, fanciful and essentially competitive', but after Sharif Hussein diverted a good deal of Ottoman attention towards Mecca, helping the MF to overcome the garrison at Bi'r ar Rummanah ('Romani') on the coast in August and thereby opening the way for the grand advance on El-Arish, Murray became more supportive.

The advance of his Egyptian Expeditionary Force through Sinai was a formidable effort of infrastructure – eventually some 400 miles of railway, 300 miles of metalled and wire-meshed roads and 300 miles of water-pipes, with drinking water pumped underneath the Suez Canal from the Sweetwater Canal in the Nile Delta, entailing the construction of filtration plants, reservoirs and pumping stations. Nevertheless, in December Murray took El-Arish, and Rafa, on the Palestine frontier, the following month.

These successes would do much to offset the failure of the

Dardanelles campaign, and the fall in April of the old fortress-town of Kut al-Amara in Mesopotamia, which came as a severe blow to the reputation of British arms, renewing fears of mutiny among Indian Muslim troops. (Lawrence himself was sent to see if there were any way of relieving Kut by 'indirect methods', including bribery.) Townshend's capitulation on 29 April after four months under siege might indeed have been fatal for British prestige had it not been for the exertions of the Arab Bureau, and then the renewed offensive from Basra by Major-General Frederick Maude, the last man to be taken off the beaches at Suvla Bay.

Back in Cairo, observing the initial setbacks to Sharif Hussein's campaign in the Hejaz, Lawrence got permission to go in person to see what could be done. 'I had believed these misfortunes of the revolt to be due mainly to faulty leadership, or rather to the lack of leadership, Arab and English,' he wrote in *Seven Pillars of Wisdom*.

> So I went down to Arabia to see and consider its great men. The first, the Sherif of Mecca, we knew to be aged. I found [his sons] Abdulla too clever, Ali too clean, Zeid too cool. Then I rode up-country to Feisal, and found in him the leader with the necessary fire, and yet with reason to give effect to our science. His tribesmen seemed sufficient instrument, and his hills to provide natural advantage. So I returned pleased and confident to Egypt, and told my chiefs how Mecca was defended not by the obstacle of Rabegh [with its blocking force of Arab regulars], but by the flank-threat of Feisal in Jebel Subh.

Lawrence's chiefs in the bureau and HQ MF accepted his recommendations and sent him back as political and military liaison officer. Though (as he freely acknowledged) there were numerous other British officers serving under the flag of the Arab Revolt – a flag designed by Sir Mark Sykes as emblematic of Arab unity – Lawrence's was in large part the deciding presence.

By early 1917, with Murray having advanced to the Palestine border and Feisal's men gaining ground, the situation looked favourable for taking the fight to the enemy rather than merely standing on the defensive, despite London's determination to give priority to the Western Front. It would not be until June, however, with Murray's replacement by Sir Edmund Allenby, that the campaign was to gain real momentum. Feisal's irregulars would continue their diversionary attacks to the very end, October 1918 – although, knowing little or nothing about the Sykes–Picot agreement, he and Sharif Hussein did so in the belief that they had been promised an Arab caliphate stretching from Egypt to Persia.

24

JULY

Sixty Thousand Casualties before Breakfast

*The terrible first day of the offensive is followed by scarcely
less terrible weeks and months of fighting on the Somme*

'It was fine, cloudless, summer weather, not very clear, for there was
a good deal of heat haze and of mist in the nights and early morn-
ings,' wrote John Masefield of late June 1916. He had served in
France as a hospital orderly before the Foreign Office engaged him
to produce war propaganda, sending him to the Somme to write an
account of the fighting for publication in America.

> At half past six in the morning of 1st July all the guns on our front
> quickened their fire to a pitch of intensity never before attained. Inter-
> mittent darkness and flashing so played on the enemy line from
> Gommecourt to Maricourt that it looked like a reef on a loppy day. For
> one instant it could be seen as a white rim above the wire, then some
> comber of a big shell struck it fair and spouted it black aloft . . .

The moment was arriving for 'the big push' which Sir Douglas
Haig had been planning since taking over as commander-in-chief

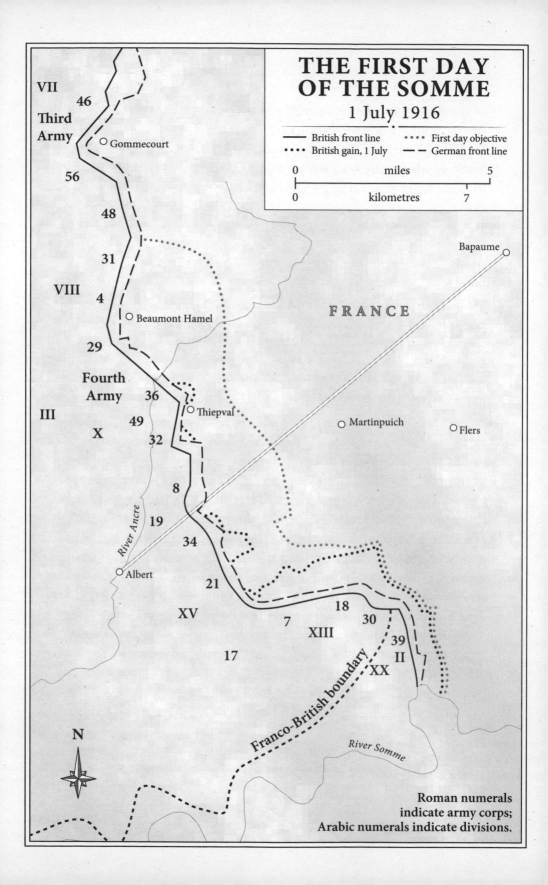

THE FIRST DAY
OF THE SOMME
1 July 1916

British front line   •••• First day objective
••• British gain, 1 July   – – German front line

0   miles   5
0   kilometres   7

VII
Third
Army
46
○ Gommecourt
56
48
31
VIII
4
○ Beaumont Hamel
29
Fourth
Army   36
III
49
X   32
8
19
34
○ Albert
21
XV
7   18   30
XIII   39
17   II
XX

FRANCE

Bapaume ○

○ Martinpuich   ○ Flers

○ Thiepval

River Ancre

Franco-British boundary

River Somme

N

Roman numerals
indicate army corps;
Arabic numerals indicate divisions.

of the BEF six months earlier. At the second inter-allied conference, in December at Joffre's headquarters in Chantilly, the British and French had agreed on a major combined offensive astride the River Somme, while Italy and Russia would mount their own offensives to coincide; but all had agreed that if in the meantime one ally came under clear threat, the others would launch diversionary attacks. The massive German offensive against the French at Verdun in February had therefore accelerated the various plans, and in the case of the Somme had significantly reduced the number of French troops taking part.

On 26 May, Joffre came to Haig's headquarters to urge him to begin his offensive without delay. For three months, said Joffre, the French had supported the whole weight of the German attacks at Verdun; 'If this went on, the French Army would be ruined.' They would not be able to hold out beyond 1 July.

Haig had been counting on 15 August, by which time he would have 200 additional heavy guns and possibly some tanks, a prototype having been demonstrated successfully in January. Going six weeks early would also carry a penalty in terms of training as well as materiel. Yet Haig felt obliged to accede to Joffre's plea. Besides, the Russians were doing a great deal to honour the undertaking they had given at Chantilly. In March they had attacked in Courland and Lithuania, an offensive which collapsed with heavy loss, and on 1 June, specifically at the request of Italy to relieve pressure on her armies in the Trentino, where the Austrians had launched an offensive, General Aleksei Brusilov had begun his long-planned attack in Polish Galicia.

There is still doubt as to exactly what the British high command thought it could achieve on the Somme. Haig had delegated planning and direction of the battle to Sir Henry Rawlinson, GOC 4th Army, a man he deeply mistrusted, setting him the task of capturing the high ground running from Montauban-en-Picardie through Pozières to Serre, and then securing positions linking Ginchy and Bapaume. The 3rd Army, to its north, would at the same time attack Gommecourt to draw away attention. An exploitation force consisting largely of three divisions of cavalry, some 30,000 horses, under Sir Hubert Gough, would thereafter pour through the gap created by the 4th Army to restore the war of movement which had been brought to an end in November 1914. To Haig the cavalryman, therefore, as C-in-C looking across the Western Front as a whole and seeking the all-important breakthrough, momentum was everything. Rawlinson the infantryman, as the tactical commander occupied by more short-term concerns, saw the attack as a more deliberate affair – rather a case of 'bite and hold'.

The problem for both men was the lack of experience in the troops who would carry out the attack, whether breaking through or 'biting and holding'. Put simply, the majority of Haig's men were green. The original BEF, largely regulars, had been destroyed as a cohesive force by the summer of 1915. Those who had survived the early battles were now filling staff appointments or commands in Kitchener's 'New Army' – the men who had answered his call to arms in 1914: 'Your Country Needs You!' These had been formed in successive tranches of 100,000, known unofficially as K1, K2 etc., each to mirror the original BEF, but this great expansion programme had never had enough instructors, materiel or time to undertake adequate training. The demand for reinforcements had brought them to France prematurely to fight alongside the remnants of the old BEF and the territorials who had volunteered to serve overseas. 'I have not got an Army in France really,' wrote Haig at the end of March, 'but a collection of divisions untrained for the field.'

How was this collection of untrained divisions supposed to deliver a crushing blow to the Germans only three months later?

The Somme does not belong to the poets, but they had a useful way with words, even in prose. In *Undertones of War* (1928), Edmund Blunden, an officer in a Kitchener battalion of the Royal Sussex, would write acerbically of the instruction issued by Haig's headquarters explaining how it was to be done: it 'assert[ed] the valuable creative principle that artillery and trench mortars cut the wire; infantry capture and consolidate the trenches. This promised to simplify the new warfare considerably.'

In fact the ambition for artillery went further. Not only would it cut the German wire in no-man's-land, it would also obliterate their fire and support trenches. Thus the infantry would not so much have to capture them, which might imply fire and manoeuvre, for which they had had scant training; they would merely have to occupy what was left of them. And because the trenches would have been destroyed, the infantry would not need to do anything but advance at walking pace across no-man's-land; so they could carry a greater weight of extra ammunition, water, rations and defence stores – up to 66 lb (30 kg) – in order to consolidate their gains.

The seven-day preparatory bombardment on the Somme certainly looked and sounded impressive: 1,500 guns firing 200,000 rounds a day (in the end, the shell count was nearer 1.7 million, since the French added their weight on the right); but because of the length of front to be attacked (18 miles in all) and the deficiencies in the number of guns for the task, their accuracy and the amount of high explosive as opposed to shrapnel, the inadequate fuses and the failure rate of ammunition (perhaps as many as one in three shells proved either duds or misfires), the German trenches would not be destroyed, nor the barbed wire in front of them cut sufficiently.

Lanes in the defensive wire laid by the British in front of their own trenches were to be cut by hand in the preceding days. In *Memoirs of an Infantry Officer* (1930), Siegfried Sassoon of the 1st Royal Welsh Fusiliers recounted how he spent a good deal of the day and night before the start of the battle crawling about trying to make wider gaps with his new wire-cutters, bought on leave at the Army and Navy Stores, so that the New Army battalion of the Manchester Regiment which was to attack from their trench might have a better chance: 'It seemed to me that our prestige as a regular battalion had been entrusted to my care on a front of several hundred yards.'

No proper testing of the theory that artillery could cut the wire and demolish the trenches had been carried out. Nor was there any plan – unlike the Germans' at Verdun – to assess the effectiveness of the bombardment before the infantry were sent over the top. Indeed, Haig specifically forbade reconnaissance on the grounds that it would 'lead to the loss of the boldest and best without result' – a strange tactical precept.

'In our trenches after seven o'clock on that morning,' wrote Masefield,

> our men waited under a heavy fire for the signal to attack. Just before half-past seven, the mines at half a dozen points went up with a roar that shook the earth and brought down the parapets in our lines. Before the blackness of their burst had thinned or fallen, the hand of Time rested on the half-hour mark, and along all that old front line of the English there came a whistling and a crying. The men of the first wave climbed up the parapets, in tumult, darkness, and the presence of death, and having done with all pleasant things, advanced across the No Man's land to begin the battle of the Somme.

The bombardment had of course told the Germans that an attack was imminent, and as soon as it switched to the support lines to allow the first wave to advance – in all, 100,000 men would go over the top that morning – German machine-gunners clambered up the ladders from their deep dug-outs in the chalk to open a devastating fire on them, supplemented by shrapnel from artillery batteries hitherto silent and undetected.

The result overall, if not without exception (the 36th Ulster Division, for example, managed to capture temporarily the formidable 'Schwaben Redoubt'), was calamitous. The north-country 'Pals' battalions – men from the same locality or trade who had been promised that if they joined up together they would stay together – fared particularly badly, and all the more tragically for the effect on the tight-knit communities at home when the telegrams began to arrive. The 1st and 2nd Barnsley 'Pals' (13th and 14th Battalions, York and Lancaster Regiment), attacking side by side in 94th Brigade, got nowhere but to a great many graves. The 1st Pals went over the top 720 strong; by the middle of the afternoon there were only

250 of them left. The 2nd Pals fared slightly better, losing 300 before the brigade commander called them off. Both battalions were lucky in one respect, however, for besides being in the support wave their brigadier was the 34-year-old Hubert Conway Rees, a regular infantryman robust enough to stop the attack. But it was too late for the battalion in front of them – the 11th East Lancashires, the 'Accrington Pals', 730 men from the close-knit cotton-mill towns of 'Blackburnshire'. After the first half an hour, 600 of them were dead, wounded or 'missing' (in other words, nothing remained of them after the shelling, for few had got far enough to be taken prisoner). Conway Rees wrote of his battalions:

> At the time this barrage really became intense, the last waves of the attack were crossing the trench I was in. I have never seen a finer display of individual and collective bravery than the advance of that brigade. I never saw a man waver from the exact line prescribed for him. Each line disappeared in the thick cloud of dust & smoke which rapidly blotted out the whole area. I saw a few groups of men through gaps in the smoke cloud, but I knew that no troops could hope to get through such a fire.

Elsewhere brigade and divisional commanders, whether from lack of information or want of Conway Rees's judgement, pressed the attacks regardless.

Some battalions famously kicked footballs into no-man's-land to lift the spirits. One Pals battalion, the 20th Northumberland Fusiliers (Tyneside Scottish), advanced as if on parade to the skirl of the pipes with all the innocence of the amateurs they still were. Pipe-Major John Wilson was 'marching erect, playing furiously, and quite regardless of the flying bullets and the men dropping all around him', wrote one man home. Wilson survived, but his uncle, in the same battalion, didn't: 'I did see poor "Aggy" Fyfe,' recalled a fellow Tynesider. 'He was riddled with bullets and screaming. Another lad was just kneeling, his head thrown right back. Bullets were just slapping into him knocking great bloody chunks off his body.'

As a man from one of the Pals battalions of the West Yorkshire Regiment wrote home: 'The battalion was two years in the making and ten minutes in the destroying.'

Sassoon, who a few weeks later would win the Military Cross, called that morning 'a sunlit picture of hell'.

The following day, Haig recorded in his diary that casualties were estimated at 'over 40,000 to date', adding that 'this cannot be considered severe in view of the numbers engaged [close on 200,000], and the length of front attacked'. The figures were unprecedented, however – almost as great as the total for the duke of Wellington's entire Peninsular campaign – and in any case were a serious underestimate. Some 40,000 had been wounded on the first day, but a further 20,000 had been killed. By comparison, those of the French and Germans had been light: the French some 1,600 killed and wounded, the Germans perhaps 12,000.

In the Battle of Loos the year before, there had been 40,000 British casualties for the gain of no significant ground, but in a fortnight's fighting, and the débâcle had led to the dismissal of the C-in-C, Sir John French. On 1 July 1916 very little ground was gained, nor was it held in the immediate German counter-attacks, but no one very senior was sacked, the blame devolving instead on regimental officers. And the Somme offensive would be pressed until the middle of November, the casualties mounting steadily, little ground being taken and no breakthrough coming. The new secretary for war, Lloyd George, would grow anxious, and then doubtful, but Haig would continue to assure him that progress was being made, that they were wearing down the Germans.

'We always felt that someone up above was ordering things, and that they probably knew more about it than we did,' wrote Captain Tom Adlam of the 7th Bedfordshire Regiment, another Kitchener battalion, who in September would win the VC: 'We just carried on.'

25

AUGUST
Exit Falkenhayn

Allied offensives on all fronts make the Kaiser begin to doubt

Of the several hundred thousand German casualties on all fronts in August 1916, the most significant was the chief of the *Oberste Heeresleitung* (supreme army command, consisting principally of the *Grosser Generalstab*, and also the Kaiser's military cabinet). But General der Infanterie Erich von Falkenhayn was not killed or wounded; he was sacked, and his dismissal would prove a turning point – perhaps *the* turning point – of the war.

Germany and her principal ally Austria-Hungary had come under increasing pressure throughout June and July. Falkenhayn's great offensive at Verdun, begun in February, had aimed at drawing in French reserves by capturing Verdun's prestigious forts, which, he calculated, were so prominent in the national consciousness that the French army would have no option but to counter-attack, and in so doing would be destroyed by massed artillery. The French had indeed obliged him, but their counter-attacks were in turn inflicting heavy casualties on the Germans. And, although the French commander-in-chief, Joseph Joffre, had desperately pleaded with

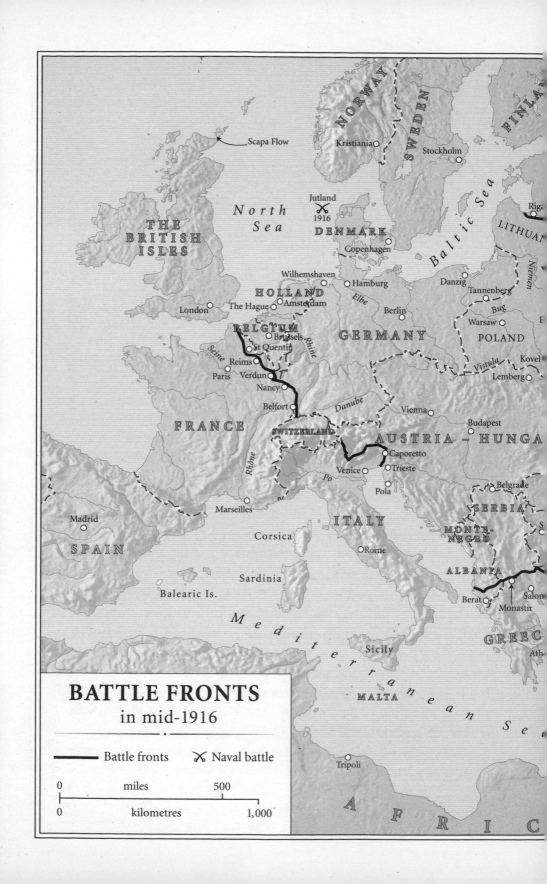

THE BRITISH ISLES

NORWAY

SWEDEN

FINLAN[D]

Scapa Flow

Kristiania

Stockholm

North Sea

Jutland 1916

Riga

Baltic Sea

LITHUA[NIA]

DENMARK

Copenhagen

Wilhemshaven

Hamburg

Danzig

Tannenberg

Niemen

HOLLAND

London

The Hague

Amsterdam

Elbe

Berlin

GERMANY

Warsaw

Bug

POLAND

BELGIUM

Brussels

St Quentin

Rhine

Seine

Reims

Verdun

Paris

Nancy

Belfort

Vistula

Kovel

Lemberg

Danube

Vienna

SWITZERLAND

FRANCE

Rhône

Po

Venice

Caporetto

Trieste

AUSTRIA – HUNGA[RY]

Budapest

Pola

Marseilles

Madrid

SPAIN

Corsica

ITALY

Rome

Belgrade

SERBIA

MONTE-NEGRO

Balearic Is.

Sardinia

ALBANIA

Berat

Salon[ika]

Monastir

M e d i t e r r a n e a n   S e[a]

Sicily

MALTA

GREEC[E]

Ath[ens]

Tripoli

A F R I C[A]

BATTLE FRONTS
in mid-1916

———— Battle fronts ✕ Naval battle

| 0 | miles | 500 |
| 0 | kilometres | 1,000 |

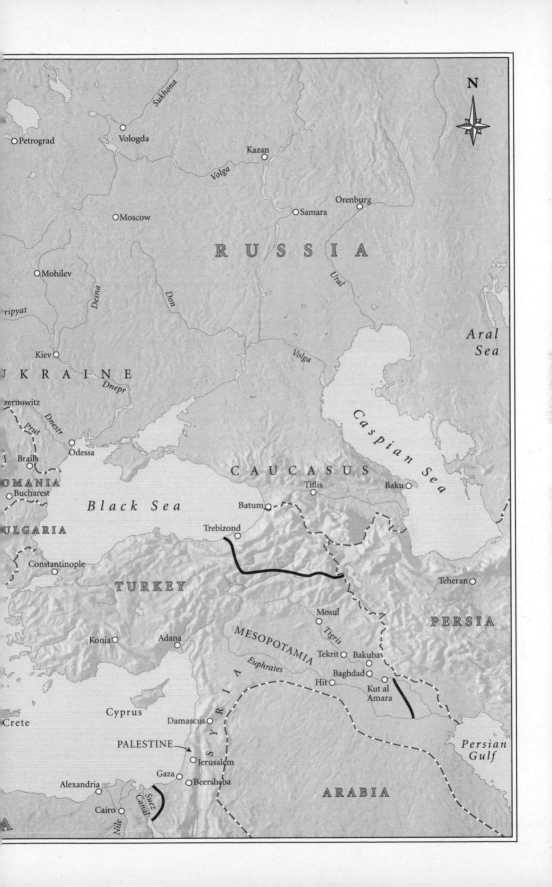

his British opposite number, Sir Douglas Haig, to bring forward the Somme offensive because he could not hang on much longer at Verdun, the French army had not broken. Falkenhayn had so far failed in his aim of 'bleeding France white'. Indeed, Verdun was proving as costly for the Germans as it was for the French.

On the Eastern Front the situation looked no more promising. On 4 June, General Aleksei Brusilov, commanding the Russian south-western army group – four armies consisting of some 600,000 men – had launched an offensive in Galicia, in what is now western Ukraine. In the first seventy-two hours his four armies advanced 50 miles, taking 200,000 Austro-Hungarian prisoners (entire Slav units surrendered) and several hundred heavy guns: infinitely more successful than the BEF's own offensive on the Somme a few weeks later, if ultimately no more fruitful.

At Joffre's urgent request, the Russians also attacked the Germans in the east, notably at Lake Naroch in present-day Lithuania, but here they were less successful, and the Germans were able to mount counter-offensives as well as reinforcing the Austrians. Nevertheless, Brusilov pressed his offensive throughout the summer, and though by the middle of August it was running out of steam, by then his four armies had taken some 375,000 German and Austro-Hungarian prisoners, a great deal of war materiel and 15,000 square miles of territory.

The cost in Russian casualties had been high – over half a million – and these would prove difficult to replace with troops of equal loyalty to the Tsar. Indeed, the offensive would prove to be the Russian high-water mark on the Eastern Front; but Brusilov's innovative tactics and operational art have earned high praise. Field Marshal Viscount Montgomery of Alamein, who in 1916 was an infantry major on the Western Front, would afterwards name Brusilov one of the seven outstanding fighting commanders of the war.

The Austrians had come under increasing pressure, too, on the Italian front. On 4 August, General Luigi Cadorna launched yet another offensive on the Isonzo river, where the future Fascist leader Benito Mussolini was serving as a corporal in the *Bersaglieri* (light infantry), and would be twice wounded, and where Ernest Hemingway would set his autobiographical novel *A Farewell to Arms*, in which an increasingly disillusioned American volunteer serves in an Italian ambulance unit. Unlike the previous five offensives here, however, all of which had ended in costly failure, this time there were marked gains, in major part owing to the masterly use of artillery – always the Italians' strongest arm (in the Crimean War *The Times*'s correspondent, William Howard Russell, had pronounced the artillery of the Piedmont–Sardinian detachment the best of the four allied armies). Before this Sixth Battle of the Isonzo, Cadorna had managed to bring forward in great secrecy 1,200 guns – 400 of them medium or heavy – and 800 bombards (heavy mortars), achieving surprise with a short (nine-hour) but intense bombardment before launching the main assault, unusually, in the afternoon. In five days the Italians forced the Austrians to abandon their bridgehead west of the Isonzo and captured Gorizia at the foot of the Julian Alps on the Slovene border.

And yet, although Austrian reserves had been sent east to counter the Brusilov offensive and further advance seemed possible, Cadorna could not exploit his victory. With no bridges left standing across the Isonzo, despite the brilliance of his engineers he could not get his artillery up quickly enough to break through the second defensive line, and on 16 August he closed down the offensive. Gorizia had cost him over 50,000 casualties – a third more than the defenders – and although these losses were fewer than the BEF had sustained on the first day of the Somme, 1 July, they came on top of the 220,000, a quarter of his then mobilized forces, suffered in the first five battles on the Isonzo. The Italian army was, however, learning. Indeed, it would now form the first 'shock troops' (preceding the famed German *Sturmtruppen*) to overcome forward defences by fire and daring – hence their nickname *arditi*, 'the daring ones', much lauded by the poet-aviator Gabriele d'Annunzio.

The British were learning, too, if not uniformly – and certainly not in the higher echelons. The attacks on the Somme had continued throughout July, the casualties mounting to 158,000, with a further 40,000 elsewhere on the Western Front, as the offensive degenerated into a series of seemingly uncoordinated localized battles that would go on throughout August. In one of these, George Butterworth, composer of *Banks of Green Willow*, was killed while in temporary command of a company of the 13th Durham Light Infantry, a 'Kitchener battalion', having won the Military Cross the day before.

The original front-line trenches were on relatively low-lying ground, overlooked – dominated, for the major part – by the German positions, especially at High Wood and Delville Wood, names immortalized in numerous regimental histories and Robert Graves's memoir *Goodbye to All That*. These gentle hills had been the objective of the first two days' fighting, Haig expecting to achieve a breakthrough so that he could launch Gough's *corps de chasse*, made up in large part of cavalry, into the open country beyond – what the less reverent officers (usually infantrymen) called 'galloping through the "G" in "Gap"'. In the event the cavalry remained penned in by barbed wire and machine guns just as surely as the 'PBI' (poor bloody infantry), only the 7th Dragoon Guards and a regiment of Indian cavalry, the 20th Deccan Horse, getting any sort of gallop – at High Wood on 14 July, and even then at a cost of 100 human casualties and 130 horses.

Fighting would continue through the whole of August and two weeks of September – gruelling fighting, some of it at night with imaginative tactics – before any of the BEF could start downhill on the far side of the ridges that had been the first day's objective, and the breakthrough would never come. A strange sort of routine set in during these weeks, at times almost surreal. In *The War the Infantry Knew*, Captain James Dunn, medical officer of the 2nd Royal Welsh Fusiliers, recorded how on 18 August

2.45pm was zero [hour] for a push through Wood Lance and High Wood by the 100th and 98th Brigades while demonstrations were made on the right and left. The gun-fire was over in little more than an hour. Through it all the Band of the 6th Welsh (Pioneers) practised: it's a good

Band, and plays good music of the 'popular' kind: a great din of guns made the strangest of obbligatos.

There were 'rumours of success everywhere', continued Dunn, but then 'At 7.30 we heard that "nothing had been gained," that "the situation is obscure".' Two days later it was the Fusiliers' turn to attack. Captain Robert Graves, not yet twenty-one, would be so badly wounded by a shell fragment through the lung that he was officially reported as having died of wounds. In fact, between 2 July and the end of August no more ground would be gained and held on the Somme than had been on the opening day of the offensive, and at the cost of a further 82,000 casualties.

The Somme was taking its mental toll, too. Dunn wrote of the increasing problem of 'shell shock', whether real, imagined or even feigned. Strange symptoms – paralysis, stuttering, inability to stand or walk, the 'shakes' – had begun appearing at the casualty clearing stations in 1915, starting a debate in both military and medical circles as to what it was, what had caused it and how it should be treated. The numbers were not then great, for the BEF in 1915 was still composed largely of regulars, or territorials who had volunteered to serve overseas – men who had been in uniform for some years, and were acclimatized to military life; Kitchener's 'New Army' battalions did not begin arriving in any numbers until the late summer. Although the battles of 1915 were bloody, they were not as relentless as those of the Somme, nor were the artillery bombardments on so industrial a scale. New drafts arriving at the front in August 1916, wrote Dunn, 'came in for enough shelling to light up the picture of "shell-shocked" and "gassed," for which two years of lurid journalese in the home papers had prepared the minds . . . so the Dressing Station near-by had many importunate applicants for admission'. He considered that 'the first duty of a battalion medical officer in War is to discourage the evasion of duty . . . not seldom against one's better feelings, sometimes to the temporary hurt of the individual, but justice to all other men as well as discipline demands it'.

The simultaneous and in part coordinated allied offensives – especially the continuing French counter-attacks at Verdun – were taking their toll on the Germans, and the Kaiser was getting anxious. Not the least of his concerns were the signs of unrest at home, in part the result of the Royal Navy's increasingly effective blockade: on 19 August, coal-miners in the Ruhr went on strike in protest at food shortages and rising prices. Then, on 27 August, the Entente gained a new ally – Romania. Bucharest, like Sofia the year before, had been wooed by both sides, but with over half the length of her border shared with Austria-Hungary, Bulgaria or occupied Serbia, and with the Black Sea closed for good to the western allies after the failure of the Dardanelles campaign, Romania had been understandably fearful of declaring her hand. In January the chief of the imperial general staff, Sir William Robertson, had minuted the foreign secretary, Sir Edward Grey, lamenting that diplomacy had not had much success of late (forgetting, rather, the Italian coup in May 1915), and Grey had replied not unreasonably that diplomacy in war depended on military success – and there had been precious little of that. But now it seemed that there *was* success – Brusilov's, Italy's, and on the Western Front. Even the nascent Macedonian front was beginning to look promising: the Bulgarians had invaded Greek territory, Athens appeared to be contemplating action (although it would be another ten months before the Greek government formally declared war), and allied reinforcements were beginning to arrive – including an advance party of a thousand Russians. On 27 August, therefore, Romania declared war on Austria-Hungary and at once sent troops into Transylvania, which had a large ethnic Romanian population. The following day, Italy, flushed with success at Gorizia and hitherto technically at war only with Austria, declared war on Germany.

It was all too much for the Kaiser. On 29 August he replaced Falkenhayn with Generalfeldmarschall Paul von Hindenburg (and his inseparable deputy Erich Ludendorff, who had parried the Russian blows with such skill), sending the former chief of the *Oberste Heeresleitung* to command the 9th Army on the Eastern Front. On the face of it Falkenhayn and his successor had much in common. Both

190

were from the old Prussian nobility, both were infantrymen and both had seen service, though Hindenburg, some fourteen years Falkenhayn's senior (he had been recalled from retirement in 1914), had fought in Bismarck's audacious wars of unification. Whereas Falkenhayn was by nature cautious and calculating, however, Hindenburg was brusquely bold.

There would be a certain irony in Falkenhayn's rustication, for the following month he launched a dazzling counter-offensive against the Romanian army, entering Bucharest on 6 December. Field Marshal Montgomery ranked him alongside Brusilov as one of the 'seven outstanding fighting commanders of the war'. The other five were Mustafa Kemal ('Atatürk'), who had thwarted the Entente's Dardanelles campaign; Ludendorff, whose success on the Eastern Front the Kaiser now hoped to see replicated on the Western; the Australian John Monash, who in August 1916 was training his new division (3rd Australian) in England after the exertions of Gallipoli and Egypt, and whose star would begin to burn bright in 1917; and the British generals Herbert Plumer and Edmund Allenby, whose time was likewise still to come.

Hindenburg, who would slowly but surely become de facto Kaiser, lost no time in making his demands known. On the last day of August he sent a letter to the war minister demanding a doubling of ammunition output by May 1917 and a threefold increase in machine-gun and artillery production. The Western Front was to be put on hold through a massive system of defences in depth until the Russians had been beaten decisively by manoeuvre, whereupon he would turn the full resources of materiel and operational art on the western allies. Crucially, too, he pressed for the resumption of unrestricted submarine warfare, backing Admiral Scheer, commander-in-chief of the High Seas Fleet repulsed at Jutland three months earlier, who had already told the Kaiser that U-boats were the only way to bring Britain down. In so doing, Hindenburg would begin the chain of events that brought the United States into the war the following spring. And once America was under arms, a German victory in the west was but a pipe dream.

191

In the meantime, however, it would be a cruel irony that while Hindenburg and Ludendorff were discarding Falkenhayn's murderous *Ermattungsstrategie* (strategy of wearing down) for one of *Vernichtungsstrategie* (strategy of decisive victories), the French and British on the Western Front were doing the opposite – if not so much by design as by default. For although Haig and a succession of French generals would continue to talk about 'breakthrough' and restoring the war of manoeuvre, the reality – that for the time being, the power of defensive weapons rendered any such breakthrough impossible – turned the offensives on the Somme and in 1917 into the strategy of attrition: what Churchill called the 'dreary process of exchanging lives, and counting heads at the end'.

26

SEPTEMBER

The Rude Mechanical

The tank goes into action – with mixed results

No weapon was ever brought to the battlefield with more impressive speed and secrecy than the tank. After a year of trial and error with various caterpillar devices, on 20 January 1916 a prototype of the ultimate rhomboid-shaped design had been demonstrated to the Admiralty Landships Committee in Lincoln. A week later, the 28-ton machine, shrouded in tarpaulins and described on the bill of lading as 'water tank for Mesopotamia', was on its way by rail to Hertfordshire to be shown to the War Office and the cabinet – and Haig's deputy chief of staff, Major-General Richard Butler, who, having watched the demonstration, asked simply: 'How soon can we have them?'

The minister of munitions, David Lloyd George, at once loosened the purse-strings. By the middle of February, Fosters of Lincoln had been contracted to build fifty, and the Metropolitan Amalgamated Railway Carriage and Wagon Co. Ltd, Birmingham, fifty more, increased in April by a further fifty. On 15 September, barely eight months after its first outing in Lincoln, the tank – the name now officially adopted – would take part in what Haig hoped would be the decisive attack of his stalled Somme offensive: the battle of Flers-Courcelette, as it became known.

Finding 'crews' – a nod to the tank's naval origins – was a novel challenge. Each tank was to be commanded by an officer, with a further seven men as drivers, gearsmen and gunners. Including supports and replacements, 150 officers and 1,000 other ranks would be needed for the initial 100 tanks. Secrecy demanded they be recruited without knowing what exactly they were volunteering for – so how were they to be found? A cover name for the organization was needed, and found: the 'Heavy Section Machine Gun Corps'. Ernest Swinton, a Royal Engineers lieutenant-colonel who had been one of the first advocates of caterpillar traction, was given charge of raising and training the new force. He at once asked the War Office to 'select and warn personally, good fighting subalterns of resource and courage, conversant with motor cars or motor cycles', then set off round the officer-cadet schools and home-based battalions scouting for talent.

Similarly secretive arrangements were put in hand to find the other ranks. Advertisements appeared in *Motor Cycle Magazine* for men who could drive 'light cars'; recruits in training for other arms were suddenly told that former plumbers and gas-fitters should report to the orderly room. The best drivers came from the stalwart Army Service Corps, whose superior discipline would prove significant.

Recruits began assembling in some mystification at Bisley in Surrey, among them a number of transferees from the Navy's armoured car detachments; then, once a few training tanks were available, they moved to Elveden Hall in Suffolk, seat of the Guinness brewing magnate the Earl of Iveagh – 15 square miles of the best pheasant shooting in the country. When the Lands Branch of the War Office telephoned Lord Iveagh to tell him of its requisition, he had sighed resignedly and said that if anyone's shoot was to be spoilt it might as well be his. Tenant farmers and labourers were uprooted, old retainers were displaced from their almshouses, and Elveden School was closed. Three pioneer battalions, many of them Welsh miners, began work creating a mile-and-a-half-long replica of the Western Front, complete with shell craters, barbed-wire entanglements, dug-outs and six lines of trenches. Security was tight. When Clough Williams-Ellis, the future architect of Portmeirion, and one of the Heavy Section's first subalterns, arrived at 'Elveden Explosives Area' (its cover name), he found cavalry, Indian troops and territorials patrolling three concentric perimeters, the area 'more ringed about than was the palace of the Sleeping Beauty'.

The first operational tanks appeared at the beginning of June. The 'Mark 1' came in two types: 'male', with two 6-pounder (57 mm) guns in side sponsons firing high explosive shells, plus three Hotchkiss machine guns; and 'female', with four heavier Vickers machine guns and a Hotchkiss. Each had 6–12 mm of armour – good protection against rifle fire and to some extent machine guns, but not much against HE. Motive power was from a 6-cylinder, 16-litre, 105 hp Daimler–Knight petrol engine driving the cater-pillar tracks through three independent gearboxes. Steering required the tank to halt momentarily to disengage a track, and the first models had tail wheels to assist, though in action these proved ineffective and were soon abandoned. On level ground the Mark 1 could make 4 mph, with a range of about 25 miles before refuelling.

Crew conditions were appalling. The combination of engine heat, noise, exhaust fumes, and violent movement as the tank crossed broken ground made men violently sick even on short jour-neys. Injuries were common. It was difficult to communicate within the tank, and almost impossible without. The commander would have to dismount to reconnoitre a path through an obstacle, or to liaise with the infantry. The War Office specification for mechan-ical reliability was a mere 50 miles between failures, as the tank was meant to be a one-off weapon whose job would be done once the infantry broke through and the cavalry let loose. Unsurprisingly, therefore, given its weight, the inexperience of the crews, and the difficulty of keeping engine and gearbox lubricated when pitched at extreme angles, breakdowns were frequent.

Nevertheless, under Swinton's direction at Elveden things slowly began taking shape, with four companies, A to D, each consisting of four sections of three tanks – two male, one female – and another tank in company reserve, formed by late July. C and D companies would entrain for the Somme on 16 August. Few of the crewmen had ever heard a shot fired in anger.

Meanwhile, at his headquarters just south of Boulogne, Haig was having to adjust his plans again. Having launched the Somme offensive six weeks earlier than planned in response to pleas from the French, under severe pressure at Verdun, in late August he began planning a climactic offensive-within-an-offensive to break the deadlock. His intention was to establish a defensive flank on the high ground north of the Albert–Bapaume road, which bisected the Somme battlefield, while pressing the main assault south of it with the aim of breaching the German rear line between Morval and Le Sars. In essence it was the same idea as that of 1 July, but on a narrower frontage (8 miles as opposed to 18 miles), with a shorter but more concentrated preliminary artillery bombardment – and now with the game-changing tanks, for which lanes 100 yards wide would be left clear of artillery fire.

There were growing concerns about loss of operational surprise, however. Once the tank was used, the Germans would gain the measure of it, adjust their tactics, increase the distribution of armour-piercing rounds which snipers already used to penetrate sentry shields, and – worst of all – develop tanks of their own. Indeed, there were fears they were already doing so. After watching a demonstration near Amiens, the Prince of Wales, a titular subaltern in the Grenadier Guards, wrote to his father, King George V: 'I enclose a rough sketch of these land submarines or "Tanks" as they are called for secrecy. The Huns have no doubt got accurate drawings of them and have by now produced a superior article!!'

Edwin Montagu, the new minister of munitions (Lloyd George having become war minister after Kitchener's death at sea in June), told the cabinet on 12 September, just three days before the fresh offensive was due to begin, that 'there are rumours the Germans are making something of the same kind' and that his French opposite number had told him that his own army had placed an order for 800 tracked machines and urged that 'we should not put ours into the field until they were ready'.

The prime minister, Asquith, whose eldest son, Raymond, was serving on the Somme, had seen the tank for himself during a recent visit. Though unsettled by Montagu's intervention he decided to leave the decision to the man on the spot – Haig. The CIGS, Sir William Robertson, agreed, though he himself believed the tank should not be used until there were many more of them, and had told Haig so.

Haig, however, was desperate for some sort of success. He told Sir Henry Rawlinson, commander of 4th Army, who if not the actual architect of the Somme offensive was certainly its clerk of works, that 'when we use them [the tanks] they will be thrown in with determination into the fight regardless of cost'.

The problem was not only of numbers, though, but of ground. The Somme was not Suffolk, certainly not after two months' bombardment. The novelist John Buchan, serving as *Times* correspondent in France, likened it to 'a decaying suburb . . . pockmarked with shell holes'. Although the tank was designed to cross broken ground, the more slowly it advanced the more vulnerable it became. Nevertheless, by the end of August fifty machines had arrived in France, and Haig decided that they would support the attack on 15 September, distributed more or less evenly across the three assaulting corps, with six held for the reserve army.

Their arrival in the forward areas just before zero hour came as a surprise to most of the infantry. Indeed, some did not see them until the attack had begun. Private Arnold Ridley of the Somerset Light Infantry – and sixty years later, Private Godfrey of BBC TV's *Dad's Army* – was severely wounded in hand-to-hand fighting that day. He recalled: 'We in the ranks had never heard of tanks. We were told that there was some sort of secret weapon and then we saw this thing go up the right hand corner of Delville Wood. I saw this strange and cumbersome machine emerge from the shattered shrubbery and proceed slowly down the slope towards Flers.'

Some thought them comical, while others were impressed by the very thing that was perceived to be their weakness: 'It was her slowness that scared us as much as anything,' a territorial told a reporter afterwards. There was something unnerving about the tank's steady, relentless advance in the face of fire. Others saw nothing at all, for only twenty-two of the fifty tanks actually reached the start line, seven of which promptly broke down.

Most of those that did get into action paid dearly. Lieutenant Basil Henriques' tank came under intense machine-gun fire, forcing him to close the viewing slits:

> Then a smash against my flap at the front caused splinters to come in and the blood to pour down my face. Another minute and my driver got the same. Then our prism glass broke to pieces, then another smash. I think it must have been a bomb right in my face. The next one wounded my driver so badly we had to stop. By this time I could see nothing at all.

When the glass shards were removed from his face at a dressing station, Henriques kept a piece to have mounted in a gold ring to give to his wife.

Where two or more tanks managed to advance together there could be distinct success. The defenders of the half-ruined sugar-beet factory at Flers were forced out by concerted 6-pounder and machine-gun fire. But overall, little ground was gained that day. Rawlinson wrote in his diary: 'A great battle. We nearly did a big thing.'

The tank had at least demonstrated its potential, and production would now be stepped up. In November the companies were expanded into battalions, and in July the following year the Tank Corps was formed – some fifteen battalions. To some extent, the concern about the loss of surprise proved over-stated. Although the Germans would occasionally use captured British and French tanks, and eventually develop their own, they failed to recognize the worth of armoured fighting vehicles until after the war. They saw the tank as something to be defeated rather than emulated.

Flers-Courcelette cost the BEF another 25,000 casualties before Haig called off the offensive a week later. Perhaps the most significant casualty – in respect of its repercussions in public life – was not a tank man, however, but an infantryman. On 17 September, H. H. Asquith's second wife, Margot, received a telephone call. 'I went back into the sitting room. "Raymond's dead," I said to the servant. "Tell the prime minister to come and speak to me."'

27

OCTOBER

'Preparedness'

*As German U-boats reach American waters,
the tide begins to turn against isolationism*

Within hours of the declaration of war at 11 p.m. on 4 August 1914, British ships had dredged up and cut the German transatlantic cables. This was not for fear of direct US intervention but to disrupt the supply of war materiel for Germany and to thwart German propaganda, which might threaten supplies to the allies. In 1940, after the fall of France, Churchill in his great 'We shall fight on the beaches' speech looked to the moment when 'in God's good time, the New World, with all its power and might, steps forth to the rescue and the liberation of the old'. In 1914 neither London nor Paris had any thoughts that the United States would send troops to France; the US army was small, and few expected the war to be a long one.

President Woodrow Wilson had declared his policy of neutrality. In an address to Congress on 19 August he warned that 'the people of the United States are drawn from many nations, and chiefly from the nations now at war. It is natural and inevitable that there should

200

be the utmost variety of sympathy and desire among them with regard to the issues and circumstances of the conflict.'

Wilson saw the conflict largely in terms of Europe's old dynastic wars, in which a New World democracy had no place save as an honest broker, for intervention would risk the still relatively young republic's cohesion (it was less than fifty years since the end of the Civil War):

> Divisions amongst us would be fatal to our peace of mind and might seriously stand in the way of the proper performance of our duty as the one great nation at peace, the one people holding itself ready to play a part of impartial mediation and speak the counsels of peace and accommodation, not as a partisan, but as a friend.

It would be some time before German 'frightfulness' – the ruthless occupation of neutral Belgium and the sinking of unarmed ships – and Berlin's clumsy meddling in Mexico led him reluctantly to the view that the conflict was more a struggle between rampant militarism and Enlightenment. Even after the sinking of the *Lusitania* in May 1915, with the death of 128 American citizens, Wilson's instinct was to persuade Germany to limit the war at sea, if only by unspecific ultimatums. At that point, Berlin had reluctantly complied, abandoning the policy of sinking without warning. In the campaign for re-election in 1916, the slogan in Wilson's camp was 'He kept us out of war!', though he never in fact promised unequivocally to stay out of it. In his acceptance speech for the Democratic nomination in September, he pointedly warned Berlin that submarine warfare resulting in American deaths would not be tolerated: 'The nation that violates these essential rights must expect to be checked and called to account by direct challenge and resistance. It at once makes the quarrel in part our own.'

There were other, more hawk-like voices. Many of these advocated not necessarily direct intervention – though some, like former President Theodore Roosevelt, one of whose sons was fighting as a volunteer with the British army in Mesopotamia, were strong advocates of joining the Entente – but 'military preparedness'. Organizations such as the American Defense League, the Army League and the National Security League were formed, championing universal military training. In 1915 military training camps for college students were set up in a number of states, and the idea of 'preparedness' began to gain traction in Congress. Wilson, however, continued to maintain that the National Guard was an adequate reserve force.

Nevertheless, in March 1916 Congress passed the National Defense Act. One of its major provisions was to grant the president power to place orders for war materiel and to force industry to comply. A Shipping Board was established to regulate sea transport and develop a naval auxiliary fleet. The Act also authorized an increase in the peacetime strength of the army to 175,000 men, and a contingency wartime strength of 300,000. Federal funds were also allocated for the National Guard, hitherto largely a responsibility of the states, and to bring it under professional supervision of the War Department. The future president Harry S Truman, who had served in the Missouri National Guard from 1905 to 1911, would rejoin when America declared war in 1917, seeing active service in France. At the same time, a Naval Act provided for construction of ten battleships, sixteen cruisers, fifty destroyers and seventy-two submarines. If the president was determined that the United States remain neutral, Congress wanted it at least to be a strongly armed neutrality.

In August 1916 Wilson conceded the establishment of the Council of National Defense, consisting of the secretaries of war, navy, labor, agriculture, interior and commerce, with the somewhat Delphic explanation that 'the Country is best prepared for war when thoroughly prepared for peace'. Then in October he appointed an advisory commission of business and industry leaders.

Yet he was increasingly frustrated by what he saw as British resistance to his calls for a negotiated end to the war, though his embryonic proposals were impossible for either side to accept (Pope Benedict XV made no progress either, and was reviled by both sides as favouring the other). There was also widespread distaste for the ruthless suppression of the 'Easter Rising' in Dublin, and its follow-up (the Irish-American vote was an important one for the Democrats), as well as anger at the blacklisting of eighty-seven US firms suspected of trading with the Central Powers.

The German decision in October to resume and intensify warfare on commerce was therefore something of an own goal. The problem was that the Battle of Jutland at the end of May had demonstrated that the German High Seas Fleet could not overcome the Royal Navy, and Admiral Scheer's hope of using U-boats to even the odds had been dashed in two subsequent attempts by the *Hochseeflotte* to draw the Grand Fleet on to a torpedo ambush. Scheer had therefore begun lobbying the Kaiser to reintroduce unrestricted submarine warfare and to expand the U-boat building programme. In October the Kaiser agreed to switch strategy from trying to wear down the Grand Fleet, instead diverting the existing U-boats to a blockade of Britain and building larger boats to take the war into the Atlantic.

The new chief of the German general staff, Paul von Hindenburg, was only too pleased to throw his weight behind Scheer's appeal to let his submarines sink merchantmen without warning, which he calculated would bring Britain to her knees in six months, for his troops and those of the other Central Powers were under real pressure. The Russian offensive led by Brusilov had made gains against the Austro-Hungarians; the German army was feeling the strain of the allied offensive on the Somme and French counter-attacks at Verdun; the campaign against the new Entente ally, Romania, was making heavy demands; and in the face of a counter-offensive by the allies on the previously inactive Macedonian front, the Bulgarians had fallen back towards Monastir in southern Serbia. However, at the insistence of the chancellor, Theobald von Bethmann Hollweg, who was anxious lest the Entente attract more neutrals – principally America – the Kaiser ruled that the U-boats must continue to issue warnings before sinking. On 24 March, a U-boat had torpedoed the *Sussex*, an unarmed Channel steamer, injuring several Americans (first reported as dead), and Wilson had threatened to sever diplomatic relations unless Germany abandoned attacks against passenger and merchant ships. Germany had complied, making the so-called 'Sussex pledge' not to attack unresisting merchant vessels without warning, but with the proviso that Washington put pressure on London to observe international law while imposing its blockade. The 'pledge' had held through the summer, but largely because the main target of the U-boats had been the Grand Fleet.

Then, on 7 October, a U-boat made a dramatic entry into American waters. One of the *Kaiserliche Marine*'s newest and largest submarines, U-53, 715 tons, put in at Newport harbour, Rhode Island. Her captain, Hans Rose, paid courtesy visits to the admirals in port, who paid courtesy visits in return while Washington decided how to handle the affair. The harbour master pre-empted the formalities, however, by suggesting to Rose that there might be a problem with quarantine regulations, whereupon he promptly returned to sea to avoid being detained.

Next morning, 2 miles off the Nantucket lightship, U-53 stopped the American steamer *Kansan* by a shot across the bow; her papers revealing no contraband cargo, Rose let her go. An hour later U-53 stopped the *Strathdene*, a British steamer, sinking her by torpedo once the crew had abandoned ship. The Norwegian steamer *Christian Knutsen*, with a cargo of diesel oil for London, went the same way. The British steamer *West Point*, bound from London to Newport News, Virginia, was stopped at 11.30 and sunk by explosive charges after the crew had taken to the lifeboats.

Alerted by the Nantucket lightship, seventeen American destroyers raced to the scene, the first arriving late in the afternoon just as U-53 intercepted the British passenger steamer *Stephano* and the Dutch merchantman *Blommersdyk* – bound for Rotterdam but with orders to put in first at Falmouth, and therefore a legitimate prize. Their crews and passengers, including several American women and children, were taken off by the destroyers while Rose used his last torpedoes to sink both ships, having asked one of the destroyers to move aside to give him a clear line of fire.

Though the sinkings were carried out under the accepted 'cruiser rules', and no one was killed, the fact that they had occurred within sight of the lightship and in the presence of US warships made for unease in Washington and consternation in the press. Under the headline 'German sea code utter disregard for neutrals', the *Cornell Daily Sun* (New York state) declared:

> We are familiar with German denunciation of a British policy which aims to blockade the Central Powers, and, as we are eloquently informed, to 'starve German women and children into submission.' As an evident sign of a nobler faith, the German Government, through its irresponsible submarine commanders, sinks the flour which is destined for the women and children in Holland.

Roosevelt thundered that Wilson's 'ostrich policy' had earned the contempt of Europe. '[His] ignoble shirking of responsibility has been clothed in an utterly misleading phrase – the phrase of a coward – "he kept us out of the war." In actual reality war has been creeping nearer and nearer until it stares us in the face from just beyond the three-mile limit.'

With U-53 the Germans had also demonstrated a hitherto unsuspected reach, which alarmed both the British Admiralty and the US Navy. Washington's concern would only be exacerbated on learning that the German legation in Mexico was in discussions with the government to establish a submarine base in Mexican waters.

Mexico had been a troublesome neighbour for some time. Since 1910 the country had been in a state of revolution. Francisco 'Pancho' Villa, one of the most prominent of the revolutionary leaders, controlled much of the north-east, and in January 1916, angered by Washington's arms embargo against him, had killed several US mining executives in Chihuahua. Then in March Villa's forces had raided Columbus, New Mexico, killing sixteen Americans. Wilson ordered an expedition to capture him, but despite receiving assurances that it would be conducted 'with scrupulous regard for the sovereignty of Mexico', the Mexican president Venustiano Carranza regarded it as a violation of sovereignty and refused support.

Brigadier-General John J. 'Black Jack' Pershing, who in due course would command the American Expeditionary Force in France, led the raid but failed to capture Villa, skirmishing instead with 'Carrancista' forces. Another cross-border raid, into Texas, by Villa's forces in May brought more US troops into Mexico and another clash with the Carrancistas, this time in a major skirmish at Carrizal on 21 June which resulted in the capture of twenty-three US soldiers. Fearing that war was imminent, Carranza proposed direct negotiations and Wilson agreed, which for the time being eased tensions. Nevertheless, Hindenburg, who increasingly had the ear of the Kaiser, saw the potential of Mexico's diverting US troops and materiel if it came to war between America and Germany, and much to Bethmann Hollweg's dismay began manoeuvring accordingly.

Woodrow Wilson would be re-elected president in November with the narrowest of majorities. A fortnight after his inaugural address in March 1917 his cabinet would agree unanimously to declare war on Germany – just as the secretary of state, Robert Lansing, had predicted: that he 'had no doubt that after the sinking of the *Lusitania* we would ultimately become the ally of Britain'.

The challenge for Washington would be how to build an army capable of taking part in modern war, and where exactly to send it.

28

NOVEMBER

Attrition

*The 'butcher's bill' on the Somme begins to raise
differing doubts among politicians*

'Are we to continue until we have killed ALL our young men?'

In November 1916, as the Somme offensive spluttered on in rain and snow, the Marquess of Lansdowne, who as foreign secretary in 1904 had negotiated the Anglo-French 'Entente Cordiale', put this question in a bleak memorandum to Asquith's coalition cabinet. In the four and a half months' fighting astride the River Somme, 420,000 British and imperial soldiers had been killed or wounded – 60,000 on the first day alone – along with nearly 200,000 French. The furthest advance made was 7 miles.

They had, however, killed a lot of Germans. Indeed, because there had been no breakthrough, the offensive had become one of attrition. Lacking sufficient artillery and opportunity for manoeuvre, this *guerre d'usure* could be carried out only by frontal attacks against an enemy in strong defensive positions. Trading life for life, even at a favourable rate of exchange, was always going to rack up a heavy butcher's bill, and although fighting techniques improved during the course of the offensive, the obsession with capturing ground, in part driven by Haig's continuing hope of breakthrough, added further to the bill drawn on the 'poor bloody infantry'.

Although called 'the Battle of the Somme', the offensive was in fact a series of smaller battles across a frontage of some 25 miles. It had been conceived originally as a combined offensive, but with the French army under increasing pressure at Verdun, the greater burden had fallen on the British. After the failure of Rawlinson's 4th Army to break through on 1 July, Gough's Reserve (later renamed the 5th) Army took over the northern part of the battlefield, and from 2 to 13 July the two in concert tried to carry the assault into the German second main defensive position in what became known as the Battle of Albert.

Sharp fighting continued across the whole front for the rest of the month, Rawlinson managing to seize 6,000 yards of the German line between Longueval and Bazentin-le-Petit. From 23 July to 5 August, three Australian divisions of Gough's army fought a costly but eventually successful battle for the village of Pozières in order to open an alternative approach from the rear to the formidable Thiepval defences, while Rawlinson also tried to support the renewed French effort towards Péronne.

By mid-September, with the assistance of the new secret weapon – the tank – Rawlinson felt ready to assault the German third line of defences. However, though Flers and Courcelette fell, the advance was limited to about 2,500 yards on a 3-mile front, the Germans holding on to Morval and Lesboeufs for a further ten days, at which point the attack finally stalled.

Throughout, Haig remained confident of a German collapse. In part this was because his chief of intelligence, Brigadier-General John Charteris, in an effort to maintain Haig's morale, had begun to downplay reports of German strength and over-state reports of German weakness. Towards the end of September he told Haig that 'the Germans may collapse before the end of the year'. Captain (later Major Sir) Desmond Morton, from 1917 one of Haig's ADCs and after the war a member of the Secret Intelligence Service (and one of

Churchill's principal advisers in his so-called 'wilderness years'), wrote of the perverse relationship: 'Haig hated being told any new information, however irrefutable, which militated against his pre-conceived ideas or beliefs. Hence his support for the desperate John Charteris, who was incredibly bad as head of GHQ intelligence, who always concealed bad news, or put it in an agreeable light.'

On 26 September Haig launched Gough's 5th Army against Thiepval Ridge, which had hitherto defied all attempts at capture. Mouquet Farm and Thiepval fell, but fighting in the infamous Schwaben Redoubt went on until the middle of October, with the Canadian Corps continuing in their desperate battle for Regina Trench until 10 November. Further south, Rawlinson had made painful progress towards Le Transloy, capturing Le Sars on 7 October, but in November the battlefield turned into a quagmire, and even Haig became doubtful that further attacks would bring about the enemy's collapse. However, he was about to attend an inter-allied conference, first with the other commanders-in-chief and chiefs of staff at Chantilly, Joffre's headquarters, and then with ministers in Paris, to discuss the strategy for 1917, and reasoned that if he could stage a late success, reducing the German salient between Serre and the Albert–Bapaume road in the Ancre sector, it would give him greater moral authority in the discussions – not least with Lloyd George, who as secretary of state for war was beginning to doubt both Haig's competence and the priority given to the Western Front as the decisive theatre of operations.

Gough, ever a 'thruster', readily agreed to one more push. On leaving his headquarters for Chantilly, Haig gave him instructions to limit his objectives in the event of serious setback, but without being specific. On 13 November, in appalling conditions, Gough attacked astride the River Ancre, north of Thiepval, and with great sacrifice the 51st (Highland) Division managed to take Beaumont-Hamel. The 63rd (Royal Naval) Division – Royal Marines, and naval reservists surplus to requirements at sea who had volunteered for land service – proved no less determined. They had seen action at Antwerp and Gallipoli, but were taking part in their first attack on

the Western Front. Novices, perhaps, they were nevertheless exceptionally well led. The commanding officer of the Hood Battalion
(their naval units were named after famous sailors – Drake, Nelson,
Collingwood etc.) was the New Zealander Bernard Freyberg, much
admired as a divisional and corps commander at El Alamein and
Monte Cassino in the Second World War. During the Ancre attack
he would win the VC – one of the fifty awarded during the Somme
offensive – and gain the nickname 'Salamander' for his ability to
live through fire. While the Naval Division captured Beaucourt,
their losses were heavy. In the Hawke Battalion, only two officers
survived unscathed. One of them, the future humorist, author and
parliamentarian A. P. Herbert, drew on the experience for his first
novel, *The Secret Battle* (1919), an unflattering picture of the way the
war was fought.

In six days' fighting on the Ancre, 5th Army lost some 22,000
men, though the Germans' losses were considerably higher as they
held on stubbornly to the northern part of the line. With mud
claiming the few available tanks and making all communication
difficult, by 18 November the battle had petered out. All it had
achieved was the creation of a most unwelcome salient, and Haig
now 'closed down' the Somme offensive.

For some, however, cut off by German counter-attacks, the fighting went on regardless. Perhaps the most tragically inspiring episode
was the stand by ninety men of the 16th Battalion Highland Light
Infantry, a 'Pals battalion' recruited originally from ex-members of
the Glasgow Boys' Brigade (the first voluntary uniformed youth
movement in the world), who were isolated in the Frankfurt Trench
near Beaumont Hamel. On 21 November the Germans sent a party
along the trench to take them prisoner, but were repulsed by small-
arms fire. The following day – on which the Glaswegians' food ran
out – the Germans attacked again, and again were seen off. The
Glasgow men continued to fortify their positions, hoping for relief
that evening, but attempts to reach them failed. On Thursday,
23 November, after a sharp artillery bombardment, the Germans

attacked once more. They were driven back by the fire of the Lewis (light machine) guns, but the bombardment had killed several men, wounded many more and destroyed part of the trench, including the makeshift water reservoir of melted snow. Next day, the Germans attacked yet again, mortally wounding Company Sergeant-Major George Lee. As he was taken down from the parapet, Lee, who had been a foreman in the Glasgow roadways department, said three words: 'No surrender, boys.'

On the Saturday a small party of Germans approached with a white flag and a captured Inniskilling Fusilier who delivered a message from the German battalion commander: 'Surrender quietly and you will be well-treated. Otherwise you may take what is coming to you.' The few unwounded Highland Light Infantrymen took a vote and decided not to reply. After dark several of them crawled out to find water, while the rest waited for the attack, but the night passed quietly.

The following morning, Sunday, with one drum of Lewis-gun ammunition left, the remnants found themselves surrounded in force. The Germans rushed the position and quickly overcame the last few defenders. Of the original ninety Highland Light Infantry, there remained only some thirty wounded, many of them badly, and a handful of unscathed men to be made prisoner. Some were taken to the German brigade headquarters for questioning. On seeing the starving, filthy, frozen and exhausted 'Pals', the interrogating officer could not believe they had held out so long: 'Who are you and where have you come from?' Defiant to the end, they answered only with their number, rank and name.

They might well have said that they were the men, or in some cases replacements for the men (for the Glasgow Boys' Brigade Battalion had lost heavily on the first day of the Somme), deemed incapable on 1 July of doing more than advance in line to take the German trenches that would have been destroyed by artillery fire.

In his despatch to London the following month, Haig claimed the Somme offensive as a considerable success:

The enemy's power has not yet been broken ... [but] despite all the advantages of the defensive, supported by the strongest fortifications, [the German army] suffered defeat on the Somme this year. Neither victors nor the vanquished will forget this; and, though bad weather has given the enemy a respite, there will undoubtedly be many thousands in his ranks who will begin the new campaign with little confidence in their ability to resist our assaults or to overcome our defence. Our new Armies entered the battle with the determination to win and with confidence in their power to do so. They have proved to themselves, to the enemy, and to the world that this confidence was justified, and in the fierce struggle they have been through they have learned many valuable lessons which will help them in the future.

The Somme has its apologists still, for the offensive was not entirely futile. The Germans found it difficult to transfer divisions to reinforce their faltering offensive at Verdun. Their new commander-in-chief, Paul von Hindenburg, began to press the Kaiser to authorize unrestricted submarine warfare to bring Britain to her knees, a desperate measure which only brought the United States into the war. Early in 1917 German troops would withdraw some 25 miles to the *Siegfriedstellung* ('Fortress Siegfried'). The British army on the Western Front – predominantly 'green' troops, the men who had flocked to the recruiting offices in 1914 – had also learned a great deal about how to fight (those, that is, who survived).

Some 130,000 British troops had been killed, however, with irreplaceable losses among junior officers and experienced NCOs. German losses remain disputed, but they were significantly less, though they too lost much 'quality'. The withdrawal to the *Siegfriedstellung* would give them better ground to hold and a shorter front, allowing them to withdraw thirteen divisions into reserve. And while Hindenburg may have been prompted to urge unrestricted submarine warfare, the naval C-in-C, Reinhard Scheer, had been pressing for it since the Battle of Jutland at the end of May, and given the increasing success of the blockade in starving Germany of food and raw materials, the Kaiser could not have resisted the pressure indefinitely.

Nor was an offensive the only or even the best way to help the French at Verdun. Sending them heavy artillery and aircraft, and taking over more of the allied line to release French troops, would have been options better suited to Haig's situation and his green regiments. Above all, persuading the French to stop playing to the Germans' game plan by mounting costly counter-attacks to recover ground of no importance except to national (or, more correctly, to Joffre's) prestige would have preserved France's fighting strength.

In his memorandum to the cabinet, Lord Lansdowne wrote: 'No one for a moment believes we are going to lose this war, but what is our chance of winning it in such a manner, and within such limits of time, as will enable us to beat our enemy to the ground and impose upon him the kind of terms which we so freely discuss?' He concluded that a negotiated peace would be preferable – a proposal for which he would be reviled by politicians and soldiers alike. Lloyd George, soon to become prime minister, drew a different conclusion, however: fight the war with better strategy and different men at the head. Unfortunately, his efforts to do so would largely fail.

The losses on the Western Front in 1916 would haunt the British and French ever after. In November 1918 the allies would be too quick to accept the Germans' call for an armistice. In 1919 they would make a bad treaty at Versailles. In the 1930s the French would adopt the catastrophic strategy of the Maginot Line, and the British the policy of appeasement.

29

DECEMBER
The Welsh Wizard

Lloyd George becomes prime minister, and Haig becomes apprehensive

Making Lloyd George war minister was 'the greatest political blunder of Henry's lifetime', Margot Asquith had confided in her diary. After the death at sea of Lord Kitchener on 5 June, the prime minister had offered the War Office to Andrew Bonar Law, leader of the Tories and colonial secretary in the coalition government, but Bonar Law declined in Lloyd George's favour.

Margot saw this as an incipient coup. The failure of the Dardanelles campaign, the humiliating surrender at Kut al-Amara in Mesopotamia, and Jutland – the strategic victory that looked like defeat – had shaken public confidence. 'We are out,' she wrote: 'it can only be a question of time now when we shall have to leave Downing Street.'

The subsequent huge losses on the Somme for no appreciable gain only compounded the sense of drift in war policy. As Churchill wrote, 'the recovery of the Germanic powers in the East [with the defeat of the Brusilov offensive], the ruin of Roumania and the beginnings of renewed submarine warfare strengthened and stimulated

214

all those forces which insisted upon still greater vigour in the conduct of affairs'. In September Asquith's son, Raymond, was killed, which made the prime minister even more withdrawn and difficult to approach. After the Somme offensive was finally abandoned in mid-November, criticism of his apparently half-hearted prosecution of the war became more vocal, echoed in a powerful editorial in *The Times* on 4 December. Two days later Asquith resigned and the King invited Lloyd George to form a government.

In France, the commander-in-chief of the British armies, Sir Douglas Haig, was in two minds about the change, writing to his wife that 'I am personally very sorry for poor old Squiff [Asquith was notoriously fond of drink]. He has had a hard time and even when "exhilarated" seems to have had more capacity and brain power than any of the others. However, I expect more action and less talk is needed now.' He was wary of Lloyd George, however, for the 'action' the new prime minister favoured might not accord with his own plans.

The government in Paris was under pressure too. French losses at Verdun and the Somme, 348,000 and 194,000 respectively, on top of the huge casualties in the opening weeks of the war and the futile counter-offensives of 1915, had brought the army close to exhaustion. On the first day of the Somme it had been 92,000 men short, but because the general staff had accelerated the call-up of 78,000 conscripts of the class of 1916, it was in reality 170,000 men below establishment. Replacements were increasingly difficult to find and to train, with even Catholic priests being called up for service as combatants. It was probably only his African troops that allowed Joffre to hang on until the fighting subsided with the onset of winter. On 12 December the prime minister, Aristide Briand, was forced to form a new administration, replacing General Gallieni as war minister with General Hubert Lyautey, the military governor of Morocco, and managed at last to manoeuvre Joffre out of his previously unassailable position by appointing him to a hollow command – 'general-in-chief of the French armies and technical adviser to the government', face-saving titles but little else – with the consolation of promotion to marshal of France.

In Russia the disintegration of the old order continued. In November the prime minister, Boris Vladimirovich Shtiurmer, was forced to resign, and on 9 December the State Council demanded the removal of the 'dark forces' and the formation instead of a government 'based on the confidence of the country'. Three weeks later, one of the most notorious of the dark forces, Grigori Rasputin, 'the mad monk', whose malign influence over the empress had become almost total, was murdered.

Yet these developments would not immediately curb the military ambitions for 1917. In mid-November, Joffre and Haig, together with the military representatives of the other allies, had agreed at the Chantilly conference to renew their offensives as soon as weather permitted. This was not what the political leaders, meeting at the same time in Paris, had wanted, believing that there could be no breakthrough on the Western Front and that the cost of the continuing strategy of attrition was too great; but they felt obliged to take the military advice nevertheless. They had favoured instead action on the Italian front, or else the Macedonian (Salonika), where a harlequin allied army – French, British, Italian, Russian and Serb – had recently begun a promising counter-offensive against the Bulgarian army. In late 1915, together with German and Austro-Hungarian troops, the Bulgarians had compelled the Serbian army, with their king, Peter, to retreat to the Adriatic through the mountains of Albania. The remnants of the Serbs had then joined the allied army on the northern Greek border, blocking the Bulgarians' advance into nominally neutral Greece. On 19 November 1916, the allies recaptured Monastir (present-day Bitola), the southernmost city of Serbia, and Lloyd George became convinced that there was now an alternative to battering against the brick wall of the Western Front.

One of those wounded during the Monastir offensive was Flora Sandes, the Yorkshire-born daughter of an Anglo-Irish clergyman. She had joined an ambulance unit in 1914 and had worked for eighteen months in a field hospital in Serbia, but during the retreat to Albania had enlisted in the ranks of an infantry regiment, rising to sergeant-major. Later commissioned and awarded Serbia's highest decoration, the *Orden Karađorđeve zvezde* (King George Star), her memoir of the retreat, with its Dunkirk-like evacuation in February 1916 and the move to Salonika via Corfu, was published in London later that year as *An English Woman-Sergeant in the Serbian Army*, with a foreword by the Serbian chief of staff, raising a good deal of money for Serb relief funds.

On 15 December, however, attention turned once again to the Western Front, where a spectacularly successful French attack at Verdun seemed to promise a change of fortune for the allies. Joffre's successor as commander-in-chief, Robert Nivelle, an artillery officer and a hero of the defence of the fortress-city (he had famously issued an order of the day which ended 'Ils ne passeront pas' – they shall not pass – a defiant slogan which in 1940 would be worn on the uniforms of the troops manning the Maginot Line), had planned in detail the attack by four divisions, with four in reserve, following a six-day bombardment by 800 guns firing over a million shells, directed in the latter stages with great precision by observation aircraft. The infantry's advance was preceded by a double 'creeping' barrage (one that progressed by successive bounds) – shrapnel from field artillery 70 yards in front of the leading troops, and HE 150 yards ahead, which then switched to shrapnel along the German second line to cut off retreat and interdict reinforcements. The German defence collapsed, with over half of the 21,000 troops in the forward divisions lost or taken prisoner in their dugouts. By the second night the French had consolidated a new line half a mile beyond Fort Vaux and 2 miles beyond Douaumont, the German line having in all been pushed back nearly 5 miles. When German officers complained about the conditions in the PoW cages, Lieutenant-General Charles Mangin, commanding the offensive, replied wryly: 'We do regret it, gentlemen, but then we did not expect so many of you.'

Briand believed that in Nivelle, a fluent Anglophone (his mother was English), he had at last found his Napoleon. He told Lloyd George that the general had sent telegrams from various places during the advance demonstrating that his objectives were being achieved exactly according to plan. Nivelle now proposed his grand design for 1917: an offensive on the Aisne, promising 'Laon in twenty-four hours and then the pursuit', with the British playing a major supporting role at Arras.

Meanwhile, in Berlin and Washington there was talk of peace. On 12 December Bethmann Hollweg, the German chancellor, called for negotiations without specific conditions or demands. On the surface, this appeared to reflect confidence in Germany's military position, the chancellor declaring that the Central Powers 'have given proof of their indestructible strength in winning considerable successes at war'. However, he knew that time was not on Germany's side. At home, the Social Democrats, the largest party, were increasingly demanding assurances that the country was fighting only in self-defence, not for conquest. Austria-Hungary, the principal ally, was becoming demoralized, notwithstanding the failure of the Brusilov offensive and the advances against Serbia and Romania.

Although Germany's armies now occupied substantial tracts of allied territory, the country faced a coalition with superior manpower resources and access to world markets, while the Royal Navy's blockade was slowly strangling her own economy and starving the home front. Desperate to break the military stalemate, Germany's military and naval leaders were pressing the Kaiser to authorize unrestricted submarine warfare, a course that Bethmann Hollweg feared (correctly) would bring the United States and possibly other neutrals into the war on the allied side. He reasoned that if the allies refused to open peace negotiations, it would be they, not Germany, who were seen as prolonging the war, thereby rallying the wavering Social Democrats to the war effort and screwing Austria-Hungary's courage to the sticking-place. Such a refusal might even mean that the United States would accept the unleashing of the U-boats – and, perhaps the greatest prize, it might spur the anti-war parties in France and Russia to press irresistibly for a separate peace.

Washington's peace initiative was more altruistically motivated.

President Woodrow Wilson, newly re-elected on a platform of keeping the country out of the war, had always seen himself as a mediator, repeatedly urging a discussion of peace terms, usually on some basis of the *status quo ante bellum* together with post-war disarmament. In 1915 and again in early 1916 he had sent his chief foreign policy adviser, 'Colonel' (an honorific peculiar to the Southern states; he had no military experience) Edward House, to Europe for talks with both sides. By way of encouragement, in May 1916 he pledged the United States to a post-war international security organization, a 'league of nations', and in December he called for the belligerents to state the exact objects for which they were fighting. In January 1917, sensing his own country's glide into war, he would make an impassioned plea for a 'peace without victory'.

Wilson was convinced that if either side won a decisive victory, this would simply re-ignite the arms races, alliances and secret diplomacy that in his view had caused the war in the first place. Sooner or later, he reasoned, another global conflict would occur: 'This is the last war of the kind, or of any kind that involves the world, that the United States can keep out of.' An end to the war that gave neither side full achievement of its aims, he believed, would enable a more enduring peace to be made through collective security. Events, however, would overtake his ideals, for once US troops were fighting in France, decisive victory could be the only object.

Notwithstanding the outcomes of the Chantilly and Paris conferences, Lloyd George was determined to take a firm grasp of strategy. The chief of the imperial general staff, Sir William Robertson, assured Haig that despite the talk of peace, prompted largely by the Marquess of Lansdowne's memorandum to the cabinet suggesting that victory was not possible without destroying the nation's vitality, the new prime minister was 'in real earnest to leave nothing undone to win the war ... [but] seemed to wish to pose as the prime instrument and mainspring of the actions of the Allies'. At their first meeting since taking office, on 15 December in the drawing room of No. 11 Downing Street, Asquith having been allowed a little grace to quit No. 10, Lloyd George told Haig that while he acknowledged the Western Front to be the primary theatre of operations, he 'could not believe it was possible to beat the German armies there – at any rate not next year'. This being the case, he wanted to transfer two divisions from France to Egypt for an attack on El-Arish and thence towards Jerusalem, and, temporarily, to send 200 heavy guns to Italy to help General Cadorna take Pola on the Adriatic.

Haig would have none of it, however: his armies were, he said, 'all engaged in preparing for next year's attacks'.

With 'Wully' Robertson strongly backing Haig, Lloyd George had little option but to concede. He would have to trust to General Nivelle's promise of 'victory without tears', and try to clip Haig's wings by placing him under command of Briand's new-found Napoleon.

Nivelle would prove to be no Napoleon, however, and 1917 would be even bloodier than 1916.

PART FOUR

1917

Defeat; and Deliverance

1 February: Germans declare unrestricted submarine warfare.

8 March: Russian revolution begins.

15 March: Russian Tsar Nicholas II abdicates.

6 April: United States declares war on Germany.

16 April: Nivelle offensive begins (preceded by Battle of Arras).

30 June: Greece officially declares war on Central Powers.

31 July: Third Ypres ('Passchendaele') begins.

24 October: Battle of Caporetto (Italian front) begins.

7 November: Bolsheviks overthrow Russian government.

11 December: Allenby enters Jerusalem.

15 December: Armistice agreed between the new Russian government and the Central Powers.

30

JANUARY
The Turnip Winter

Economic warfare – the Royal Navy's blockade of Germany – begins to bite

By 1917, Germany had become, like Frederick the Great's Prussia (according to Voltaire – or, as some have it, Mirabeau), 'an army with a country attached to it'. A century earlier, in his seminal work *Vom Kriege* (On War), the Prussian military theorist Carl von Clausewitz had concluded that 'war is an act of force . . . [which knows] no logical limit'. In January 1917, Germany's military leaders, to whom the Kaiser was now in total thrall, were about to prove Clausewitz right – and with catastrophic results.

In his memoirs, General Erich Ludendorff, the power behind the military throne of the chief of staff and effectual viceroy, Field Marshal Paul von Hindenburg, wrote that with the Entente's rejection of President Wilson's peace initiative in December, 'the war had to continue and to be decided by force of arms. It was to be Victory or Defeat.' Because the struggle was therefore now existential, 'the results were further preparations on a large scale, the maintenance of our determination to fight . . . and at the same time the employment of

223

every weapon in Germany's arsenal'. The German army, he believed, was 'completely exhausted on the Western Front, [nevertheless] our worn-out troops would have to take the offensive as early as possible, and on a greater scale than in the autumn of 1916, if they were to achieve ultimate victory'.

Ludendorff knew that the odds were increasingly against them. Although the Entente offensives of 1916 had all been checked, ultimately, 'the outlook for the coming year was exceedingly grave. It was certain that in 1917 the Entente would again make a supreme effort.' French losses at Verdun and on the Somme had been appalling, 'but she possessed in her colonies extraordinary resources of manpower'. Britain's army was yet to reach its full potential, and the Russians, in reorganizing their forces in the wake of the failed Brusilov offensive, had actually increased their strength. With the cooperation of the exiled Romanian army, re-equipped and retrained by the French, and Austro-Hungarian prisoners of war forming their own Slavic national contingents to fight for the Entente, the Russian bear looked as dangerous as ever. 'In every theatre of war the Entente was able to add to her numerical superiority enormous additional resources in every department of technical supply, and to destroy our troops on a still greater scale than had been achieved on the Somme and at Verdun.'

German strength, on the other hand, was diminishing. Verdun and the Somme had taken serious toll of the army, and the Royal Navy's blockade was sapping morale at home. Ludendorff railed against the civil authorities' lack of resolution to organize ruthlessly for war: 'The law left untouched labour that should have been devoted to the state.' Only men between the ages of seventeen and forty-five were liable for service. At Ludendorff's bidding, Hindenburg now demanded that the liability be extended to men between fifteen and sixty years, and, with certain exceptions, women. He largely got his way, and the so-called Hindenburg Programme introduced comprehensive control of labour, with a consequent doubling in output of war materiel.

Food production remained inadequate, however. Malnutrition,

even starvation, became widespread in the so-called *Kohlrübenwinter* – 'Turnip Winter' – of 1916–17, the blockade exacerbated by the strange inability of the civil authorities to regulate agricultural practice and prices. Farmers fed grain to their animals although its nutritional value as bread was four times that of grain eaten indirectly through meat (the 2 lb loaf had been enough for the pre-war working man's day). Prices incentivized farmers to slaughter stock rather than breed, so that there was a compounding shortage of animals and therefore of manure – resulting in smaller harvests and the need for more fertilizer to be produced by industry at the expense of explosives and other war materiel. Black-market prices rose, and *Reibekuchen mit Rübenkraut* (potato cakes with sugar beet syrup) – still today a curious favourite of German Christmas markets – became a staple in the towns (workers in rural areas tended to fare better). Ironically, it had been the Royal Navy's blockade of Napoleonic Europe a century earlier, cutting off the supply of cane sugar from the West Indies, that had stimulated the growth of beet sugar extraction. Soldiers returning to Germany for leave were shocked to find their families famished. Absenteeism and desertion increased, occasionally with offers of intelligence to the Entente.

Food was not only in short supply at home. Military rations were repeatedly cut, and the high command became increasingly concerned about the monotony of the diet. When the German army launched its last-ditch offensive on the Western Front in March 1918, many a unit's progress faltered on coming across bounteous allied ration dumps. There was also insufficient corn for the army's horses, which were quickly being worn out, so that industry had to produce more mechanical transport instead at the expense of armaments and aircraft production. In turn, the mechanical transport needed more fuel, placing even greater demands on logistics at the front. The cavalry were progressively demounted, their horses sent to artillery and transport units (the shortage of cavalry would play a part in the failure of the March 1918 offensive).

In January 1917, Ludendorff's assessment was bleak in the extreme: 'We could not contemplate an offensive ourselves, having to keep our reserves available for defence. There was no hope of a collapse of any of the Entente Powers. If the war lasted our defeat seemed inevitable.' Indeed, the army 'would not have been able to exist, much less carry on the war, without Roumania's corn and oil.'

The Russian revolution in March (February in the Russian, Julian, calendar) took Berlin by surprise, and would in large part be the German army's saving in 1917.

However, there was one weapon in Germany's arsenal that had yet to be fully employed. In October 1916 submarine warfare against merchant shipping, suspended after the sinking of the *Lusitania* the previous May, had been resumed, but under the so-called 'cruiser rules', with ships stopped, searched and then sunk only if carrying contraband and after the crews had been allowed to take to the lifeboats – a time-consuming and dangerous practice. After the Battle of Jutland on 31 May 1916, with the German surface fleet more or less confined to Wilhelmshaven and the Royal Navy's economic blockade therefore unchallenged, Admiral Henning von Holtzendorff, chief of the imperial naval staff, proposed a counter-blockade by U-boats, sinking without warning any merchant ship within designated 'exclusion zones'. Britain relied on imports of food and war materiel, and unlike Germany had no land borders across which a minimal supply could be maintained. In 1916 the *Kaiserliche Marine* had built over a hundred powerful new submarines able to range into the Atlantic, and a base for the lighter ones at Zeebrugge whence the cross-Channel transports could be attacked. Holtzendorff reckoned he could sink 600,000 tons of shipping per month. Two of Germany's leading economists, Gustav von Schmoller and his pupil Max Sering, a specialist in agrarian economics, stated that this would result in food riots, severe distress in trading areas and the collapse of the British economy, especially if Zeppelins bombed the grain depots in the Channel ports. Britain would therefore be forced to sue for peace, Holtzendorff argued, in which case France could not continue the fight.

The issue was decided on 9 January at a conference at GHQ in Pless Castle (present-day Poland), presided over by the Kaiser.

Theobald von Bethmann Hollweg, the increasingly marginalized chancellor, was sceptical of the naval and economic arguments and fearful of the reaction of neutrals – principally the United States, whose trade with the Entente was considerable, but also Denmark and the Netherlands. After the recent victories in Romania, however, Ludendorff was confident that Denmark and the Netherlands would have no appetite for war, and proposed merely that cavalry patrols on these borders be increased.

The chancellor seemed reassured, asking only that 'military measures which are to be taken with regard to the neutral boundaries, and particularly with regard to the Danish border, be such as not to carry the implication of excessive menace'. Indeed, he conceded: 'We should be perfectly certain that, so far as the military situation is concerned, great military strokes are insufficient as such to win the war. The U-boat war is the "last card." A very serious decision. But if the military authorities consider the U-boat war essential, I am not in a position to contradict them.' What, though, if America were to declare war?

Admiral Holtzendorff jumped up. 'I guarantee on my word as a naval officer that no American will set foot on the Continent!' It was an ill-judged echo of Admiral St Vincent's remark in the Napoleonic wars: 'I do not say the French cannot come [to Britain], I only say they cannot come by sea.' The same hubris, too, would prompt Reichsmarschall Goering to boast in 1939 that 'if one enemy bomber reaches the Ruhr, you may call me Meyer'.

Hindenburg, however, backed his naval counterpart emphatically: 'The war must be brought to an end rapidly, although we would be able to hold out still longer, but haste is needed on account of our allies [who were beginning to falter]' – to which Ludendorff added that the U-boats would bring 'some relief for the western front. We must spare the troops a second battle of the Somme.'

Besides, Hindenburg declared, 'We can take care of America. The opportunity for the U-boat war will never be as favourable again.'

The chancellor looked out of the window at the frozen pond in the park below, rubbed his hand over his clipped grey hair in a familiar gesture of uncertainty, then found his voice: 'Of course, if success beckons, we must follow.'

With his military advisers, and now also the chancellor, urging it, the Kaiser's decision was but a formality. Unrestricted submarine warfare was to begin on 1 February, he said, and 'with the utmost vigour' – at which point he signed the order and, followed by the high command, marched from the room to lunch.

Moments later Baron von Reischach, the *Oberhofmarschall* (Lord Chamberlain), entered the room and found Bethmann slumped in a chair. 'What's the matter?' he asked. 'Have we lost a battle?'

'No,' replied the chancellor, 'but *finis Germaniae*. That's the decision.'

In fact the *finis* was rather slower to begin than feared. The United States broke off diplomatic relations with Germany on 3 February, but President Wilson said he would take no further action unless Germany committed 'overt acts' by actually sinking American vessels. On the same day, the grain ship *Housatonic* was torpedoed off the Scillies. Ironically, she bore the same name as the first ship ever sunk by a submarine – the USS *Housatonic*, sunk by the Confederate submersible *Hunley* off Charleston, South Carolina, in 1864. But the grain ship *Housatonic* was sunk under cruiser rules, by Hans Rose of U-53, who had paid a 'courtesy visit' to Newport, Rhode Island the previous October before sinking several neutrals within sight of the Nantucket lightship a few days later. Rose stopped the *Housatonic* with warning shots, then sent his crew aboard to open the sea-cocks. They returned to the submarine with armfuls of soap, explaining that it was in short supply in Germany owing to the demands of the munitions industry for glycerine. Only when the *Housatonic*'s crew were in the lifeboats did Rose hasten her to the bottom with a torpedo.

Indeed, it would take another eight sinkings – and the discovery, through the so-called Zimmerman telegram (the 'suicide note written in farce'), that Germany was encouraging Mexico to invade – to provoke Congress into a declaration of war on 6 April.

Even so, it looked at first as if Admiral Holtzendorff's promises would be fulfilled. In January, under cruiser rules, his U-boats sank 368,000 tons of shipping; in February they sank 540,000; in March they almost reached the projected figure of 600,000 tons, and in April sank 881,000. Holtzendorff's mistake, however, was to assume that the Royal Navy – and soon the US Navy – would find no answer to the threat. Initially the Admiralty was reluctant to introduce convoys in the Atlantic, not least because the Grand Fleet needed the escort destroyers, but in May, Admiral Jellicoe, now the first sea lord, conceded to the demands of the prime minister, David Lloyd George. With the introduction of improved depth charges, a primitive hydrophone (developed by the New Zealand physicist Sir Ernest Rutherford) and more float planes, sinkings quickly fell back to pre-February levels.

Nor had Holtzendorff been alone among professional naval officers in believing that unrestricted submarine warfare would be decisive. In June 1917, a still sceptical Jellicoe told the war cabinet that nothing could be done to defeat the U-boats at sea, and that unless the army could capture their bases on the Belgian coast it was 'improbable that we could go on with the war next year for lack of shipping'.

However, by the end of the year the 'Dover Barrage', the mine and steel-netting barrier laid north of the Dover Straits, had been much strengthened, effectively closing the straits to submarines operating out of Zeebrugge and Ostend. Between May 1917 and November 1918, over two million American troops would be transported across the Atlantic in convoy, with fewer than 700 killed as a result of U-boat attacks.

Bethmann had been right: after 9 January 1917, it was *finis Germaniae*. The only questions were how, exactly, and when.

31

FEBRUARY
Biblical Terms

Lloyd George tries to turn attention to a land he knows

Raised in the strong evangelical tradition of Welsh Nonconformity, David Lloyd George had probably the best grasp of biblical geography of any British prime minister in history. At the Versailles peace conference after the war, he reduced the French premier, Georges Clemenceau, to silence by suggesting the British mandate in Palestine should run 'from Dan to Beersheba'. It was perhaps not surprising, then, that on becoming prime minister at the end of 1916, dismayed by the continuing slaughter on the Western Front, he should turn his eyes east to the Holy Land.

Initially he had to play his cards close to his chest, for the Germans on the Western Front could obviously not be beaten in Palestine, and the allied generals, not least the chief of the imperial general staff, Sir William Robertson, were intent on continuing their war of attrition in France. Lloyd George's motives were undoubtedly mixed. He had an instinctive dislike of the Turks and wanted Britain to play a greater role in the Middle East after the war. Diverting troops eastwards would also limit the generals' ability to mount offensives in France. Above all, perhaps, he wanted a victory somewhere – anywhere – to raise public morale in what was clearly going to be a long and bloody fight. 'Jerusalem by Christmas' (1917) became his objective.

However, the Ottoman Empire – its ethnic Turkish troops especially – had so far proved a far tougher adversary than expected. In January 1916 the Dardanelles campaign had ended in the humiliating (if brilliantly conducted) evacuation of the Gallipoli peninsula, and then in April the British army suffered one of its worst ever defeats when 10,000 British and Indian troops were forced to surrender at Kut al-Amara in Mesopotamia after a four-month siege. Yet Lloyd George had reason to be optimistic. General Sir Archibald Murray's meticulous logistic planning for the advance of the Egyptian Expeditionary Force from the Suez Canal across the Sinai desert into Southern Palestine was beginning to yield rewards. In December, Murray's British, Anzac and Indian troops, few of whom were regulars, had taken El-Arish, opening up the coastal road, and then, in January, Rafa on the Gaza frontier. It looked as if Lloyd George would indeed have a great victory for the public to celebrate, and long before Christmas.

The shame of Kut was also being expunged. The fortress-town, gateway to Baghdad, was about to be retaken. The campaign in Mesopotamia was primarily about oil, discovered just before the war in large quantities around Basra and Mosul; but there were also other considerations. Success here would discourage any Turkish attempts to foment discontent among India's Muslims, demonstrate that the British were still in control and encourage an Arab revolt against Ottoman rule which would ease the threat to the Suez Canal and hasten the defeat of the Ottoman Empire. Baghdad, therefore, Mesopotamia's administrative capital, some 300 miles upstream of Basra, was – and remained – a considerable prize.

After the surrender of Kut in April, London had taken over control of the campaign from Delhi, removing Lieutenant-General Sir John Nixon as head of the Mesopotamian Expeditionary Force and instructing his replacement, Lieutenant-General Sir Frederick

Maude, to consolidate around Basra. Maude, a systematic Cold-streamer and experienced general, ignored these instructions and began instead to plan the recapture of Kut. By December, having gathered reinforcements to form two corps (50,000 men), thoroughly reorganized his logistic support and at last put the medical services on a footing comparable with those on the Western Front, he persuaded the reluctant 'Wully' Robertson to authorize an advance.

Progress was slow initially because of heavy rain and Robertson's insistence – under the shadow of the Somme – on minimizing casualties. Nevertheless, on 24 February 1917 Maude drove the Turks from Kut, harrying their retreat with a flotilla of Royal Navy gunboats. Barely pausing to consolidate, two days later he renewed the advance and on 11 March took Baghdad.

With Mesopotamia apparently all but won and the Egyptian Expeditionary Force now through Sinai, it looked as if Britain was set to knock Turkey out of the fight, thereby changing the course of the war in the southern Balkans, drawing in precious Austrian and German reserves from both Western and Eastern Fronts and relieving pressure on Russia, about to erupt in revolution. Buoyed up with his success in taking Rafa, and believing Ottoman morale to be crumbling, on 26 March Murray launched a hasty offensive at Gaza, gateway to Palestine. However, the Turks, advised by the Bavarian Colonel Friedrich Kress von Kressenstein, and alerted by aerial reconnaissance to the attempts at encirclement, were not yet done. Murray, highly regarded as a staff officer but lacking the vital energy of a commander, tried to direct the battle from his headquarters railway carriage at El-Arish, 50 miles away. His divisional commanders, dismayed by mounting casualties and what appeared to be strong defences (though in fact they were thin), broke off battle after a single day's fighting.

The stakes were high, and Murray's report encouraged London to order another assault. The second Battle of Gaza, in mid-April, would be a more deliberate affair, in which tanks were used for the first time in the Middle East – but just eight of them, widely separated in a frontal assault 'to frighten the life out of them [the Turks]'.

Without adequate artillery support – though with another innovation, gas shells – against strengthened defences, the attack was no more successful than frontal assaults in France, and almost as bloody. In June, Murray would be relieved – as he had been from his two previous appointments – and replaced by Sir Edmund Allenby, whom Field Marshal Haig had just removed from 3rd Army in France.

Never did Haig do better service than in sacking Allenby from his European command. In November, adopting a plan devised by Lieutenant-General Sir Philip Chetwode, John Betjeman's future father-in-law, he would break through the Gaza defences by a surprise attack at Beersheba – where Abraham and Isaac had dug their seven wells, as Lloyd George would have known, and which now proved a vital watering place for the Desert Mounted Corps, foremost in the subsequent advance.

On 11 December Allenby would enter Jerusalem, dismounting to walk through the Jaffa Gate, a gesture received well by both Jews and Arabs. He had delivered Lloyd George what the prime minister called 'a Christmas present to the nation'. General Maude would not live to hear of it, however: he died in November, of cholera – by coincidence in the same house in Baghdad in which Colmar von der Goltz had succumbed to typhus eighteen months earlier.

32

MARCH
Alberich

Spirits soar as the Germans withdraw to the Hindenburg Line

'One night when we weren't being shelled we heard that the old Hun, as we called him, had pulled out his heavy howitzers and gone.' Henry Williamson, author of *Tarka the Otter* (1927), recalled the surprise and hopefulness in the trenches in March 1917 when Operation Alberich began. Not long afterwards, 'we saw the Bengal Lancers trot past us . . . a wonderful sight'.

As an 18-year-old territorial in the London Rifle Brigade, Williamson had volunteered to serve in France, spending the winter of 1914–15 in the trenches before being evacuated, sick. On recovering he was commissioned into the Bedfordshire Regiment, but specialist training and more sickness kept him in England during the Somme offensive. In March 1917, by then a lieutenant with the Machine Gun Corps, he was in the line just south of Arras when the Germans began pulling out. However, rumours that 'the Hun was packing up altogether' soon proved wide of the mark. Operation Alberich was a strategic withdrawal to more defensible ground.

The losses at Verdun and the Somme in 1916, and the Austrian setbacks on the Eastern and Italian fronts, had left the German army much weakened and short of artillery ammunition. Its 154 divisions on the Western Front were ranged against 190 French, British and Belgian (many of them much stronger than the Germans'), soon to be reinforced by the *Corpo Expedicionário Português* (Portuguese Expeditionary Force – some 55,000 infantry and supporting arms) and their independent heavy artillery corps. Against these forces, and certain that the allies would renew their attacks, in January 1917 Hindenburg decided to go onto the strategic defensive until he could find more troops. He told the Kaiser that they must 'let the U-boat commanders show what they can do'.

His chief of staff, Erich Ludendorff, advocated falling back to a new line of defence – the *Siegfriedstellung* ('Siegfried Fortress-Position') – to eliminate two salients between Arras and St-Quentin, and between St-Quentin and Noyon, which had been formed during the Somme offensive. The line – at its furthest point, some 30 miles back, and 90 miles long – had been reconnoitred as early as August 1916 in case of an allied breakthrough, and rudimentary trenches dug. Hindenburg now ordered that stronger defences be prepared. Not surprisingly, to the Entente these would become known as the 'Hindenburg Line'.

On ground of their own choosing, well away from the day-to-day fighting, industrial construction techniques could be used instead of digging under fire. Several hundred thousand men, including German and Belgian civilians and 50,000 Russian PoWs, laboured on the *Siegfriedstellung* throughout January and February. The defences consisted not merely of trenches (some of them 5 metres deep and 4 metres wide) but pillboxes – *Mannschafts-Eisen-Beton-Unterstände* ('iron-reinforced concrete shelters for troops'). These allowed machine guns to dominate the ground, obviating the need to rely on massed infantry rifles. Many were sited on reverse slopes, making them difficult to pinpoint, with a line of lightly defended outposts a mile or so in front to slow down any attack. It was a looser system of defence than the rigid lines of the Somme, making a 'battle zone' up to 4 miles deep, better able to absorb attacks, and in turn making the attacker more vulnerable to counter-attack. As the war went on, anti-tank ditches were also dug.

As well as providing the defenders with better ground to hold, by eliminating the two salients the move to the Hindenburg Line shortened the front by some 25 miles, releasing thirteen divisions into reserve.

The allies were not unaware of the activity. As far back as October the RFC had reported new trench lines far behind the Somme front, and the following month aerial photography revealed a complete new line of defences, 70 miles long, from Bourlon Wood north to Quéant, Bullecourt, the Sensée river and Héninel, joining the German third (reserve) line near Arras. This in itself was not indicative of the scale of Alberich; the British, too, were constructing precautionary fall-back positions. Even the forcible evacuation of thousands of French civilians (perhaps as many as 125,000, while the elderly, women and children were left behind with minimal rations) revealed nothing definite, for the Germans had never shown any qualms about uprooting potential spies and *francs tireurs* in the forward areas.

As winter drew on – the worst winter of the war, the frozen ground so hard that bursting shells were lethal at several times the usual distance – the construction was increasingly masked by bad flying weather. GHQ concluded that the work was tactical and routine. Indeed, until late January it is probable that Ludendorff – and thus Hindenburg – intended withdrawing to the new line only if there were an actual allied offensive. Besides, Field Marshal Haig and the new French commander-in-chief, Robert Nivelle, doubted that any soldier would willingly abandon ground, especially that on which he had spilled so much blood, however valueless or however much of a liability that ground had become. This assumption harked back to their historical understanding of battle – that he who was in possession of the ground at the end of the fighting was the winner. Ludendorff himself was only too aware of the moral effect of withdrawing, writing in his memoirs: 'It implied a confession of weakness bound to raise the *morale* of the enemy and lower our own.'

When at last, in March, Nivelle realized that the Germans were indeed retiring, and his staff warned that his own plans for an offensive would be seriously derailed as a result, he declared that 'if he had whispered orders to Hindenburg, the latter could not have better executed what he desired'. And as late as 17 April, Haig would tell the director of military operations at the War Office that it would be 'the height of folly for the French to stop [their offensive] now, just when the Germans had committed the serious fault of retiring, meaning to avoid a battle, but had been forced to fight against their will'.

However, the 'Alberich manoeuvre' was not merely a withdrawal; it also involved a scorched-earth operation. Nothing of use to the allies was to be left standing in the country abandoned. Houses were to be destroyed – whole towns and villages razed to the ground – railways dug up, bridges blown, road junctions mined, wells fouled or filled in (some may have been poisoned), even fruit trees cut down, and booby traps – ranging from simple pieces of duckboard in trenches which, when stepped on, would detonate grenades, to a huge delayed-action mine under Bapaume town hall – laid to make the allies wary of following up too quickly. Three- and six-inch steel 'crow's feet' – caltrops – were sown in the river bottom at every ford to puncture horses' hooves.

The operation was indeed well named. In German mythology, Alberich was the malevolent dwarf who guarded the treasure of the *Niebelungen*, and was eventually overcome by the hero Siegfried. Crown Prince Rupprecht of Bavaria, commanding the group of armies in the northern sector, learning of the scale and methods of the proposed operation, was appalled and contemplated resigning. He only stayed his hand because he thought his departure might suggest that a rift had developed between Bavaria and the rest of Germany. Churchill wrote that the Germans 'left their opponents in the crater fields of the Somme, and with a severity barbarous because far in excess of any military requirements, laid waste with axe and fire the regions which they had surrendered'.

Ludendorff saw the position rather differently:

We had to put up with the fact that the Entente turned our exceedingly thorough demolition of the territory and dispersal of the population to account, in order once more to call us Huns, and to play the organ of their propaganda with all the stops pulled out. One cannot blame them. Nevertheless, we had acted in accordance with the laws of warfare, and had not even gone as far as the belligerents in the American Civil War.

The actual withdrawal took place between 16 and 20 March and yielded more French territory than any action since the counter-attack on the Marne in September 1914. Indeed, it seemed at first to be an excellent opportunity for the British and French cavalry, including the Indian regiments that Henry Williamson saw, to have their long-awaited gallop at the enemy. But in following up the Germans – as far as their aggressive rearguards permitted (their artillery was perfectly ranged on every bridge and crossroads) – cavalry and infantry alike were shocked at the conditions wrought by the weather, their own guns and the scorched-earth policy. The divisional history of the 62nd (West Riding) Division, in which Williamson was serving, records that

> trenches as such did not exist, for they had been obliterated by the con-
> centrated fire of the guns . . . The front line was held by a series of posts
> and dugouts which somewhat resembled islands in a sea of mud. Shell
> holes pock-marked the ground, often overlapping one another and
> where pathways existed between them they were but a few inches
> wide. The holes were full of water and more than one man lost his life
> through slipping off the narrow pathway into the slimy mass which
> engulfed him.

The problem of getting up supplies was prodigious. After a while even the stocks of insulated telegraph cable, on which the entire system of communications relied, ran out. The Royal Engineers, ever resourceful, did their best to recover German wire, using wine bottles with the bottoms knocked out as insulators, fixed on pea-sticks. Pursuit was inordinately slow. Indeed, the cavalry frequently found themselves having to mark time while necessaries were got forward for the infantry and artillery, as well as having the greatest difficulty themselves finding feed and water for the horses. The Wiltshire Yeomanry reported that between 20 and 29 March, through shortage of forage, they lost twenty-two horses dead and thirty-five unfit for service.

Nor had the horses started the pursuit in the best of condition. Because of shortages of, and interruption to, shipping that winter, in part owing to the U-boats, the forage ration for the cavalry had been severely cut – from 12 lb of both oats and hay per day to 9 lb of oats and 6 lb of hay. It was not restored until late April, when in addition certain amounts of bran (not a great nutrient) and linseed were issued as a supplementary ration. The 9th Lancers had used thatch from their billets in lieu of hay.

Nevertheless, there were several brisk actions. On 27 March, the Canadian Cavalry Brigade, commanded by Brigadier-General J. E. B. (Jack) Seely, the former British war minister (who shared initials with the great Confederate cavalry leader J. E. B. Stuart), was ordered to take what remained of the village of Guyencourt. In the course of doing so, Lieutenant Frederick Harvey, of Lord Strathcona's Horse, won the VC – dismounted, displaying the skill that had made him an Irish rugby international. His citation recounts that

> a party of the enemy ran forward to a wired trench just in front of the village, and opened rapid fire and machine-gun fire at a very close range, causing heavy casualties in the leading troop. At this critical moment, when the enemy showed no intention whatever of retiring, and fire was still intense, Lt. Harvey, who was in command of the leading troops, ran forward well ahead of his men and dashed at the trench, skilfully manned, jumped the wire, shot the machine-gunner and captured the gun.

But in truth, in the two years of trench warfare the BEF as a whole had lost the habit of movement. Later that year, when again they were able to break out from the trenches – temporarily – General Edmund Allenby, commanding 3rd Army, would say they were like 'blind puppies', unable to make use of ground.

The British and French needed eight weeks to rebuild the roads, bridges and railways in the abandoned area before they could launch their own spring offensive – exactly as Ludendorff had intended.

As the year wore on, the Hindenburg Line would be progressively strengthened, extending eventually from the North Sea to the Vosges, in five distinct zones, or *Stellungen*, each bearing a name from German mythology: Wotan, Siegfried, Alberich, Brunhild and Kriemhild, with supporting lines Hunding and Freya. These were formidably strong positions in which to hold out against allied attacks, and to garner strength for their own great offensive in 1918.

Meanwhile, as the Germans settled into their new fortress-quarters, they were to receive an unexpected windfall. On 15 March (2 March in the old Julian calendar), as revolution swept through Petrograd, the Tsar abdicated. With the imperial Russian army and navy disintegrating, Ludendorff promptly withdrew ten divisions from the Eastern Front.

The following month, however, German fortunes would take a turn for the worse with the entry of the United States as 'co-belligerents' on the side of the allies. Berlin's window of opportunity to defeat what remained of the Entente would begin to close. Everything now depended on the U-boats' ability to starve the British, keep the Americans at arm's length and buy time for one last throw of the dice on the Western Front.

33

APRIL

The Cruellest Month

The great French 'Nivelle offensive' fails dismally, and with it the British, though the Canadians show their mettle

'Battles are won by slaughter and manoeuvre,' wrote Churchill. 'The greater the general, the more he contributes in manoeuvre, the less he demands in slaughter.'

After the Somme, the new prime minister, David Lloyd George, came to the same conclusion. His commander-in-chief on the Western Front, Sir Douglas Haig, offered only a repeat of the costly frontal attacks of 1916. Lloyd George thought him 'brilliant – to the top of his boots'.

But who might replace him?

In October 1914, as both sides dug in and stalemate developed, Lloyd George, then chancellor of the exchequer, called on General Noël Castelnau, commander of the French 2nd Army. How many troops did he have? asked the future prime minister. Nine army corps, was the answer. That was more than Napoleon had ever commanded in a single battle, replied 'LG'.

'Ah, Napoleon, Napoleon,' said Castelnau, with a sigh; 'if he were here now, he'd have thought of the "something else".'

In January 1917 the French prime minister, Aristide Briand, having finally managed to sideline the long-serving commander-in-chief Joseph Joffre, began singing the praises of a new Napoleon – Robert Nivelle. Like Napoleon, Nivelle was an artilleryman, and he appeared to have mastered the potential of the 'creeping barrage', which at last promised to allow the infantry to break through the German defences. At the inter-allied conference in Rome that month Briand told Lloyd George and Paolo Boselli, the Italian prime minister, that during the counter-offensive at Verdun in December, Nivelle had sent telegrams from various places during the advance demonstrating that his objectives were being achieved exactly according to his plan. Briand was sure that the grand offensive his new C-in-C was planning would be decisive. When the Italian C-in-C, Luigi Cadorna, suggested instead a combined offensive against the Austrians on the Italian front, 'LG', wary of promised breakthroughs in France, was at once enthusiastic. However, the chief of the imperial general staff, the gruff ranker General Sir William Robertson, argued that the priority must remain the Western Front. Unfortunately, Cadorna backed down, apparently impressed by Anglo-French military solidarity.

Lloyd George met Nivelle in Paris on his way back to England and, reassured by his confidence, invited him to London. Later that month Nivelle addressed the war cabinet in perfect English (his mother was British) and made a strong impression. When he left, Colonel Maurice Hankey, the cabinet secretary, wrote in his diary: 'Lloyd George would like to get rid of Haig, but cannot find an excuse.'

Instead, he proposed subordinating the BEF to the French high command for the coming offensive. Haig – since 1 January, by the express wish of the King, Field Marshal Haig – refused, arguing that Nivelle could rely on his best support but could not order him precisely how and when to give it. Lloyd George backed down, with some face-saving formula for all parties, but the episode left a bitter taste in Haig's mouth and did nothing to improve the prime minister's view of his new field marshal.

In March Nivelle began issuing peremptory instructions nevertheless, to which Haig objected both as a matter of military principle and because he did not 'believe our troops would fight under French leadership'. Resignations threatened, Haig writing in his diary that he 'would rather be tried by court martial', and although things quietened down, the row led to Briand's resignation.

It was while all this was going on that the Germans had decided to fall back to the *Siegfriedstellung* or 'Hindenburg Line'. As information about the move came through, many of Nivelle's own subordinates began urging him to abandon his plans. General Joseph Micheler, commanding the army group formed to exploit the anticipated victory, argued that the Germans were now in too strong a position. They had many more troops and artillery available for counter-attack, including those now being transferred from the Eastern Front after the Tsar's abdication and the near-collapse of the Russian army. He begged Nivelle to stand on the defensive instead and send troops to Italy to gain a victory there before the Germans did.

Nivelle was not deterred, however: 'Laon in twenty-four hours and then the pursuit. You won't find any Germans in front of you.'

Indeed, the more his generals voiced their concerns, the more vaunting became his predictions. They would break through 'with insignificant loss' and in three days at most would be in open country on their way to the Rhine: 'Nous les verrons Verdunés,' he claimed: 'We shall see them "Verdunned".'

On 24 March, Paul Painlevé, France's new war minister and a future prime minister, visited Haig and 'questioned [him] closely about Nivelle'. Haig was guardedly supportive, writing in his diary that 'I was careful to say that he struck me as a capable general, and that I was, of course, prepared to co-operate with whoever was chosen by the French government to be their C-in-C . . . my relations with Nivelle are and always have been *excellent*.'

Haig's sense of soldierly solidarity when faced with a politician (especially 'an extreme socialist', as he described Painlevé) prevented his speaking his mind. Perhaps with the offensive only a fortnight away he believed the die was cast, and any doubts expressed only likely to do harm. It was a catastrophic mistake.

Still Painlevé was not convinced. Having heard the discordant voices (traditionally shriller in the French army than in the British), he tried to persuade Nivelle to heed his generals. This was an impossible proposition, and nonsensical too, for either a C-in-C was to be trusted to come to the best military judgement or he was not, in which case dismissal was the only option.

Nivelle threatened to resign. Painlevé, though a brilliant mathematician, could not find the formula or the confidence to – in effect – dismiss 'the victor of Verdun', and backed down. He would count it as the costliest mistake of his long political career.

At first things seemed to go well for the Nivelle offensive. The BEF, in its supporting role, was to make a preliminary attack along a 15-mile front at Arras and at Vimy Ridge to draw German reserves away from the coming French assault on the ridge of the Chemin des Dames above the River Aisne. This it began on 9 April, Easter Monday, in a snowstorm, spearheaded by 3rd Army under Sir Edmund Allenby. An early casualty was the poet and most lyrical of writers on the English countryside Edward Thomas, thirty-nine years old, not long commissioned and only recently arrived in France, who was killed in a forward observation post, spotting for the guns of his heavy battery.

Progress was encouraging nonetheless. The 9th Scottish Division advanced 4 miles, and the Canadian Corps under the British Lieutenant-General Julian Byng took Vimy Ridge, the dominating heights above the Artois plain, in one of the finest feats of arms in the entire war. This success did not come cheap, however. In the three days' fighting it took to consolidate their gain, some 10,500 Canadians – or 'Byng Boys' as they were soon known – were wounded, and 3,600 killed (the Germans, defending fiercely, suffered 20,000 casualties). What had given the assaulting infantry their chance was an unprecedentedly accurate three-week bombardment, during which many of them were able to shelter from the counter-fire unobserved in tunnels hewn in the chalk of Arras. Isaac Rosenberg, one of the few acknowledged greats of the war poets not to have been commissioned, was serving with the 11th Battalion, The King's Own, a 'Bantam battalion' (consisting of men under the 1914 minimum height of 5 feet 3 inches). In a letter home he wrote: 'We've been in no danger – that is, from shell-fire – for a good long while, though so very close to most terrible fighting. But as far as houses or sign of ordinary human living is concerned, we might as well be in the Sahara Desert.'

Once the attack began, a very precise creeping barrage screened the infantry's advance. It was devised and coordinated in large part by Major Alan Brooke – who in the Second World War would rise to become Field Marshal Lord Alanbrooke, Churchill's 'master of strategy'. British artillery techniques had by this stage become quite sophisticated, including gas shells that neutralized much of the German artillery. On the other hand, the few tanks available were dogged by mechanical failure.

Exploiting success was another matter, however, not least because of the congestion behind the British front, caused in part by the very troops who were to have been the instrument of exploitation – the mass of cavalry, which instead became a target for the enemy's guns. Fighting then descended to what it had been on the Somme – a slogging match, with mounting casualties on both sides (the Australians suffering particularly badly at Bullecourt due to the inveterate self-assurance of the 5th Army commander, Sir Hubert Gough). When the battle ended on 15 May, losses in the BEF had risen to 150,000. Indeed, the daily casualty rate was the BEF's heaviest of the entire war. The following month, Haig sacked Allenby. 'The Bull', as he was known, not entirely affectionately, had fallen foul of those both above and below him. His subordinate commanders felt he had pushed them too hard, while Haig blamed him for failing to break through. It would prove to be one of the most felicitous of Haig's decisions, however. Reassigned to command in Palestine, by Christmas Allenby would take Jerusalem from the Turks.

The French attack, when it came on 16 April – delayed several days by bad weather – faltered almost at once. The German defences were largely on the reverse slope of the Chemin des Dames and therefore hidden from observation, except by air, and although the French had mustered 1,000 aircraft, superior German fighter tactics and bad weather had negated the advantage (the BEF itself lost seventy-five aircraft in the five days preceding its attack). Nivelle's artillery bombardment, by an unprecedented number of batteries, was much less successful than he had predicted, leaving the German machine-gunners to dominate the crest. The French infantry failed to keep up with the creeping – in fact, more a 'running' – barrage, which advanced too quickly at 100 yards a minute, and the attack could get no further than the top of the ridge. By nightfall the infantry had advanced just 600 yards instead of the 6 miles promised in Nivelle's schedule. Of the 132 French tanks massed for the attack (mainly Schneiders), in action for the first time, 57 had been destroyed and 64 had become irretrievably bogged down in the mud.

As Micheler had warned, the Germans had been able to increase the number of divisions on the Aisne substantially – indeed, by a factor of four, so that the French were barely at parity, let alone with the usual superiority of three to one reckoned necessary in the attack. Operational security had also been poor, with divisional orders in some cases being copied down as far as battalion level, so that as soon as the Germans began taking prisoners they were able to piece together Nivelle's intentions. There were even suggestions that Nivelle's critics had leaked the plans – a suggestion that would have been unbelievably far-fetched but for the fevered state of the post-Verdun French army, which within a month would see widespread mutinies.

By 26 April, over 95,000 French wounded had passed through the casualty clearing stations. When the offensive was abandoned a fortnight later, the total number of casualties, dead and wounded, had risen to 187,000. Nivelle's days were numbered.

But who was to succeed him? Paris was badly shaken, and the right answer – the infantryman Philippe Pétain – seemed unthinkable, for he had long been the outsider, refusing to subscribe to the orthodoxy of *offensive à outrance* ('offensive to the utmost') and insisting on the power of the defensive. But some, at least, could see his qualities. At the end of April, the *Times* war correspondent, Charles à Court Repington, wrote anxiously to Lloyd George from Paris:

> I hear that influence is being brought to bear on your side of the water to oppose the appointment of Pétain to the chief command on the ground that he holds certain views which, in fact, he does not hold . . . [I] ask you not to credit the silly chatter which attributes to him a want of go and resolution.
>
> He sees the situation clearly . . . He will not promise the moon as others have done. In this last French offensive our friends have lost 120,000 men, equal to two thirds of the French class of a year, and are much depressed. Pétain foretold the failure to the War Council . . . He sees that we are practically on an equality with the enemy, and must wait until you in England, and the Americans, provide the superiority of force necessary for victory . . . He is against trying to do much with little, and prefers to do little with much . . . He will most certainly support Haig in every way, for the arrest of this mad Rheims offensive [Nivelle's] does not at all imply quietism and want of activity . . . Believe me that he is the best general in France.

Repington, dubbed by his detractors 'the Playboy of the Western Front', was wrong about many things during the course of the war, but not this. Although Pétain, who replaced Nivelle on 15 May, would not be able to contribute much in manoeuvre, he had the sense and courage to stop demanding slaughter.

Unfortunately, as the baton now passed to the British on the Western Front, Haig would not see things the same way.

34

MAY

All Goes Quiet on the Western Front

While the armies lick their wounds,
the allied high commands try to work out 'what next?'

In the wake of the failure of Nivelle's 'mad Rheims offensive', as Repington called it in his letter to Lloyd George, another inter-allied conference was held, in Paris on 4 May, at which 'LG' found himself having to put heart into the new French government, especially its head, Alexandre Ribot, prime minister for a fifth time since 1892. The BEF was now in some respects co-equal with the French army, if not in size then certainly in terms of fighting capability (and Britain's wider war effort – naval and economic – was also now vast); but it was still not strong enough to achieve any significant offensive success on its own. Ribot assured 'LG' that the French nation was still in the fight, but the French army had serious problems of morale to put right first. This job would fall to Pétain, and he would do it well, not least by heeding what every *poilu* was saying – that they would defend the trenches but they would not attack. He told Ribot that the only rational course was to stand on the defensive until conditions changed in favour of the offensive, which to his mind meant more British troops, but principally the arrival of the Americans – and tanks.

Haig, still offensively minded, saw all this as a green light to switch his own effort back to Flanders, and the scheme to take Ostend and Zeebrugge, the viperous nests of U-boats. The previous November, Asquith – then still prime minister – had told the CIGS, Robertson, that there was 'no operation of war to which the War Committee would attach greater importance than the successful occupation, or at least the deprivation to the enemy, of Ostend, and especially Zeebrugge' – and Lloyd George had, of course, been a member of that committee. Now, with 'LG' humbled – hamstrung, even – by having placed his faith in Nivelle, Haig turned the steering wheel to head north-west and put his foot confidently on the accelerator, telling General Sir Herbert Plumer, 2nd Army commander, to dust off the plans he had made a year ago (before, at Joffre's request, Haig had switched the effort to the Somme) for a preliminary attack to take the Messines–Wytschaete Ridge.

The lull in offensive operations was certainly a boon for the RFC, which had suffered so many losses in the previous month that it had become known as 'Bloody April'. Its numerical superiority over the *Deutsche Luftstreitkräfte* – 385 fighters to 114 – had been negated by the Germans' superiority in aircraft technology, organization and pilot training. The Albatros D.II and D.III outclassed most of the RFC's planes except the French SPAD VII and the Sopwith Pup and Triplane, which were few in number and spread along the front. The new generation of allied fighters was not yet fully ready for service, and attempts to rush new aircraft into action proved disastrous. On the first patrol undertaken by the Bristol F2a (a plane that in time was a match for the Albatros), four out of six were shot down in an encounter with five Albatros D.IIIs led by Manfred von Richthofen, the 'Red Baron', who commanded one of the innovative *Jagdstaffeln* (hunting squadrons). During that one month, the RFC lost a third of its fighter force (losses three times those of the Germans), the flying life-expectancy of its pilots falling to just seventeen and a half hours.

'Bloody April' would force the RFC to change its approach to aerial combat, just as the losses over the Somme had forced the Germans to do the year before. It was now accepted that well-trained pilots flying the best planes were more important than mere numerical superiority, and pilot-training schools were reorganized with experienced veterans as instructors.

The consequences of the 'mad Rheims offensive' were also felt further afield. As agreed at the Chantilly conference in November, the Italians had been due to make their own, concurrent, offensive on the Isonzo to keep the German–Austrian alliance at full stretch; but this had been delayed by organizational problems, and it was not until 10 May that the tenth Isonzo offensive was opened on a frontage of 25 miles: thirty-eight Italian divisions against fourteen Austro-Hungarian. By the end of the month the Italians had advanced to within 10 miles of Trieste, but a counter-offensive recovered virtually all lost ground. Cadorna finally closed down the offensive on 8 June, having suffered 157,000 casualties; the Austro-Hungarians lost only half that number. (A simultaneous offensive by French, British and Serbian troops on the Macedonian front was no more successful in its objectives, though much less bloody.) Morale in the Italian army had taken a serious blow, and Cadorna would attempt to restore it by massing his greatest number of divisions yet along the Isonzo for one further attempt to break through towards Trieste.

Meanwhile in Russia, although the provisional government announced that it would stay in the war, troops and peasants were declaring for the anti-war Bolshevik party in increasing numbers. On 16 April, Vladimir Lenin had returned from exile in Switzerland in a special train organized by the Germans. By November his leadership of the Bolsheviks would bring an armistice on the Eastern Front.

Only at sea – and across the Atlantic – did there appear to be good news for the allies. Finally, after much opposition from Sir John Jellicoe, the first sea lord, the Admiralty agreed to introduce the convoy system for merchant ships making the crossing from North

America. The decision would have an almost immediate impact: U-boat losses rose, while the rate of merchant ship sinkings fell equally dramatically. And although it would be several months before Admiral Holtzendorff's promise to the Kaiser that 'on my word as a naval officer . . . no American will set foot on the Continent' would be proved an idle boast, those American troops were already gathering. On 12 May, General John 'Black Jack' Pershing – who would prove one of the most thoughtful but resolute commanders in France – was appointed commander of the American Expeditionary Force. He had surmised something was afoot when on 3 May, at his headquarters on the Rio Grande, from where he was conducting operations on the Mexican border, he had received a cryptic telegram from the father of his late wife, Senator Francis E. Warren of Wyoming: 'Wire me today whether and how much you speak, read, and write French.'

On 18 May, Congress passed the Selective Service Act, enabling the registration and selective draft of men aged between twenty-one and thirty. By November 1918, Pershing would have at his call some two million troops.

35

JUNE
Messines

*Victory in a well-planned, well-executed set-piece battle,
but a false promise of future success*

At the beginning of 1917 the commanding officer of the Australian
3rd Division, Major-General John Monash – not a soldier by profession but a civil engineer – had astutely characterized the Western
Front as above all an 'engineering problem'. Yet GHQ seemed to be
tackling it as mobile operations at the halt. Haig continued to think
in terms of a breakthrough that would restore the war of movement
last experienced in the late summer of 1914, a war in which for
some reason he believed the allied armies would have the advantage. Monash and a few others, their voices necessarily muted
because there could be no open dissent, thought the situation more
akin to siege warfare.

Indeed, the Western Front, with its continuous line of trenches
from the North Sea to the Swiss border, had become the largest
siege in history. The Germans laid siege to France, the allies to
German-occupied Flanders and northern France. And like a gigantic ravelin of some medieval fortress, the German salient south of

Ypres, formed during the fighting in October 1914, threatened, and in some places overlooked, the movement of troops to its north.

For over a year the commander of 2nd Army, General Sir Herbert Plumer, had been working on plans to straighten out the line at Ypres, and much preparatory tunnelling work by the Royal Engineers (with Canadian, Australian and New Zealand engineers), assisted by former coal-miners in the infantry battalions, had been carried out. Undermining fortifications had long been one of the staples of siegecraft. In 1215 King John had famously laid siege to Rochester Castle, tunnelling under the great tower and hollowing out a large cavity, the roof supported with props. Into this his siege-workers packed brushwood and fattened pigs; they then set the chamber alight, and down came the tower. In the seventeenth century, gunpowder had added an explosive dimension to military mining, which soon developed into a specialist arm. Eventually, in 1856, the Corps of Royal Sappers and Miners were incorporated into the Royal Engineers.

With Haig now turning his attention to a major offensive at Ypres, eliminating the German salient became a priority, and he gave Plumer approval to mount a limited operation in early June to take the high ground east of Wytschaete and Messines.

Though Plumer, usually somewhat ponderous, could at times become emotional and even impulsive, he was a meticulous, experienced infantryman. His appearance – slightly portly, with bushy white moustache – entirely belied his capability. Haig almost sacked him shortly after becoming commander-in-chief, but had since developed a solid respect for his fellow officer. With the cloud of the Somme hanging over 4th Army commander, Sir Henry Rawlinson, 'Plum' was the only infantryman to whom he could turn at that level. Nevertheless, bruised by the experience of the Somme, and by Arras in April, Haig was anxious not to see another operation stalled through 'phasing', with deliberate operational pauses, and urged all speed in the attack. This suited Plumer, who although thoroughly realistic about what could be expected of infantry, wanted as short a battle as possible. Initially suggesting three days, as the furthest objective was just 3 miles he finally agreed to Haig's preference for a single day.

Such an ambitious aim would rely on the successful detonation of all the mines more or less simultaneously, followed immediately by the occupation of the shattered German defences. For no student of history, as Plumer and his fellow generals were, would have forgotten the disastrous delay before the Union infantry's attack at Petersburg in the American Civil War after the annihilating explosion of the long-tunnel mine under the Confederate defences.

In the wake of the detonation of the nineteen mines at Messines, therefore, Plumer planned for his infantry to advance in strength protected by a creeping barrage 700 yards deep which progressed at the rate of 50 yards a minute (half that of Nivelle's disastrous barrage at the Chemin des Dames in April), with tanks to help overcome any remaining strongpoints, and gas or flammable bombs from the new man-portable Livens projectors.

Three army corps would take part in the attack – two British (IX and X), and II Australian and New Zealand (Anzac) under command of Lieutenant-General Alexander Godley, an Anglo-Irish officer who had been commandant of the New Zealand Military Force (largely militia) before the war. Each corps comprised four infantry divisions, three of which would take part in the initial assault, with the fourth in reserve.

By early June, twenty-one mine shafts, a total of nearly 9,000 yards of tunnels, had been driven under the German lines across a front of nearly 12,000 yards, and packed with 400 tons of ammonal explosive at depths of between 50 and 100 feet.

Plumer had also studied the lessons of the Somme, not least the necessity of not taking it for granted that massed artillery achieved results. Precision was essential. With the help of the RFC, therefore, a very precise preliminary bombardment was opened on 8 May, followed by a heavier one beginning on 21 May. Some 2,300 guns and 300 heavy mortars fired in all around three million shells. The RFC and French air service had been able to provide the gunners with accurate maps of German artillery positions, and during the bombardment helped correct the fall of shot. By the time the infantry attacked on 7 June, 90 per cent of German guns in and around Messines had been destroyed.

It was by no means easy for the allied gunners, however. Captain Cyril Dennys, in a Royal Artillery heavy howitzer battery, spoke of the particular difficulties and danger of operating near Ypres. The guns could not be placed in a pit because the water level was too high, so a platform had to be made and sandbag walls built for protection. The ground was so devastated

> that the usual camouflage netting might give you away. So we would make the position look as untidy as the surroundings. We used to throw around bits of old sackcloth, sandbags, rum jars – and instead of putting the implements, the battery hand spikes and levers and things in neat order, we used to throw them about. We were told to do this by the RFC pilots. They said, 'For God's sake don't have any kind of order. Have your battery positions as untidy as you can and never allow your men to approach the guns along the same track, or they'll make a path that will be visible from the air.'

A long bombardment signalled to the enemy the intention to attack, of course, but Plumer turned this to his advantage. When a bombardment stopped suddenly, the Germans would at once scramble up the ladders of their deep dug-outs to man the machine guns in anticipation of attack. Plumer therefore timed zero hour, when the mines were to be detonated, at 3.10 a.m., when there was just enough light for a man to be seen from the west at 100 yards, but for the bombardment to cease at 2.50. The Germans, expecting attack, would rush to their defensive positions and then be caught by the explosions.

There was a thunderstorm in the evening of 6 June, but by midnight the sky had cleared, and at 2.00 a.m. the RFC began overflying the German lines to mask the sound of the tanks as they drove up to the start line. By 3.00 a.m. the infantry had reached their forward trenches largely unnoticed, thereby not attracting enemy shelling, and at 3.10 – zero hour – the nineteen mines were detonated over a period of twenty seconds, which magnified the shock and terror in the German lines, for the forward troops had known for months of the tunnelling and become increasingly apprehensive.

'The whole hillside rocked like a ship at sea,' recalled one Australian sapper. 'Then when we got to look at the craters, we saw there were lumps of blue clay as big as small buildings lying about . . . We thought the war was over.'

Major-General Charles Harington, Plumer's chief of staff, had shared that same sense of apocalypse when, at the final conference the day before, he said: 'I do not know whether or not we shall change history tomorrow, but we shall certainly alter geography.'

In London, Vera Brittain, auxiliary nurse and writer (of, among other works, her memoir *Testament of Youth*, covering the war years), felt 'a strange early morning shock like an earthquake.' Lloyd George heard it in 10 Downing Street. It was reportedly heard even in Dublin. The combined near-simultaneous explosions were the loudest man-made sound to that date.

Some 10,000 German troops were killed instantly. Those who survived unscathed were very badly shaken. Some positions were abandoned. Others were surrendered without a shot. But by this stage in the war, German defences had become 'elastic', designed to absorb punishment. The most forward line was relatively lightly defended, and troops were authorized to retire to more heavily defended lines half a mile behind if they came under heavy pressure – acting in effect as reconnaissance patrols, for communications (still predominantly line) were always precarious.

The combination of the artillery preparation, the mines, the creeping barrage and the tanks, and the improved organization and tactics of the infantry, quickly paid off. By 5 a.m. almost all Plumer's initial objectives had been taken. Only on the extreme left was there any appreciable delay as the territorials of the 47th (London) Division struggled to cross the Ypres–Comines Canal. The second phase of the attack began soon afterwards with the reserve divisions carrying on from where the initial attackers were consolidating, supported by tanks and field artillery that at last had their opportunity to gallop forward.

As was standard practice, the Germans counter-attacked the following day, but without success, and indeed with the loss of more ground. The counter-attacks continued, but with decreasing force, until 14 June, by which stage the entire Messines salient was in allied hands.

Messines was probably the finest set-piece action of the war, demonstrating what combined-arms planning and tactics could achieve. And although it begat over-optimism in Haig's plans for his big offensive at the end of July, it was a great boost to morale.

It was certainly not without cost, though: 2nd Army suffered some 24,000 casualties, including over 3,500 who were killed or died of wounds. But the Germans lost probably 35,000, including 7,000 prisoners. Compared with the 60,000 casualties on the first day of the Somme the year before (for the most limited territorial gains), the 'butcher's bill' seemed reasonable.

One of the most poignant losses was that of the Irish Nationalist MP Major Willie Redmond. His brother John, leader of the Irish Parliamentary Party, had urged fellow Nationalists to enlist to further the cause of home rule by proving their loyalty to the King. In November 1914, Willie Redmond had himself made a celebrated speech in Cork, standing at an open window of the Imperial Hotel. Speaking to the crowd below, he ended by shouting: 'I do not say to you, "Go" – but,' – taking off his hat – 'grey-haired and old as I am, I say "Come, come with me to the war!"'

By June 1917 he was a major in the Royal Irish Regiment, in the 16th (Irish) Division consisting in large part of former members of the Irish Volunteers, who had been formed before the war to counter the Ulster Volunteers raised to resist home rule. On 7 June, the 16th (Irish) advanced towards Wytschaete alongside the 36th (Ulster) Division consisting in large part of former Ulster Volunteers. The 57-year-old Redmond, a devout Catholic, was hit by shell splinters and fell in no-man's-land. He was found by an Antrim Protestant, Private John Meeke, a stretcher-bearer with the Ulster Division.

257

Though coming under machine-gun fire, Meeke managed to bandage Redmond's wounds before himself being wounded, whereupon Redmond ordered him to leave him and take cover. Meeke refused and managed to get him back to an aid post, but Redmond died that night of wounds.

At his burial next day, the Ulster Division formed a guard of honour.

36

JULY

'Passchendaele'

Ever more slaughter in Flanders fields

'Every brook is swollen and the ground is a quagmire. If it were not that all the records of previous years had given us fair warning, it would seem as if Providence had declared against us.'

So wrote Haig's chief of intelligence, Brigadier-General John Charteris, on 31 July 1917 at the beginning of the Third Battle of Ypres, commonly called 'Passchendaele' after the village and ridge that would become the culminating objective before the offensive was finally called off in November.

In the fortnight's preparatory bombardment, 3,000 guns fired four and a half million shells on the German defences. That barrage cost £22 million – in today's prices, £1.7 billion. The results overall were mixed. On the drainage system of west Flanders, however, they were tragically spectacular. As reclaimed marshland, the Ypres area was bound to revert to swamp if the system were destroyed. Worse still, according to Charteris, the records showed that in Flanders 'the weather broke early each August with the regularity of the Indian monsoon' – and in 1917 the weather proved true to its record.

259

Third Ypres followed a depressing pattern of strategic thinking on the Western Front – a pattern that had produced ever greater slaughter. In four and a quarter years' fighting on the Western Front, the allies 'spent' (casualties and losses) nearly eight million men, and the Germans (and to a limited extent Austrians) over five and a half million. Of all those years, 1917 was perhaps the bloodiest.

The strategy for 1917 had been determined at the inter-allied conference at Chantilly in December the previous year. At the urging of Joseph Joffre, the French commander-in-chief, he and his allied counterparts – British, Russian and Italian – agreed to apply again the same strategy that had failed in 1916. They would mount syncopated offensives on the three principal fronts to try to stretch the enemy to breaking point, and then exploit the situation that presented itself. All their training convinced them that, in the words of the British army's *Field Service Regulations*, 'decisive success in battle can be gained only by a vigorous offensive'. Haig in particular believed that the chief factor in success was, as *FSR* stated, 'a firmer determination in all ranks to conquer at any cost'.

The problem was that the situation on the Western Front had not materially changed since December 1914, when it seemed 'quite likely', as Churchill had written to Asquith, 'that neither side will have the strength to penetrate the other's line in the Western theatre'. The overwhelming advantage lay now, as it had then, with the defender.

Nevertheless, a weak French government acquiesced in Joffre's strategy, though the prime minister, Aristide Briand, despairing of the casualties at Verdun, managed to manoeuvre him out of command in the field, replacing him with Robert Nivelle, a man he called 'a new Napoleon'. Unfortunately, Lloyd George, who had just replaced Asquith in No. 10, fell for Briand's confidence – and, indeed, Nivelle's, not least for the latter's ability to explain himself in perfect English. Having lost confidence in Haig after the Somme offensive, 'LG' threw his weight behind Nivelle's proposed spring offensive on the Aisne and told Haig to put aside his misgivings and support the 'new Napoleon'. When that offensive failed, spectacularly, Haig emerged in a morally stronger position with London. He therefore began to develop his own ideas for a breakthrough near Ypres, ostensibly to clear the Belgian coast and thereby substantially reduce the menace from the U-boats – an enterprise that would resound strongly with the cabinet's conclusion in November that 'there is no operation of war to which the War Committee would attach greater importance than the successful occupation, or at least the deprivation to the enemy, of Ostend, and especially Zeebrugge'.

This war cabinet minute was not in itself a requirement for an offensive, rather an attempt to limit the ambitions for offensive action, and with the failure of the Nivelle offensive, the cabinet wanted to avoid another major blood-letting in 1917. However, by May that year, with Russia beginning to fall apart in revolution, the French army barely answering to discipline, the Italians increasingly hard pressed and no prospect of American relief for at least six months, they recognized that Britain would have to bear the burden not merely at sea and in the Middle East, but on the Western Front. There seemed to be no alternative to Haig's plans to reach the sea.

Nevertheless, a month before it was due to begin, Lloyd George warned Haig that 'a great attack which fails in its objective while entailing heavy casualties must necessarily discourage the British Army' as well as having a grave effect on public opinion in both Britain and France, and that the cabinet 'must regard themselves as trustees' for those serving and must see that they were 'not sacrificed on mere gambles'.

Haig assured the cabinet they need have no worries. And indeed, preparations seemed to go well. On 7 June, the British 2nd Army under General Sir Herbert Plumer launched a meticulously planned operation at Messines just south of Ypres with the object of straightening out the Ypres salient and taking the high ground that commanded the British defences and rear areas further north. From here Haig intended to launch his 'Northern Operation' – an advance to Passchendaele Ridge and thence, in conjunction with landings

261

from the sea, including tanks, to the Belgian coast as far as the Dutch frontier south of the Scheldt.

Notwithstanding the success of the Messines operation, Lloyd George remained apprehensive. In his memoirs he wrote bitterly about Haig's over-optimism: 'The capture of the Messines Ridge, a perfect attack in its way, was just a useful little preliminary to the real campaign, an *apéritif* provided by General Plumer to stimulate the public appetite for the great carousal of victory which was being provided for us by GHQ.'

He was not alone in his concern. Ferdinand Foch, the new French chief of the general staff, told the senior British liaison officer, Henry Wilson, that 'the whole thing was futile, fantastic and dangerous'. Philippe Pétain, who had replaced Nivelle as commander-in-chief, believed that 'Haig's attack towards Ostend was certain to fail', and with heavy casualties.

However, the British CIGS, 'Wully' Robertson, who had risen from the ranks and had a reputation for bluff common sense, told the cabinet that Haig's plan 'should secure us against this mistake'. Haig himself assured the cabinet that he was 'fully in agreement . . . that we ought not to push attacks that had not a reasonable chance of success, but that we ought to proceed step by step'. He himself had 'no intention of entering into a tremendous offensive involving heavy losses' – although, as he told the cabinet, 'if the fighting was kept up . . . for six months Germany would be at the end of her available manpower'.

Still the war cabinet hesitated, but at this point Haig found an unlikely ally. Admiral Sir John Jellicoe, the first sea lord, said that nothing could be done to defeat the U-boats at sea, and that unless the army could clear the Belgian coast the losses of shipping were likely to be such as to render it impossible for Britain to prosecute the war for another year. Few but Jellicoe believed this, for most of the submarines were operating from bases in Germany, principally the island of Heligoland (which in 1890 Britain had exchanged for Zanzibar), but Haig was not a one to look a gift horse in the mouth.

Eventually the war cabinet gave him the go-ahead after he

promised he would halt the offensive if it became clear that his objectives could not be obtained. However, the criteria for judging whether those objectives were being obtained were not specified. The judgement would be Haig's, and Haig had a tendency to believe that failure to make progress was primarily a sign of lack of determined leadership.

As if to reinforce Haig in his conviction that his great 'Northern Offensive' was not only practicable but necessary, on its very eve he learned that three Russian armies – some sixty to seventy divisions – were in full retreat along a 150-mile front. Under the terms of the December agreement, a major offensive against one ally would bring about a prompt counter-offensive by all the others. He therefore felt justified in telling Pétain, who was nursing the French army back to fighting health after the terrible losses of 1916 and early 1917, that the policy the French C-in-C was advocating of standing on the strategic defensive until 1918, when the Americans would arrive in strength, would only serve the Germans, allowing them to concentrate all their reserves in the east and knock Russia out of the war before the winter. Now, Haig proclaimed, was 'the critical moment of the war'.

Clearly, therefore, he would press the offensive in Flanders with even greater determination than the cabinet envisaged, for as well as the questionable objective of relieving the U-boat threat, it now had a major strategic purpose.

In any case, he was confident of a breakthrough, telling his army commanders that 'opportunities for the employment of cavalry in masses are likely to offer'. And Hubert Gough, commanding 5th Army, a cavalryman and a 'thruster', was the man to create those opportunities. Gough rewrote the plan that Plumer had earlier devised, making provision to take rapid advantage of ground the Germans abandoned – one of the lessons of the Somme – and setting more ambitious objectives for the first day. Tanks in large numbers were to help the infantry forward. Tank supply had been stepped up after the Somme, and the Tank Corps, hitherto the Heavy Branch of the Machine Gun Corps, came formally into being on 27 July.

However, Tank Corps staff officers had been surveying the going for several weeks and were far from confident that the ground was suitable. The destruction of the drainage ditches had, wrote one, turned the Steenbeck, a stream that ran parallel to the front line, into 'a wide moat of liquid mud'.

The attack was scheduled to begin on 28 July, but was postponed for three days because Gough had not quite completed his preparations. On 28 July it began to rain heavily. Nevertheless, of the 136 tanks committed to the attack, all but two managed to reach the start line, which was itself a mechanical triumph.

Zero hour was 3.50 a.m., first light, to minimize the Germans' advantage in observation from the higher ground. A layer of unbroken low cloud meant that it was still dark when the infantry advanced – fourteen divisions, with the support of a French corps on the left, and one of Plumer's on the right, on a frontage of 11 miles.

Progress was mixed. Lieutenant Edmund Blunden MC, of the 11th Royal Sussex, advancing on the left, recalled:

> We rose, scrambled ahead, found No Man's Land a comparatively good surface, were amazed at the puny tags and rags of once multiplicative German wire, and blundered over the once feared trench behind them without seeing that it was a trench . . . German dead, so obvious at every yard of a 1916 battlefield, were hardly to be seen.

Towards the centre, north-east of Ypres itself, things were not so promising. Here the ground was more open, rising gently and dotted with fortified farms and concrete pillboxes that had scarcely suffered during the bombardment. The infantry had to overcome these one by one, with the help of those tanks that could get forward over the cratered and waterlogged ground. By the end of the day's fighting, half the tanks had been knocked out by fire or become 'bogged'.

German reserves poured forward throughout the day. Gough had planned that the RFC, which had had a gruelling two months' combat against the odds, would interdict their movement by bombing, and by machine-gunning – 'strafing' (from the German imprecation *Gott strafe England* – 'May God punish England') – but the low cloud largely prevented it.

Many of the initial gains in the centre and south were either lost to German counter-attacks or could not be exploited because of the exhaustion of the troops. The greatest success was achieved on the northern flank, by the French, and by XIV Corps under the diminutive but capable Lieutenant-General the Earl of Cavan, a Grenadier who had been recalled from retirement as a colonel in 1914 and who would go on to command an Anglo-Italian army with notable success in 1918 during the final offensive on the Italian front.

But nowhere was there any appreciable gain of more than 2 miles. Still Haig reported to the War Office that evening that the results were 'most satisfactory'.

The offensive would continue, though it would never get near the coast, in what Blunden would describe as a 'slow amputation'. Casualty figures are still disputed, but were probably around a quarter of a million on each side.

Blunden would survive the three and a half months' fighting at Third Ypres, and the war. Two of his fellow poets (though their names are not inscribed on the memorial in Westminster Abbey) did not survive the first day. Lance-Corporal Francis Ledwidge of the Royal Inniskilling Fusiliers, a fervent Irish Nationalist who had nevertheless answered the call to arms, was killed by artillery fire. Private Ellis Humphrey Evans of the Royal Welsh Fusiliers, better known by his Bardic name 'Hedd Wyn', a reluctant conscript, was fatally wounded by shrapnel. In September, he would be posthumously 'chaired' (made chief bard) at the national Eisteddfod, at which Lloyd George, a Welsh speaker, was present.

37

AUGUST

'O for a beaker full of the warm South'

*British reinforcements on the Italian Front find the food
strange and the fighting every bit as murderous*

As Field Marshal Sir Douglas Haig's armies battled throughout August with the Germans and the weather at Third Ypres (Passchendaele), for others, attention was being called to the warm south. In April, ten batteries of field guns and howitzers had been sent from France to strengthen the Italian army's artillery on the Isonzo, and several more of heavier calibre joined in August, some direct from England.

For most gunners, the change was welcome. Hugh Dalton, who would become Clement Attlee's chancellor of the exchequer in 1945, but who in August 1917 was a lieutenant with a siege battery on the Italian front, expressed his delight at his new theatre of war: 'What worlds away is this country with its wonderful cloudless sunshine from the dismal flat lands of the Western Front!'

While the other ranks shared Dalton's sentiments as to climate and scenery, however, they were not best pleased with the rations. On the Western Front the Army Service Corps fed them good

British fare, but in Italy they were victualled by the *Regio Esercito Italiano* (Royal Italian Army): less beef, bacon, cheese and tea than they were used to in France, supplemented instead by macaroni, rice, coffee and red wine. The wine – 'Key-Auntie', as they were told to pronounce it – was appreciated, but many a letter home complained of the monotony of pasta and stew.

Haig had not wanted to send them anyway. He protested vehemently to the chief of the imperial general staff, Sir William Robertson, when given the order, arguing that it would jeopardize his coming offensive at Ypres; but Lloyd George was chary of the continued promises of breakthrough on the Western Front and wanted to shift the effort south, to either Italy or Salonika – or both. The Italian commander-in-chief, Luigi Cadorna, had also begun to warn that with the disintegration of the Eastern Front since the overthrow of the Tsar in February, there was a heavy buildup of not only Austro-Hungarian but also German troops on the Italian front. He was keen to mount another major summer offensive on the Isonzo, as promised at the inter-allied conference at Chantilly in November. It would be his eleventh offensive south-east towards Trieste (in Slovenia, then a province of the Austro-Hungarian empire) since Italy entered the war in May 1915: bloody, attritional fighting, sometimes with promising, but all too often temporary, gains.

In the Tenth Battle of the Isonzo, from 10 May to 8 June, Cadorna's *grigioverdi* ('grey-greens', the colour of their uniform) had almost broken through to Trieste, but were then pushed back almost to their starting lines by Austrian counter-attacks. Though Tenth Isonzo had inflicted heavy losses on the enemy, Cadorna now doubted he could mount an eleventh offensive unless reinforced. However, while the French and British had made contingency plans to send reinforcements if the Italians were attacked in overwhelming strength, as also agreed at Chantilly, both Robertson and his French counterpart, Ferdinand Foch, dug their heels in and refused anything more than artillery for an offensive.

Cadorna went ahead nevertheless, having managed to assemble fifty-one divisions and 5,200 guns. His object once more was the

Carso, the limestone plateau beyond the Italian bridgehead at Gorizia which had been captured exactly a year before. The preliminary bombardment – a single day, but intense – opened at 6 a.m. on 18 August. Unlike the struggle with the mud of Passchendaele, however, Dalton recalled that

> one had to guard against a dust cloud being raised by the blast of the guns, thus giving away our position to the enemy. To prevent this, we formed a chain of men every half hour to pass water-buckets from hand to hand, from the river just behind us down the sunken road, to lay the dust in and around the gun pits. But under an Italian August sun the ground soon grew parched and dusty again.

The Italian 3rd Army, under the duke of Aosta, son of King Amadeus of Spain (of the House of Savoy) and cousin of the Italian king, Emmanuele III, made good progress initially along the coastal plain, and 2nd Army under Luigi Capello, an outspoken general with a reputation as both a self-publicist and a 'butcher', advanced 7 miles in short order, taking five mountain peaks, over 20,000 Austro-Hungarian (and some German) prisoners, and most of the Bainsizza plateau south-east of Tolmino. However, 2nd Army's progress was so rapid that they outran their artillery and supplies, and Capello halted the advance to regain balance.

It was an unfortunate decision, for the Austro-Hungarians were probably at breaking point. By the time he resumed the offensive, resistance had stiffened, and his attacks, particularly in the mountains, were beaten back with heavy loss. Aosta's 3rd Army likewise was fought to a standstill. Cadorna again asked for heavy artillery to be sent from France, but the answer once more was 'no'. On 12 September he called off the offensive.

The 'butcher's bill' was a heavy one. The Italians admitted to 166,000 casualties: 40,000 dead, 108,000 wounded and 18,000 missing (prisoners of war or men subsequently accounted killed), losses some 25 per cent greater than in Nivelle's disastrous spring offensive on the Aisne. Morale in the Italian infantry fell noticeably. But the

Austro-Hungarians had taken serious casualties too, some 110,000: 15,000 dead, 65,000 wounded, 30,000 missing. Moreover, an additional 30,000 had been taken prisoner – a sure sign of collapsing morale – and a third of their artillery had been destroyed or captured.

Cadorna was now determined to mount a twelfth – and decisive – offensive as soon as he could make good his losses and gain reinforcements from the British and French. These both Robertson and Foch continued to refuse, having little faith in the remaining fighting spirit of the Italian army. Indeed, Haig demanded the return of 'his' artillery now that Cadorna's forces had gone back on to the defensive.

Unfortunately, however, the Austro-Hungarian high command would not wait for Cadorna to mount his Twelfth Battle of the Isonzo. Reinforced by more troops and up to 1,000 guns drawn from the disintegrating Eastern Front, as well as by five high-grade German divisions, including the *Alpenkorps*, in October they would strike a blow centred on Caporetto that would send the Italians in full retreat almost as far as Venice. Many more troops would then be sent from France to help them consolidate on the Piave than Cadorna had asked for in the summer (and with them, to the relief of 'Tommy', would come the Army Service Corps – and 'better' rations).

Meanwhile, during Cadorna's eleventh blood-letting on the Isonzo, London and Paris found themselves troubled by another Italian – the Pope, Benedict XV. Cardinal Giacomo della Chiesa had been elected to the papacy on 3 September 1914 at the comparatively young age of fifty-nine, probably for the very reason that the conclave of cardinals wanted a vigorous pope to deal with what Benedict himself would call 'the suicide of civilized Europe'. In his first encyclical letter, in November 1914, he had asked, albeit with a degree of circumlocution, but clearly referring to the invasion of neutral Belgium: 'Surely there are other ways and means whereby violated rights can be rectified. Let them be tried honestly and with good will, and let arms meanwhile be laid aside.'

But he had been more direct in his summary of the human

condition of Christian Europe: 'Race hatred has reached its climax; peoples are more divided by jealousies than by frontiers; within one and the same nation, within the same city there rages the burning envy of class against class; and amongst individuals it is self-love which is the supreme law over-ruling everything.'

Since he had made no concrete proposals, his appeal had brought no material response. He had then turned his efforts to limiting the war's spread, conducting behind-the-scenes diplomacy to prevent war between Italy and Austria. And because British diplomatic efforts were being made at the same time to persuade Italy to declare war on the side of the Entente, Benedict's initiative made him no friends in London.

In late 1915, after the Italians had entered the war, he had tried to broker a peace directly between Belgium, France and Germany. This foundered on the pact made in September 1914 by the Triple Entente powers (Britain, France and Russia) 'not to conclude peace separately during the present war'. Having failed in this, he had issued another general appeal for a negotiated peace, which was no better received than the first.

Benedict continued his efforts throughout 1916 and into the following spring, when he tried also to keep the Americans out of the war; and then, in August 1917, when it seemed as if all sides must be growing exhausted, he issued his most significant 'peace note'. In a preamble, he said that he wished

> no longer to dwell upon the general, as the circumstances suggested to us in the past: we want now to descend to more concrete and practical proposals, and to invite the governments of the belligerent peoples to agree upon the following points, which appear to be the bases of a just and lasting peace, leaving to the same governments to apply them at a specific level and to complete them.

These 'following [seven] points' ranged widely, and probably influenced President Woodrow Wilson's own 'Fourteen Points' speech of January 1918 proposing a basis for lasting peace (which, just as unrealistically as the Pope, if every bit as worthily, he called 'peace without victory').

Benedict's August peace note fell on no more fertile ground than his earlier initiatives. He had no influence in Russia, an Orthodox country, which was anyway imploding. Germany, though it had a sizeable Catholic population, especially in the south, was essentially Protestant, the land of Luther. France was as much anti-clerical as it was staunchly Catholic. Besides, Catholicism did not equate with ultramontanism: 'Holy Father, we do not want your peace,' was the message of one preacher in the church of La Madeleine in Paris. Austria-Hungary, the great Catholic empire, had long lost its soul to Berlin. Britain in many ways was still too close to the Spanish Armada and the Gunpowder Plot to regard Rome with anything but suspicion. And, indeed, Haig's diaries are disparaging of 'the Catholic people [certain officers]' whose hearts, he believed, were not in the fight. As for the Italians, their goal – the reason they had entered the war in the first place – was their ultimate unification, the repossession of *Italia Irredenta*, the parts of the territory still in Austrian hands; and it was, moreover, only forty-seven years earlier that Rome had been liberated from papal rule – by troops commanded by Cadorna's father. The Italian government mistrusted Benedict's motives, too (not entirely without reason), believing that in a negotiated settlement he would try to recover some of the former papal states. Italian newspapers suggested his name should not be 'Benedetto' ('blessed') but 'Maledetto' ('accursed').

Benedict's peace initiative would even be cited as one of the reasons for the Italian collapse at Caporetto. This, however, was another convenient excuse to distract from the failure of the Anglo-French high commands to regard the war on the Italian front as a continuation of that on the Western Front. Only with the 'crisis of the war', as Haig called it – the great last-ditch German offensive in spring 1918 – would the interrelationship of the two fronts be acknowledged by the creation of a *generalissimo*, Marshal Foch, to take supreme command of both.

38

SEPTEMBER
'Boom'

As Zeppelins and Gothas bomb London with impunity,
a new air service is conceived to counter them

While fatherhood of the Royal Air Force is usually attributed to Major-General Sir Hugh (later Marshal of the RAF Lord) 'Boom' Trenchard, who led the Royal Flying Corps on the Western Front, a paternity case could equally be brought against the South African Lieutenant-General (later Field Marshal Sir) Jan Smuts. In September 1917, daylight raids on London propelled his paper on the reorganization of aviation to the top of the war cabinet's agenda.

Jan Smuts had been a successful Boer commando leader in the South African War a decade and half earlier, but with the creation of the Union of South Africa in 1910 as a self-governing domin-ion, he had done much towards reconciliation. Indeed, in many ways he was as much an imperialist as his former adversaries. In 1914, when defence minister, he had put on uniform and taken command in the field against a Boer insurrection, then led opera-tions against German South-West Africa (now Namibia), and later in German East Africa. In the spring of 1917 he came to London to take part in the first imperial conference of the war.

In late 1916, during the Somme offensive, Sir Douglas Haig, commander-in-chief of British armies on the Western Front, began pressing urgently for twenty more squadrons of aircraft. These could not be found, however, without borrowing from the Royal Naval Air Service (RNAS), and it became clear that something was wrong with the supply of equipment and trained personnel for the two separate air services. While the RFC was preoccupied with the war in France, the RNAS was growing anxious about the air defence of its dockyards and arsenals in Britain. Raids by 'Zeppelins', the generic name for German airships irrespective of manufacture, and by Gotha bombers, were increasing, including attacks on civilian targets. The RNAS had taken offensive action against the Zeppelins from the start, bombing the airship sheds at Cologne and Düsseldorf in October 1914. The success of these prompted the director of the Admiralty's air department, Captain (later Rear-Admiral Sir) Murray Sueter, to commission the aircraft manufacturer Frederick Handley Page to produce a longer-range machine capable of dropping a heavier bomb – as Sueter put it, 'a bloody paralyser of an aircraft'. The result was the Handley Page Type O, the first British strategic bomber, which came into service towards the end of 1916. Twin-engined, with a crew of four or five, it had a range of 700 miles, eight hours' endurance and a top speed of just under 100 mph, and could carry 2,000 lb (907 kg) of bombs.

The RNAS was, however, divided between those advocating long-range bombing and those who saw the priority as cooperation with the fleet. Meanwhile, air defence of Britain remained the responsibility of the RFC, though the army believed that operations in France and Flanders had priority. Zeppelins had bombed London in 1915 and 1916, killing 500 people, and the RFC had been forced to allocate – divert – twenty-seven squadrons, with over 400 aircraft and some 17,000 officers and men, to air defence. The Royal Artillery, too, increasingly had to divert anti-aircraft guns and searchlights to cover London.

273

The airships countered by attacking at dusk and in darkness, using factory and street lighting as guides before enforcement of the blackout (first ordered in London in October 1914 and extended across the whole of England in February 1916). The defending aircraft found them difficult to attack because they flew high and their top speed was about equal to their own. At the start of the war, aircraft could not climb fast enough to intercept a Zeppelin before bombs were dropped, and, defended by five machine guns, it was a dangerous enemy to close with. Nevertheless, it was an early model, a BE2c biplane, flown by Lieutenant William Leefe-Robinson, that brought down the first airship over England, at Cuffley in Hertfordshire on the night of 2 September 1916. Leefe-Robinson repeatedly circled the Zeppelin, which was illuminated by several searchlight beams, firing at close range into its belly until it caught fire. For this action, he was awarded the VC.

The Germans' periodic ascendancy in aerial combat on the Western Front – notably the so-called 'Fokker scourge' from June 1915 until the allies produced comparable fighters ten months later, and then 'Bloody April' (1917), when the German 'flying circuses' gained temporary mastery again – was a growing concern of both GHQ in France and the War Ministry in London.

The press began to agitate, too. On 31 October 1916, *The Times* thundered at Lord Curzon's Air Board, which had been formed in May to improve coordination:

It is a week since we called attention to the deplorable deadlock which has paralysed the Air Board, and everything which has come to our notice since has continued that warning. In our opinion the Board was always doomed to failure. We described it when it was appointed as 'one more stopgap, which can only succeed by a miracle'; and the miracle has not happened. The fact is that the Air Board has never possessed the willing confidence and cooperation of both the Services concerned, and it was never invested with the formal authority required to override them. That it has existed for months without open and notorious scandal we attribute, first, to the energy with which it has faced an impossible task; and, second, to the supremacy which our airmen have lately achieved at the front. The public, and perhaps the Government, have been obsessed with this temporary triumph. There has been no long view of the reaction which will follow unless the organization of the Air Services – and especially the design, construction, and purchase of machines for both – is placed on a satisfactory footing.

Reaction of a sort came soon enough, as Zeppelin raids on London increased, almost with impunity. More RFC aircraft were diverted from the Western Front and elsewhere to cover the capital and east coast ports, and there was talk of forming a separate air ministry, and a separate air service, better to focus on air defence and strategic bombing. For the prime minister was acutely aware of his growing political predicament. The Passchendaele offensive was going nowhere but to even more graves, while the Germans were ranging almost at will over England; and the effects of the Royal Navy's blockade of Germany – which were steadily but surely undermining the enemy's ability to fight – were not discernible to the man in the street (or, indeed, to many senior military officers). A display of determination to deal with the aerial raiders by forming a separate force, and giving the Germans a taste of their own medicine by bombing, which would also supplement the work of the blockade, made both political and military sense.

Lloyd George was not without opposition at home when it came to strategic bombing, especially when it involved civilian deaths, which looked like reprisals. Bishops in the House of Lords spoke against it (as they would in the Second World War, notably after the bombing of Dresden). In April 1917, in retaliation for the sinking of two hospital ships, the RNAS bombed Freiburg. The Bishop of Ely declared bluntly that 'a policy of reprisals is essentially wrong.' On 13 June, 162 civilians were killed and 400 injured, including many children, in a daylight raid on London by fifteen Gothas. Seventy-two tons of bombs fell within a one-mile radius of Liverpool Street Station, while others fell at Fenchurch Street and in the East End. At a service for children killed in their schoolroom, the Bishop of

275

London, Arthur Winnington-Ingram, a strong supporter of the war effort from the outset (he had been a chaplain to the London Rifle Brigade – territorials – since 1901), echoed the protests, saying that he did not believe 'the mourners would wish that 16 German babies should lie dead to avenge their dead'.

RFC and RNAS aircraft had been barely able to get within striking distance of the bombers. When the Gothas returned on 7 July, the defenders made better contact, but only one was destroyed and the casualty list was still high at 57 killed and 193 injured. The *Daily Mail* reported that Britain had not been 'so humiliated since the Dutch Fleet sailed up the Thames in 1667' and called for the heads of those responsible.

The clamour for reprisals against German cities was as loud in Parliament as it was in the popular press and at Speakers' Corner in Hyde Park. William Joynson-Hicks, MP for Manchester North, and later a notably authoritarian home secretary, told Lloyd George: 'Every time the Germans raid London, British airmen must blot out a German town.'

Lloyd George decided he had to act. In June he had co-opted Smuts to the war cabinet, and now he asked him to carry out a study into the air defence of Britain, the air organization generally, and the arrangements for the higher direction of aerial operations. Smuts agreed at once. Indeed, he had already been consulting widely. The new chairman of the Air Board, Lord Cowdray, told him that aircraft production had so improved in late months that by 1918 there would be 3,000 machines surplus to known requirements, which would amply sustain an independent strategic bombing force. Within a month (on 17 August), Smuts had submitted his principal report to the war cabinet, recommending:

> We must create the new directing organization – the new Ministry and Air Staff which could properly handle this new instrument of offence, and equip it with the best brains at our disposal for the purpose. The task of planning the new Air Service organization [amalgamating

the RFC and RNAS] and thinking out and preparing for schemes of aerial operations next summer must tax our Air experts to the utmost.

The report met with a mixed response. The RFC and RNAS did not want to lose the connection with their respective services. Nor did Field Marshal Haig, and Admiral Sir David Beatty commanding the Home Fleet, want to lose command of their supporting aircraft, though the CIGS, Sir 'Wully' Robertson, and the first sea lord, Sir John Jellicoe, had no strong objection. Lloyd George began to have second thoughts, and, his spirits low with the news from France of the faltering Passchendaele campaign, in early September took a holiday. The press, not knowing of the actual Smuts report but hearing rumours of dissension in government and among senior officers, again began pressing for action, not least when the Germans mounted heavy attacks on London and the east coast over four successive nights at the end of September.

On 1 October the War Cabinet authorized retaliatory raids on Germany, though these proved slow in materializing. The following week, the cabinet received a paper showing that German aircraft production was increasing alarmingly, and on 15 October, during continued questions in Parliament, Andrew Bonar Law, Leader of the House of Commons, sensing serious disquiet, hinted at the formation of a separate service. It was confirmed in an official announcement the following day.

Much to Lloyd George's relief, but to the dismay of many, including 'Boom' Trenchard, who at this time opposed the concept of an independent strategic bombing force, in November the Air Force Bill would pass through Parliament with little opposition.

The Royal Air Force would formally come into being on 1 April 1918. The initials 'RAF', said those who opposed its creation still, stood for 'Royal April Foolers'.

39

OCTOBER
Caporetto

*A humiliating collapse of the Italian Front presages
victorious recovery a year later*

In October 1917, Freya Stark, who would later find fame as an explorer and travel writer, was a 24-year-old nurse with the British Red Cross on the Italian front. Her field ambulance just outside Gorizia lay close to the junction of the 2nd and 3rd Italian Armies, which for two years had been launching a succession of bloody offensives astride the Isonzo River. Some of these had made gains, some had been repulsed, and the eleventh, in August, had almost broken through on the coast towards Trieste, then a city of the Austro-Hungarian empire.

The Austrians had to date been standing on the defensive on this, their south-western, front in order to concentrate their efforts against the Russians and Serbs. With Russia in the grip of Bolshevik revolution and her army disintegrating, with Serbia over-run, and with Berlin willing to help, it was possible now to go on to the offensive. Indeed, it was not just possible; it was necessary. Another offensive by the Italians might just succeed.

When the Austrian offensive was launched, on 24 October, across the entire front from Lake Garda to the Gulf of Trieste, but with especial force at Caporetto (today Kobarid, Slovenia) in the Julian Alps, 20 miles north of Gorizia, it would precipitate a general retreat that was only halted a few miles from Venice. 'Caporetto', as the whole battle (strictly, Twelfth Isonzo) is popularly known, became a byword for national calamity and humiliation.

Freya Stark would be lucky not to be taken prisoner. Separated from the main body of her unit, five days after the Austrians struck, in darkness and with only what she could carry, she managed to cross one of the last bridges over the Tagliamento just hours before Italian engineers blew it up. Though already exhausted by long hours of nursing the mounting casualties, she would have another 60 miles to cover until reunited with the rest of her field ambulance beyond the Piave River.

In mid-October, aerial reconnaissance and other intelligence had alerted the Italian commander-in-chief, Luigi Cadorna, to the buildup of enemy troops, and he had therefore instructed his army commanders to adopt a defensive posture rather than continue with plans for a further offensive. The newly appointed commander of 2nd Army, Luigi Capello, who had distinguished himself in the Italo-Turkish War in Cyrenaica in 1912 and in successive battles of the Isonzo, disagreed with Cadorna's strategy. His defensive measures were half-hearted to say the least, and not helped by his succumbing to a kidney infection in the days before the Austrians struck.

Nor was the northern part of 2nd Army's front, in which Caporetto stood, expected to be the Austrian *Schwerpunkt* (main effort). Indeed, it was viewed as something of a quiet sector and used almost as a rest area. Some of the units there were considered unreliable: many conscripts were disaffected factory workers from Turin, where there had been a general strike in August (in which the Italian Marxist Antonio Gramsci was active), with much violence. Officers in several units of 2nd Army were reportedly in fear of their lives, and many conscripts had agreed among themselves that if the Austrians attacked they would at once surrender.

In August, the German commander-in-chief, Paul von Hindenburg, by now in effect viceroy, had become increasingly anxious about Austria-Hungary's staying power. The empire – war-weary and fissile, composed as it was of disparate nationalities whose grievances seemed to be increasing – looked on the brink of collapse. Consequently, the new, young emperor, Charles I (Franz Joseph had died the previous November), and his new chief of staff, Arthur Freiherr Arz von Straußenburg, had little difficulty in persuading Berlin to come to their aid. There is no evidence that Hindenburg believed an offensive could knock the Italians out of the war completely, but a heavy blow might unnerve them to the point of abandoning future offensive plans. Sixteen divisions – nine Austrian and seven German, including the Austrian Edelweiss Division and the German *Alpenkorps*, specialist mountain troops – were therefore secretly assembled to form a new army, the 14th, under the German General Otto von Below.

The following month, experts from the *Grosser Generalstab* in Berlin, led by the chemist Otto Hahn, who would win the Nobel Prize for his discovery of nuclear fission in 1938, went to the Italian front to reconnoitre suitable areas for an attack by chlorine–arsenic and phosgene gas. They recommended Caporetto, where the junction of valleys on the upper reaches of the Isonzo, and the likely weather, would most favour the discharge. A good road running west to the Venetian plain also favoured the sector.

In the event, bad weather delayed the attack for two days, but on 24 October the wind dropped, and fog settled across much of 2nd Army's front. At 2 a.m., 900 *Gasminenwerfer* – mortars firing gas shells – were triggered electrically, at once shrouding the defences at Piezzo in the valley north of Caporetto in deadly vapour. Knowing that their gas masks were effective for at best two hours, many troops simply fled, though 600 were killed. Austrian troops were able to cross the Isonzo unopposed and begin the outflanking movement. All then remained quiet until 6 a.m., just before dawn, when a mortar bombardment was directed at the trenches over much of the 12-mile front, with particular intensity at Caporetto and downstream at

280

Tolmino. Forty minutes later, 2,000 artillery pieces opened fire, targeting especially the road along which reserves were already moving up to reoccupy the abandoned defences.

At 8 a.m. two large mines were detonated under strongpoints on the heights either side of the valley, and the Austrian–German infantry attacked using specialist 'storm-troop' tactics and the new model Maxim light machine gun. Mountain troops infiltrated the strongpoints and batteries along the crests of the ridges to protect the flanks of the main attack, laying reinforced telephone cable as they did so to maintain contact with the artillery. Among the German troops taking part was Leutnant (later Field Marshal) Erwin Rommel, whose Württemberg Mountain Battalion took three peaks south of Caporetto and 9,000 prisoners in just over two days. Rommel himself won the coveted *Pour le Mérite* honour for his aggressive spirit, and used the experience of the assault to develop his own ideas about offensive tactics, of which he wrote in his 1937 book *Infanterie Greift An* ('Infantry Attacks'), which was said to have helped persuade Hitler to give him command of an armoured division in 1940.

For the Italians, it was almost impossible to hold out against this well-planned and well-executed attack. Although they beat back the enemy on either side of Below's main thrust, the penetration – up to 15 miles by nightfall – began to throw 2nd Army into disarray. Many troops, believing the situation lost, threw away their weapons, declaring hopelessly: 'Andiamo a casa!' (We're going home!)

As the offensive gained momentum in the following days, and 2nd Army troops on the flanks of the main thrust fell back so as not to be cut off in the parallel valleys, Below's divisions reached the open plain, the high road to the great valley of the Po, and for a while it looked as if there would be a complete collapse. Cadorna ordered a general retreat, hoping to stabilize the front on the Tagliamento, but 2nd Army had in effect disintegrated.

No army in full retreat is a pretty sight, and the stories of Italian indiscipline (and worse) are unedifying, but in truth there would be similar scenes in Sir Hubert Gough's 5th Army in March 1918, when the Germans launched their great *Kaiserschlacht* offensive on the Western Front. The Italian army did rally, and largely of its own will and capability. Fortunately, to the right of 2nd Army was the duke of Aosta's 3rd Army, with its right flank on the Gulf of Venice. Aosta's men had withstood the attacks on their front, and now as they withdrew to avoid envelopment they were able progressively to take over enough of the front to make a junction with 4th Army, commanded by Mario di Robilant. Di Robilant, withdrawing from the Carnic Alps west of 2nd Army, had been able to take up a strong defensive position on Monte Grappa and extend east to the Piave, which was fortuitously swollen by the autumn rains. Here, in the second week of November, his and Aosta's 3rd Army were at last able to bring Below's 14th Army and that of the Austrian General Svetozar Boroević to a complete halt.

Meanwhile, putting into action the contingency plans drawn up earlier in the year, eleven French and British infantry divisions, plus heavy artillery and aircraft, were rushed to Cadorna's aid from the Western Front. Although – with the exception of some of the artillery – they would not arrive in time to take a direct part in the fighting along the Piave, they helped strengthen the front subsequently and, with further reinforcements, would take part in the counter-offensives the following year which led to the Austrians suing for peace.

For the time being, however, the price of sending allied divisions from France was to be Cadorna's sword. On 8 November he was replaced by his former chief of operations Armando Diaz, a humane and highly respected Neapolitan, who would now have to play the part of Pétain after Verdun, nursing Italian morale back to health.

Diaz's task was prodigious. When the fighting died down in late November, the army had retreated over 100 miles. The 670,000 men of 2nd Army were widely scattered: over 280,000 of them were prisoners of war and a further 350,000 were simply absent, while 40,000 were dead or wounded. Over 3,000 artillery pieces and a similar number of machine guns had been lost, along with huge quantities of munitions, food, animal fodder, petrol and medical supplies. By contrast, Austrian–German casualties, killed and wounded, were around 70,000.

While Diaz's task was as urgent as Pétain's before him, therefore, it was also more complex, not least in respect of the army's reputation. Commanding Freya Stark's field ambulance was George Macaulay Trevelyan, described later as 'probably the most widely read historian in the world'. Writing of Caporetto, he concluded:

In order to understand the nature of the phenomenon, before inquiring into its causes, it is necessary to realize that there were three distinct categories of conduct among the Italian troops. To confuse any one of these three categories with either of the other two is to misunderstand the whole affair.

First, there were a few regiments who, in accordance with a previously-formed intention, abandoned their duty, and surrendered on purpose. This was 'Caporetto' in the narrower and more strictly accurate sense, for it was only in that geographical zone that such betrayal occurred; but unfortunately Caporetto was the key to the whole strategic position.

When, consequently, a general retreat had been ordered, the second category of conduct was observable in a much larger number of men . . .

[Second Army] carried out irreproachably the difficult retirement across the Isonzo gorge and out of the hills; but as they proceeded over the plain, hustled by the victorious enemy pouring down on their flank from Cividale, they were gradually infected by the sense that all was lost . . .

The last scenes of the Second Army were a sad falling from what the same men had shown themselves two months before.

The third and largest category of all consisted of the troops who did their duty throughout. Most of, though not quite all, the Third Army from the Carso, and the Fifth, First, and Fourth Armies on the Cadore and Trentino fronts, saved Italy by holding fast where required, and retreating in order where necessary, so that the shorter line was successfully established in the early days of November.

Many heroic feats of individual companies, regiments, and divisions illumined the worst hours of the Retreat. And some of the finest of these were performed by units of the Second Army itself, both in the mountain region of Matajur above Caporetto, and in the plain of Udine.

When Freya Stark herself crossed the Piave and stumbled into Padua to be reunited with her field ambulance, she had not bathed for a month, nor rested in sixty-four hours. She was amazed to find the place full of shops selling 'ordinary things', and people going about their business despite the growing number of military refugees. After taking a bath and some sleep, she ventured out and in one of the shops bought a chiffon blouse. 'It was the most frivolous and unwarlike thing to catch my eye,' she wrote in her diary. She had already written, 'I weep so easily now.'

40

NOVEMBER
Cambrai

The first mass tank attack gains spectacular results, but they are overturned in an impressive German counter-offensive

'Just a line. A big battle has begun & we are taking the leading part. In fact it could not have taken place without us . . .' wrote Lieutenant-Colonel J. F. C. 'Boney' Fuller, on the staff of the Tank Corps, to his mother on 20 November 1917. 'I believe the attack was one of the most magnificent sights of the war, great numbers of Ts forging ahead in line of battle followed by infantry . . . Elles our General led the battle in a T, flying our colours. I am glad to say he has returned safely, though the flag has been shot to tatters.'

The Battle of Cambrai was born of the disappointments of Third Ypres (Passchendaele). In July, just before the opening of his great offensive to break through at Ypres and capture the Channel ports, Field Marshal Sir Douglas Haig, a cavalryman, told his army commanders that 'opportunities for the employment of cavalry in masses are likely to offer'. Meanwhile, on the other side of no-man's-land, the German chief of staff, General Erich Ludendorff, an infantry-man, was convinced that 'trench warfare offered no scope for cavalry'. Indeed, he wanted to dismount them and give their horses to the artillery and transport: 'The wastage in horses was extraordinarily high, and the import from neutral countries hardly worth the consideration.'

But while Ludendorff saw the Western Front as siege warfare on an industrial scale, Haig, as a fellow general put it, regarded it as 'mobile operations at the halt'. Ever since succeeding Sir John French (also a cavalryman) as commander-in-chief in December 1915, he had constantly sought a return to the war of movement of 1914. In his view – and that of the army's 'bible', *Field Service Regulations* – decisive success in the field was to be achieved only by robust attack. In Haig's view, this meant an offensive leading to breakthrough followed by rapid exploitation, in which cavalry would be of the first importance.

Both sides had tried to break through in 1915, but without success, leaving their cavalry champing at the bit in frustration. It was the same again in 1916, first for the Germans at Verdun, and then for the British and French on the Somme. Fortunately, away from the front, minds had been at work on the problem of how to penetrate the German lines. In February 1915, Winston Churchill, then first lord of the admiralty, impatient with the War Office's lack of interest in mechanical trench-crossing devices, had himself set up the 'Admiralty Landships Committee' to investigate their potential. Seven months later, in September 1915, the first design was tested; by December a completely new and improved version was produced; and in January 1916 this first 'tank' was demonstrated to the War Office – which was sufficiently impressed to place an order for 100 of them, equipped with either 6-pounder cannon or Hotchkiss and Vickers machine guns. Thirty tanks went into action in the middle of September during the Somme battles; although most of them broke down prematurely, or were engulfed in the mud, nevertheless Haig recognized their worth and ordered several hundred more.

Opinions as to how the new weapon was to be used were divided. Some officers in the Heavy Section, Machine Gun Corps, the unit responsible for fielding the tank, believed from the outset that they should be used en masse and with a degree of independence. Inter-communication was only by hand or flag signals, however, and reliability remained a problem. Fosters, the Lincoln firm responsible for the development work, had been contracted for engineering tolerances of just 50 miles between breakdowns, which – allowing for movement to the start line from the railheads – did not envisage any great part in advancing. The War Office, and moreover Haig's GHQ, saw tanks essentially as battering rams to crush the initial defences – the multiple trench lines and fortified positions – in order to allow the cavalry to break out.

Haig certainly had high hopes of them at Third Ypres. He had some 140 available for the offensive, all but two of which made it to the start line without mishap. But the mud of Passchendaele would prove even worse than that of the Somme; soon the tanks were stuck fast, and once again the cavalry stood waiting in vain for the breakthrough.

Morale in the new Tank Corps, formed from the Machine Gun Corps on 27 July, fell, as did the confidence of the rest of the army in the tank. The corps needed to be given a fighting chance, on ground specially chosen – better drained and not pock-marked with shell craters. HQ Tank Corps therefore proposed an offensive towards Cambrai. However, planning for Cambrai – originally conceived as a raid, a limited action to show what the tank could do in the right conditions – soon fell prey to the continuing ambition for breakthrough and restoration of the war of movement. Not the least in ambition was another cavalryman, General Sir Julian Byng, recently appointed to command of 3rd Army after Haig had sacked Edmund Allenby, and now given responsibility for the battle as a whole. In 1757, one of his ancestors, Admiral John Byng, had faced a firing squad – *pour encourager les autres* – for failing to press his attack on a French fleet off Minorca. General Byng was not going to make the same sort of mistake.

He decided to throw all his divisions into the attack, and all his allotted fighting tanks – 380 of them (the Tank Corps now had 476 machines in all, including spares and various specialist tanks) – leaving himself without reserves. Haig placed virtually the entire Cavalry Corps, some 27,500 cavalrymen and their support troops, under Byng's command, with the intention that they should 'pass through and operate in open country'.

The preparations were prodigious. Some of the regiments had to march long distances to the assembly areas – the Queen's Bays, for example, 106 miles in five night marches. Oats and hay for the horses – 270 tons – had to be pre-positioned. 'Cavalry track battalions' were formed, largely of Indian NCOs and sowars (troopers) recently arrived in France as reinforcements, to make gaps in the barbed wire and fill in or bridge the trenches and shell holes to help get the cavalry forward in the wake of the advancing tanks and infantry. With pick and shovel, assisted by tanks fitted with grapnels to tear up the wire, they were expected to clear paths 60 yards wide to a depth of 5 miles, bridging twenty-six successive lines of trenches.

The battle began well. On 20 November, in an obliging morning mist and before a single artillery round had been fired, the massed tanks answered to the command 'Driver, advance!' Favoured by the absence of the usual artillery notification, and their own quite remarkable success in concealment during the build-up (aided by the RFC's local air superiority), the tanks took the Germans wholly by surprise. When the following infantry reached the forward trenches they found flasks of hot coffee at the firing step – breakfast hastily abandoned. On a 6-mile front, checked only at Flesquières, by midday Byng's divisions were able to penetrate 5 miles into the defences of the Hindenburg Line – further to date than anywhere on the Somme or in Flanders. By early afternoon, only a half-finished fourth line stood between 3rd Army and open country, and here there was a wide-open gap for several hours.

An advance of 5 miles, even a relatively easy one, was tiring, however. By now the tanks were crewed by men exhausted by noise, fumes and concussive vibrations, or were out of action owing to breakdown or enemy fire. The infantry could make no further progress without them, and if the infantry could make no progress, the cavalry certainly couldn't. Besides, for whatever reason – poor communications, lack of 'dash' in regiments that had been inactive for three years (recriminations would follow) – the cavalry were slow getting forward.

And they certainly *were* expected by the Germans. Leutnant Miles Reinke of *2 Garde-Dragoner Regiment* wrote home: 'We waited for several regiments of cavalry to sweep up and drive us towards Berlin. But this didn't happen, much to our surprise.' Indeed, expecting to be over-run at any minute, they had even abandoned Cambrai itself.

With no reserve of tanks and infantry to renew the attacks, Byng told his spent troops to dig in, and the cavalry, when they did come up in the afternoon, to hold along the St-Quentin Canal. German reserves began pouring into the breaches, and the following morning, after a night of icy rain, the British faced the predictable counter-attacks.

Haig sent more divisions to Cambrai, but it was too late. Byng's renewed attacks on 22 and 23 November quickly petered out, while with impressive speed, and largely undetected, the Germans massed twenty divisions for a counter-offensive. These came out of the morning mist on 30 November after a short, intense bombardment consisting of high explosive, gas and smoke – but with almost no tanks, for the Germans did not rate them. Using new infiltration techniques they thrust at both flanks of the salient created by 3rd Army's advance, breaking through in the south. Byng's infantry put up a resolute defence, and disaster was averted, but only with considerable loss, including Brigadier-General Roland Boys Bradford VC, MC – at twenty-five the youngest brigade commander of modern times, who had been in command for just three weeks.

Byng was now forced to abandon the greater part of his original gains. German casualties at Cambrai were around 50,000; the BEF's were 45,000 (of which 10,000 were dead), yet with nothing to show for it, just the sense of a 'near miss', a demonstration of what the tank could do in the attack if well handled. The church bells, which had rung in England on the first day to announce a resounding victory, had sounded prematurely.

A board of inquiry was held in London to examine how the spectacular initial success had turned into another costly reverse. Byng survived, as did Haig, though the perceived intelligence failures led to the dismissal of his chief of intelligence, Brigadier-General John Charteris.

However, the tank had at last proved itself. Production was now stepped up, and faster types were developed. From Cambrai on, it was seen as an essential element in the all-arms battle, which was itself the key to any sustained success on the Western Front.

As 'Boney' Fuller wrote to his mother, Brigadier-General Hugh Elles had led the Tank Corps into the battle 'flying our colours', which were 'shot to tatters'. The flag was in fact almost as famously improvised as the 'Star-Spangled Banner' at the defence of Fort McHenry. Nothing had been done about distinguishing colours for the Corps, and so just before the battle Elles went into a French shop to find material for a flag. Although stocks were small, he managed to buy some lengths of brown, red and green silk, which were then sewn together and flown from his tank, *Hilda*. Fuller suggested that the colours typified the struggle of the Corps – 'From mud, through blood to the green fields beyond.'

Ever after, the flag has been flown with the green uppermost.

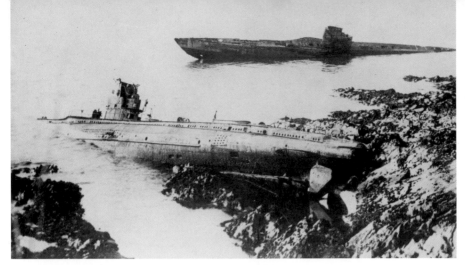

Above U-boat warfare: U-86 wrecked after the war. Initially German U-boats operated under the Hague Convention's 'cruiser rules', by which the passengers and crew of an unarmed ship were warned before attack so that they could take to the lifeboats. After the Kaiser finally re-authorized unrestricted submarine warfare in January 1917, some U-boat commanders were pitiless in their attacks. On 27 June 1918, U-86 torpedoed the Canadian hospital ship *Landovery Castle*, then surfaced and machine-gunned the survivors in the lifeboats. In all, 234 medical officers, nurses, orderlies, wounded troops and seamen died. There were just 24 survivors.

Right The pilot and observer of an RE8 biplane of 59 Squadron RFC are briefed before a mission, St-Omer, 1917. In 1914 the RFC and RNAS could muster around a hundred aircraft for operational service. By the end of the war, the RAF, formed by amalgamating the separate services on 1 April 1918, had some 22,000 aircraft.

Left 'Lafayette we are here!' General John J. 'Black Jack' Pershing, C-in-C American Expeditionary Force, arrives at Boulogne in June 1917. The entry of the US into the war was the certain guarantee of ultimate victory, but exactly how this was to be achieved would cause much allied disagreement – as would President Wilson's ideas about the peace terms to be offered the Germans.

Above The collapse of the Eastern Front: Russian troops captured in the final 'Kerensky' offensive of July 1917, named after the chairman of the Russian provisional government. It was singularly ill-timed, after the February revolution: calls for peace were increasing, especially in the army, whose material capability and morale had been rapidly deteriorating since autumn 1916. The Germans were now able to transfer troops to the Western Front, and to reinforce the Austrians on the Italian front.

Left An army in defeat: the Italian front, October 1917. Reinforced by 'crack' German divisions, and using poison gas to devastating effect, the Austro-Hungarian army mounted a huge surprise offensive in the Julian Alps, with its *Schwerpunkt* (point of greatest effort) at Caporetto, now Kobarid in Slovenia. British and French heavy artillery, aircraft and then troops were rushed from the Western Front to help stem the tide, but the Italians were eventually able to halt the offensive on the Piave. The loss of sovereign territory was humiliating; however, a year to the day, the Italians would launch a counter-offensive that knocked Austria out of the war.

Right Ottoman machine guns in Palestine. General Sir Edmund Allenby's arrival as C-in-C in July 1917 reinvigorated the British and imperial troops of the Egyptian Expeditionary Force, which in the autumn swept north through Gaza and by Christmas had taken Jerusalem.

Above left 'Good God, did we really send men to fight in that?' Haig's chief of staff is meant to have said when he saw the ground over which Third Ypres ('Passchendaele') was fought. Men of the 4th Australian Division on a duckboard track passing through the remains of Chateau Wood, near Hooge in the Ypres salient, October 1917 – a landscape which Paul Nash's modernist *The Menin Road* (painted 1919) could hardly make more nightmarish.

Above right His 'Christmas present to the nation' (and to Lloyd George): Allenby entering Jerusalem on foot by the Jaffa Gate on 11 December 1917, the gesture of a shrewd, confident and arguably great commander. 'Only one man rides into Jerusalem,' he said simply (Jesus of Nazareth had, of course, entered the city on a donkey on Palm Sunday via the Golden Gate, on the east side).

Left Who was giving orders to whom? The Kaiser (*centre*) remained the commander-in-chief of the German army, but from late 1916 Hindenburg (*pointing*), chief of the *Grosser Generalstab*, began increasingly to direct the entire war effort, including industrial policy. Meanwhile, Ludendorff (*right*) acted increasingly as commander-in-chief of the armies in the field, directing military strategy. Ludendorff suffered a nervous collapse in October 1918, and shortly afterwards resigned. The Kaiser abdicated on 9 November. Hindenburg remained in post until July 1919. In 1925 he would become the second elected president of the German Reich.

Above A war of movement at last: Canadian troops on the Arras–Cambrai road, September 1918, with an abandoned Renault FT light tank, during the three-month allied counter-offensive – the 'Hundred Days' – which brought the Germans on the Western Front to their knees.

Left British Mark V tanks, carrying fascines to assist in trench and ditch crossing, advancing during the 'Hundred Days'.

Left British and Italian troops passing abandoned Austrian artillery in the Val d'Assa, 2 November 1918, after the victory at Vittorio Veneto. The following day, Vienna accepted the Italians' terms for an armistice.

Above left To the victors . . . The Generalissimo, Foch (*third from left*) with his Western Front C-in-Cs: to his left Pershing, his right Haig, and on Haig's right, Pétain.

Above right To the victors . . . The fourth C-in-C, Diaz, who nursed the Italian army back to health after Caporetto, then on the battle's anniversary launched a counter-offensive that expelled the Austrians from Italian soil and brought about their complete collapse. (The C-in-C of the Macedonian front, Franchet d'Espèrey, answered in effect directly to the French government, not to Foch.)

Left To the victors . . . the 'Big Four' at the Paris peace conference, 1919: Lloyd George talking to Orlando; Clemenceau ('Le Tigre') facing the camera squarely; and Wilson in elegant profile. Making peace as allies would prove every bit as tricky as making war, not least because Wilson sought a new approach to international relations in the post-war world – his famous 'Fourteen Points' – whereas the European allies were more concerned with weakening Germany.

THE ART OF WAR

No war before or since has been painted so much and in so many different styles. Official war artists were appointed early in the fighting to record the supreme human endeavour.

Above *Canadian Artillery in Action*: a 6-inch howitzer on the Somme, July 1916, depicted by the Toronto-born Kenneth Forbes. A combatant officer in the (British) Machine Gun Corps, he had been wounded and gassed, and thereafter appointed an official war artist. The painting shows the exhausting 'industrial' nature of the gunners' work – as well as the danger.

Below *The Zeebrugge Raid*, 23 April 1918, by Charles de Lacy. HMS *Vindictive* landing men on the mole by night, with others going ashore from the *Iris*, a Mersey ferry, behind; star shells illuminate the action, in which many a VC was won.

Above *Made on the Wing*: RAF scouts leaving their aerodrome on patrol over the Asiago Plateau, Italy, 1918, by Sydney Carline. Himself a pilot, Carline sketched the scene in watercolours from the observer's seat in the fourth aircraft.

Above *Charge of the [Australian] 3rd Light Horse Brigade at the Nek*, Gallipoli, 7 August 1915, by George Lambert. As a diversion in support of an attack by New Zealand troops, the 3rd Light Horse were ordered to take the Turkish trenches at 'the Nek', a narrow, sheer-sided ridge, at first light. The artillery bombardment was ineffective and the Turks stood-to their machine guns. Despite the losses in the first wave, the Australians pressed the attack, suffering nearly 400 casualties in a very restricted area. The attack, if not a model of tactical judgement, became a symbol of defiant Australian courage.

Above 'Good God, did we really send men to fight in that?' *The Menin Road*, by Paul Nash.

Below The man on whom it all depended, whether British, French, Italian or American – the NCO. *Grenadier Guardsman* (1918) by Sir William Orpen. The model was Sergeant Stanley Burton, of Hulme, Manchester – at the time of the painting, 35 years old. He had joined the Grenadiers in 1902; recalled to the colours in 1914, he was promoted sergeant in 1917 and won the Military Medal in July that year at Third Ypres.

41

DECEMBER

'How the devil can we finish this war?'

*Another year of failed allied offensives closes
with dismal prospects for the next*

New Year's Eve on the Western Front in 1917 was an occasion for 'fireworks'. In *Undertones of War*, Edmund Blunden, who had joined the army in 1915 almost straight from school and was now a captain in the Royal Sussex, with a Military Cross from the Somme, and still not fully recovered from being gassed in November, wrote of the 'successions of coloured lights . . . but the sole answer to the unspoken but importunate questions was the line of lights in the same relation to Flanders as at midnight a year before. All agreed that 1917 had been a sad offender. All observed that 1918 did not look promising at its birth.'

It was certainly true of the Western Front – and indeed the Eastern and Southern: each new offensive in 1917 had failed. What was left of the Eastern Front was falling apart as Russia descended into civil war. On 15 December an armistice was signed between the new Bolshevik government and the Central Powers, and from the Baltic to the Black Sea the guns fell silent. On the Southern Front(s)

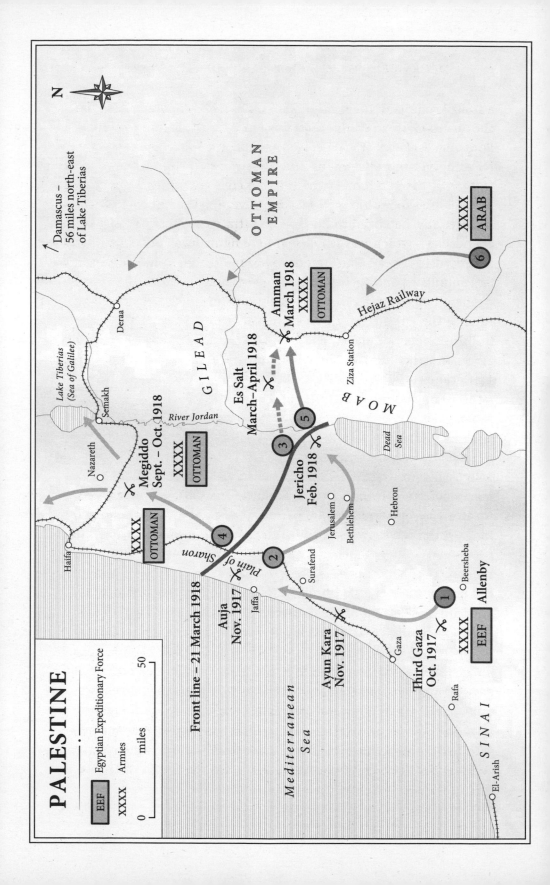

a sizeable chunk of the north Italian plain lay in enemy hands after the Austro-German counter-offensive in October, and in December Romania, isolated after the Russian collapse, gave up the fight, releasing yet more Germans and Bulgarians for the Macedonian front. On the Western Front, the French were still licking their wounds after the ruinous Nivelle offensive, and the British, now the stronger ally, had been stopped in their tracks at Third Ypres (Passchendaele) – which was why the line of lights in Flanders had not advanced in a year. The Americans were arriving, but not yet in large numbers, and their troops were very green.

There had been good news further afield, however: Jerusalem, whence the Ottomans exercised their rule in Palestine, had fallen to British and Dominion troops of General Sir Edmund Allenby's Egyptian Expeditionary Force. Allenby himself entered the city on 11 December by the Jaffa Gate on the western side, but on foot rather than mounted in the traditional fashion of the victorious general. 'Only one man rides into Jerusalem,' he said simply, though Jesus of Nazareth had entered the city on 'Palm Sunday' via the Golden Gate, on the east side.

Jerusalem had fallen without a shot, too. Allenby had simply outmanoeuvred the Turks, and within a mere six months of arriving in theatre. Having been relieved of command of 3rd Army in France in June, in the wake of the failure to make progress at Arras, he had been chosen by Lloyd George to replace the hapless Sir Archibald Murray after the second failure to break through the Turkish defences at Gaza, which held the key to Palestine. Murray had been a serial failure – first as chief of staff of the BEF in 1914 under Sir John French, then as CIGS in London, and now as a commander-in-chief. He was, however, a methodical planner; it had been his eye for detail that had mastered the immense logistical challenge of crossing the Sinai desert and got the EEF to the other side. On the other hand, Allenby, 'the Bull', brought dynamism to the campaign. Although he was now facing Field Marshal Erich von Falkenhayn, who had worsted the Romanians in September before being made commander-in-chief of the Ottoman army group in Palestine,

Allenby was well served by his three corps commanders: the infantryman Lieutenant-General Edward Bulfin, the cavalryman Philip Chetwode, and the Australian Henry Chauvel – 'Light Horse Harry' – who, unusually even in the higher ranks of the Australian forces, was a regular.

In early November, Allenby broke the Gaza defences by a surprise attack at Beersheba, whose famed wells would prove invaluable to Chauvel's Desert Mounted Corps of 'Anzac' light horsemen and British Yeomanry. Now the pace could quicken, for hitherto, especially during the transit of Sinai, water had been a constant problem, and much reliance had had to be placed on the slower-moving camel for both reconnaissance and logistics.

Having opened the door to Palestine at Gaza, Allenby now pressed his advance on two axes, one towards Jaffa, the other towards Jerusalem. On 12 November four divisions of the Ottoman 8th Army counter-attacked in front of Wadi Sara Junction on the Jaffa–Jerusalem railway, but were held by the Australian Mounted Division fighting dismounted. In turn, the following day, Bulfin's XXI Corps, augmented by elements of Chauvel's, attacked and dislodged 8th Army who were deployed in hastily constructed but naturally strong defences. This and the failure of the Turk rearguards to check XXI Corps' follow-up in the coming days forced 8th Army out of Jaffa, while 7th Army withdrew into the Judean Hills to defend Jerusalem.

Despite a series of counter-attacks in the coming days checking the first attempt to surround Jerusalem, on 8 December Chetwode's corps, which had relieved Bulfin's in the advance, took the heights to the west of the city, and the Turks, now threatened with envelopment, gave up the ground that evening.

Exactly what happened the following morning is the subject of much anecdote. The mayor of Jerusalem, Hussein Salim al-Husseini, wanting to spare the city from bombardment, rode out to deliver the Ottoman governor's letter surrendering the city to Allenby's forces, but had difficulty finding anyone to accept it. In his memoir *The Romance of the Last Crusade: With Allenby to Jerusalem*, Major Vivian

Gilbert of the Machine Gun Corps recounts how the mayor's first attempt to hand over the letter – to a foraging cook, a certain Private Murch of 'one of the London regiments', met with failure. Murch's commanding officer had sent him into the village of Lifta to find eggs for breakfast. The cook, 'a miserable specimen', his clothes 'covered with grease and filth', wearing a misshapen helmet 'at least one size too small', and in boots so worn that his 'very big red toe' stuck out of one of them, got lost and stumbled into the mayor's party.

In broken English al-Husseini addressed him: 'Where is General Allah Nebi? I want to surrender the city please. Here are the keys; it is yours!'

'Murch' (Gilbert appears to have disguised his true identity) is supposed to have replied, in rich Cockney: 'I don't want yer city. I want some eggs for my hofficers!'

The mayor rode on and some time later came across two scouting sergeants, James Sedgewick and Frederick Hurcomb, of the 19th Battalion, London Regiment (Territorials). They too refused to take the letter, but sent word of it back. Eventually Brigadier-General Charles Watson, commanding the 180th (London) Brigade, came forward, found the mayor and rode with him to the city where a small but jubilant crowd met them outside the Jaffa gate. Watson formally accepted the surrender and returned to his headquarters, only to learn that the divisional commander, Major-General John Shea, a Bengal Lancer, was on his way to take the surrender instead. Watson therefore rode back to Jerusalem with the keys and asked the mayor to wait for General Shea.

Shea arrived by car not long afterwards and was warmly greeted by a now larger crowd. The mayor once again surrendered the city and both he and the general gave short speeches, to loud cheers.

On returning to his headquarters, Shea telegraphed to Allenby: 'I have the honour to report that I have this day accepted the surrender of Jerusalem.'

Allenby, however, appreciating that the moral significance of taking Jerusalem was far greater than its military importance, immediately telegraphed back that he would 'himself accept the surrender of Jerusalem on the 11th inst'. Shea again returned the keys to the mayor, and two days later Allenby made his pointedly humble entry. It was a gesture not lost on the Arabs, who had seen the Kaiser enter the city on a white horse during his visit to the Holy Land twenty years before.

Although it would be another ten months before the whole of Palestine was occupied, the fall of Jerusalem was indeed a fillip to British morale. In one respect, however, Britain's troubles here were only just beginning, for there were conflicting promises to be reconciled. Grand Sharif Hussein ibn Ali al-Hashimi, guardian of the holy city of Mecca, had been given to understand that by siding with Britain and the western allies against Constantinople, he would win unity and independence for the Arabs at the end of the war; in particular, that London would recognize the independence of a united Arab state comprising the Arab provinces of the Ottoman Empire, including all of Palestine. In May 1916, however, Britain, France and Russia had reached a secret agreement in which the major part of Palestine was to be 'internationalized', and in subsequent developments a letter sent secretly by Arthur Balfour, secretary of state for foreign affairs, to the British Zionist Baron de Rothschild promised support for the establishment in Palestine of a 'national home' for the Jewish people. The 'Balfour Declaration' would become one of the future League of Nations' first and thorniest problems.

To the high command on the Western Front, however, Palestine was a sideshow, for it occupied few Germans: only in France and Flanders could Germany be beaten, for that was where Germany's strength lay (though not, of course, its weakness). Yet how was the German army to be beaten after three years of failed offensives? General Émile Fayolle, who had been appointed to command the French central army group when Philippe Pétain was made commander-in-chief, before being sent to Italy in the wake of Caporetto, confided bleakly to his diary: 'How the devil can we finish this war?'

There were indeed some voices suggesting that the allies – in particular Britain – could not do so without self-defeating losses, and therefore should not try to end the war by force of arms. The most compelling of the advocates for a negotiated peace was the Marquess of Lansdowne, who in November 1916, as the Somme offensive dragged on with increasing losses, had put a memorandum before the cabinet forcing them to confront the scale of slaughter of the country's young men, arguing that continuing the war would destroy the nation's vital strength, and proposing that peace be negotiated on the basis of the *status quo ante bellum* – in other words, without annexations or reparations.

The memorandum was not well received, and when Lloyd George became prime minister the following month, Lansdowne was quietly dropped from the cabinet. For many months, however, he continued to try to persuade his former colleagues of his argument, before deciding to mount a public campaign. He invited the editor of *The Times*, Geoffrey Dawson, to publish a letter outlining his proposals for a negotiated peace, but Dawson decided that publication was not in the national interest. Lansdowne then offered the letter to the *Daily Telegraph*, which published it on 29 November 1917:

> We are not going to lose this war, but its prolongation will spell ruin for the civilised world, and an infinite addition to the load of human suffering which already weighs upon it ... We do not desire the annihilation of Germany as a great power ... We do not seek to impose upon her people any form of government other than that of their own choice ... We have no desire to deny Germany her place among the great commercial communities of the world.

The letter was almost universally condemned as 'a deed of shame'. It was also probably unrealistic, for later research suggested that the German government's minimum peace terms would have been incompatible with Lansdowne's proposals, which would have been summarily rejected by Berlin. Field Marshal Haig, for one, countered by saying that the prospects for 1918 were 'excellent'.

If Haig's prediction was necessarily confident – he had the

morale of an army to maintain – it was nevertheless disingenuous. On 28 December, writing in his diary of his first proper meeting with General John J. ('Black Jack') Pershing, commander-in-chief of the American Expeditionary Force (AEF), Haig recorded that he had told the US general that he was expecting a huge German offensive to be mounted in the spring, that the 'crisis of the war would be reached in April', and that he had one question for Pershing: how might the AEF help?

What Haig could not yet have appreciated, however, was that there was soon to be a sea change in the allied direction of the war. On 16 November Georges Clemenceau, at seventy-six still the most dynamic of all French politicians – he was not known as 'the Tiger' for nothing – became prime minister. From an office in the war ministry, rather than the Matignon, the premier's traditional residence, 'Le Tigre' declared his policy in the simplest of terms: 'Je fais la guerre' – 'I [intend to] make war.'

He had once said that war was too important to be left to the generals; and he was now determined that he (and Lloyd George) would direct the strategy in the year ahead.

PART FIVE

1918

Finis Germaniae

3 March: Russia signs (peace) Treaty of Brest-Litovsk.

21 March: Germany launches spring offensive.

15 July: Second Battle of the Marne begins.

8 August: Battle of Amiens ('the black day of the German army').

21 August: Beginning of the 'Hundred Days' (allied counter-offensive).

24 October: Battle of Vittorio Veneto (Italian front) begins.

30 October: Turks sign Armistice (throughout Middle East); Bulgarians sign Armistice (fighting on Macedonian front effectively ceases).

3 November: Austria-Hungary signs Armistice (Italian front).

9 November: German Kaiser Wilhelm II abdicates and flees Germany.

11 November: Germany signs Armistice at Compiègne.

42

JANUARY
Peace without Victory?

'And I said to the man who stood at the gate of the year:
"Give me a light that I may tread safely into the unknown."'

King George VI made these lines famous by including them in his 1939 Christmas broadcast to the Empire. They begin the poem 'God Knows', written by the English missionary Minnie Haskins, later a tutor at the London School of Economics, and published privately in 1912. Had they been spoken by George VI's father, George V, at Christmas 1917, they would have been scarcely less apt. But unlike January 1940, at the gate of the year in 1918 there was indeed a man with a light wishing to share it: President Woodrow Wilson.

Yet Wilson was not so much answering the despairing question that the French General Émile Fayolle had confided to his diary as the new year came – 'How the devil can we finish this war?' – as proposing how the enemy might be persuaded to end it. The United States had entered the war in April 1917, Wilson insisting on the (largely symbolic) term 'co-belligerent' rather than 'ally' to define his country's status in the conflict, but up to now the US had been not so much a 'co-belligerent' as a non-belligerent. Except at sea,

301

and in the air, US forces had seen little fighting. The American Expeditionary Force, under General John 'Black Jack' Pershing, was still in formation and training. The US army was having to expand even more rapidly than the British army had had to do in the first year of the war, the intention being to put a million men into the field by the end of 1918, starting from a regular army strength of at most 150,000.

Wilson's light by which to tread safely into the unknown came in the form of the 'Fourteen Points', which he put to Congress on 8 January 1918. The United States, he said, had entered the conflict as 'a war for freedom and justice and self-government'. While this was designed in part to appeal to domestic idealism, his intention was also to exploit the fragility of the enemy's 'multinationality'. The Central Powers principally comprised three multinational empires: the German Hohenzollern (the most homogeneous, but not without internal tensions), the Austro-Hungarian Hapsburg (the most polyglot, culturally and religiously diverse), and the Ottoman Turkish, which even before the war resembled the Roman Empire in its over-extended, terminal stages.

Wilson deliberately played to the growing ethnic unrest in the Austro-Hungarian Empire by promising independence and self-determination for all the nationalities involved, extending this to include those of the former Russian Empire, which since the Bolshevik Revolution in November 1917 was in a state of incipient civil war and had withdrawn from the allied war effort to negotiate a separate peace.

Eight of the Fourteen Points addressed specific territorial issues, the most important of which was that Alsace and Lorraine should be returned to France. The other six addressed the future conduct of international relations, prescribing an end to secret treaties; reciprocal and free trade; limits on national armaments; impartial adjudication of competing colonial claims; and 'freedom of the seas', an objective that would have the distinction of being opposed by Britain, France and Germany alike. Most significant, however, was Wilson's fourteenth point, that 'a general association of nations must be formed under specific covenants for the purpose of affording mutual guarantees of political independence and territorial integrity to great and small states alike' – the League of Nations.

'The day of conquest and aggrandizement is gone by,' he declared, and it was 'this happy fact, now clear to the view of every public man whose thoughts do not still linger in an age that is dead and gone, which makes it possible for every nation whose purposes are consistent with justice and the peace of the world to avow now or at any other time the objects it has in view.'

In Wilson's call for a just and stable peace there were echoes of Pope Benedict XV's 'peace note' of August 1917, in which he called for 'peace without victory' – a note given short shrift by both the allies and the Central Powers. In truth, though, while Wilson's Fourteen Points offered a measure of succour to nationalists in the Austro-Hungarian Empire, who increasingly equated peace with their coming independence, they would do little to hasten the end of the war. They would, however, form the agenda for the peace conference in Paris that followed.

For the time being, largely at the urging of the British prime minister, David Lloyd George, the allied leaders strove to arrive at a more unified strategic approach to the war. At their emergency meeting at Rapallo in November 1917, after the débâcle at Caporetto, when the Italian army was thrown back almost to the Venetian lagoon, the French, British and Italian prime ministers approved the creation of a 'supreme war council' at Versailles to coordinate military policy, initially with respect to Italy, but also with a view to the strategy for the Western Front in the coming year. Lloyd George would rule out any idea of a renewed offensive in Flanders, advocating a policy of strategic defence until such time as the AEF could take to the field in strength and preferring any offensive to be against the Turks in Palestine and Mesopotamia instead. With intelligence of the transfer of increasing numbers of German troops from the Eastern to the Western Front, and knowing that the Germans could not afford to let the relative strengths (by some measures, 192 allied divisions to 169 German) turn decisively against them, especially with the continued erosion of civilian morale in Germany itself, all the allied leaders expected that the German chief of staff – effectively commander-in-chief – Erich Ludendorff, would mount a major offensive in early spring, and that, in Field Marshal Haig's words, the 'crisis of the war would be reached in April'.

For those in the trenches and the rest areas, however, January 1918 was just another month to be endured, the chief vexation now being not so much the Germans as the weather. Leonard Ounsworth, a gunner in a heavy battery of the Royal Garrison Artillery, recalled:

> The thaw started on January the 15th, with rain as well – so complete that the ground just collapsed. The end of the dugout just fell in and buried one of the cooks – he'd have suffocated if we hadn't got him out in time. Four of the guns were moved to Sorel [Somme] that day. They couldn't have picked a worse one for it, because by the time we got there the ground was an absolute quagmire.

Keeping up morale became an even greater priority: one way was foraging for ordnance, which was increasingly lucrative, with the shortage of metal in Britain putting a premium on salvage. In the Cambrai sector, Major Andrew Bain of the 7th Argyll and Sutherland Highlanders, a territorial battalion, recorded:

> I made a sort of salvage-price list, and distributed this to the four battalions in my brigade. It said 'For every rifle you'll be credited with two pounds; for a shell case, six pence; for ammunition about two pence a dozen for spent cartridge cases.' And that mounted up enormously. One month, the 6th Gordons, by just combing over the ground and picking up everything that was there, collected about six thousand pounds [£450,000 in today's prices].

With little prospect of serious action for a month or so, more leave could also be granted, sometimes for apparently exigent reasons. Captain Cyril Dennys of the Royal Garrison Artillery described how although he himself was 'very young', he believed that the sexual aspect worried some of the older men quite a lot. I mean, it made them jumpy. I remember there was one case where a captain who was getting on in age applied for special leave. You could get a week's special leave to go to Paris or somewhere. On his leave chit he was asked for his reason. He put quite boldly sexual starvation. And to everyone's surprise and delight he got his leave.

For the American Expeditionary Force, however, it was a time to familiarize themselves with trench routine and patrolling before the expected German offensive, although Pershing feared that 'the long period of trench warfare had so impressed itself upon the French and British that they had almost entirely dispensed with training for open warfare', and was determined therefore that the latter should be the focus of the AEF's training as soon as they were able to look after themselves when in the line.

There were practical problems, however. With the direct approach that had characterized American military thinking for at least half a century, Pershing saw his route on to German soil – key to winning the war – as the shortest distance between two points. That was through Lorraine (or, since 1871, 'Lothringen' to the occupying Germans), which meant that his starting place, and therefore the AEF's concentration area, had to be behind Verdun and the St-Mihiel salient: 'If the American Army was to have an independent and flexible system it could not use the lines behind the British–Belgium front nor those in rear of the French front covering Paris.'

When Pershing had visited GHQ on 28 December, however, Haig had asked him how the AEF might help in the event of a German offensive, 'the crisis of the war', for there were now almost 200,000 American troops in France, although as yet only one division had appeared at the front. Pershing was single-minded in his determination to keep the AEF as a discrete army under his own command, ready for the great offensive when the time came – and indeed, President Wilson had told him to keep his distance from the BEF – but Pershing was also a realist. Haig recorded in his diary, with evident relief, the AEF commander-in-chief's agreement that, if the situation became critical, he was ready to 'break up American divisions and employ battalions and regiments as draft to fill up our divisions'.

Who was to decide that the situation was critical was, of course, another matter.

There is no record of a comparable undertaking to the French, but while this does not signify any unwillingness, it does perhaps suggest a nascent, and not altogether surprising, Anglo-American 'special relationship' of the kind that was already developing between the respective intelligence branches. President Wilson's concern to keep the AEF at a distance from the BEF (exacerbated by the view of the CIGS, Sir William Robertson, who had urged that American troops be incorporated in units of the BEF as if they were simply British) and to look instead to the French, as the 'old ally', was all very well, but the *Grand Quartier General*, the French general staff, had proved reluctant to share intelligence. The head of the AEF's G2 (intelligence) branch, Brigadier-General Dennis Nolan, had therefore been turning increasingly to Brigadier-General John Charteris at GHQ, whom he found a much readier collaborator (though in January Charteris would be sacked because of the findings of the committee of inquiry into the failure of intelligence at Cambrai). Besides, the language and organizational differences with the French were already proving a hindrance to training, and so later that month Pershing decided to accept Haig's offer to take 150 battalions into the BEF to train. Initially one American battalion would be allotted to each British brigade, after which they would be progressively grouped into American regiments, the AEF's equivalent of brigades, and divisions.

By the end of January 1918, although inter-allied bickering and the mistrust between the British military leadership and Lloyd George continued, and while there was no consensus on precisely how and when the war would end, there was at least the confidence that unless 'the crisis of the war' was mishandled, there would come a peace with victory for the allies. The secretary for war, Lord Derby, went so far as to bet Lloyd George a hundred cigars to a hundred cigarettes that the war would be over by the next new year.

43

FEBRUARY
Doughboys

As the Russian front disintegrates further,
on the Western Front the Americans fire their first shots

In August 1917 the Pope had made his appeal for peace, declaring his neutrality to be 'appropriate to him who is the common father and who loves all his children with equal affection'. It brought him little filial warmth in response. In February 1918 it would be the turn of the Kaiser to speak of sacred matters: 'War is a disciplinary action by God to educate mankind,' he told the citizens of Bad Homburg, gathered in the courtyard of the castle, his summer residence for thirty years and now the place of his February *Kur*.

He had good news for them: the new People's Republic of Ukraine, detached from the Russian Empire in the wake of the Bolshevik takeover, had on the previous day signed a peace treaty. It signalled ultimate victory, he said, and in the meantime would bring them more bread, for Ukraine always had a surplus of grain. (In many parts of Germany, the flour was by now being supplemented with potato peelings and sawdust.) It was, indeed, the *Brotfrieden* – the bread peace. But he warned them too that Ukraine was 'shaken by a civil war . . . [and] could be overrun by the Bolsheviks and large parts of the grain could be carried away by the Red Army'.

Indeed, at the council of war that followed, the recent armistice with the Russians would be temporarily overturned in order to force the hand of the new government. Since the middle of December, the guns had been formally silent from the Baltic to the Black Sea (and less formally since the November ceasefire), but the peace negotiations at Brest-Litovsk were being deliberately drawn out, said Richard von Kühlmann, secretary of state for foreign affairs. General Max Hoffmann, chief of staff in the east and the guiding brain of the *Grosser Generalstab* throughout the campaigns against Russia, was convinced that both German and Austro-Hungarian forces must immediately take to the offensive again, 'otherwise these brutes [Bolsheviks] will wipe up the Ukrainians, the Finns, and the Balts, and then quickly get together a new revolutionary army and turn the whole of Europe into a pig-sty'.

The Kaiser agreed. There was, he told the war council, a worldwide conspiracy against Germany by Bolsheviks supported by President Woodrow Wilson, Freemasons and 'international Jewry'.

Not only was his proto-fascism a faulty assessment, however, it was inconsistent with recent German policy. It was Berlin that had brought Lenin by train from Swiss exile to Petrograd, and Berlin that had given financial backing to the Bolsheviks, including secret subventions to their newspaper *Pravda*. As for the Jewish conspiracy, what of the (by general estimate) 100,000 Jews serving in the German army, 12,000 of whom were killed in action and 18,000 of whom were awarded the Iron Cross?

Hoffmann was given the green light nevertheless, and on 18 February some fifty-two German and Austro-Hungarian divisions crossed the ceasefire line in *Unternehmen Faustschlag* (Operation Fist Punch). They quickly occupied Dvinsk in Latvia and Lutsk in north-western Ukraine, and soon found themselves advancing along the Russian railway lines against virtually no opposition. 'It is the most comical war I have ever known,' Hoffman wrote in his diary. 'We put a handful of infantrymen with machineguns and one field gun onto a train and push them off to the next station. They take it, make prisoners of the Bolsheviks, pick up a few more troops and go on. This proceeding has, at any rate, the charm of novelty.'

Lenin and his commissar for foreign affairs, Leon Trotsky, a Ukrainian Jew, gave in at once, telegramming Hoffmann to accept all the peace conditions demanded at Brest-Litovsk. With an open road before him, however, Hoffmann was not inclined to accept the capitulation, and prevaricated over the paperwork. On 20 February, German troops entered Minsk, the first city of Belarus and an important railway junction on the Warsaw–Moscow line, taking nearly 10,000 prisoners. 'There is no fight left in them,' wrote Hoffmann. 'Yesterday one lieutenant with six men took prisoner six hundred Cossacks.'

Indeed, during the next two weeks German troops would take the Ukrainian capital, Kiev, and Narva, the easternmost city of Estonia, less than 90 miles from Petrograd. When a German plane bombed the Fontanka embankment close to the Summer Palace, the Bolsheviks' governing council began quitting the city for Moscow, which was declared the new capital on 12 March. With the support, however, of the 39-year-old former editor of *Pravda*, Joseph Stalin, Lenin just managed to persuade his council to accept whatever terms the Germans offered, and on 3 March the Russian delegates at Brest-Litovsk were instructed to sign the punitive treaty that brought the war on the Eastern Front to an end, giving up Finland, Estonia, Latvia, Lithuania, Poland, Belarus and the whole of Ukraine.

Erich Ludendorff, in effect the C-in-C of the entire German army, could now switch even more divisions to the Western Front for what he intended to be the decisive offensive. And they would take with them an extra 2,500 artillery pieces and 5,000 machine guns captured in the recent fighting.

Meanwhile, in London, matters were coming to a head over the terms of reference of the British representative at the new supreme war council at Versailles – in effect a *generalissimo*'s headquarters, controlling among other things the planned inter-allied reserve of thirty

divisions. Although Lloyd George had been one of its chief propo-
nents, the prime minister now found himself lumbered with three
points of advice and decision – Versailles (where the permanent
British representative was Sir Henry Wilson), GHQ in France (Haig),
and the CIGS (Robertson). Maurice Hankey, secretary of the war
cabinet, was at the council's meeting at the end of January and
recorded that 'all gave different advice [creating] a worse state of
chaos than I have ever known in all my wide experience'.

In the end, 'Wully' Robertson, who had never been a supporter
of the idea of a supreme war council (he called it 'the Versailles
Soviet'), resigned, whereupon Lloyd George made General Sir Henry
Wilson CIGS, and appointed in his place at Versailles – double-
hatted as deputy CIGS for supposedly greater control – Sir Henry
Rawlinson, lately commander of 4th Army. This would do little to
ameliorate the problem of differing advice, but it did at least remove
one thorn from Lloyd George's side, for he had found Robertson
increasingly difficult to work with of late.

For the rest, February on the Western Front continued as quietly
as January, with just raiding and local attacks. For the Americans,
however, it was the opportunity to see a little instructive action at
last. In mid-January, the 1st US Division had entered the line in the
St-Mihiel salient (French sector), the first complete division to do
so. On discovering this, the Germans had launched several raids,
killing, wounding or capturing a number of US troops. 'This thing
of letting the Boche do it all is getting on the nerves,' noted one
officer in his diary: it was certainly not 'the American way'.

On 13 February the AEF got its first opportunity to strike back,
albeit in a limited way, when several artillery batteries took part in
a six-hour bombardment prior to a French attack at Butte de Mesnil
in Champagne. Then, ten days later, just south of Laon, two officers
and twenty-four enlisted men took part in a raid alongside French
troops, capturing several dozen Germans. In its report of the
action, *The Times* commented that although 'the actual occasion
was not of much importance, February 23 is one of the dates that
will always be remembered in the history of the war'.

Another memorable date would be the fifth, but for a more melancholy reason – the loss of the former luxury liner *Tuscania*, pressed into service as a troopship, to a German torpedo off the north coast of Ireland, and with her of 166 US servicemen, the first to be killed on their way to Europe, together with 44 of her British crew. The German submarine UB-77 had sighted *Tuscania*'s convoy during the day and shadowed them until early evening, then under cover of darkness had fired two torpedoes, the second of which struck home, sending her to the bottom in four hours.

Elsewhere on the Western Front, one of the most famous – and certainly most controversial – American soldiers of the twentieth century was about to become the first to be decorated by the French. On 26 February, Colonel Douglas MacArthur, chief of staff of the US 42nd Division – 'the Rainbow Division' – had sought permission of the general commanding the line at Réchicourt to accompany a trench raid that night. His dress surprised both the raiders and one of the 42nd Division's ADCs who had slipped away to join in 'the picnic' as he called it. Instead of a steel helmet MacArthur wore his service cap, and rather than pistol, knife or club – the preferred weapons of a trench raid – he carried his riding whip. 'It's the orders you disobey that make you famous,' he told the ADC.

He was right. The raiders had a hard fight, but they returned at dawn with a large bag of prisoners, including a colonel whom MacArthur had taken in his personal charge and prodded back to the trenches with his riding whip. Though the seat of MacArthur's immaculate riding breeches was left behind on the wire, General de Bazelaire greeted the 38-year-old trench-raider with a kiss on both cheeks and pinned on him a Croix de Guerre. The story made the *New York Times* the following week, together with the opinion of the Rainbow Division's commanding general that 'Colonel MacArthur is one of the ablest officers in the United States Army and one of the most popular'. A fortnight later MacArthur would win the US Distinguished Service Cross in one of the 42nd Division's own raids, and by the end of the war was commanding the division whose name he himself had suggested – 'Rainbow' because it was made up of militia units from across America, rather than, as most of the others, recruited from a single state.

The AEF, for all their greenness, not least among the officers, were certainly creating an impression; and at the time of lowest ebb in allied morale – after the fruitless losses of 1917, and facing a massive and desperate German offensive – the impression alone was reassuring. When General Pershing visited GHQ at the end of December, Haig had been particularly impressed by his ADC, 'a fire-eater, [who] longs for the fray'. He was Captain (later General) George S. Patton.

As for the 'doughboys' themselves, they had, wrote Vera Brittain in *Testament of Youth*, 'an unusual quality of bold vigour in their swift stride'. While serving as a nurse at the British base at Étaples she saw for the first time a contingent of them marching down the road:

> They looked larger than ordinary men; their tall, straight figures were in vivid contrast to the under-sized armies of pale recruits to which we had grown accustomed. At first I thought their spruce, clean uniforms were those of officers, yet obviously they could not be officers, for there were too many of them; they seemed, as it were, Tommies in heaven. Had yet another regiment been conjured from our depleted Dominions? I wondered, watching them move with such rhythm, such dignity, such serene consciousness of self-respect. But I knew the colonial troops so well, and these were different; they were assured where the Australians were aggressive, self-possessed where the New Zealanders were turbulent.
>
> Then I heard an excited exclamation from a group of Sisters behind me. 'Look! Look! Here are the Americans!'
>
> I pressed forward with the others to watch the United States physically entering the war, so God-like, so magnificent, so splendidly unimpaired in comparison with the tired, nerve-racked men of the British Army.

Yet Pershing was still determined to take his time, and to keep the AEF as a discrete force rather than – except for training – integrating its divisions in allied corps. Notwithstanding his accommodating response to Haig's question when they had met on 28 December, he continued to stand aloof from allied planning, and would certainly not commit troops to the inter-allied reserve.

In mid-December, the French high command had noted a 'crisis of pessimism' among its *poilus*, and by mid-February the postal censors were reporting growing doubts about the Americans, and the *poilus*' 'anxiety' as to whether US cooperation would 'shorten the war or prolong it'. The late-February morale report observed bleakly: 'The depth of weariness is obvious.'

44

MARCH
Kaiserschlacht

The Germans' last hope of victory: a million-man offensive in the West

In his memoirs, General Erich Ludendorff, the man who by early 1918 was effectively running the German war effort and wielding increasing power over German politics and industry, wrote that at this point 'the condition of our allies and of our Army all called for an offensive that would bring about an early decision. This was only possible on the Western Front.'

The Royal Navy's blockade was beginning to cripple German civilian morale, as well as constricting supplies for the front. One deserter, Heinrich Fleischer, volunteered to work for the British Secret Service Bureau after going on leave to Berlin and finding his family 'white and emaciated, with nothing to eat but turnips and watery potatoes'.

If Ludendorff could not force a decision on the Western Front by the end of the year, a million and more newly arrived Americans would be poised to decide matters in 1919.

With the signing of the peace treaty with the Bolshevik government at Brest-Litovsk on 3 March, Ludendorff could now turn his

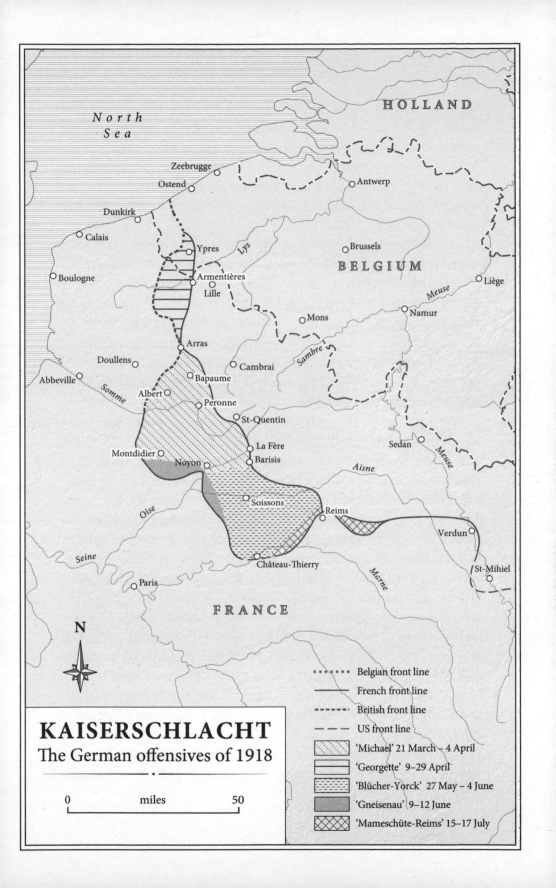

HOLLAND

North Sea

Zeebrugge
Ostend
Antwerp
Dunkirk
Calais
Ypres
Lys
Brussels
Boulogne
Armentières
Lille
BELGIUM
Liège
Meuse
Mons
Namur
Arras
Doullens
Cambrai
Sambre
Abbeville
Bapaume
Somme
Albert
Peronne
St-Quentin
Montdidier
La Fère
Sedan
Noyon
Barisis
Meuse
Aisne
Oise
Soissons
Reims
Verdun
Seine
Château-Thierry
St-Mihiel
Marne
Paris

FRANCE

N

KAISERSCHLACHT
The German offensives of 1918

0   miles   50

Belgian front line
French front line
British front line
US front line
'Michael' 21 March – 4 April
'Georgette' 9–29 April
'Blücher-Yorck' 27 May – 4 June
'Gneisenau' 9–12 June
'Mameschüte-Reims' 15–17 July

back on the Russian front and transfer the remaining troops to France. 'I set aside all idea of attacking in Macedonia or Italy. All that mattered was to get together enough troops for an attack in the west,' he wrote. When he told the Kaiser that he planned to assemble 900,000 men for what would be called *Die Kaiserschlacht* – the Kaiser's battle – the reply was: 'Add another hundred thousand and make it a million.'

By withdrawing troops from the Macedonian front, and other measures, he was just able to do so. In January there had been 169 German divisions in the west against 192 allied ones. By March 1918 there were 191 (although the Americans were beginning to field more divisions too). Not only would *Die Kaiserschlacht* be, in Ludendorff's words, 'one of the most difficult operations in history', it would be the largest. He had also told the Kaiser that 'the state of training of the Army for attack enabled us to contemplate doing so about the middle of March'.

The training was as significant as the numbers. During the winter, the army had been forming units of elite *Sturmtruppen*, 'storm[ing] troops', to spearhead the offensive. 'The whole line of thought of the Army had to be diverted from trench warfare back to the offensive,' wrote Ludendorff, for they had stood on the defensive on the Western Front since mid-1916, when the attempt to break the French at Verdun had begun to falter. 'It was necessary to emphasize the principle that men must do the work not with their bodies alone but with their weapons. The fighting line must be kept thin, but must be constantly fed from behind.'

The light machine gun was to be the principal weapon in this new doctrine of the offensive, together with the flame-thrower and the rifle. The *Sturm* teams would be made up of men under thirty-five, including picked riflemen, who were withdrawn from routine duties and given better rations. Their task was not to overpower but to infiltrate, bypassing strongpoints to penetrate deep into the enemy's defences, leaving pockets of resistance to the second wave of more legionary infantry. They would prove formidably effective, but might have been even more so had they had the support of tanks. The one consolation to the allies was that the Germans had simply not thought these worthwhile enough to put into serious production, even after the experience of Cambrai, and fielded only a few dozen 'A7s' (named after the war ministry department responsible, the *Allgemeines Kriegsdepartement, Abteilung 7*), together with the same number of captured British Mark IVs. 'They were merely an offensive weapon, and our attacks succeeded without them,' reckoned Ludendorff.

Sturm tactics without sound operational strategy could not be enough, however. In December, Ludendorff's strategic adviser, Lieutenant-Colonel Georg von Wetzell, head of the operations section of the *Oberste Heeresleitung* (supreme army command), had written an appreciation of the situation on the Western Front. He was not greatly impressed with the expertise of the British army (including its imperial troops): the artillery, he said, 'like the British tactics as a whole, is rigid and stiff'. He thought the French much nimbler, 'just as skilful in the tactical use of their artillery as of their infantry', and their 'use of ground in the attack ... just as good as in the defence'. Their losses at Verdun in 1916 and the setbacks of the Nivelle offensive in 1917 had clearly taken their toll, though, and Wetzell thought the French 'not such good stayers as the British'. With the British, he concluded, 'we have a strategically [at GHQ level] clumsy, tactically rigid, but tough enemy in front of us'. The Third Battle of Ypres – Passchendaele – despite (perhaps even because of) all its terrible slaughter, showed that although French strength was on the wane, with growing British material strength and resolve, the Germans would now face an even harder fight.

Wetzell also pointed to the problem of maintaining the momentum in an advance through what he called the 'shot-to-pieces battle area' that had been left by the German withdrawal to the Hindenburg Line a year earlier, and the subsequent fighting. Moving forward the artillery would be especially slow. The logistical problems, already grave, would increase as the advancing troops got further from the railheads and depots, exacerbated by the shortage of both draught horses and mechanical transport (the Germans had 23,000 motor lorries, most with iron-rimmed wheels, compared with the allies' 100,000 with rubber tyres). Wetzell accordingly concluded that there would have to be 'operational pauses' in the offensive so that the supporting arms and services could catch up with the leading troops. These, however, would give the enemy time to reorganize their defences, aided by 'the excellent railway communications behind the front'. He warned, therefore, against hoping for a rapid breakthrough, urging instead a series of coordinated simultaneous attacks, in the hope that somehow the allied line could be prised apart.

For once, however, the allies would not be taken by strategic surprise. Any appreciation of the Germans' military situation could not fail to conclude that they now saw the war as a race with the American Expeditionary Force, whose drafts were arriving in the many thousands each month. Nor could aerial reconnaissance fail to pick up the signs of the German buildup, any more than the signals intercept service could miss the increased radio and telegraph traffic. Besides, by this stage in the war the allies had extensive human intelligence sources in Belgium and the occupied areas of France. The Secret Service Bureau operated a number of collection systems, one of the most successful of which was *La Dame Blanche* (named after the spectral harbinger of downfall in European myth), a network of train-watchers able to supply information on the movement of individual divisions, from which the bureau, together with the War Office's military intelligence directorate and the intelligence branch in GHQ, was able to put together a detailed German order of battle in north-west France and Flanders. The French had similar arrangements, including agents whom they inserted by air behind enemy lines.

On 19 February, *The Times* published a despatch from Harry Perry Robinson, its new war correspondent (its previous correspondent, the celebrated Colonel Charles à Court Repington, having resigned in a dispute with the proprietor, Lord Northcliffe, who wanted to distance the paper from Haig after the setback at Cambrai). Robinson explained:

The German offensive is now undoubtedly very near. Evidence accumulates daily, especially convincing being the statements of prisoners taken recently . . .

An immense amount of training for the attack has been going on. Of that we have been assured by our airmen. To escape observation, much of the training is being done in remoter areas . . .

The training is largely in the nature of open fighting, for the Germans seem to count on breaking our lines and getting the warfare into the open country behind, in which they are going to be aided by the use of gas, tanks and trench mortars. There will probably be no obliterating bombardment such as has preceded most of our great attacks, but in the days before the assault counter-battery shooting, both with gas and high-explosive shells, and long spells of destructive fire on trenches, communications, billets, and so forth. Immediately before the attack there will be only a short burst of fire, behind which men are to come over in one grand rush, while immense numbers of mobile guns and trench mortars will push up behind the supporting troops.

R. C. Sherriff, who served as a captain in the East Surreys, put the words of many a front-line soldier into the mouth of Lieutenant Osborne in his 1928 drama *Journey's End*, set in the run-up to *Die Kaiserschlacht*: 'We are, generally, just waiting for something.'

But GHQ did not know where, exactly, the Germans would attack. Ludendorff considered three options: in Flanders, to capture the remaining Channel ports; in the east, abreast Verdun, where the weakened French might this time be overwhelmed; or at the junction of the allied line between Arras and St-Quentin. The advantage of striking at the junction was that the enemy might retreat in diverging directions – the French to cover Paris, and the British along their lines of communication to the Channel ports, giving the latter very little manoeuvre room.

Forecasting the enemy's moves – as opposed to identifying his options and the relative merits of each – is more an art than a science, and therefore subject to the full range of human frailties. The forecast made by the 'E' (Enemy) Group of the British military staff at the allied supreme war council at Versailles would prove to be reasonably accurate, but was largely dismissed by GHQ as a result of the friction between the two headquarters.

To meet the expected attack, Haig, in order to cover the Channel ports, concentrated his strength in the north, while the French, to cover Paris, strengthened their positions to the south of the British. Three British armies – from right to left, 3rd (Byng), 1st (Horne) and 2nd (Plumer) – covered the two-thirds of Haig's front from Cambrai to the sea, some forty-six divisions in all. General Sir Hubert Gough's 5th Army, with just fourteen divisions, held the remaining third, from Cambrai to the Oise (4th Army, having had so many divisions withdrawn in late 1917, existed on paper only). Haig had thereby insured against the worst case, and had also strengthened Arras, a natural bastion and key communications centre, but in doing so he had left the junction with the French relatively weak. To compensate for this, GHQ sought to deceive the Germans with contrary intelligence, not least through the press. The *Times* article of 19 February accordingly also stated: 'So far as our front is concerned, especial attention is being given to sectors between Arras and St Quentin.'

Gough was not the subtlest of generals, and after Passchendaele morale in 5th Army was not the highest. In consequence, and also because 5th Army was relatively weak in numbers, Gough did not arrange his defences in the sort of depth that the Germans had at Third Ypres, and which Haig himself had stipulated. Gough appears to have believed rather more in the inherent superiority of a strongly held front line, and also that his infantry lacked the capacity for counter-moves under fire if held back in depth. Besides, GHQ's intelligence assessment was that the Germans had stood on the defensive for so long, and taken such a beating at Passchendaele, that they had lost the edge in offensive spirit. Consequently, nine out of ten of Gough's battalions were disposed within 3,000 yards of the front line – well within range of field artillery, and liable to be over-run or bypassed before they could adjust.

It was at this point of junction between 5th Army and the French that Ludendorff chose to strike – with the army group of the Crown

Prince. As late as 16 March, however, GHQ was sure that 'no significant attack is expected south of the Bapaume–Cambrai road'. A week's shelling across the whole allied front had given nothing away, and nor would its sequel in the five days following.

Then, at 4.40 a.m. on 21 March, a massive bombardment – the new German technique of the *Feuerwaltz* (fire-waltz), a mixed bombardment of high explosives, smoke, tear gas and poison gas – was opened on the foremost trenches and artillery positions along 40 miles and more of 3rd and 5th Armies' front. Operation Michael (after the archangel depicted in Christian iconography in armour with fiery sword in hand, trampling a dragon), the first phase of *die Kaiserschlacht* had begun. At nine o'clock, Hartwig Pohlmann, an officer in the 36th (Prussian) Division, left his dug-out after what he described as 'a little breakfast' ready for the advance, but could see nothing. 'It was thick fog. I thought, how can we attack in this?'

At 9.35, the creeping barrage began and Pohlmann told his soldiers

> to hang on with one hand to the belt of the man in front, but they couldn't do that for long because the ground was very rough and we had to creep through barbed wire. So soon there was a pell-mell, but everyone knew that they had to go straight on . . . As we advanced through the fog we suddenly heard guns firing behind us. We realised we had come out behind a British battery . . . One of my men laid a hand on the shoulder of the British officers and said, 'Cease fire.' They were stunned.

If Pohlmann's recollections were coloured by the years, they certainly illustrate the confusion into which 5th Army was thrown that morning. In just five hours, the Germans had fired a million shells at 5th Army's sector – over 3,000 a minute. The British line began to collapse, though there were many stubborn – heroic – pockets of resistance. Near St-Quentin, the 16th Manchesters, a 'New Army' battalion, were holding the line at what became known as Manchester Hill. Their commanding officer was Lieutenant-Colonel Wilfrith Elstob, who was not yet thirty. A parson's son from Sussex, Elstob had been commissioned in the first wave of volunteers in 1914 and promoted successively within the same battalion. He had told his men: 'Here we fight, and here we die.' The citation for his posthumous VC, won that day, ran:

> For most conspicuous bravery, devotion to duty and self-sacrifice . . . During the preliminary bombardment he encouraged his men in the posts in the Redoubt by frequent visits, and when repeated attacks developed controlled the defence at the points threatened, giving personal support with revolver, rifle and bombs. Single-handed he repulsed one bombing assault driving back the enemy and inflicting severe casualties. Later, when ammunition was required, he made several journeys under severe fire in order to replenish the supply. Throughout the day Lieutenant-Colonel Elstob, although twice wounded, showed the most fearless disregard of his own safety, and by his encouragement and noble example inspired his command to the fullest degree. The Manchester Redoubt was surrounded in the first wave of the enemy attack, but by means of the buried cable Lieutenant-Colonel Elstob was able to assure his Brigade Commander that 'The Manchester Regiment will defend Manchester Hill to the last.' Sometime after this post was overcome by vastly superior forces, and this very gallant officer was killed in the final assault, having maintained to the end the duty which he had impressed on his men . . . He set throughout the highest example of valour, determination, endurance and fine soldierly bearing.

At two o'clock Gough gave the order to 'give ground' – to begin fighting a delaying action while the heavier guns were pulled back to escape capture. Soon, however, under the continued pressure of the *Sturm* troops and the sheer weight of artillery fire, 5th Army was in full retreat. By nightfall, after the Germans had fired some 3.2 million artillery and mortar rounds – at that time the greatest bombardment in history – the rearmost lines had been breached in several places, and the defenders south of St-Quentin driven right out. Within twenty-four hours the Germans would take nearly 150 square miles of the Western Front in some of the most spectacular advances of the war. It was not without cost, however: they had suffered some 40,000 casualties. British casualties were roughly the same, including 21,000 taken prisoner.

A young officer in the 2nd Yorkshire Regiment (Green Howards), Herbert Read – later Sir Herbert Read, the art critic and writer, and one of the thirteen war poets commemorated by name in Westminster Abbey – described in a letter to his future wife the frantic days that followed:

> We were rushed up to the line in the early hours of the morning, and from then and for six days and nights we were fighting as I never dreamt I would fight – without sleep – often without food and all the time besieged by hordes of the Boche. The Colonel was wounded during the second day and I had to take command of the battalion. We were surrounded in our original position and had to fight our way through. We took up position after position, always to be surrounded. On the whole the men were splendid and there were many fine cases of heroism. But our casualties were very heavy and we who have come through may thank our lucky stars eternally.

One of the thirteen poets who did not come through was Private Isaac Rosenberg. In 1915 he had enlisted in a 'Bantam battalion' consisting of men under the minimum (in 1914) height of 5 feet 3 inches. The Bantams were originally intended not for combat but for labour and support duties. Such had been the losses the previous year, however, that in March 1918 Rosenberg found himself with the 1st King's Own, a pre-war regular battalion, and on 1 April this diminutive Jewish infantryman from the East End was killed during night fighting near Arras. The American literary critic and Second World War infantry officer Paul Fussell would call Rosenberg's 'Break of Day in the Trenches' the greatest poem of the war.

Although there would be recriminations, 5th Army put up as much of a fight as could reasonably be expected in the circumstances. A German report stated: 'The [British] 7th Corps covered the retreat of the main body even to the extent of being destroyed itself.' Gough, however, would pay the price, not least because in

323

part the circumstances were of his making. He was relieved of command on 28 March and replaced by Henry Rawlinson, brought back from Versailles.

At the end of December, Haig had told General Pershing that the crisis of the war would come in April. At the end of March, the crisis looked as if it were already come.

45

APRIL

'Backs to the Wall'

The Germans almost break through in Flanders,
forcing Haig famously to reach for his pen

The massive attack on General Sir Hubert Gough's 5th Army front on 21 March was potentially as shattering for the cohesion of the allied line as the Austro-German attack in October had been on the Italian front at Caporetto. So ferocious was the initial artillery assault and so innovative were the German infiltration tactics that by 25 March three British divisions – the 16th (Irish), 36th (Ulster) and 66th (East Lancashire) – each with losses of over 7,000, had practically ceased to exist.

Unlike at Caporetto, however, the Germans on 5th Army's front, while able to infiltrate and bypass locally, were unable to make the big, bold, fast outflanking moves that had destroyed the unity of the Italian line in the Alps and astride the Isonzo. Lacking both cavalry (for a great many of Ludendorff's regiments had been de-horsed to provide draught animals for the artillery and transport) and tanks, when 5th Army began to withdraw – even at times precipitately – the Germans could move no faster than their quarry.

One of the reasons was that a year earlier, in their own withdrawal to the Hindenburg Line, they had devastated the ground over which they now advanced.

It was the very problem that had prompted Ludendorff's strategic adviser, Lieutenant-Colonel Georg von Wetzell, to warn, during the planning of *die Kaiserschlacht*, against expectations of rapid breakthrough. Ludendorff had accordingly set no precise objectives, saying only that he intended to 'punch a hole into [their line]. For the rest, we shall see.'

After all, it had worked for him, and for Hindenburg, in Russia in 1914. And indeed, the men on the receiving end of Ludendorff's massive punch – both those of Gough's 5th Army and, increasingly, those to the north, on the right wing of Byng's 3rd Army – struggled to stem the German advance. Lieutenant Ulick Burke of the 2nd Devons, which though a regular battalion was by 1918 made up largely of conscripts, and whose officers in the main had joined since 1914 – men of Kitchener's 'New Army' – described the disorientating experience of those days of constant retreat:

> Then we halted, stayed where we were. We did as much defence work as possible and waited for them to come. Then they'd come on and we'd get the order – after we'd shot and killed quite a few – to retire. Well, we were retiring and retiring and we were never still. You never knew where you were going to pick up any food, where you were going to pick up ammunition, and some of the men got windy and really would have run. Now if an officer or a sergeant had behaved like that, the whole lot would have panicked. The only thing that kept them there was respect for your bravery and your attitude; you knew what you were doing and you were saving them all you could. And that kept them steady.

It was dispiriting, too, to be abandoning ground taken the year before. Sergeant-Major Richard Tobin, of the 7th (Hood) Battalion, 63rd (Royal Naval) Division, in Byng's 3rd Army, remembered how in late March they 'dropped into a trench . . . we knew of old. We had started to retreat on 21 March, and here we were back in the trench we had started to attack from on November the 13th, 1916.'

For this was the old Somme battlefield.

Here and there the speed of 5th Army's retreat actually became something of a problem for the Germans, for large parts of Gough's ordnance stores, with their abundant food and quantities of rum, brandy and whisky, had to be abandoned. For troops on increasingly short and unattractive rations, even the elite *Sturmtruppen*, it was sometimes simply too much to resist. As more than one historian has been unable to resist saying, the advance was slowed not so much by lack of German fighting spirit as by the abundance of Scottish drinking spirit.

Meanwhile in Paris something close to panic began taking hold, with Pétain, the French commander-in-chief, saying the war was as good as lost. The civilian population was already unnerved by bombing (on 8 March, Gothas had dropped 100 bombs on the city, precipitating the flight of 200,000 Parisians to the country), and the Germans were shelling the suburbs, now within the 70-mile range of their specially made Krupp railway guns.

The crisis, however, at last galvanized the allied leadership. On 26 March General Foch, the French representative at Versailles, had been instructed, in the words of the memorandum signed by Clemenceau and the allied plenipotentiaries, 'to coordinate the action of the allied armies on the Western Front'. Specifically, he was to form a common reserve and to use it to guard the junction of the French and British armies and to plug the potentially fatal gap that would have followed a German breakthrough. A fortnight later, with Paris looking as if it might fall, Foch was formally appointed *généralissime* (more usually, *generalissimo*): supreme commander. He now had strategic direction of all the allied armies on the Western Front, including the Americans, and in June his remit would be extended to cover the Italian front as well. This appointment meant that Ludendorff could not now divide the French and British armies, because Foch saw their cohesion as the greater priority than Haig's of covering the Channel ports. If it became necessary – and Foch told Haig and the supreme war council that he didn't believe it would – the armies would retire as one towards the Somme.

In this, Foch would be proved right. Ludendorff had indeed punched a hole into the allied line, but his offensive, 'Michael', had run out of steam. Despite attacks on the French line to fix their reserves in place, Pétain had, if somewhat belatedly, moved significant reinforcements to ease the pressure on Amiens, which was key to the continued cohesion of the allied line. Determined allied counter-attacks, including a magnificent mounted charge by a squadron of Lord Strathcona's Horse (Canadian Cavalry Brigade) at Moreuil Wood, together with the strengthening of a new line of defence, and handy reserves, halted the *Kaiserschlacht* just short of the city. After a fortnight's advances, in some places over 40 miles, on 5 April Ludendorff brought Operation Michael to a close.

Total British losses, including dominion troops, were 178,000, including over 75,000 taken prisoner, plus 1,300 guns and 200 tanks, while the French lost 77,000 and the Germans 240,000. But Amiens and Arras stood firm. Ludendorff would now turn his attention instead to the north, French Flanders, with the aim of pushing 1st Army (Horne) and 2nd Army (Plumer) back against the Channel ports.

The northern sector of the British line had been thinned out to reinforce the Somme, and the weakest link in this weakened sector was the Portuguese Corps, which held the front in the plain of the River Lys. Their morale was probably the poorest of any corps in the entire allied line, not least for the fact that home leave arrangements had largely broken down with the problem of shipping created by the need to bring US troops to Europe, and the submarine menace.

On 9 April, therefore – Ludendorff's fifty-third birthday, for which the Kaiser came to lunch at the *Oberste Heeresleitung* at Avesnes-sur-Helpe and presented him with a bronze figure of his imperial self – Operation Georgette began. After a short, sharp *Feuerwaltz* bombardment – high explosive, poison gas and smoke – fourteen

divisions of Prince Rupprecht of Bavaria's army group (General Ferdinand von Quast's 6th Army) attacked along a 10-mile front towards
the Lys at Armentières. Four divisions of well-rested *Sturmtruppen*
assailed the Portuguese sector. So ferocious had been the bombardment, and so skilled was the assault troops' attack, that within an
hour the Portuguese front line – apart from a few isolated positions –
was taken, along with 6,000 prisoners.

The British troops on either side of the three-and-a-half-mile
hole thereby opened up in the allied line were also soon on the
retreat to avoid being outflanked – just as had happened at Caporetto. The Germans had released 2,000 tons of mustard and
phosgene gas, incapacitating over 8,000 men, of whom many were
blinded. The following day, Armentières fell (and despite a stout
defence, Bailleul, across the Lys to the north-west, on the road to
Dunkirk, would fall on the fifteenth). On the same day, Plumer's
men were driven from Messines, whose capture he himself had
masterminded nine months earlier, and would soon give up Passchendaele Ridge too, which had been won at such debilitating cost
in November. The Germans now began to commit their reserves,
and the situation became critical.

So alarmed was Haig that on 11 April he issued a 'Special Order
of the Day':

> Three weeks ago to-day the enemy began his terrific attacks against us
> on a fifty-mile front. His objects are to separate us from the French, to
> take the Channel Ports and destroy the British Army.
>
> In spite of throwing already 106 Divisions into the battle and endur-
> ing the most reckless sacrifice of human life, he has as yet made little
> progress towards his goals.
>
> We owe this to the determined fighting and self-sacrifice of our
> troops. Words fail me to express the admiration which I feel for the
> splendid resistance offered by all ranks of our Army under the most try-
> ing circumstances.
>
> Many amongst us now are tired. To those I would say that Victory
> will belong to the side which holds out the longest. The French Army is
> moving rapidly and in great force to our support.

There is no other course open to us but to fight it out. Every position must be held to the last man: there must be no retirement. With our backs to the wall and believing in the justice of our cause each one of us must fight on to the end. The safety of our homes and the Freedom of mankind alike depend upon the conduct of each one of us at this critical moment.

In fact, Foch remained firm in his conviction that the offensive was nothing more than a huge diversion in preparation for something more substantial elsewhere, and gave Haig only limited support. And although both 1st and 2nd Armies were forced to give ground, they were making the Germans pay dearly for it. Hauptmann Stefan Westmann, a medical officer with an assault battalion in Quast's 6th Army, described the sheer weight of machine-gun fire they faced, 'which was so terrific that the losses were staggering. We got orders to lie down and seek shelter. Nobody dared lift his head because they would machinegun us for any movement. The British artillery opened up and the corpses, the heads and the arms and legs flew about and we were cut to pieces.'

He also recalled his astonishment when his battalion over-ran a British field hospital near Merville: it was

completely intact and there I saw for the first time since years the abundance of material, of equipment which we didn't know anymore about. Amongst other things I found cases full of surgical gloves. The German doctors had to operate with their bare fingers. They had to go into the purulent and contaminated wounds with their bare hands and the only thing to wash our hands with was a kind of sand soap. Two parts of sand, one part of soap. And here I found actually thousands of pairs of rubber gloves.

The war of materiel was beginning to show in every way.

Despite the initial success of Georgette, the Germans managed to advance only some 8 miles. Ludendorff closed down the offensive on 29 April, and began to think of a new line of attack – as Foch had predicted, against the French sector.

Casualties on both sides in April had been huge. In five weeks the BEF – technically now the 'British Armies in France' – had lost some 236,000 men (20,000 of them dead and 120,000 taken prisoner), the French around 90,000; but the Germans had lost an irreplaceable 348,000.

Although it was not yet apparent, the 'crisis of the war', which Haig had foretold in his discussion with General Pershing in December, and which he believed had come at the Lys, was past. The Germans had exhausted themselves, and were continuing to do so. They had also taken ground they could not possibly hold against a major counter-offensive by such abundantly equipped and well-supplied troops as the allies.

The appeal had already gone out to the Americans, however, to do all they could to hasten into the field. The chief of the army staff in Washington, General Peyton C. March, at once stepped up mobilization and declared: 'I am going to get the men to France if they have to swim.'

46

MAY

The Cruel Sea

A supreme effort is made to protect US convoys from U-boats

General March would baulk at nothing in his determination to strengthen the American Expeditionary Force. Troopships now sailed into the Atlantic filled to overflowing: tiers of bunks, each shared by three men, sleeping in shifts, reached the overhead (ceiling). Under March's leadership, from May until the Armistice in November, the US War Department despatched over a million and a half men to France.

Getting them there was one thing, however; getting General 'Black Jack' Pershing, the AEF's commander-in-chief, to commit them to battle was another. Even as the great German offensive looked set to continue, and with over half a million Americans already in France, he was adamant that he would not integrate trained battalions within British brigades, insisting instead on building them steadily into separate US brigades, divisions and corps. Haig gave vent to his frustration in his diary: 'I thought Pershing was very obstinate, and stupid. He did not seem to realise the urgency of the situation . . . [He] hankers after a "great self contained American

Army".' As the AEF had no commanders of divisions and corps, nor staffs, Haig believed it 'ridiculous to think such an Army could function alone in less than 2 years' time!'.

It had, after all, taken that long for the BEF to expand into something of the same; but the difference was that the BEF had made that transformation while also doing a great deal of fighting, in the course of which a very large number of men, and, crucially, of experienced officers, had been killed. At a meeting of the supreme war council at Abbeville on 1 May, attended by both Clemenceau and Lloyd George (as well as the Italian prime minister, Vittorio Emanuele Orlando, who had sent several divisions and aircraft to fight under French command), General Ferdinand Foch angrily demanded of Pershing: 'You are willing to risk our being driven back to the Loire?' Pershing, fearing that the French and British might be fought to exhaustion by the end of 1918, and that a great American army would then be needed to win the war in 1919, replied: 'Yes, I am willing to take the risk.' He was not, he said, willing 'to fritter away our resources in this manner'.

Though Foch was Generalissimo, this did not give him the power to direct how individual units and formations were to be used. His authority was to 'coordinate the action of the allied armies on the Western Front.' Lloyd George tried one final time, asking: 'Can't you see that the war will be lost unless we get this support?' Pershing was adamant, however. 'Gentlemen,' he replied forcefully, 'I have thought this programme over very deliberately and will not be coerced.'

But while the arguments went on as to how best the Americans could help win the war, the process of getting them to France looked increasingly vulnerable to demoralizing, even debilitating, losses at sea.

Operating out of Ostend and Zeebrugge, and from the specially constructed base on Heligoland in the German Bight, U-boats had initially had easy access to the English Channel. Almost as soon as war began, however, the Royal Navy had instigated counter-measures in the narrower waters, including the 'Dover Barrage', a belt of minefields and submarine nets between the Belgian coast and Dover, guarded by the 'Dover Patrol'. In late 1917 this had been shifted further south, and searchlights installed, to cover the 22 miles between Folkestone and Cap Gris Nez, so that by May 1918 the Channel was effectively closed to U-boats entering from the north.

The problem remained, however, the exit into the Atlantic via the Shetland–Norway gap. At the allied naval conference of September 1917 it was agreed to close this gap with mines, despite the technological and logistic challenge of mining water 900 feet deep. The component parts of 100,000 of the newly developed Mark 6 'antenna' mine, effective at the assumed maximum submarine depth of 200 feet, were to be manufactured in the United States and assembled in Scotland.

The Mark 6, a 34-inch diameter steel sphere with a buoyancy chamber and 300 lb of TNT, was a highly sophisticated device. The mine was connected to its 800 lb anchor box by a steel mooring cable coiled on a reel. Its depth below surface was controlled by allowing the cable to unwind as it was dropped from the minelayer until on reaching the bottom a sensor locked the reel so it would pull the buoyant mine below the surface, whereupon a float extended the antenna above the mine.

Ten rows of mines were laid at a depth of 80 feet to threaten U-boats on the surface, while submerged craft were targeted by four rows of mines at 160 feet and another four rows at 240 feet. Each mine had two safety devices to render it inert on detaching from its mooring cable. The first was an open switch in the detonation circuit that was closed by hydrostatic pressure 25 feet below the surface. The second was a spring that pushed the detonator away from the explosive charge into the buoyancy chamber unless compressed by hydrostatic pressure. Each mine contained a battery with a two-year life connected to a detonating circuit which could be initiated by any one of five parallel fuzes, four of which were conventional horns in the mine's upper hemisphere. Each horn contained a glass ampule of electrolyte to connect an open circuit if broken by bending the soft metal horn. The fifth and wholly innovative fuze was a long copper wire antenna with a float extending above the mine. A ship's steel hull that touched the antenna would form a battery, the seawater acting as an electrolyte to complete a circuit, with an insulated copper plate on the mine's surface actuating a detonating relay. The mines had five separate spring-loaded safety switches in the detonating circuit, held open by salt pellets that took twenty minutes to dissolve in sea water after the mine was laid overboard.

The US Navy, with Royal Navy support and cover, started laying mines in June 1918, and by November some 56,000 were in position. Within a month of beginning they had claimed the first U-boat. After the war the Admiralty calculated that twenty-three U-boats in all were lost to the 'Northern Barrage', and that it had also been a significant deterrent. The mines further demoralized the German surface fleet, too, whose mutiny in October would be a major factor in the call for an armistice. The cost of the mines was $80 million ($1.3 billion at today's prices) – harbinger of the American way of war.

Besides the minefields, the convoy system introduced in May 1917 was paying dividends. Not only did the escorts provide a strong deterrent to attack, with the improvement of depth charges and development of special equipment such as hydrophones, the convoys became an active means of destroying submerged craft. Aircraft were also an increasing deterrent to surface passage by U-boats, especially when in early 1918 the Germans shifted their attacks to coastal waters in an attempt to sink vessels after the convoys had dispersed to their intended ports of call.

Nevertheless, with the German High Seas Fleet effectively blockaded at Wilhelmshaven, the *Kaiserliche Marine* had no choice but to continue the submarine offensive. In May, Scheer sent six of the new long-range U-boats to operate in American coastal waters. By the end of the war these had sunk nearly a hundred ships, but they were mostly sailing vessels or small steamers, with no effect on General March's transportation plans.

The Admiralty, though, was not satisfied with largely passive measures. The justification for Haig's Third Ypres offensive – 'Pass-chendaele' – the previous year had been in part the prospect of taking Ostend and Zeebrugge and clearing out Holtzendorff's 'nest of vipers'. After the failure of the offensive to get anywhere near the ports, and the *Kaiserliche Marine*'s concentration on attacking in coastal waters, in January the first sea lord, Sir John Jellicoe, was relieved – sacked – for what was perceived as growing defeatism. His successor, Admiral Sir Rosslyn Wemyss, instructed Vice-Admiral Roger Keyes, the new commander of the Dover Patrol, to undertake more vigorous operations in the Channel. Keyes, one of the few senior naval officers to come out of the Dardanelles campaign with any credit, needed no urging. The most spectacular demonstration of the new offensive spirit came in April with the 'Zeebrugge Raid', aimed at blocking the entrances to the Bruges (Brugge) ship canal in Zeebrugge harbour and to Ostend harbour some 15 miles down the coast, as well as inflicting as much damage as possible on both ports.

Devised and led by Keyes personally, the operation involved some seventy-five ships and began with superb symbolic timing at one minute past midnight on St George's Day, 23 April. A force of Royal Marines was to mount a diversionary attack on the mile-long Zeebrugge Mole, destroying the gun batteries, seaplane station and defences, in order to draw the Germans' attention from the main object, the blocking of the ship canal. The action was pure Nelson. The little force was carried to the mole by the old cruiser *Vindictive* and two River Mersey passenger ferries, the *Daffodil* and *Iris II*. *Daffodil*'s task was to push *Vindictive* hard up against the mole, then to pull alongside the mole and disembark her marines.

The Germans, if not actually expecting the attack, were alert nonetheless. A smokescreen that had been laid by motor launches to cover the approach had been dispersed when the wind changed direction half an hour before the vessels arrived, and *Vindictive* came under fire as she approached, with many casualties among the storming party. *Daffodil* managed nevertheless to push *Vindictive* against the mole, but could not then disengage, and her marines had to disembark via the cruiser. *Iris II* was unable to land her marines directly on the mole either, and tried to get alongside *Vindictive* instead, but was only able to get a few men off before having to pull away.

At a quarter past midnight, the viaduct connecting the mole to the shore was severed by the submarine HMS C3 to prevent the Germans from counter-attacking. C3's commanding officer, Lieutenant Richard Sandford, son of the Archdeacon of Exeter, ran his boat, packed with high explosive, between the iron pillars of the bridge, had the crew taken off by motor boats, then set the fuzes. He was just able to get away before the explosion.

Meanwhile, three concrete-filled blockships were scuttled in the narrow access channel, though not in the intended positions. In the event, they would only obstruct the canal for a few days, for the Germans removed two piers on the western bank of the canal and dredged a channel through the silt near the sterns of the blockships, which allowed them to get two U-boats past at each high tide. The attempt to block the harbour at Ostend failed altogether when the blockships grounded too far out.

Keyes would make a second attempt in poor weather on 9 May, this time with *Vindictive* as the main blockship; but she too settled in the wrong position, and the entrance remained open.

Casualties at Zeebrugge were heavy for the numbers engaged: over 200 killed and missing, and 400 wounded. Not surprisingly, although in strict terms a failure, the operation was promoted as a victory, with the award of eight VCs, including one for Sandford of the C3, and numerous other decorations for gallantry. The 4th Battalion Royal Marines were deemed to have acted collectively with such valour that two of the VCs were awarded by ballot under rule 13 of the Victoria Cross Warrant, the last time that awards were made by this procedure.

Ludendorff was not to be distracted by pinpricks, however. Besides, he did not believe that the *Kaiserliche Marine* would now achieve anything worthwhile. This was, indeed, the ultimate reason for his great *Kaiserschlacht* offensive. On 27 May he renewed the attack, but this time in the direction of Paris – calling it Operation Blücher–Yorck after the duke of Wellington's great Prussian partner in scourging the French at Waterloo, and Field Marshal Ludwig Yorck, who with Blücher had led the Prussians in the storming of Paris the year before (and in whose honour Beethoven's *Yorckscher Marsch* is named). On a 24-mile front astride the old Aisne battlefield, in the early hours of the morning, 4,000 guns began yet another *Feuerwaltz* bombardment with HE, gas and smoke. In the French sector, along the Chemin des Dames, the Germans broke through to a depth of 12 miles, annihilating four divisions in the process. In just six hours, between Soissons and Rheims, the Germans reached the Aisne, destroying another four French and four British divisions. By the end of the following day a 40-mile-wide, 15-mile-deep salient had been driven into the allied line, and on the fourth day Ludendorff's men reached the Marne near Château-Thierry.

Elsewhere, however, the Germans were not having it all their own way. On 28 May the first entire American brigade would go into attack, at Cantigny on the Somme. The French army provided air cover and additional artillery support – a preliminary bombardment and then a creeping barrage – plus a dozen tanks and the new flame-thrower, which proved particularly effective. The Americans took the village and a hundred prisoners, though not without loss. It was, however, as great a symbolic success as a tactical one, and Pershing gave the order that no inch of Cantigny was to be surrendered. In the next three days the Germans made no fewer than seven counter-attacks, with poison gas, but the Americans held despite mounting casualties – over 1,000 by the time they were relieved, including 200 killed. The brigade commander, the 50-year-old Iowan Colonel Hanson E. Ely, recalled: 'They could only stagger back, hollow-eyed with sunken cheeks, and if one stopped for a moment he would fall asleep.'

Cantigny gave warning – to the Germans and allies alike – that the Americans, though recently arrived and still green in Western Front fighting, were not to be taken lightly. It also gave force to Pershing's argument for an independent US army command. At the meeting of the supreme war council at Versailles on 1 June, Pershing revealed that the planned strength of the AEF in 1919 was now 100 divisions. Although the point was not discussed, such a figure would place Pershing in the driving seat, perhaps even as *generalissimo*. It would also place President Wilson in an almost unassailable position from which to dictate terms of peace.

For the time being, though, Haig fumed in his diary, 'the ignorance of the Americans in all things connected with an Army [was] appalling'.

47

JUNE

The Bread Offensive

The war takes a turn in the allies' favour in Italy and the Balkans

While Ludendorff's attention was focused primarily on the *Kaiser-schlacht*, his continuing offensive on the Western Front, he was only too well aware of the interconnection of the four discrete European fronts. In the east, fighting had effectively come to an end with the Treaty of Brest-Litovsk in March, and what troops remained there were a force of observation, except in Finland, where the Bolsheviks were reluctant to cede independence under the terms of the treaty. Ludendorff had sent the Baltic Division to assist the former Tsarist General Carl Gustav Mannerheim, later President of Finland, to eject the remaining Russian troops and put down the Finnish communists. By the end of May, German troops held both Vyborg (western Russia) and Narva (Estonia), respectively north and south of the Gulf of Finland. These Ludendorff intended to use as bases for an advance on Petrograd if it became necessary to overthrow the Bolshevik government, or to prevent the British troops sent to Murmansk in support of the 'White Russian' (anti-Bolshevik) forces from doing so themselves.

The Italian and Macedonian fronts had been quiet for many months, but Ludendorff was content: 'they formed the protection of our flanks, the Macedonian Front at the same time protecting the flank of Austria-Hungary', he wrote in his memoirs. This seemingly distant backwater was, however, rather less secure than he supposed, for morale in the poorly fed and ill-equipped Bulgarian army, which, with a stiffening of German generals, formed the major part of the Macedonian front, was beginning to ebb.

The capitulation the previous month of the Romanians, who after the Russian collapse were effectively surrounded and unable to continue the fight, had at first seemed propitious. The Romanian army, if not exactly agile, had been numerically strong. In July the previous year they had fielded eighty infantry and nineteen cavalry divisions and over 900 artillery batteries – some 800,000 men, with around a million in immediate reserve. The Treaty of Bucharest, signed on 7 May, allowed Ludendorff to withdraw several divisions from the Balkans, which added to his own reserves for the *Kaiserschlacht*. This, however, immediately weakened Bulgarian enthusiasm for the fight, for many army officers, seeing the Turks as the traditional enemy, had anyway tended to favour the Entente. Allied strength on the Macedonian front had received a boost in late 1917, too, with the entry of Greece into the war, and at the end of May the Royal Greek Army, though fielding only ten divisions, roundly defeated the Bulgarians in a two-day battle at Skra-di-Legen, north-west of Salonika.

The other factor on the Macedonian front was Serbia, which the Austrians and Bulgarians had over-run in 1916. The country remained turbulent, but extreme repressive measures had largely kept it in check. The Serbian army, though, having been evacuated via Albania and Montenegro by the Italian navy, had then been re-equipped by the allies and was also biding its time in Macedonia. Indeed, the manpower ratio on this southernmost front was now around three to two in the allies' favour (720,000 Serbian, French, British, Greek and Italian to 575,000 Bulgarian, German and Turk) – with even better ratios in artillery (two to one) and aircraft (ten to one).

Nevertheless, in March, the Austrians – who might have been

expected to reinforce their allies in the Balkans – had instead sent reinforcements to the Western Front to support the *Kaiserschlacht*: first artillery and then, in accordance with the new treaty of mutual assistance signed in May (the *Waffenbund* – literally, 'weapons federation'), several divisions. With ammunition in short supply, however, the artillery had soon returned to the Italian front; and the Austro-Hungarian army had received a boost after Brest-Litovsk with the repatriation of several hundred thousand prisoners of war, although some, notably the Czecho-Slovaks, heeding President Wilson's promise of national determination, had decided to join the allies – or, at least, the White Russians – instead. (Jaroslav Hasek, author of the semi-autobiographical comic novel *The Good Soldier Schweik*, was a member of this 'Czecho-slovak Legion' until, disillusioned, he defected to the Red Army.)

Yet while the boost in manpower was obviously welcome, it increased the logistic difficulties – notably food supply – with which the Austrians had been struggling for some time. Still, the Austrian chief of staff, General-Oberst Arthur Arz von Straußenburg, felt ready to go on to the offensive once more against the Italians, who were now strengthened by French and British divisions and holding firm positions on the Piave, to where they had withdrawn after the débâcle at Caporetto in October. Numerically, the two sides were evenly matched, but the Austrians' supply situation had become so acute that Straußenburg saw the offensive in part as the solution to his problems, for the north Italian plain beyond the Piave was a veritable storehouse. Indeed, the army began speaking of it as *das Brot Offensiv* – the bread offensive.

Meanwhile on the Western Front, Ludendorff, having closed down Operation Blücher–Yorck, the renewed offensive towards Paris, on 11 June, and then on 14 June its adjunct Operation Gneisenau, launched five days before astride the Oise, began hoping that 'relief on the Western Front might be secured in Italy itself'. The cost of the *Kaiserschlacht* was already enormous, with very little strategically to show for it. The Germans had lost 160,000 men in Operations Blücher–Yorck and Gneisenau alone, and although the allies had lost as many, they at least had had the satisfaction of success in halting the offensives.

Ludendorff's hopes of relief were soon to be dashed. On 15 June, the Austrians attacked, directing their main effort between Asiago, at the foothills of the Alps, and the sea. Straußenburg had some fifty-eight divisions available – almost 950,000 men, as many as Ludendorff had had at his disposal for the *Kaiserschlacht*. Facing him were fifty-seven divisions, but with a slight advantage in artillery – some 7,000 guns in all – and a considerable superiority in the air, with nearly 700 aircraft, including five squadrons of the newly formed RAF.

Two of the five British divisions hurriedly despatched to Italy in the aftermath of Caporetto had been recalled to the Western Front in March when the *Kaiserschlacht* began, but two were in the line. These held a front of about 5 miles south of Asiago, with the third remaining division in reserve, although influenza had rendered many troops sick. On 15 June the British divisions found themselves hard pressed opposing the Austrian main effort. In his despatch on the fighting, their corps commander, General the Earl of Cavan, one of the most capable senior British officers of the war – soon to be appointed to command a newly formed 10th (Anglo-Italian) Army – described how his front was attacked by four Austrian divisions:

[The line] was held by the 23rd Division on the right and the 48th Division on the left. On the front of the 23rd Division the attack was completely repulsed. On the front of the 48th Division the enemy succeeded in occupying our front trench for a length of some 3,000 yards, and subsequently penetrated to a depth of about 1,000 yards. Here he was contained by a series of switches [alternative positions], which had been constructed to meet this eventuality. On the morning of June 16th the 48th Division launched a counter-attack to clear the enemy from the pocket he had gained; this attack was completely successful, and the entire line was re-established by 9 a.m.

During the initial Austrian assault, Lieutenant Edward Brittain of the 11th Sherwood Foresters, brother of Vera Brittain, auxiliary nurse and author of *Testament of Youth*, was killed leading a local counter-attack. Brittain had won the Military Cross on the Somme and was highly regarded in the battalion, but it later emerged that his letters to England, intercepted by the censor, revealed that he had engaged in homosexual activity with one of his soldiers and that his commanding officer, Lieutenant-Colonel Charles Hudson, had been told in confidence that Brittain would face court martial when the battalion came out of the line. Hudson warned him obliquely, and it has been suggested that as a result Brittain put himself in the way of fire that first morning. Hudson himself, at twenty-six already with a DSO and bar as well as the MC, and barely four years older than Brittain, would win the VC that same morning, and be badly wounded in the course of doing so.

Opposite them was Lieutenant Ludwig Wittgenstein of the Austrian artillery, alumnus of Trinity College Cambridge and at twenty-nine already a philosopher of note. Almost killed directing the fire of his battery, he was decorated for bravery a third time.

Despite some local successes, however, the Austrians made no real progress that morning, or in the following days. Italian morale had recovered dramatically after Caporetto, in large part owing to the efforts, and personal qualities, of the new commander-in-chief, Armando Diaz. Under his leadership, commanders at all levels had taken to heart the lessons of Caporetto, adopting more 'elastic' tactics for the defence. Cavan himself noted that the

> High Command had ample reserves available and handled the situation with coolness and decision. Steps were at once taken to deprive the enemy of the gains which he had made. Torrential rains brought the Piave down in flood and added to the embarrassments of the enemy. Many of his bridges were washed away, and those which remained were constantly bombed by British and Italian aviators.

On a similar note, George Macaulay Trevelyan, who in 1918 was commanding the British Red Cross contingent in Italy, commented approvingly: 'Above all, the reserves were well handled, here locally as well as by Diaz on the grand scale. The Bersaglieri *ciclisti* were hurried up on their "push bikes" along the lanes to the threatened spot time after time, and never in vain.'

After a week, Straußenburg called off the offensive and withdrew his hard-won bridgeheads back north of the Piave. His casualties had been woefully heavy: nearly 12,000 dead, 80,000 wounded and 25,000 made prisoner. The allies had suffered too, with 8,000 dead, 30,000 wounded and nearly 50,000 made prisoner (many of whom were also wounded), but they remained masters of the field. As Cavan wrote:

> Not only was the original front line entirely re-established, but that portion of the right bank of the Piave, between the Piave and the Sile Rivers which had been in Austrian hands since November, 1917, was cleared of the enemy. Captured orders and documents proved beyond doubt that the enemy's plans were extremely ambitious, and aimed in fact at the final defeat of the Allied forces in Italy. The result was a complete and disastrous defeat for Austria.

Ferdinand Foch, the *generalissimo*, whose powers to coordinate and direct the allied armies now extended to the Italian front as well, pressed Diaz to mount a general counter-offensive to follow up his success. Diaz successfully argued against it, however. Like Pershing, he would not be hurried. When he mounted his grand offensive, he intended it to be decisive rather than merely exploitative. Besides, he argued, once the allies crossed the Piave they would face the same logistic problems that had confronted the Austrians. For the time being, therefore, content to bank the undoubted boost in morale his defensive victory had gained, Diaz ordered only limited actions to seize better start positions from which to launch his decisive offensive when the moment came. He could afford to take his time; the repulse was a catastrophic blow to the Austrian army's own morale and cohesion. From now on internal ethnic tensions would play an increasing part in the collapse of Austrian resistance.

Nor was it just on land that Italian morale received a boost that month. Just before the Austrian attack, the *Regia Marina* (Royal

Italian Navy) had sent the *Szent István* to the bottom of the Adriatic – the only dreadnought on either side to be sunk at sea by direct action. The allies had been strengthening the Otranto Barrage, making it almost impossible for even U-boats to get through the straits into the Mediterranean. The new commander of the *Kaiserliche und Königliche Kriegsmarine* (Austria-Hungary's 'Imperial and Royal' Navy), Rear-Admiral Miklós Horthy, who after the war would become Regent of Hungary, decided to force the barrage by bringing the blockade ships to battle. During the night of 8 June, Horthy left the naval base at Pola on the Istrian coast (in modern Croatia) with two of his four dreadnoughts, *Viribus Unitis* and *Prinz Eugen*, for the attack on the barrage, while his other two dreadnoughts, *Szent István* and *Tegetthoff*, were to sail the following evening to rendezvous with him further down the coast. At first light on 10 June, two Italian motor torpedo-boats (*Motoscafo armato silurante* – MAS) under Lieutenant-Commander Luigi Rizzo, returning from patrol off the Dalmatian coast, spotted smoke from the *Szent István* and *Tegetthoff* group making for the rendezvous. Rizzo at once turned his boats towards the smoke, closed rapidly to penetrate the escort screen and made a run for the dreadnoughts.

MAS 21's two torpedoes ran wide of *Tegetthoff*, but MAS 15's hit the *Szent István* abreast her boiler-rooms. Both boats then evaded pursuit by dropping depth charges in their wake.

Szent István's aft boiler-room quickly flooded, giving her a ten-degree list to starboard. Counter-flooding of the portside trim cells and magazines reduced the list somewhat, but the crew were unable to plug the holes, and the captain therefore steered for the coast at low speed. Water continued to penetrate the forward boiler room and eventually all but two of the ship's twelve boilers were doused, cutting off power for the pumps. In a further effort to counter the list her captain ordered the turrets to be trained to port and their ready ammunition thrown overboard. *Tegetthoff* then tried to take her in tow, but had to abandon the attempt when it became clear that *Szent István* was about to founder. She capsized just after six o'clock, some two and a half hours after being struck, with the loss of eighty-nine crew. The number would have been far higher had not the *Kriegsmarine* changed its policy just before the war to require all seamen to be able to swim.

Horthy called off the attack on the barrage and his fleet returned to Pola, where it remained for the rest of the war. Days before the Armistice, a second of his dreadnoughts, the *Viribus Unitis* ('United Forces', the personal motto of the former emperor, Franz Joseph), would be sent to the bottom – sunk at anchor by Italian frogmen in a daring raid. By then, however – although, with the Austro-Hungarian Empire disintegrating so rapidly, the *Regia Marina* was unaware of it – *Viribus Unitis* had been handed over to the provisional Yugoslav navy.

Soon after *Szent István's* sinking, a Russian dreadnought was also sent to the bottom by torpedo – but one fired from a Russian destroyer. The *Empress Catherine the Great*, launched in 1914 for the Imperial Russian Navy's Black Sea Fleet, had been renamed after the February 1917 Revolution *Svobodnaya Rossiya* ('Free Russia'). When the Treaty of Brest-Litovsk was signed, she had slipped out of Sevastopol for the greater security of Novorossiysk on the eastern shore of the Black Sea, but was scuttled on 18 June when the Germans demanded she be handed over under the terms of the treaty.

The writing was well and truly on the wall for the German *Kaiserliche Marine* too. After a fruitless foray into the North Sea in April to attack a convoy, in which the battle-cruiser *Moltke* was almost sunk by a torpedo fired by the Royal Navy's submarine E42, the High Seas Fleet was to remain inactive at Wilhelmshaven for the rest of the war. Throughout, the Imperial German Navy had lost none of its dreadnoughts, though they in turn had failed to sink any of the Grand Fleet's, with the exception of HMS *Audacious*, which had struck a mine off the north coast of Ireland. Only after the Armistice were any of the Germans' dreadnoughts sent to the bottom – by hand of their own crews interned at Scapa Flow.

48

JULY

Friedensturm

*The Germans are finally halted on the Marne,
and Foch declares it time to go on the counter-offensive*

By the middle of July 1918, the great and desperate German offensive on the Western Front – *die Kaiserschlacht* – had begun to stall. The military correspondent of the *Berliner Tageblatt*, Lieutenant-General Armand Baron von Ardenne, tried to put a favourable gloss on the situation:

> Our three great battles of assault from March 21st to July 15th caused the enemy losses amounting to 1,225,000 men. On July 15th our attempted surprise failed, and, despite his losses, the enemy's numerical superiority had increased. Then the German command, swift as lightning and without the least hesitation, knew how to find the transition to the now necessary, although momentary, defensive. That was a strategic masterpiece that merits admiration.

The 'strategic masterpiece' was no more than acknowledging reality, but credit was still due to the operations section of the *Oberste*

Heeresleitung, and in particular to its head, Lieutenant-Colonel Georg von Wetzell. During the planning for *die Kaiserschlacht* Wetzell had warned Ludendorff not to expect – and therefore not to attempt – any spectacular success, proposing instead that they take the line of least resistance rather than going for the seemingly most significant objectives. This offered the possibility of progressively prising apart the allied line. Ludendorff had accepted this in principle, but in the event had proved reluctant to break off attacks that appeared to be going well against what he considered to be important objectives. Having failed to make any significant progress in April against the northernmost sector of the British line (Operation Georgette), he had then devised a diversionary attack on the Aisne, hoping thereafter to be able to mount a second thrust towards the Channel ports. This part of the line was held by the French 6th Army under General Denis Duchêne and included the British IX Corps, which had been sent to what was supposed to be a quiet sector to recover from the March battles. It soon became apparent that an attack was imminent, however, and to counter the German infiltration tactics, but contrary to instructions, Duchêne massed his troops in the forward trenches. The three British divisional commanders, having suffered the penalties of forward defence against the new German tactics in Flanders, protested. Duchêne, an experienced infantryman, remained adamant.

The attack – Operation Blücher–Yorck – began at 1 a.m. on 27 May with another huge *Feuerwaltz* bombardment by some 3,700 German guns, saturating the gun emplacements, cutting field telephone lines and isolating the headquarters, and disorientating the defenders. Captain Sidney Rogerson of the Royal Sussex Regiment, attached to 23rd Brigade headquarters, described the scene:

> Crowded with jostling, sweating humanity the dugouts reeked, and to make matters worse headquarters had no sooner got below than the gas began to filter down. Gas masks were hurriedly donned and anti-gas precautions taken – the entrances closed with saturated blankets and braziers were lighted on the stairs. If gas could not enter, neither could the air.

The bombardment inflicted devastating casualties. The Germans were able to take the dominating ridge of the Chemin des Dames, while further east, near Rheims, they broke through and were across the Aisne in six hours. By 6 June they were within shelling distance of Paris, and Ludendorff, exhilarated by the prospect of reaching the capital (where the government was once again contemplating decamping to Bordeaux) tried to extend the offensive westward (Operation Gneisenau) to draw yet more allied reserves south, and to join up with his salient at Amiens. However, the French were ready for this, with defence in depth along the River Matz.

It was during Operations Blücher–Yorck and Gneisenau that the US Marine Corps fought its first large-scale action since its founding in 1775. For three weeks the 4th Marine Brigade, alongside the 3rd Infantry Brigade in Major-General Omar Bundy's 2nd US Division, checked the Germans at Belleau Wood, on the Marne. For the United States it was the largest battle since Appomattox (1865) in the Civil War. General 'Black Jack' Pershing, commanding the American Expeditionary Force, is supposed to have said afterwards: 'The deadliest weapon in the world is a United States Marine and his rifle.' It echoed a German intelligence report that described the marines as 'vigorous, self-confident, and remarkable marksmen'.

As before, in mid-June the combination of over-extended supply lines, exhaustion, stiffening allied resistance and counter-attacks brought the German advance to a halt, but at this point Ludendorff, either through desperation or, with Paris so close, genuine miscalculation, finally gave up on Wetzell's concept of seeking the most promising axis of advance. Seeing it was now or never, he gambled on sheer mass, and artillery bluster, though it would take him a month to garner the strength to do so. His grandiloquently named *Friedensturm* (peace offensive), he told the commanders of 1st, 3rd and 7th Armies, would draw the allied reserves south from Flanders, knock out the BEF, expand the salients and bring the Entente (and Americans) to the negotiating table.

By now, though, the allies were getting the measure of the new German tactics. Duchêne himself had been removed from 6th Army and replaced by the colonial artillerist Jean Degoutte, who after the Armistice would command the French Army of the Rhine, and the commander-in-chief, Philippe Pétain, insisted on what he called 'a recoiling buffer defence'. The idea was that, just as the hydraulic railway buffer absorbs impact, the lightly held forward defences would yield to the storm troops, who, outrunning the cover of their own guns and their impetus spent, would be stopped on a strong position in rear and pummelled by the defenders' artillery – the very system the Germans themselves had used to such effect at Third Ypres.

The *Friedensturm* opened on 15 July, but, warned by air reconnaissance and German prisoners, the French were ready. The warning did not come without cost, however, for aerial combat and 'strafing' of ground troops had been intense, and aircraft losses high. Earlier in the month, Major James McCudden VC, DSO and bar, MC and bar, MM – at 23, one of the most decorated British airmen or indeed British soldiers – had been killed in a crash following an engine failure; and before the month was out, one of the RAF's highest-scoring 'aces' and another of its most decorated officers, Major 'Mick' Mannock VC, DSO and two bars, MC and bar, was also dead, killed in a dogfight over the German lines. The day before the *Friedensturm* began, former President Theodore Roosevelt's fourth and youngest son Quentin, not yet twenty-one, was shot down and killed. (His other three sons were also in action, with the infantry and artillery.)

The loss of surprise had gone hard with the Germans. Herbert Sulzbach, adjutant of an artillery regiment in the 9th (Prussian) Division, recalled how the 'first French prisoners came in and told us they knew of our offensive. Our mood was not good after we heard this.' The French heavies shelled the *Sturmtruppen* even before they had left their primitive trenches. Machine guns cut them down savagely in the loose-knit forward defence zone, and then as they ran on to the main position – in the open, and beyond the covering range of their own guns – they were pulverized by every manner of artillery, not least the famous quick-firing *soixante-quinze*, tailor-made for the job.

East of Rheims the offensive stuttered bloodily to a halt, and although on 16 July, to the west of the city, under cover of darkness and smoke, the Germans did manage to get across the sacred Marne (the battle would be known officially as Second Marne) to threaten the Rheims–Epernay road – where the newly arrived 8th Italian Division suffered heavy casualties – by next day here too the attacks had petered out.

On 18 July, the French, with nine US divisions now fighting alongside them, and with British support on their left, counter-attacked. This time they used 'the Cambrai key' (so called after the British tank attack at Cambrai in November 1917): no preparatory bombardment to give away what was coming, enabling the tanks to gain the advantage of surprise, and then exceptional weight of artillery fire on the support trenches and battery positions. Crown Prince Wilhelm, the German army group commander, summed up the tactical shock: 'Without artillery preparation, simply following the sudden rolling barrage, supported by numerous deep-flying aircraft and with unprecedented masses of tanks, the enemy infantry – including a number of American divisions – unleashed the storm against the 9th and 7th Armies at 5:40 in the morning.'

Herbert Sulzbach recalled how his battery

> moved into the front line and were attacked by a barrage which was absolutely unbelievable. It was the worst barrage and the worst gunfire I ever heard, and I had been through the Somme and everything else since then . . . the gas attacks [were] fearsome. The gas stuck into the high grass so that even our horses had gas masks.

The French tanks were smaller, faster and more agile than the earlier models, too – the new Renault 'FT' (all Renault projects had a two-letter product code bearing no particular significance), armed with a 37 mm cannon or Hotchkiss machine gun in a revolving turret. (The British 'Whippet' tank, which mounted four machine guns and could make 8 mph, the speed of a trotting horse, had first gone into action in late March.) Aircraft in the ground attack role added to the Germans' discomfort. Sulzbach noted: 'Their aircraft were flying very low and seeing everything that we were doing and bombing us in daylight.'

Yet somehow the Germans managed to rally, and despite French advances of 5 miles on the first day, their counter-attack was eventually halted. For the Americans in particular, the Marne counterattack was another sharp and salutary blooding. The Germans, especially when cornered, were still lethal – even to the bravest, corn-fed 'doughboy' if he was a novice in battlecraft, as many hastily trained recruits were. The French, by contrast, were now perhaps too wary; or, as the former infantry officer, historian of the war and military theorist Basil Liddell Hart put it, 'unlike the Americans they suffered too much from experience'.

Nevertheless, German casualties in the Marne battles were well over 100,000, with 25,000 more taken prisoner, and the critical loss of nearly 800 guns. Ludendorff was forced to abandon his Flanders stroke planned for 20 July, and his front was now over-stretched and under-fortified. It ran (in places meandered) over 300 miles – 70 more than when he had launched the *Kaiserschlacht*. Instead of the formidable defences of the Hindenburg Line and elsewhere, there were now vulnerable salients and primitive entrenchments. His losses since April had been staggering: perhaps as many as a million dead, wounded or missing. As early as 8 May, the chief of staff of Crown Prince Rupprecht's army group, Generalleutnant Hermann von Kuhl, had confided the grim state of affairs to his diary:

> Our supply of reinforcements and replacements is virtually exhausted . . . I doubt if further major offensives will be possible . . . The Americans are on their way. I am really doubtful if we shall be able to force a decision. We are not going to achieve a breakthrough – and then there is the issue of horses and the supply of oats.

The men on the ground knew it too, no matter how unprepared they were to admit it openly. Herbert Sulzbach said simply: 'We realised something had gone wrong, our losses were enormous . . . We realised it was the beginning of the end.'

Foch, however, the *generalissimo*, knew exactly what he had to do. On 24 July he told Haig, Pershing and his own senior officers: 'The moment has come to abandon the general defensive attitude forced upon us recently by numerical inferiority and to pass to the offensive.'

49

AUGUST

The Black Day of the German Army

The allies go on the counter-offensive

For nearly four years the guiding principle of the allied commanders – the thrusting Foch, the cautious Pétain, the doggèd Haig – had been that only offensive operations could decide matters. *Field Service Regulations*, the British Army's 'bible', held that the chief factor in success was 'a firmer determination in all ranks to conquer at any cost'. But *Field Service Regulations* also made it clear that the situation had to be favourable for offensive action to be advisable: 'If the situation be unfavourable for such a course [a vigorous offensive], it is wiser, when possible, to manoeuvre for a more suitable opportunity.'

For nearly four years, however, the allies – Italy included, perhaps even Italy especially, if not for quite as long – had persevered with the doctrine of the offensive when the situation was not so much unfavourable as futile. Now, in the high summer of 1918, having lost countless hundreds of thousands of men in repeated attempts to make the situation fit the doctrine, rather than the other way round, the allies found themselves in a position where the situation

355

really had – at last – changed to fit the doctrine. The high-water mark of *die Kaiserschlacht*, Ludendorff's own great and desperate offensive to knock out the Entente before the Americans arrived in overwhelming numbers – indeed, the high-water mark of the entire four-year German offensive in the west – was now visible; and soon would be heard its 'melancholy, long, withdrawing roar'.

The failure of Ludendorff's attack on the Marne in July – the *Friedensturm* or 'peace offensive' – would prove to be the *Kaiserschlacht*'s final battle. The subsequent German retreat to ground that they could hold was Foch's signal to begin the counter-push, if cautiously at first.

He had already been planning to reduce the salient at St-Mihiel, near the sector of the American buildup, and also to push the Germans back at Amiens to free the railway lines there from German artillery fire, for they were critical to the movement of reserves and supplies. Meanwhile Haig had been making his own plans (proposed by Henry Rawlinson) to attack at Amiens. When the BEF had at last managed to halt its own retreat after Ludendorff's offensive had broken 5th Army's front, Rawlinson's 4th Army had closed the gap astride the Somme, forming a junction with the French to the south. Throughout June, the British III Corps on the left, under Lieutenant-General Richard Butler, who had risen four ranks since commanding the 2nd Lancashire Fusiliers in 1914, and the Australian Corps under John Monash on the right, had made vigorous local counter-attacks. What these showed was that the tactics developed for offensive operations in the light of the experience of Third Ypres – re-organization of the platoon into assault parties and Lewis light machine-gun teams, well-rehearsed techniques of fire covering movement, and better all-arms coordination – were indeed battleworthy. The attacks also showed that the open, firm ground south of the Somme was especially suitable for a larger offensive.

Foch agreed to Haig's plan to attack at Amiens but insisted that the French 1st Army to the right also take part. Rawlinson objected at first as he wanted to use tanks instead of a preliminary bombardment – 'the Cambrai key' – so as not to sacrifice surprise, and the French 1st Army hadn't enough. The obvious compromise was reached: the French would not launch their attack until forty-five minutes after 4th Army went into action, so that their own bombardment would not begin before 4th Army's zero hour. North of the Somme III Corps would attack, with the Australian Corps under John Monash to their right astride the river, and the Canadian Corps under the 42-year-old Lieutenant-General Sir Arthur Currie to the right of the Australians and alongside the French. (In his memoirs, Lloyd George claimed that he seriously considered Currie, a militia officer – in civilian life an estate agent – as a replacement for Haig.) The Canadians, who were generally reckoned to be the best corps on the Western Front, were brought from Flanders especially for the operation. The move was conducted in great secrecy for, given the corps' reputation, had they been discovered the Germans would have assumed an attack was imminent. As deception, two Canadian battalions and a casualty clearing station were sent to Ypres with scant concealment, as well as a wireless unit to serve false signal intelligence to the German intercept stations.

By early August, aerial reconnaissance and artillery sound-ranging had located nine out of ten of the German batteries in the area. With the improved mathematical methods for 'predicted fire', these could be struck at zero hour without prior 'registration', the older technique of establishing the exact range and bearing by fire beforehand – visually observed, usually from the air, corrected, and the coordinates recorded. The disadvantage of registration was that it told the batteries they had been located, and prompted them to move. It also told the higher command that an offensive was probably imminent. Besides the mathematical improvements, predicted fire required very precise locating. Aerial photography was crucial, but sound-ranging had also become significant. The system developed had been one of the more impressive technical advances in gunnery during the war. Pairs of microphones were used to determine the bearings to the source of the sound. By calibrating the observed flash of the gun with the time of the sound's arrival at the microphone, the range could be calculated, and the intersection of the bearings gave the battery's location. The method had been perfected by the 28-year-old Australian Lawrence Bragg, who in 1915 had won the Nobel Prize in physics, and had subsequently been commissioned in the Royal Artillery.

Rawlinson's fire plan was devastating. At zero hour, as the tanks gained the initial surprise, 2,000 guns would open up counter-battery fire, bombard the German reserve trenches, and provide a creeping barrage for the infantry to shelter behind in the advance. A total of 450 tanks would take part, the Canadian and Australian corps each being allocated a brigade of 108 Mark Vs (the latest model), thirty-six Mark V 'Star' tanks adapted to carry a section of infantry with a light machine-gun team – and twenty-four unarmed tanks for ammunition resupply. A battalion of fifty Mark V tanks was allocated to III Corps, while a hundred 'Whippet' tanks each with four machine guns and a speed of up to 8 mph, plus several score armoured cars, were attached to Lieutenant-General Charles Kavanagh's Cavalry Corps, which, as at Cambrai, was to be held in close reserve for exploitation. Seventy more Whippets were sent to the French.

The security measures taken to mask the noise created by the deployment of all these machines were imaginative. In 1980, as the SAS prepared to storm the Iranian Embassy in London to release the hostages held by a group of armed militants, the noise of drilling as fibre-optic surveillance cables were introduced into the building was masked by getting air-traffic control to reroute passenger jets low overhead on their approach to Heathrow. It was a much-celebrated ruse, but not a new one. The night before the attack at Amiens in August 1918, the RAF's Handley Page bombers flew for hours over the front to drown the noise of the tanks coming forward.

On 8 August, just after first light, and in thick fog, the attack began. Private James Southey of the Australian Corps wondered

how we were going to get on. But, forward we pushed, and met comparatively slight opposition. Some Germans surrendered quickly. Others fought to the end. As we pushed on wondering where we were, the sun broke through and we began to see countryside that we hadn't seen for quite a time. It was unscarred, all sorts of cultivated land, and we began to feel, 'By Jove, the war's coming to an end. We're getting through.' And we had a feeling of great uplift about the whole job.

In the centre the Australians and Canadians advanced quickly – 3 miles by mid-morning – and by dusk, aided by the RAF's constant 'strafing' of the roads to harry the Germans as they withdrew and intercept reserves as they came forward, they had punched a 15-mile-wide hole in the forward defences south of the Somme. In all, that day, Rawlinson's 4th Army took 13,000 prisoners, and the French 3,000. A further 14,000 Germans had been killed or wounded. Losses in 4th Army – British, Australian and Canadian – were by no means light, however: nearly 9,000, including many tank crews. Corporal Harry Brice of the Canadian Engineers recalled coming across one tank that had been destroyed along with its crew by a German 5.9 howitzer that had depressed its barrel to fire at 15 yards' range. In doing so, it had also killed every one of the German gunners. As Private Southey said, some just fought to the end.

The cavalry had not been able to 'gallop through the "G" in "Gap"', however, for despite the success in punching a hole in the forward defences, no true gap had been made – or, at least, none that could be kept open. The Tank Corps staff had suggested letting the Whippets go ahead on their own, but both Haig and Rawlinson preferred to keep them in close support of Kavanagh's horsemen, for the lesson of Cambrai was that without machine-gun support the cavalry would be stopped in the rear of the battle area before being able to get a gallop in open country. Nevertheless some Whippets did break through into the German rear areas, playing havoc with the artillery. One of them, *Musical Box* (crews invariably named their machines, a nod, perhaps, to the tank's naval origins), commanded by Lieutenant Clement Arnold, roamed at will for nine hours, shooting up a battery, an observation balloon, an infantry battalion's camp and a divisional transport column, before being knocked out and set alight by an artillery round. The driver was killed as they tried to escape, but Arnold and his gunner were taken prisoner – and would have been despatched on the spot had it not been for the intervention of a German infantry officer, Ritter Ernst von Maravic. In gratitude as they were rescued from the homicidal *Feldgrauen*, Arnold gave Maravic his watch, a 21st-birthday present from his father. In 1931, Maravic made contact with Arnold, visited him and returned the watch.

In his memoirs, Ludendorff called Thursday, 8 August 'der schwarze Tag des deutschen Heeres' – the black day of the German army (literally, of the German armies). It was not so much the ground that the allies had taken, although that itself was impressive, as that the morale of his troops had so evidently buckled. Men had surrendered without a fight; and, as among the Russians in 1917, fleeing troops had shouted 'You're prolonging the war!' at officers who tried to rally them, and 'Blackleg!' (*Streikbrecher*) at reserves moving up.

When he received Ludendorff's report, the Kaiser said: 'I see that we must strike a balance. We are at the end of our reserves. The war must be ended.'

But while Wilhelm hoped to gain favourable terms, principally by appealing to President Wilson and his 'Fourteen Points', the proposals about which Britain and France had been so lukewarm, Ludendorff knew that the army would now face the hardest fight to prevent catastrophic defeat. His professional sense told him that the only feasible option was a strategic retreat like that of Operation Alberich (the withdrawal to the Hindenburg Line the previous year) to dislocate the allies' now inevitable counter-offensive. Indeed, some of Ludendorff's officers were already urging this very course. But how could he ask the army to retreat over the very ground that was still wet with their blood – and when he had just promised them victory (or at least peace) in the last big push?

To the allies, meanwhile, rapid and decisive victory did not yet seem a foregone conclusion. On 25 July, Henry Wilson, chief of the imperial general staff, had issued a memorandum entitled 'Military Policy 1918–19', in which he stated that '1st July 1919 should be taken as the date by which all preparations are to be completed for the opening of the main offensive campaign'. Indeed, even after such a promisingly large bag of prisoners on the first day, the Amiens attack had petered out in the days that followed, for the old problem of the Germans' being able to seal the breach faster than the attackers could exploit it had still not been overcome. Foch urged Haig to renew the attack, but Haig had at last learned the lesson of the Somme and Third Ypres – not to slog away at hardening resistance. Instead of returning to GHQ, however, the great and palatial 'War Office' at Montreuil-sur-Mer, Haig stayed near the front, forming a tactical headquarters, and showing a greater readiness to listen to his army and corps commanders when they advised against delivering unprepared attacks on new German positions. He now switched the main effort back north, to Julian Byng's 3rd Army, which had been preparing to attack at Bapaume, but told him to do '[no] more attacking than was absolutely necessary. Our object is to keep the battle going as long as possible, until the Americans can attack in force.'

On 21 August Byng launched his attack, and three days later 1st Army under Henry Horne joined in the general offensive north of Rawlinson's recuperating 4th Army. This rash-like spread of attacks now forced Ludendorff to do what his advisers had urged earlier – withdraw to the old Hindenburg Line as far south as Soissons.

But this time there would be no opportunity for the delaying tactics of Alberich – the demolitions, booby traps and general 'scorched-earth' policy that had made of it what Wetzell had called the 'shot-to-pieces battle area'. Nor would they be allowed to withdraw unharried: this time they would be pressed every mile of the way, not least from the air.

It was the beginning of what would come to be known as the 'Hundred Days' – a reference to Napoleon's bid for victory in 1815 (though he, of course, was unsuccessful) – which would culminate in the eleventh-hour ceasefire of 11 November.

50

SEPTEMBER
The Return Push

The Americans at last attack in strength

In September the Americans were at last ready to fight as a separate entity, rather than single divisions in support of the British or French. On 10 August, the American 1st Army had formally come into existence under command of General John J. – 'Black Jack' – Pershing himself, who also remained commander-in-chief of the growing American Expeditionary Force. 1st US Army comprised in all some 300,000 troops, and its first object would be to take the St-Mihiel salient, between Verdun and Nancy. In 1914 the Germans had driven this triangular wedge into the French lines towards the Meuse, effectively severing direct rail communications between Paris and the easternmost part of the Western Front. Reducing the salient would be the Americans' first independent task of the war.

Pershing decided to do this with two 'super corps' each consisting of four or five divisions, and a third of three divisions, with two smaller French corps in support. The main attack was to be made against the south face by the US I and IV Corps, with a secondary thrust against the west face along the heights of the Meuse by the smaller V Corps (including the French 15th Colonial Division). To fix the enemy in the salient, a holding attack against the apex would be made by the French II Colonial Corps, and in reserve Pershing would hold three strong American divisions.

To maintain air superiority and provide close air support, some 1,500 aircraft were placed under Pershing's operational control, 40 per cent of them flown by American crews, the remainder by British, French and Italian. Nine bomber squadrons of the RAF were also placed at Foch's call.

Pershing's Field Order No. 9, dated 7 September, was straightforward: 'The First Army will attack at H hour on D day with the object of forcing the evacuation of the St. Mihiel Salient.' It was the first time that the terms 'D Day' and 'H Hour' were used.

Ludendorff, however, increasingly short of men and bracing for the coming counter-offensive, had already decided to withdraw from the salient to shorten the line. By D Day, therefore – 12 September – much of the German heavy artillery had already been withdrawn, and the Americans' progress was deceptively swift. The assault was led by a body of over 400 tanks, largely French, but including an American brigade of 140 Renault FT light tanks commanded by Colonel George S. Patton, whose 3rd Army in the Second World War would famously skirt the same ground in short order. Patton wrote to his father afterwards that 'in war as now waged there is little of the element of fear, it is too well organized and too stupendous'.

Nevertheless, the infantry fighting was no less visceral than elsewhere, not least for its taking place in the foulest weather. Private di Lucca, of the 42nd US Division (the 'Rainbow' Division), described how, in the darkness, because of the deluge of rain that had filled the trenches the night before, 'we had to form a line by holding each other by our raincoats ... during a terrible barrage which had started fifteen minutes earlier. Everything was coming down – trees, stones, rocks, everything came over our heads in the trenches'. At dawn they went over the top. The Germans, di Lucca recalled:

came out of their trenches [and] we met one another like a bunch of animals. We lost our senses; we charged them with our bayonets. I saw a German, a six-footer, coming towards me – why he picked me I don't know. Anyway, I saw him coming. I don't know what gave me the idea, what gave me the strength, but as soon as he came near me, I turned my rifle by the butt, broke his thrust and I hit him on the chin. All of a sudden he was bleeding. He let go his arm, put his hand towards his chin to find out where the blood came from. That gave me a clear spot: I turned the rifle and I hit him in mid chest with the bayonet. I left the bayonet there till he fell down.

By 13 September, the leading units of the US 1st Army had met up with the French troops advancing from the west, and three days later, having nipped off the salient completely, Pershing halted the offensive. Its objective had been achieved with remarkably light casualties. Colonel George C. Marshall, Roosevelt's chief of army staff in the Second World War and afterwards Secretary of State in the Truman administration, was in September 1918 one of the operational planners in Pershing's headquarters, and had been anxious about US public opinion. He had reckoned that

fifty thousand (50,000) casualties was the percentage normally to be expected and hospitalization was prepared accordingly. Nevertheless, if we suffered that many casualties during the brief period involved, the American people, not accustomed, as were our Allies, to such huge payments in human life, would have seized upon the criticism of any Allied official as a basis for condemning our own Commander in Chief.

The actual figures proved to be a fraction of the worst estimate: some 4,000 Americans had been killed and 3,000 wounded – over twice as many casualties as the Germans; but the Germans had also had 15,000 men taken prisoner, and lost 450 guns.

In fact, Pershing had wanted to continue the offensive towards Metz, but this, along with Haig's own more northerly push, would have meant offensives on diverging axes, which, while posing a real danger to the Germans, would have failed to concentrate the allied effort. Pershing reluctantly agreed therefore to realign his axis of advance north and further west towards Sedan, which would mean attacking through the particularly difficult sector east of the Argonne forest. Unfortunately, not having time to switch all his experienced divisions to this new axis, he would have to use green ones. And these would pay the price.

When news of Haig's intention to attack the Hindenburg Line reached London, the cabinet feared another Passchendaele. The CIGS, Henry Wilson, sent Haig a telegram warning of the consequences of high casualties. In his diary, Haig sneered at his masters as 'a wretched lot of weaklings'. Fortunately for Haig, Foch now covered his back by issuing the simple directive: 'Everyone is to attack (Belgians, British, French and Americans) as soon as they can, as strong as they can, for as long as they can.'

London (and Paris) had appointed Foch to be *generalissimo*; they must now live with the consequences.

Foch's design was for a gigantic pincer attack on the great German salient between Verdun and Ypres – the ejection, no less, of the 'Boche' from France. The right pincer was to be the Americans in the Meuse–Argonne to draw away reserves from the Cambrai–St-Quentin sector and threaten the Germans' railway communications through Lorraine. The left (British) pincer would, if driven deep enough, likewise threaten the lines of communication through the Liège corridor. The French would support each pincer on the inner flanks, while a further attack by a combined Anglo-Belgian force at Ypres would tie down any loose German reserves.

On 28 September Pershing was able to mass nearly 3,000 guns for a three-hour bombardment of the lightly held German forward defence zone before advancing on a 20-mile front. In theory, the odds in his favour were overwhelming – almost ten to one – but his expectations of progress were to prove unrealistic. His green troops largely fell into the trap set up by the Germans' elastic defence, pushing on rather too rapidly without adequate artillery cover, and in the centre the advance began to falter. As Pershing's orders had been for the whole line to advance together, the rapid progress made by his troops on the flanks was soon to no avail, and the fighting developed into a slogging match. And in forest fighting, the defender always has the advantage. The situation report issued by 1st Army for 29 September read: 'It would seem that our troops are not well organized for an attack. The gaining of the objectives for the present, does not seem possible without undue losses unless time is taken to reorganize and prepare for a concentrated, simultaneous attack.'

Nevertheless, there were some notable examples of sheer fighting spirit. Perhaps the most famous was that of Sergeant Alvin York – memorably portrayed by Gary Cooper in Howard Hawks' 1941 film *Sergeant York* – a pacifist-leaning draftee from Tennessee who killed fifteen Germans and took no fewer than 132 prisoners all in the same frenzied firefight.

When eventually Pershing called a halt, in mid-October, 1st Army had suffered 100,000 casualties – almost the strength of the entire United States regular army before the war. No one who had seen green troops in action for the first time was surprised, but the scale of the losses, on a par with those incurred in the offensives of 1916 and 1917, and for equally little gain, was a shock none the less. Contrary to Marshall's fears, however, American public opinion did not immediately falter, or lose confidence in Pershing.

The BEF's pincer had been rather more effective, exploiting the lines of least resistance to pierce the German front and threaten strongpoints from the flanks. On 27 September, after a thunderous overnight bombardment in which, said a sergeant-major of the Irish Guards, 'Even the wurrums themselves are getting up and crying for mercy,' and again with the help of the early-morning mist, 3rd Army's left and 1st's right attacked on the Canal du Nord, penetrating on a narrow front and then spreading out fan-like to break down the sides of the breach. By nightfall the following day they had reached Cambrai, beyond the northern edge of the Hindenburg Line, thereby threatening to turn it. Stiffening German resistance brought things to a standstill, however.

The baton was now passed to Rawlinson's 4th Army, on the right of Byng's 3rd, which had been preparing to assault the line with 3rd

Army's support, but now found the roles reversed. A two-day bombardment had prepared the way: 1,600 guns, one for every 3 yards, the first eight hours with gas driving the defenders under cover, the next day and a half with high explosive keeping them below ground to avoid the need for further gas, which would have hindered the attackers when they went forward. On 29 September, one British and two American divisions of Monash's Australian Corps (the more recently arrived Americans having been attached for training) spearheaded Rawlinson's attack on a 9-mile front. Again, the Americans pressed bravely but without the battlefield 'savvy' that the British had acquired the hard way. They gained their objectives but at much cost, and had to be rescued by the Australians.

Meanwhile, in a move that would have been familiar to the duke of Wellington's men in the Peninsular War, the British 46th Division, under cover of the smoke-thickened morning mist and using collapsible boats (and life-belts taken from Channel ferries), managed to get across the St-Quentin Canal near Bellenglise and, with scaling ladders, climb the 50-foot scarp to capture the machine-gun posts which were supposed to command the obstacle. The Germans were taken entirely by surprise. Sappers following close behind patched up several bridges that had been only partially demolished. Then, thanks to the much improved staffwork at divisional and corps level, instead of the attacking troops continuing until exhausted, with the consequent loss of momentum, a fresh division was passed through to carry the advance beyond the rear line of the Hindenburg defences.

The 46th, originally a Midland territorial division, had had a poor reputation since the Somme, but had been reinvigorated by the arrival only weeks before of the forty-year-old Gerald Farrell Boyd, 'the ranker general', who had enlisted in the Devonshire Regiment after failing the entry exam for the Royal Military Academy Woolwich. Having won the Distinguished Conduct Medal in the Boer War as a sergeant, he had been commissioned into the East Yorkshire Regiment, and in 1914 had been serving as a captain on the staff – a promotion since the outbreak of war of five ranks.

With tactical opportunities now presenting themselves, regimental, brigade and divisional leadership was all-important. Lieutenant-Colonel Bernard Vann MC, an Anglican priest who had originally tried to join up as a chaplain but had been turned down because of prejudice against clergy from the Church of England's Anglo-Catholic wing, commanded one of Farrell Boyd's battalions, the 6th Sherwood Foresters. In September 1914, Vann, a Cambridge graduate who had played professional football for Derby County, had enlisted instead in the Artists' Rifles, and the following April had been commissioned in the Foresters. Almost four years to the day after enlisting, as he led his battalion in the attack at Bellenglise, he won the VC, in the words of the citation:

> For most conspicuous bravery, devotion to duty and fine leadership during the attack . . . On reaching the high ground above Bellenglise the whole attack was held up by fire of all descriptions from the front and right flank. Realising that everything depended on the advance going forward with the barrage, Col. Vann rushed up to the firing line and with the greatest gallantry led the line forward. By his prompt action and absolute contempt for danger the whole situation was changed, the men were encouraged and the line swept forward. Later, he rushed a field-gun single-handed and knocked out three of the detachment. The success of the day was in no small degree due to the splendid gallantry and fine leadership displayed by this officer.

He would not learn of the decoration, however, for four days later he was killed leading yet another attack.

The 46th's breaching of the Hindenburg Line was one of the outstanding divisional actions of the war. It, and other successes at Ypres, now meant that the BEF were at last breaking into open country. Foch told Haig that the Germans could not resist the attacks for much longer, not least with the Americans going on the offensive continuously and 'learning all the time'. He was quite certain of it, indeed: 'Soon they will crack.'

51

OCTOBER

Tout le monde à la bataille!

*The Central Powers are assailed on all fronts,
and the Kaiser's regime crumbles*

At the culminating point of the battle of Waterloo, when his battered but defiant infantry had seen off Napoleon's last desperate attempt to break the allied line, the duke of Wellington took off his hat and waved it in the air to signal the whole line to advance. On 11 September 1918, Generalissimo Ferdinand Foch had done the same with his order: 'Everyone is to attack (Belgians, British, French and Americans) as soon as they can, as strong as they can, for as long as they can.'

Accordingly, across the entire Western Front, the allies had seized on the exhausted and much demoralized Germans and begun pressing them relentlessly. By the first week of October, the British (including all the dominion troops) were into open country. Two weeks later, in the Meuse–Argonne region, the Americans broke through the so-called Kriemhild Line and now threatened the great German railway base at Metz. The line's name proved to be prophetic, for Kriemhild, the wife of Siegfried in the Niebelung legends, was struck by a mighty sword-blow but said she felt no pain. It was only when she stooped to pick up a ring that her body fell into pieces. Everywhere, indeed, the increasingly desperate and erratic Ludendorff, de facto commander-in-chief of the German armies on all fronts, gave ground. His reserves were being pulled this way and that; a third of the entire German army spent September and October in or near slow-moving trains.

Even the dormant Macedonian front – tended by 'the gardeners of Salonika', as Clemenceau called them, for 'all they do is dig' – had come to life. Ludendorff had famously derided Macedonia as his greatest internment camp, but the allies had been steadily building up strength. They had lost the token Russian contingent there after the Treaty of Brest-Litovsk in March, but by that time had gained ample compensation in the nine divisions of the Greek army, Greece having in June 1917 finally been persuaded to join the Entente. By September 1918, the allies' advantage in manpower, artillery and aircraft on this southernmost front was overwhelming. The Bulgarians had begun to see the writing on their wall and were already preparing to quit Macedonia when the French General Franchet d'Espèrey, commanding the 'Allied Armies of the East', launched a two-pronged offensive in the middle of September, in which a Franco-Serbian army broke through at Dobro Pole. The fleeing Bulgarians were badly mauled by allied aircraft in the Kosturino and Kresna passes, and morale collapsed. The allies took Skopje, the capital of Macedonia, at the end of the month, by which time Bulgarian deserters had already reached Sofia and, with the Agrarian National Union, proclaimed a republic. The provisional government asked for an armistice, which Franchet d'Espèrey conceded on 29 September.

Austria's southern flank was now wide open, and Franchet d'Espèrey, who had made his name in the great counter-attack on the Marne in 1914, urged the supreme war council to let him press on north, believing that with an army of 200,000 he could cross Austria and Hungary, mass in Bohemia covered by the Czech Legion and take Dresden. Instead, Versailles told him to open up communications with Russia through Romania, while the Serbs retook their capital, Belgrade. The whole of the Central Powers' southern front was being systematically taken apart at the seams.

Ludendorff was literally prostrated by the news of the Bulgarian surrender. By some accounts he fell to the floor, foaming at the mouth. He told the Kaiser that the Bulgarian armistice had 'fundamentally changed the situation in view of the attacks being carried out on the Western Front', for to shore up his Balkan ally he had sent east his strategic reserve – several divisions – that could otherwise have been kept in France.

The situation in Germany itself was also becoming very ugly. The *Kaiserliche Marine* was increasingly restive, there were food riots in the major cities, and communist sentiment was rife and openly expressed. Indeed, to forestall revolution, the Kaiser sent for Prince Maximilian of Baden, a former major-general and prominent liberal, to be chancellor. On 3 October, the German government resigned.

Three days later, Haig visited Foch, who showed him one of the Paris newspapers, in which 'in large type was printed a note from Austria, Germany and Turkey, asking for an armistice at once, and stating their readiness to discuss conditions of peace on the basis of President Wilson's 14 points'.

It was somewhat premature, but in truth Ludendorff could find no succour from his remaining allies. With the climactic battle of Megiddo – ancient Armageddon, which according to the Book of Revelation was the place of the great battle at the end of time – Sir Edmund Allenby had chased the Turks out of Palestine, while in Mesopotamia, Lieutenant-General Sir William Marshall was about to make a final, successful push to secure the oil fields at Mosul. When the Bulgarians surrendered, the British Army of Salonika (Macedonia), under the shrewd Aberdonian Sir George Milne, turned east towards Constantinople. With nothing to stop Milne entering the Turkish capital, Enver Pasha and his cohort fled for Berlin, and on 15 October what remained of the Ottoman government asked for terms.

Next it would be the turn of the Austro-Hungarians to fall. Under Armando Diaz's judicious leadership, the Italians had roundly defeated their summer offensive on the Piave, Vienna having gambled what strength remained on a knockout blow. With French, British and American help, Diaz would now mount what would prove the decisive counter-offensive, launching it with exquisite theatrical timing, calculated to lift his own men and further depress the Austrians, on 24 October, the anniversary of Caporetto. The battle, known as Vittorio Veneto, after the small town at the furthest reach of the Italians' thrust, is sometimes dismissed as a walkover, the Austrians' morale having sustained a fatal blow at the Piave, but the Italians still suffered 30,000 casualties in the process.

Allied air power now began to assert itself conclusively. The ground-attack ('strafing') squadrons were never busier, even on the most distant fronts. Troops, guns and transport in the open were far easier targets than those in the years of entrenchments. In Palestine on 21 September the Turks had been caught in a defile north-east of Nablus and subjected to five hours' bombing and strafing, which, according to the official report, left them 'a dispersed horde of trembling individuals, hiding for their lives'. After the Italian victory at Vittorio Veneto at the end of October, the Conegliano–Pordonone road – the Austrians' principal escape route – was rendered impassable by aerial bombardment night and day. On the Western Front, although the terrain did not form many such defiles, the attacks were relentless nevertheless.

They were not pursued without cost, however; nor was the defensive fighting that preceded them. Between March and November 1918, for example, No. 80 Squadron RAF was in almost continuous action. Its average strength in pilot officers was twenty-two, and during this time a total of 168 officers were struck off strength (for all causes), a monthly attrition rate of 75 per cent. So high was the price the squadrons paid in those months that the losses would influence the RAF's post-war doctrine. Hugh Trenchard, the chief of the air staff, became convinced that the ground-attack role was not cost-effective, and would instead develop the concept of strategic bombing, the belief that the heavy bomber could win future wars without the aid of armies or navies.

With the steady collapse of all fronts, including the home, Prince Max of Baden had arrived in Berlin not a moment too soon. As the new chancellor, his first instinct was to ask for time to take stock, arguing that to seek an armistice was to make any peace initiative impossible. But on 3 October, with Ludendorff in despair, protesting 'I want to save my army' (a psychiatrist was called to Army headquarters after his foaming breakdown), Field Marshal Hindenburg, the titular chief of army staff and in effect pro-Kaiser, wrote: 'As a result of the collapse of the Macedonian Front . . . there is, so far as can be foreseen, no longer a prospect of forcing peace on the enemy.' Instead he insisted on an immediate appeal for an armistice.

A week later, however, Ludendorff had recovered his composure somewhat. The allies' advance on the Western Front was beginning to slow, and the resistance of his own troops seemed to be stiffening. Indeed, by 17 October there was such an improvement in the reports from the front that he felt able, without risk of precipitating rout, to order a general withdrawal to more secure positions to continue the fight.

Berlin's strategy now was to separate President Wilson from the other allied leaders, to try to negotiate with him on the basis of his apparently more conciliatory stance, rather than submit to what would be the far tougher terms of the Franco-British Entente. Wilson was not going to fall for that, however: he was determined that the German army be eviscerated to make sure there was no possibility of revanchism, although his reply to the German overtures confirmed his commitment to the 'Fourteen Points'. Ludendorff, whose mood swings must have been giving his psychiatrist and colleagues increasing cause for concern, but who realized the probable severity of the armistice conditions, now insisted that the war be carried on. When he learned that Berlin was not prepared to do this, he offered his resignation, which the Kaiser accepted on 26 October.

The long and, on the face of it, successful Hindenburg–Ludendorff partnership was finally broken – and acrimoniously – when the

Kaiser 'ordered' the field marshal to remain at his now largely ceremonial post. As the two men left the imperial presence, Hindenburg
tried to console his old friend. Ludendorff, however, believing that
Hindenburg should have insisted on resigning too, snapped back:
'You have treated me very shabbily.'

Adding to the ignominy of his 'betrayal', with revolution in the
wind (workers' risings were spreading throughout Germany),
Ludendorff had to lie low until, a week later, he was able to slip out
of Germany for Sweden disguised in blue spectacles and a false
beard.

Revolution was one thing, however; mutiny another. The
Hochseeflotte – the German High Seas Fleet – had not made any sortie in strength since April. This prolonged inactivity while the army
and submarine service were heavily engaged had done much to
undermine both the morale of the ratings and the self-respect of
the officers. Local mutinies had already resulted in executions,
exacerbating the tensions, when the naval command conceived the
truly Wagnerian solution of a *Tod Reit* ('Death Ride') – a desperate
sortie by the entire fleet, some eighteen battleships, five battle-
cruisers and supporting craft, with the aim of bringing every one of
the Royal Navy's ships to battle.

The *Hochseeflotte* assembled in Schillig Roads, Wilhelmshaven,
on 29 October to sortie the following day. That evening, however,
the crews convinced they were to be sacrificed to sabotage the
armistice negotiations, discipline dissolved. Next day, Admiral
Franz von Hipper, who had succeeded Reinhard Scheer in command of the *Hochseeflotte* in August, cancelled the operation and
ordered the squadrons to disperse in the hope of quietening things
down. When *III Geschwader* (3rd Battle Squadron) returned to Kiel,
however, their crews helped spark the more general mutiny of
3 November, which in turn spurred widespread military and civil
upheaval, and a general strike in Berlin.

A Soviet Germany looked imminent.

52

NOVEMBER

The Eleventh Hour

The Central Powers collapse, and Germany signs the Armistice

At the end of October, with the German army in retreat on the Western Front, the Kaiser had left the *Berliner Stadtschloss* for the *Oberste Heeresleitung* at Spa in Belgium (quartered, ironically, in the Hôtel Britannique). Ostensibly to avoid the Spanish flu sweeping the capital, in truth it was because army headquarters was a safer place to be, not so much for Wilhelm II's health as for his life: the atmosphere in Berlin was as metaphorically febrile as it was literally.

On 2 November, the Austro-Hungarian army rapidly disintegrating, Emperor Karl I (as Karl IV, King of Hungary) abdicated. Next day, Vienna accepted the austere terms demanded by the Italians in return for an armistice. For two and a half years the Royal Italian Army had battled alone against the Austro-Hungarians – and then the Germans too – at altitudes never before seen, until the humiliating collapse of their Alpine front at Caporetto in October 1917. They had recovered by their own resourcefulness, with a little help from the French and British, and the following summer had defeated what was meant to be the Austrians' knockout blow. They had even

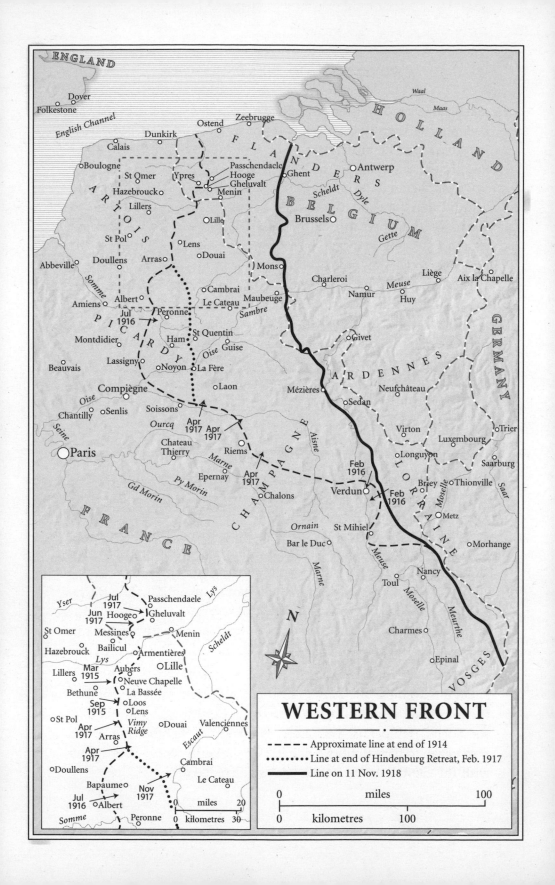

ENGLAND

Dover
Folkestone

English Channel

Calais
Boulogne
St Omer
Hazebrouck
Lillers
St Pol
Doullens
Abbeville
Amiens
Albert
Montdidier
Beauvais
Lassigny
Compiègne
Chantilly
Senlis
Soissons

Paris

Seine

Dunkirk
Ostend
Zeebrugge

FLANDERS

Ypres
Passchendaele
Hooge
Gheluvalt
Menin

Ghent

HOLLAND

Waal
Maas

Antwerp

BELGIUM

Scheldt
Dyle

Brussels

Gette

ARTOIS

Lille
Lens
Douai
Arras
Cambrai
Le Cateau
Maubeuge

Mons

Charleroi
Namur
Huy

Liège
Aix la Chapelle

Meuse

GERMANY

Jul
1916
Peronne
PICARDY
Ham
St Quentin
Oise
Guise
Noyon
La Fère
Laon
Ourcq
Apr
1917
Apr
1917

Sambre

Givet

ARDENNES

Mézières
Sedan
Neufchâteau

Virton
Longuyon
Luxembourg
Trier
Saarburg

Chateau
Thierry
Riems
Marne
Epernay
Apr
1917
Chalons

CHAMPAGNE

Aisne

Feb
1916
Verdun
Feb
1916

Briey
Thionville
Metz

Saar

LORRAINE

Moselle

Py Morin
Gd Morin

FRANCE

Ornain
Bar le Duc

St Mihiel

Morhange

Marne

Meuse

Nancy
Toul

Moselle
Meurthe

N

Charmes

Epinal

VOSGES

Inset map

Yser
Lys
Jul
1917
Passchendaele
Jun
1917
Hooge
Gheluvalt
St Omer
Messines
Menin
Hazebrouck
Bailicul
Lys
Scheldt
Lillers
Mar
1915
Aubers
Armentières
Lille
Neuve Chapelle
Bethune
La Bassée
Sep
1915
Loos
Lens
St Pol
Apr
1917
Vimy
Ridge
Arras
Douai
Valenciennes
Escaut
Apr
1917
Doullens
Cambrai
Bapaume
Nov
1917
Le Cateau
Jul
1916
Albert
Somme
Peronne

0   miles   20
0   kilometres   30

WESTERN FRONT

– – – Approximate line at end of 1914
· · · · · Line at end of Hindenburg Retreat, Feb. 1917
—— Line on 11 Nov. 1918

0   miles   100
0   kilometres   100

managed to send divisions to France to help stem the *Kaiserschlacht*, Ludendorff's own desperate final offensive, before launching their fight-back on the anniversary of Caporetto, recapturing all their lost ground and more in the battle known as Vittorio Veneto.

On the day that the last imperial Habsburg was leaving the Schönbrunn Palace for good, the German minister of the interior came to Spa to ask the Kaiser to abdicate too. Wilhelm rejected the idea out of hand. It would, he said, bring anarchy. Indeed, he declared his intention to lead his troops back to Germany in person to forestall revolution, and to go at once to the front to gauge for himself the troops' morale.

As ever, at the front the Kaiser saw what he wished to see. One of his personal staff, Count Detlef von Moltke, recounted: 'Near Ghent representatives from eleven divisions were greeted and decorated. The presence of the Kaiser had not been announced and the fresh and hardy and orderly appearance of the troops was all the more gratifying. The spontaneous enthusiasm of the soldiers on seeing their Commander-in-Chief was also most encouraging.'

Picked men about to receive decorations for bravery are not the best indicators of the general state of morale, but their commander-in-chief would return to Spa resolved to – as he saw it – do his duty to the army and the country.

That same day, 4 November, as fighting continued with barely remitting intensity – as if the frustrations of the trench years were being made up for with a vengeance – the most celebrated of the war poets, Lieutenant Wilfred Owen, was killed. He had recently returned to duty after convalescent leave in England, and died leading his platoon of the 2nd Manchesters during the crossing of the Sambre–Oise Canal. Only days earlier, Owen had been recommended for the Military Cross, which would be gazetted the following year.

On 5 November the Kaiser returned to Spa, where he learned of the *Hochseeflotte*'s mutinies at Kiel, the general strike in Berlin and the Social Democrats' vociferous demand for his abdication. He now began to have doubts, not helped by faltering communications with the capital. As Detlef von Moltke recorded:

Railroad connection with Germany began to be irregular and broken. Soon it ceased altogether. No train crossing the Rhine. Telegraphic and telephonic connection with Berlin became difficult. It appeared to be under some sort of censorial control and confidential messages could no longer be trusted. Finally we had to have recourse to air service. Two airships flew to Berlin, but none returned.

If communications with Berlin were difficult, Berlin had no difficulty communicating with Spa. On 9 November, the new chancellor, Prince Max von Baden, telegraphed that the Kaiser must abdicate, or else the cabinet would resign: 'revolution was extending on all sides, and the Social-Democrats could no longer hold the radicals under control,' Moltke recorded; 'the city and town officials in the large cities on the coast and in the western and southern portions of the Empire had assumed independent authority and . . . the Rhine and the great magazines of munitions and food along and east of this line had been seized by the revolutionists'.

The Kaiser, who had been joined by the Crown Prince, whose army group was covering the Ardennes approaches south of Liège, asked Hindenburg if he thought the unrest could be put down by force of arms. The Kaiser said that he himself was inclined to wait for the outcome of the peace feelers put out to the allies, and then lead the army back in person into Germany without announcing specifically that he would employ force against the revolt. However, Lieutenant-General Wilhelm Groener, who had replaced Ludendorff as *Erster Generalquartiermeister*, in effect commander-in-chief, told the Kaiser that the revolt had turned against him personally: 'The army will march home in peace and order under its leaders and commanding generals, but not under the command of Your Majesty, for it no longer stands behind Your Majesty.'

The Kaiser became angry. So did the Crown Prince's chief of staff, Major-General Friedrich von der Schulenburg, who was certain that 'no soldier of any rank would desert the Kaiser in the face of the enemy'.

Groener, a relatively low-born Württemberger, was neither impressed nor intimidated by the Junker's response: 'I have other information,' he replied stonily. Earlier and secretly, he had summoned fifty senior officers to Spa to discuss the feasibility of the Kaiser's plan.

At this darkest of moments, the telephone rang. Baron von dem Bussche, under-secretary at the foreign ministry, was calling from the chancellor's office to say that if the Kaiser did not abdicate at once the socialist Karl Liebknecht would be proclaimed 'President of the Republic'.

Wilhelm conceded. He would abdicate as emperor, he said, but remain King of Prussia. The news was telephoned to Berlin, but the message came back almost immediately: 'Too late. We can no more make use of that. By order of the Chancellor.'

The Wolff Telegraphic Bureau, the principal German news agency, then put out a communiqué which pre-empted further discussion: 'His Majesty, the Emperor and King, has abdicated, the Crown Prince has renounced the succession. Prince Max has been appointed Regent, and Representative Ebert [leader of the Social Democrats, and a moderate], Chancellor.'

That night the Kaiser left by train for exile in the Netherlands.

Meanwhile an armistice had to be negotiated. On 7 November Berlin had sent a telegram to the allied *generalissimo*, Ferdinand Foch, requesting a meeting. The following day the German delegation, headed by Matthias Erzberger, leader of the Catholic Centre Party, crossed the front line in five cars and were escorted for ten hours to Foch's private train in the forest of Compiègne, 35 miles north of Paris.

Erzberger was handed the list of allied demands. They amounted to complete surrender and demilitarization. He was given seventy-two hours to agree. There was to be no negotiation.

There were practical problems in communicating the military details to Spa, however. The 22-year-old Rittmeister (captain of cavalry) Count Wolff-Heinrich von Helldorf, one of the interpreters, volunteered to take them, but on reaching the crossing point at the front line, he found the fire too heavy and telephoned Compiègne to say he would have to wait till first light. Major-General Detlef von Winterfeldt, the German military representative, at once began making alternative arrangements: a French aircraft, trailing two white streamers in the hope of not being shot down, would fly them to Spa with the other interpreter. Eventually, though, Helldorf was able to slip through the lines in darkness, reaching Spa in mid-morning on the 9th, so the unique experiment of an airborne flag of truce was never attempted.

The following day, Sunday, Hindenburg sent the new chancellor, Ebert, a message urging that the armistice be signed even if the conditions he had just read could not be improved on. Meanwhile he set about composing new instructions for the delegation at Compiègne to try to negotiate better terms.

On receiving Hindenburg's message, Ebert telegrammed Erzberger instructing him to accept the terms as modified by Hindenburg's forthcoming proposals.

Ebert's telegram was followed soon afterwards by a much longer one from Spa specifying the improvements that Hindenburg sought to the military details. The delegation asked for time to decipher these before meeting the allied delegates to agree the final wording of the armistice document.

Tired, apprehensive men, laborious communications, and uncertainty as to what was really happening in Berlin made a classic recipe for misunderstanding. No sooner had the staff finished deciphering Hindenburg's instructions than a second telegram arrived from Berlin authorizing them to agree the original, unmodified, terms. To make matters worse, this was sent *en clair*, entirely compromising the improvements that Hindenburg sought. A note of farce then entered the proceedings when the allied delegation read the telegram and saw that it appeared to be signed not by Reichskanzler Ebert but by Reichskanzler Schluss. Foch did not know the name. He telephoned Paris. They didn't know the name either. Erzberger was summoned to explain. 'Schluss,' he told them, simply meant 'end of message'.

Nevertheless it was several hours before the German delegation were ready for the final meeting.

Shortly after two o'clock in the morning on Monday, 11 November, the parties assembled in the dining car of Foch's Wagon-Lits train. For the allies, there were Foch himself, the supreme commander, and the (British) first sea lord, Admiral Sir Rosslyn ('Rosie') Wemyss, and their principal staff officers. For the Germans, there were Erzberger, Count Alfred von Oberndorff from the foreign ministry, and their army and navy advisers Winterfeldt and Captain Ernst Vanselow.

Erzberger was in no position to make any conditional demands because the allies now knew that his instructions from Berlin were to accept the terms as given. He therefore tried reasoning, his concerns principally for the economic well-being of Germany. Starvation among the civil population would be exacerbated, he argued, if they were to surrender all the road transport and rolling stock as demanded. Foch was prepared to make a few concessions, as long as the central element of the Armistice – the surrender of territory – remained unaltered. If the Germans did not actually have 2,000 aeroplanes to surrender, he would settle for what they said they had – 1,700. If they couldn't without unwarranted hardship surrender 10,000 road vehicles in a fortnight, he would accept 5,000 over a longer period. He was certainly content to let them keep 5,000 of the 30,000 machine-guns demanded in order that they could fight the Bolshevists at home (and to grant some leeway in quitting Russia where 'Reds' threatened). And, as Lettow-Vorbeck's little army remained undefeated in East Africa, Foch was prepared to allow them time to withdraw rather than demanding immediate surrender.

'Rosie' Wemyss was rather less inclined to be accommodating when it came to the naval terms. Captain Vanselow, the naval representative, chosen probably for his legal acumen (before the war he had collaborated with the Swiss legal scholar Eduard von Waldkirch on the *Handbook of International Law*), pointed out that the *Kaiserliche Marine* did not possess 170 U-boats to surrender. Wemyss simply took back the document, crossed out the figure and wrote 'all submarines'.

Vanselow then said that the *Hochseeflotte* at Wilhelmshaven and Kiel should be accorded the same honours as Lettow-Vorbeck, as they too had never been defeated in battle.

'They have only to come out,' replied Wemyss tartly.

Erzberger and Oberndorff complained at the stipulation that the Royal Navy's blockade was to continue until a final treaty was agreed, claiming that this was unfair to Germany's women and children.

'Unfair?' snapped Wemyss. 'You sank our ships indiscriminately too.'

Indeed, some 11 million tons of allied and neutral shipping had been destroyed during the course of the war. Nevertheless, he said he would refer the matter to London.

The talking continued for almost three hours, until just after five o'clock the Germans said they were ready to sign. A fair copy of the signatory page was typed at once – with the rest to be typed up later – and signed by the delegates at twenty minutes past five, but officially recorded as five o'clock, to come into effect six hours later, at 11.00 a.m. Paris time – 'the eleventh hour of the eleventh day of the eleventh month'.

This demanded no mean effort of communications, on both sides. No official warning orders had been issued that hostilities might end soon, although the word was out that the Germans were seeking terms. On the contrary, offensive action continued across much of the front, if more cautiously than in the weeks before, as the allies could not afford to give the enemy occasion for second thoughts.

At 9.30 a.m. Private George Ellison of the 5th Royal Irish Lancers was killed in the outskirts of Mons, where the British army had fought its first battle of the war. Ellison, forty years old, from Leeds, in Yorkshire, had enlisted young but had left the army in 1912 on marrying, when he became a miner. Having a reserve liability, though, he was recalled to the colours in 1914, rejoining the Lancers, one of the first regiments to see action at Mons. Private George Ellison was the last soldier from Britain to die before the Armistice came into force.

The ceasefire order reached Captain Harry Truman of the US 129th Field Artillery just before ten-thirty. He sent at once for his battery sergeant, 'Squatty' Meisburger, who found the future president of the

United States of America 'stretched out on the ground eating a blue-berry pie. Where he got the blueberry pie I don't know . . . His face was all smeared with blueberries. He handed me a piece of flimsy and said between bites, "Sergeant, you will take this back and read it to the members of the battery."'

Truman was following the old military maxim: bad news comes from the top; good news is passed down the chain of command.

But there were thirty minutes still to go, and they had a lot of ammunition prepared for use. In the next half-hour they fired as much of it as they could – 164 rounds.

At two minutes to eleven, the last soldier of the British Empire to die before the ceasefire was killed: Private George Price, twenty-five years old, of the 28th Saskatchewans (Canadian Expeditionary Force). His battalion had been ordered to secure the bridges on the Canal du Centre near Mons.

At 11 a.m. precisely the 15th Hussars, Field Marshal Sir John French's old command, a regiment that like many in the cavalry had hung on to its cherished traditions throughout the war, mus-tered its remaining trumpeters, fished out their obsolete instruments from the baggage, and sounded 'Cease Fire'. It was an extraordinary moment, for the ceremonial call (all calls were ceremonial, for the trumpet had long ceased to be carried in the field) had not been heard for over four years. Moreover, the regiment was mustered not a dozen miles from where they had heard the first shots fired on 22 August 1914.

In London, Lloyd George released the news at 10.20 a.m. A hun-dred and forty miles away in Shrewsbury near the Welsh border, as the church bells began ringing out the ceasefire at eleven o'clock, Wilfred Owen's mother received the telegram informing her of her eldest son's death.

Private George Ellison's widow, Hannah, would not learn for sev-eral more days that her husband had been killed that morning.

Some 700,000 servicemen from Britain and Ireland had been killed during the war, or had died while in the King's service, and 200,000 more from the dominions and India. In volume 4 of *The World Crisis*, published eleven years later, Winston Churchill reflected on the scenes of celebration he witnessed in London on Armistice Day:

> Who shall grudge or mock these overpowering entrancements? Every allied nation shared them. Every victorious capital or city in the five continents reproduced in its own fashion the scenes and sounds of London. These hours were brief, their memory fleeting; they passed as suddenly as they had begun.
>
> Too much blood had been spilt. Too much life-essence had been consumed. The gaps in every home were too wide and empty. The shock of an awakening and the sense of disillusion followed swiftly upon the poor rejoicings with which hundreds of millions saluted the achievement of their hearts' desire. There still remained the satisfactions of safety assured, of peace restored, of honour preserved, of the comforts of fruitful industry, of the home-coming of the soldiers; but these were in the background; and with them all there mingled the ache for those who would never come home.

Conclusion

The War to End All War?*

It is not possible to live in an English village – or indeed a Scots, Irish or Welsh one – without being aware of the Grim Reaper's harvest in the years 1914–18. The war memorials not only enumerate but also name the price of victory, sometimes in whole families of sons. The cost was indeed high – high enough in blood for Britain, but twice as high for France. How could it be otherwise with so many men under arms and for so long?

Need it have been *so* high, however? That is the question I address in *Too Important for the Generals* (2016). I maintain that it need not have been.

Was it a war of German aggression; were the Germans truly deserving of the *Kriegsschuld* (war guilt) verdict of the Paris peace conference of 1919, the basis of their agreement to pay reparations? Article 231 of the Treaty of Versailles specified:

> The Allied and Associated Governments affirm and Germany accepts the responsibility of Germany and her allies for causing all the loss and

* In August 1914, the celebrated British author and social commentator H. G. Wells wrote a number of articles in the London papers, which subsequently appeared as a book entitled *The War That Will End War* – giving rise to the phrase 'The War to End All War.'

385

damage to which the Allied and Associated Governments and their nationals have been subjected as a consequence of the war imposed upon them by the aggression of Germany and her allies.

One historian, the Australian Christopher Clark, Regius Professor of History at Cambridge, has recently asserted otherwise. In *The Sleepwalkers: How Europe Went to War in 1914* (2012), he absolves Germany from peculiar guilt. The book sold well in Germany, because, said the German historian Hans-Ulrich Wehler, it served a 'deep-seated need [on the part of German readers], no longer so constrained by the taboos characteristic of the later twentieth century, to free themselves from the burdensome allegations of national war guilt' (*Frankfurter Allgemeine Zeitung*, 6 May 2014). Indeed, on the recommendation of the British ambassador in Berlin – who seems unilaterally to have repudiated Article 231 of the Treaty of Versailles – Clark received a knighthood for services to Anglo-German relations.

One wonders what the late Lady Thatcher would have made of this. She famously believed that too many ambassadors had 'gone native' in their eagerness to empathize. With a nod to Nietzsche, Professor Margaret MacMillan called her own meditation on the subject *The Uses and Abuses of History* (2009).* Perhaps there is scope for a further volume: *The Uses and Abuses of Historians*.

For a robust refutation of this revisionist idea of German innocence (which was, of course, an idea begun in Germany in the 1920s, and one that served the rise of the Nazis), it is well to consult the Anglo-German historian John Röhl's biography of the Kaiser.† I draw extensively on Professor Röhl's research in *1914: Fight the Good Fight* (2013), for it is compelling.

Indeed, there is a simple – but not simplistic – story that in a way sums up the whole question. In *The Origins of Totalitarianism* (1951), the German-born American political theorist Hannah Arendt relates

* Friedrich Nietzsche, *On the Use and Abuse of History for Life* (1874).
† Volume 3, *Into the Abyss of War and Exile, 1900–1941* (London, 2014).

an exchange between Clemenceau and the German representative at the Versailles conference: 'What, in your opinion, will future historians make of this troublesome and controversial issue?' asked the German. To which Clemenceau replied: 'This I don't know. But I know for certain that they will not say Belgium invaded Germany!'

It is not a case of there being two narratives, a British one and a German one, for that is to relativize the issue of truth versus falsehood in history. The facts of a case are not always apparent, but where they are, opinion must take note. The controversy is not so much between Britain and Germany as between truth-tellers and ideologues in both countries.

If for France and Britain, then, the First World War was not of their making, was the peace they made at Versailles as good as it might have been?

When the final treaty was signed, Marshal Foch despaired that it was 'not a peace but a twenty-year armistice'. He would die just ten years later – just ten years before his prophecy was proved true. In June 1944, writing in her syndicated daily newspaper column, 'My Day', First Lady Eleanor Roosevelt put it bluntly: 'We gave up unconditional surrender the last time ... and now [in the war with Germany and Japan] we have sacrificed thousands of lives because we did not do a thorough job.'

She was right – as indeed were her husband, President Franklin D. Roosevelt, and Winston Churchill in their declared policy 'this time' of unconditional surrender. As Cicero wrote: 'War should be so engaged in that nothing but peace should appear to be aimed at.'

For while it is still argued just how directly the Treaty of Versailles led to the Second World War, the Paris conference (its grander sessions held in the hall of mirrors at the Palace of Versailles) made a peace that was on the one hand too harsh and on the other too lenient. The allies' exhaustion after four years' fighting – the cost they had borne in blood and treasure – demanded territorial and financial reparations from the Kaiser and his Second Reich. Yet that same exhaustion conceded too much in the arrangements for the future self-government of Germany. And, being so exhausted, the allies would have no will in the years that followed to maintain armies great enough either to enforce the harshness or to safeguard the leniency. Foch saw it plainly. So did the young British Brigadier-General Archibald Wavell – later Field Marshal the Earl Wavell, of Second World War fame – who in 1919 wrote: 'After the "war to end war" they seem to have been pretty successful in Paris at making a "peace to end peace".' Others were saying the same, in several different languages.

If all do not agree that the war itself was *not* futile, despite its excessive cost, most seem to agree that the promise of peace was truly tragic. And so the debate as to the war's ultimate futility will go on.

The Tiger: "Curious! I seem to hear a child weeping!"

Annex A

THE ARMISTICE TERMS

Among its thirty-four clauses, the armistice contained the following stipulations:

Western Front:

- Termination of hostilities on the Western Front, on land and in the air, within six hours of signature.
- Immediate evacuation of France, Belgium, Luxembourg, and Alsace-Lorraine within 15 days. Sick and wounded may be left for Allies to care for.
- Immediate repatriation of all inhabitants of those four territories in German hands.
- Surrender of 5,000 artillery pieces, 25,000 machine guns, 3,000 mine-throwers, 1,700 aircraft (including all night bombers), 5,000 railway locomotives, 150,000 railway carriages and trucks, and 5,000 road vehicles.
- Evacuation of territory on the west side of the Rhine plus 30 km (19 miles) radius bridgeheads on the east side of the Rhine at the cities of Mainz, Koblenz and Cologne within 31 days.
- Vacated territory to be occupied by Allied and US troops, maintained at Germany's expense.
- No removal or destruction of civilian goods or inhabitants in evacuated territories and all military matériel and premises to be left intact.

- All minefields on land and sea to be identified.
- All means of communication (roads, railways, canals, bridges, telegraphs, telephones) to be left intact, as well as everything needed for agriculture and industry.

Eastern and African Fronts:

- Immediate withdrawal of all German troops in Romania, and in what were the Ottoman Empire, the Austro-Hungarian Empire and the Russian Empire back to German territory as it was on 1 August 1914. The Allies are to have access to these countries.
- Renunciation of the Treaty of Brest-Litovsk with Russia and of the Treaty of Bucharest with Romania.
- Evacuation of German forces in Africa.

At sea:

- Immediate cessation of all hostilities at sea and surrender intact of all German submarines within 14 days.
- Listed German surface vessels to be interned within 7 days and the rest disarmed.
- Free access to German waters for Allied ships and for those of the Netherlands, Norway, Denmark and Sweden.
- The naval blockade of Germany to continue.
- Immediate evacuation of all Black Sea ports and handover of all captured Russian vessels.

General:

- Immediate release of all Allied prisoners of war and interned civilians, without reciprocity.
- Pending a financial settlement, surrender of assets looted from Belgium, Romania and Russia.

Annex B

THE WAR FOR CIVILIZATION:
THE RECKONING

Country	Total mobilized forces	Killed	Wounded	Prisoners and missing	Total casualties	Casualties as % of forces
ENTENTE AND ASSOCIATED POWERS						
Russia	12,000,000	1,700,000	4,950,000	2,500,000	9,150,000	76.3
British Empire	8,904,467	908,371	2,090,212	191,652	3,190,235	35.8
France	8,410,000	1,357,800	4,266,000	537,000	6,160,800	73.3
Italy	5,615,000	650,000	947,000	600,000	2,197,000	39.1
United States	4,355,000	116,516	204,002	4,500	323,018	7.4
Japan	800,000	300	907	3	1,210	0.2
Romania	750,000	335,706	120,000	80,000	535,706	71.4
Serbia	707,343	45,000	133,148	152,958	331,106	46.8
Belgium	267,000	13,716	44,686	34,659	93,061	34.9
Greece	230,000	5,000	21,000	1,000	27,000	11.7
Portugal	100,000	7,222	13,751	12,318	33,291	33.3
Montenegro	50,000	3,000	10,000	7,000	20,000	40.0
Total	**42,188,810**	**5,142,631**	**12,800,706**	**4,121,090**	**22,062,427**	**52.3**
CENTRAL AND ASSOCIATED POWERS						
Germany	11,000,000	1,773,700	4,216,058	1,152,800	7,142,558	64.9
Austria-Hungary	7,800,000	1,200,000	3,620,000	2,200,000	7,020,000	90.0
Turkey	2,850,000	325,000	400,000	250,000	975,000	34.2
Bulgaria	1,200,000	87,500	152,390	27,029	266,919	22.2
Total	**22,850,000**	**3,386,200**	**8,388,448**	**3,629,829**	**15,404,477**	**67.4**
GRAND TOTAL	65,038,810	8,528,831	21,189,154	7,750,919	37,466,904	57.6

FURTHER READING

For an understanding of the war as a whole (even if contentious) – John Terraine's *The First World War: 1914–1918* (1984), though now rather dated, is a fine counter to the 'Lions led by Donkeys' school of Great War historiography. Sir Hew Strachan's (short) *The First World War* (2004) and Sir Michael Howard's shorter-still *The First World War* (2003, reissued as *The First World War: A Very Short Introduction* in 2007) are magisterial. So is Sir John Keegan's *The First World War* (1998). Niall Ferguson's *The Pity of War* (1998) poses interesting questions, but I prefer the answers in Strachan's, Howard's and Keegan's books. For straight chronology, with only the lightest touch of commentary (some of it poetical), Martin Gilbert's *First World War* (1994) is unbeatable. His *First World War Atlas* (1970) is indispensable.

The Western Front, which of course dominates British consciousness of the war, has generated books enough to sink a battleship. A number of British historians have made it almost their life's study. Gary Sheffield's work on Field Marshal Haig is crucial to any understanding of the conflict: his edition, with John Bourne, of *Douglas Haig: War Diaries and Letters 1914–1918* (2005) is as important as the probably better-known *Alanbrooke Diaries 1939–1945* in revealing the preoccupations of high command at any time. On the particular battles – First and Third Ypres ('Passchendaele') and the Somme – there has been much recent scholarship, but I still believe that General Sir Anthony Farrar-Hockley's two books – *The Somme* (1966) and *Ypres 1914: Death of an Army* (1967) are pacey, faithful and full of soldierly insight. *Passchendaele: A New History* by Nick

Lloyd (2017) is very fine. So is William Philpott's *Bloody Victory* (2009), on the Somme, as is his more general *Attrition: Fighting the First World War* (2014). On the final victories, Peter Hart's *The Last Battle: Endgame on the Western Front, 1918* (2018) is compelling, although he is considerably more approving of Haig's generalship than I am. For the French, of course, Verdun was the Somme and Third Ypres rolled into one; on these, Alistair Horne's *The Price of Glory* (2007) is essential.

The war in Africa is best read in two books: Hew Strachan's *The First World War in Africa* (2004) and Edward Paice's *Tip & Run: The Untold Tragedy of the Great War in Africa* (2007). The war in the Middle East has over the years produced many great books, not least of course that from the pen of T. E. Lawrence (of Arabia): *The Seven Pillars of Wisdom*. And *Allenby: A Study in Greatness* by General Sir Archibald Wavell, published in 1940 (to considerable criticism in some quarters, the feeling being that the C-in-C Middle East ought to be concentrating on beating the Italians rather than poring over page proofs), remains highly regarded. Of more recent scholarship, Rob Johnson's *The Great War and the Middle East* stands out.

Mark Thompson's *The White War: Life and Death on the Italian Front* is excellent.

Alan Palmer's *The Gardeners of Salonika* (2011) is a very fine account of the virtually unheard-of Macedonian Front.

And Gallipoli? Robin Prior's *The End of the Myth* (2009) and Peter Hart's *Gallipoli* (2011), each with its own focus and conclusions, are good places to start. L. A. Carlyon, an Australian author remarkably kind to the British, also offers a powerful account in *Gallipoli* (2002).

The Royal Navy has been less well served than the Army, for fairly obvious reasons: the work of blockade and counter-blockade is tedious and largely uneventful in comparison with the war on land, and, aside from the battles of Coronel, the Falklands and Jutland, there were no dramatic sea battles. So much of the story is about the preparations, and Robert Massie's *Dreadnought: Britain, Germany and the Coming of the Great War* (1991) is still the best analysis. Mike Farquharson-Roberts' *A History of the Royal Navy:*

World War I (2014) is concise, scholarly and readable, and has the added advantage of being written by a former Surgeon Rear-Admiral. As for Jutland, 'As well write the history of a ball,' as the duke of Wellington said of Waterloo. So many ships, so many salvoes – so many books. Nigel Steel and Peter Hart make sense of it – to me at least – in *Death in the Grey Wastes* (2012).

As for the service that saw the greatest acceleration and change – that of the air – E. R. Hooton's *War Over the Trenches: Air Power and the Western Front Campaigns 1916–1918* (2010) is definitive – and readable.

There were, of course, no British troops on the Eastern Front (though some found their way there in the wake of the Revolution). Norman Stone is a historian who, as they say, 'excites opinion'; I myself think his *The Eastern Front 1914–1917* (2008) is matchless in its Russian perspective – and entertaining.

PICTURE ACKNOWLEDGEMENTS

Any illustrations not specifically credited below are in the public domain or the copyright holder is unknown. Every effort has been made to trace copyright holders; any who have been overlooked are invited to get in touch with the publishers.

Section 1

Page 1: (*top*) The Print Collector/Getty Images; (*middle*) Library of Congress; (*bottom*) © Bundesarchiv, Koblenz Inv.-Nr.: Bild 183-R04335.

Page 2: (*middle*) National Maritime Museum, Greenwich, London; (*bottom*) The York Press.

Page 3: (*top*) © IWM (Q 57328); (*middle*) © The rightsholder (Q 67819); (*bottom*) © IWM (HU 95834).

Page 4: (*top*) GL Archive/Alamy Stock Photo; (*middle*) © TopFoto; (*bottom*) Forces War Records: https://www.forces-war-records.co.uk.

Page 5: (*top*) Bettmann/Getty Images; (*middle*) Popperfoto/Getty Images; (*bottom*) Archives/AFP/Getty Images.

Page 6: (*top*) https://www.learning-history.com; (*middle*) https://www. learning-history.com; (*bottom*) Karl Bulla/ullstein bild via Getty Images.

Page 7: (*top*) ullstein bild/ullstein bild via Getty Images; (*middle*) Military History Collection/Alamy Stock Photo; (*bottom*) https://rarehistorical photos.com.

Page 8: (*top*) Bain News Service/Ian Dagnall Computing/Alamy Stock Photo; (*middle*) New York Public Library/Science Source; (*bottom*) Science History Images/Alamy Stock Photo.

PICTURE ACKNOWLEDGEMENTS

Section 2

Page 9: (*top*) National Archives, USA; (*middle*) © IWM (Q 12167); (*bottom*) Keystone/Hulton Archive/Getty Images.

Page 10: (*top*) © IWM (Q 86646); (*middle*) Hulton Archive/Stringer/Getty Images; (*bottom*) Courtesy Library of Congress, Prints & Photographs Division, LC-DIG-ppmsca-13709-00127.

Page 11: (*top left*) Australian War Memorial; (*top right*) Universal History Archive/UIG via Getty Images; (*bottom*) Everett Collection Historical/Alamy Stock Photo.

Page 12: (*top*) Library and Archives, Canada; (*middle*) Henry Guttmann/Hulton Archive/Getty Images; (*bottom*) © IWM (Q 25968).

Page 13: (*top left*) SeM/Universal Image Group via Getty Images; (*top right*) Popperfoto/Getty Images; (*bottom*) Bettmann/Getty Images.

Page 14: (*top*) *Canadian Artillery in Action*, *c*.1915 (oil on canvas) by Kenneth Forbes (1892–1980)/Canadian War Museum, Ottawa, Canada/Bridgeman Images; (*bottom*) National Maritime Museum, Greenwich, London.

Page 15: (*top*) *British Scouts leaving their Aerodrome on Patrol, over the Asiago Plateau, Italy, 1918* (oil on canvas), Carline, Sydney (1888–1929)/Imperial War Museum, London, UK/Bridgeman Images; (*bottom*) *The Charge of the 3rd Light Horse Brigade at the Nek, 7 August 1915, 1924* (oil on canvas), Lambert, George (*fl.c.*1897)/Australian War Memorial, Canberra, Australia/Bridgeman Images.

Page 16: (*top*) *The Menin Road, 1919* (oil on canvas), Nash, Paul (1889–1946)/Imperial War Museum, London, UK/Bridgeman Images; (*bottom*) The History Collection/Alamy Stock Photo.

Illustration in text p. 388
'Peace and Future Cannon Fodder', cartoon by Will Dyson, *Daily Mail*, May 1919, © John Frost Newspapers/Alamy Stock Photo.

Endpapers
Peace Palace Library, Netherlands.

Index

*Page numbers in **bold type** refer to maps.*

Abbeville, supreme war council at 333
Adlam, Capt. Tom 182
Admiral Ganteaume, French merchant
    ship 49
Admiralty, 'Room 40' intelligence
    centre 161
Admiralty Landships Committee
    193, 286
aerial reconnaissance 77–8, 79, 91,
    318, 357
  and photography 56, 80
  at Verdun 133
Africa, war in 82–8
Air Board 274–5
air defence 273
air warfare 76–81
  aerial combat 80
  air support 363
  and anti-aircraft artillery 80, 273
  civilian targets 77, 275–6
  ground attack ('strafing')
    352–3, 372
  strategic bombing 79, 264–5, 275–6,
    277, 372–3
aircraft 76, 81
  British 78, 80; Handley Page bombers
    273, 358
  fighters 249
  French 246
  German 80, 249; Fokker 274; Gotha
    273, 275, 328

increased production 276
  for reconnaissance 77–8, 91
airships, German 76–7, 79
Aisne, river 21
  German advance to 338, 349–50
  proposed offensive 218, 246–7
Albania 104, 216–17
Alberich *see* Operation Alberich
Albert, Battle of 208
Albert, King of the Belgians 22
Alcock, Capt. John 81
al-Husseini, Hussein Salim, mayor of
    Jerusalem 294–5
Allenby, Gen. Sir Edmund 174, 239
  Battle of Megiddo 371
  in Jerusalem 233, 293, 295–6
  and Nivelle offensive 244, 245
Alsace-Lorraine 302
  French defences 10, 12
American Defense League 202
American Expeditionary Force (AEF) 251
  1st US Army 362–3, 364, 366
  I Corps 362
  IV Corps 362
  V Corps 363
  1st US Division 310
  42nd US Division 311–12
  at Cantigny 338
  Marne counter-attack 353
  mobilization 331, 332
  at Western Front 305–6, 318

INDEX

Amiens 328
  allied attack at 356–61
ammunition
  for Dardanelles 73
  shortages 45, 56–8, 71–3
Amphion, HMS 11
Anglo-Japanese naval treaty (1902) 24
Anglo-Persian Oil Company 109
Antwerp
  aerial bombing of 79
  defence of 22–3
'Anzac' Corps (Australian and New
    Zealand Army Corps)
  II Corps 254
  Australian Corps 357, 358, 359
  Desert Mounted Corps 294
  in Egypt 171
  Gallipoli 62, 64, 65
Aosta, Gen. the Duke of, Italian 3rd
    Army 268, 283
Arab Bureau, Cairo 170, 173
Arab Revolt 170–1, 172
Arbuthnot, RAdm. Sir Robert 163
Ardenne, Lt-Gen. Armand
    Baron von 348
Arendt, Hannah 386–7
Argonne forest 365–6
Armentières, fall of 329
Armistice (Nov. 1918)
  and ceasefire 382–3
  negotiation 379–82
  terms of 387–8, 389–90
Army League (US) 202
Arnold, Lt Clement 359–60
Arras, Nivelle offensive 244
Arras–St-Quentin junction 319–20
  German *Kaiserschlacht* at 321–4
artillery
  gas shells 233, 245
  Italian 187
  for Italian front 266
  Krupp railway guns 327
  Livens projectors 254
  and 'predicted fire' 357
  for Somme offensive 177, 179–80

sound-ranging 357–8
  at Verdun 133
Artois 71
Asiago, Austrian attack on 343–5
Asquith, H. H., prime minister 215
  and BEF 10–11
  and Churchill 18, 22, 43
  coalition ministry 57, 67, 73–4
  and French 15, 118–19
  and submarine warfare 141
  and tanks 197
Asquith, Margot 199, 214
Asquith, Raymond 197, 199, 215
Attlee, Clement 94, 113, 117
Attlee, Laurence 117
Aubers Ridge 55, 72
Audacious, HMS 142, 347
Australia 24
  see also 'Anzac' Corps
Austria-Hungary
  disintegration of Empire 347
  and Eastern Front 126
  demoralization grows 218
  nationalist unrest 302, 303
  and Serbs 20, 102
  surrender to Italy 375, 377
  and *Waffenbund* treaty 342
Austro-Hungarian army
  counter-offensive into Italy 293
  defeat at Vittorio Veneto 372
  and Isonzo 267, 268–9, 279, 281
  and Italian offensive 341–5
Austro-Hungarian Navy 346–7

Baghdad 110, 111, 231–3
Bailleul, fall of 329
Bain, Maj. Andrew 304
Balfour, Arthur, MP 73, 129, 296
Balfour Declaration 296
Balkans **103**
Bapaume, mined 237
Baratov, Gen. Nikolai 113
Barlow, Raymond, Air Mechanic 11
Barrès, Auguste-Maurice 135
Basra 31, 109, 110–11, 169, 232

INDEX

Bauer, Korvettenkapitän Hermann 143
Baynes, Sir John, *Morale* 58
Bazelaire, Gen. de 311
Beatty, VAdm. David 159
  Battle of Jutland 161–4
Beck, Capt. Frank 93
Beersheba 233, 294
BEF *see* British Expeditionary Force
Belfort 132
Belgium
  and defence of Antwerp 22–3
  intelligence sources 318
  invasion 7
Belgrade 371
Bell, Gertrude 170
Belleau Wood 350
Bellenglise, attack at 368
Below, Gen. Otto von 280, 281
Belridge, Norwegian tanker 50
Benedict XV, Pope 202
  call for truce 36–7
  peace note (Aug. 1917) 269–71, 303
Berlin, general strike 374
Bethmann Hollweg, Theobald von,
  German chancellor 203, 206, 229
  call for peace negotiations 218
  and submarine warfare 227–8
Birdwood, Lt-Gen. William 64, 90
Birrell, Augustine, chief secretary for
  Ireland 152
Black Prince, HMS 163
Blixen, Karen 87
Blücher, German cruiser 49
Bluebell, HMS 151
Blunden, Edmund, MC 264, 265
  Undertones of War 178, 291
'Boer revolt' 84
Bonar Law, Andrew 214, 277
Boselli, Paolo, Italian prime minister
  242
Botha, Louis, South African prime
  minister 24, 47, 82
Bowes-Lyon, Capt. the Hon.
  Fergus 100
Boyd, Gen. Gerald Farrell 367–8

Bradford, Brig.-Gen. Roland Boys,
  VC 289
Bragg, Lawrence 358
Breslau, German cruiser 24
Brest-Litovsk, Treaty of 308–9, 314, 340
Briand, Aristide, French prime minister
  215, 243
  and Nivelle 217–18, 242, 260–1
Brice, Cpl Harry 359
British army
  conscription 120
  in Ireland 153–5
  Irishmen in 149, 257–8
  'Pals' battalions 180–2
  reinforcements (1914) 22
  reservists 10–11
  training 178
  voluntary recruitment ('New
    Armies') 44, 64, 97
British army units
Armies, corps and divisions
  1st Army 55, 320, 328, 330, 361
  2nd Army 55, 261, 320, 328, 330
  3rd Army 177, 320, 326, 361
  4th Army 177–8, 208, 356–7, 359,
    361, 366–7
  5th Army 208, 210, 320, 321–4
  10th (Anglo-Italian) Army 343–4
  II Corps 13, 14
  III Corps 356, 357
  VII Corps 323–4
  IX Corps 90–1, 254, 349
  X Corps 254
  XIV Corps 265
  XXI Corps 294
  Machine Gun Corps 286–7
  Tank Corps 198, 263–4, 287–8, 359
  9th Scottish Division 244
  10th (Irish) Division 91
  11th (Northern) Division 91
  15th (Scottish) Division 98
  16th (Irish) Division 257, 325
  29th Division, Gallipoli 64, 65, 66–7
  36th (Ulster) Division 257–8, 325
  46th Division 367–8

Divisions (cont.)
  47th (London) Division 98
  51st (Highland) Division 209
  63rd (Royal Naval) Division 64,
    209–10
  66th (East Lancashire) Division 325
Other formations
  15th Hussars 383
  16th Battalion Highland Light
    Infantry 210–11
  16th Manchester Battalion 321–2
  Army Service Corps 194
  Cavalry Corps 358, 359
  Dublin Fusiliers 154
  Leinster Regiment 154
  Royal Irish Regiment 154
  Desert Mounted Corps 233
  Imperial Camel Corps 172
  Royal Artillery 273
  Royal Engineers 253
British Expeditionary Force (BEF) 11, 15
  enlargement 55, 68
  reinforcements 32–3
  see also British army
Brittain, Lt Edward 343–4
Brittain, Vera 256, 312
Brooke, Maj. Alan (later Lord
    Alanbrooke) 245
Brooke, Rupert 22
Brown, Lt Arthur Whitten 81
Brunton, Sgt David 17
Brusilov, Gen. Aleksei 19, 128, 137, 203
  in Polish Galicia 177, 186
Buchan, John
  Greenmantle 95
  on Somme 197
Bucharest, Treaty of (1918) 341
Bulfin, Lt-Gen. Edward 294
Bulgaria 45, 203, 341
  entry into war 93–4, 104, 117
  and Macedonia 104, 216
  surrender 370, 371
Bundy, Maj.-Gen. Omar 350
Burke, Lt Ulick 326
Bussche, Baron von dem 379

Butler, Lt-Gen. Richard 130, 193, 356
Butte de Mesnil 310
Butterworth, George 188
Byng, Lt-Gen. Sir Julian 90, 244–5,
    287–90, 361

Cadorna, Gen. Luigi 186–7, 220, 242
  and Caporetto 279–82
  Isonzo river campaign 74–5, 250,
    267–8, 269
Cambrai, Battle of 286–90
  German counter-offensive 289
Campbell, Lt-Cdr Gordon, VC 139,
    141, 146
Canadian Expeditionary Force 68
  8th Brigade 70
  Canadian Corps 209, 244–5, 357, 359
  Lord Strathcona's Horse 328
Canal du Nord 366
Cannon, Pte Jim 13
Canopus, HMS 25, 27–9
Cantigny, American brigade at 338
Capello, Gen. Luigi 268, 279
Caporetto, Battle of (Twelfth Isonzo)
    269–70, 271, 278–84
Carden, VAdm. Sackville, and
    Dardanelles campaign 51
Carnaris, Lt Wilhelm 30
Carnarvon, HMS 29
Carranza, Venustiano, Mexican
    president 205–6
Carrizal, Mexico 206
Casement, Sir Roger 147, 149–51, 156
Castelnau, Gen. Noël de 241–2
  Champagne offensive 95–6
  Verdun 134
casualties 383–4, 392
  African 85
  American 364, 366
  Amiens 359
  Arras–St-Quentin 323
  Austrian 345
  Caporetto 282–3
  civilian 80–1; in German
    naval raids 35

from disease 105–6
Eastern Front 126–7
first 11, 18
First Ypres 31, 33, 68
Flanders 328, 331
Flers-Courcelette 199
Gallipoli 66–7, 93, 94, 116
Isonzo river campaign 75, 268–9
Italian 187, 372
Ludendorff's operations 342
Mesopotamia 114
Messines 257–8
Neuve Chapelle 58
Nivelle offensive 246
officers, at Loos 99–100
'Passchendaele' 265
Russian 186
Second Marne 353
Second Ypres 71, 72
Somme 182, 187–8, 207–8, 212
Verdun 136, 138
Vimy Ridge 244, 245
Zeebrugge 337
Caucasus 24
Cavan, Lt-Gen. the Earl of 265
   at Asiago 343–5
Cer Mountain 20
Chantilly, inter-allied conferences at
   1915 117–18, 123, 125, 177
   Nov. 1916 209, 216, 250, 260
Chaplin, Charlie 59
Charleroi 79
Charles (Karl) I, Emperor 280, 375
Charteris, Brig.-Gen. John 37, 97–8,
   119, 208–9
   dismissal 290, 306
Château-Thierry 338
Chauvel, Gen. Henry 294
Chemin des Dames 244, 246, 254,
   338, 350
Chester, HMS 162
Chetwode, Lt-Gen. Sir Philip
   233, 294
chlorine gas
   British use 97–8

at Caporetto 280–1
German use at Ypres 69, 74
Christmas truce (1914) 36, 38–40
Churchill, Winston, first lord of the
      Admiralty 18, 28
   and aircraft 78
   at Antwerp 22
   on Armistice Day 384
   and Dardanelles 45–6, 51–3, 62–3, 67
   and German fleet 115
   on Macedonia 108
   moved from Admiralty 117
   and naval power 159
   optimism 35–6
   orders Grand Fleet to Scapa Flow 10
   and submarine warfare 143
   and tanks project 123, 129, 286
   and Treaty of Versailles 387
   on war strategy 43–4, 214–15, 241
Clark, Christopher 386
Clausewitz, Carl von, On War 223
Clayton, Capt. Harold, VC 66
Clemenceau, Georges 106, 230, 298, 333
   at Versailles 387
Collingwood, HMS 163–4
Comet, gunboat 112
Committee of Imperial Defence, 'Red
      Book' 10
communications
   aircraft 79
   telegraph cable 238
Condé Canal 13
Congreve, Brig.-Gen. Walter 39, 40
Congreve, Capt. Billy, VC 34
Connolly, James, ICA 156
Connolly, 'Captain' Sean 152
conscription (in Britain)
   calls for 59
   introduction 120
Constantine, King of the Hellenes 104
Constantinople 45–6, 51, 371
convoy system, shipping 145, 229,
   250–1, 335
Cookson, Lt-Cdr Edgar, VC 112
Coolidge, John, US diplomat 49

Cornell Daily Sun newspaper 205
Cornwell, Boy 1st Class Jack, VC 162
Coronel, Battle of 25, **26**, 27–31
Cowan, Col. Henry 153, 154
Cowdray, Lord 276
Cradock, RAdm. Sir Christopher 25, 27–8
Crewe, Lord, viceroy of India 110
Ctesiphon 112
Currie, Lt-Gen. Sir Arthur 357
Curzon, Lord, Air Board 274–5
Czecho-Slovaks 342

Daffodil, ferry 336–7
Daily Mail 276
Daily Telegraph 297
Dalton, Hugh 266
d'Annunzio, Gabriele 187
Dardanelles 45–6, **60–1**, 116
  see also Gallipoli
Dawson, Geoffrey, editor of
  The Times 297
de Gaulle, Capt. Charles 135
de Havilland, Geoffrey 78
de Valera, Eamon 155
Dease, Lt Maurice, VC 13, 149
Defence, HMS 163
Degoutte, Gen. Jean 351
Dennys, Capt. Cyril 265, 304–5
Derby, Earl of, secretary for war 306
Derfflinger, German battleship
  162, 164
Deville, Gen. St Claire 57
di Lucca, Pte 363–4
di Robilant, Gen. Mario 282
Diaz, Gen. Armando 282, 344–5
  and Battle of Vittorio Veneto 372
Dobell, Maj.-Gen. Charles 85–6
Dogger Bank, Battle of 49
Dorrell, Sgt-Maj. George, VC 16
'Dover Barrage' 229, 333–4
Dreadnought, HMS 159
Dresden, German cruiser 30
Dublin, in Easter Rising 152–6
Duchêne, Gen. Denis 349, 350–1

Duke of Edinburgh, HMS 163
Dunn, Capt. James, *The War the
  Infantry Knew* 188–9

East Africa 24
  see also German East Africa
East Prussia 14
Easter Rising, Dublin 147–56, **148**
  reprisals 156
Eastern Front 34, 48, **124**, 186
  resumption of action 340–7
Ebert, Friedrich, as chancellor
  379, 380
Edmonds, Sir James 119
Edward, Prince of Wales 196
Edwards, Rifleman Frank 98
Egypt 167
  Arab Bureau 170, 173
Egyptian army 52
Egyptian Expeditionary Force 172,
  231, 232
El Qurnah, Iraq 110, 111
El-Arish 172, 220, 231
Elles, Brig.-Gen. Hugh 123, 128, 130,
  285, 290
Ellison, Pte George 382, 383
Elstob, Lt-Col. Wilfrith, VC 321–2
Elveden Hall, Suffolk 194–6
Ely, Col. Hanson E. 338
Emden, German cruiser 24, 27, 30
Empress Catherine the Great, Russian
  destroyer 347
Enver Pasha, Turkish war minister 64,
  112, 371
Erzberger, Matthias 379, 380, 381
Evans, Pte Ellis Humphrey 265

Falkenhayn, Gen. Erich von 19, 137
  and chlorine gas, use of 69
  dismissal 183, 190–1
  Eastern Front 126
  on Gallipoli 94
  at Loos 96
  in Palestine 293
  and Romania 191

and Serbia 104
and Verdun 132, 135, 136, 138
Falkland Islands 29
Farnborough, HMS 139, 141, 146
Fayolle, Gen. Émile 296
Feisal bin Hussein (later King of Iraq) 173–4
Feldkirchner, Oberleutant zur See Johannes 141
Field Service Regulations (British army) 260, 286, 355
Fifi, HMS 87
Finland 340
Fisher, Adm. of the Fleet Lord (Jacky) 28
  and Dardanelles campaign 51, 116
  Jutland 163
  and submarines 141
Flanders
  drainage system 259, 264
  German advances in (1918) 325–30
Fleischer, Heinrich 314
Flers-Courcelette, Battle of 194, 198–9
Foch, Gen. Ferdinand 23, 71
  and armistice 379
  and artillery for Isonzo 267
  and counter-attack at Amiens 356–7
  and Diaz 345
  final offensive 365, 369–70
  and Haig 262
  offensive near Arras 95, 96
  and offensive strategy 354
  and Operation Georgette 330
  and Pershing 333
  as supreme commander (*généralissime*) 327–8
  and Treaty of Versailles 387
Foster & Co. Ltd, Lincoln 129, 193, 287
France
  and colonies 86, 224
  government and war in 1916 215
  and papal peace note 271
Franchet d'Espèrey, Gen. 370–1
Freiburg 275
French, Gen. Sir John 12–13, 15
  and air reconnaissance 77–8, 79

and allied offensive 54, 55
and ammunition shortages 56, 71–2
dismissal 74
on gas, use of 70–1
and Joffre 17–18, 22, 37–8, 45
at Loos 96, 98–9
at Neuve Chapelle 55
resignation 118–19, 120
at Ypres 23, 32
French army
  1st Army 356–7
  2nd Army 21–2, 134
  5th Army 12, 16
  6th Army 21, 349
  II Colonial Corps 363
  15th Colonial Division 363
  colonial troops 46, 64, 85
  Corps Expéditionnaire d'Orient 64
  counter-attacks (1918) 352–3
  morale problems 248–9, 261, 313
  mutinies 137, 246
  and offensive strategy 43–4
  in retreat 15
French Equatorial Africa 86
Freyberg, Gen. Bernard, VC 210
Friedensturm (July 1918 peace offensive) 350–2, 356
Friend, Maj.-Gen. Sir Lovick 152
Fuller, Lt-Col. J. F. C. 'Boney' 285, 290
Fussell, Paul 323

Gallieni, Gen. Joseph 17, 18, 215
Gallipoli campaign 59, **60–1**, 62–7
  end of 116
  Suvla Bay 89–94
Gallipoli peninsula 51–2, 59, 64–5
  Anzac Cove 65, 92
  Cape Helles 64, 65, 91, 94
gas
  at the Lys 329
  see also chlorine gas
Gaza, second Battle of 232–3, 293
George V, King 38, 118
George VI, King 301
  as Sub-Lt Prince Albert 163–4

German army 203
  1st Army 12–13, 14
  2nd Army 12
  6th Army 329, 330
  7th Army 294, 352
  8th Army 14, 294
  9th Army 352
  advance to south-east 17
  advances in Flanders 325–6
  Alpenkorps 269, 280
  Baltic Division 340
  cavalry horses 225
  and Eastern Front 48, 125–6, 186
  and *Kaiserschlacht* **315**, 316–22
  lack of materiel 327, 330
  Operation Fist Punch (against Russia)
    308–9
  retreat from Amiens 360–1
  retreat from Marne 356
  Schutztruppe (Africa) 84, 88
  strategic withdrawal (Operation
    Alberich) 234–8
  Sturmtruppen 316–17, 327
  transfer of troops to Western Front
    303–4
  transport 317–18
  at Verdun 186
  view of tanks 198, 316–17
German East Africa 47, 86–8
German Navy 347
  auxiliary vessels 115
  High Seas Fleet (*Hochseeflotte*) 31, 35,
    48–9, 144
  losses 30
  mutiny 335, 371, 374
  raids on Scarborough and ports 35
  relative strength 160–1, 165–6
  see also submarine warfare
German South-West Africa (Namibia)
  24, 82, 84–5
Germany
  African colonies 47, 82
  airships 76–7
  armistice with Russia 308
  and 'dreadnought race' 142–3, 159

and Eastern Front 34
  economic blockade 161, 190, 203,
    218, 223–6, 314
  and guilt for war 385–7
  and Irish revolt 149, 151
  and Mexico 201, 205–6
  and papal peace note 271
  resignation of government,
    1918 371
  unrest 190, 373, 378
Gilbert, Maj. Vivian 294–5
Glasgow, HMS 27, 28, 29
Gneisenau, German cruiser 27, 29, 30
Godley, Lt-Gen. Alexander 254
Godley, Pte Sidney, VC 13
Goeben, German battle-cruiser 24
Goltz, Baron Colmar von der, Turkish
  army 112–13, 233
Good Hope, HMS 27, 28
Gorizia 137, 187, 268, 279
Gorringe, Maj.-Gen. George 111
Gough, Gen. Sir Hubert
  178, 208
  and German 1918 offensive 320,
    321–4
  and 'Passchendaele' 263
  Thiepval 209
Gramsci, Antonio 279
Graves, Robert 189
  Goodbye to All That 188
Great Britain
  declaration of war 7
  and papacy 270
  'war council' 44–5
  see also British army
Great Yarmouth, Zeppelin raid 77
Greece 45, 104
  declaration of war 190
  defeat of Bulgarians 341, 360
Grey, Sir Edward, foreign secretary 11,
  190
Groener, Lt-Gen. Wilhelm 378–9
Grunshi, Pte Alhaji 85
guerrilla warfare 86–7
Gumbinnen, Battle of 14

Haber, Franz, and chlorine gas 69
Haeckel, Ernst, on spread of war 46
Hague Conventions
  on poison gas 69
  on submarine warfare 49
Hahn, Otto 280
Haig, Gen. Sir Douglas 13
  on Americans 339
  attack on Hindenburg Line 365
  as C-in-C 123, 125
  and Cambrai 285, 286–9
  Charteris and 208–9
  and Sir John French 118, 120
  and gas, use of 97–8
  and German 1918 offensive 320
  and Indian Corps 96
  on Lloyd George 209, 215, 241,
    242–3
  at Neuve Chapelle 55, 56–8
  and Nivelle 243–4, 260–1
  'Northern Offensive' 261, 262–3
  and offensive at Amiens 356
  over-optimism 262
  and Pershing 297–8, 305–6, 312–13
  and plans for Somme 135–6, 175,
    177–8, 186
  plans for Western Front 128, 219–20,
    252
  and Plumer 253
  and RAF 273, 277
  and Somme 182, 196, 211–12
  'Special Order of the Day' (April
    1918) 329–30
  and tanks 286–7
  on withdrawal 236
Hall, CSM Frederick, VC 70
Hamilton, Gen. Sir Ian
  and Dardanelles campaign 51–2, 63,
    64–5
  dismissal 94
  and Suvla Bay 89–94
Hammerle, Oberleutnant zur See Max
  144
Hampshire, HMS 116
Hankey, Col. Maurice 44–5, 242

  and Dardanelles 62–3
Harington, Maj.-Gen. Charles 256
Harvey, Lt Frederick, VC 239
Hase, Georg von 162
Hasek, Jaroslav, *The Good Soldier
  Schweik* 342
Haskins, Minne 301
Hatfield Park, tank demonstration
  129–30, 193
Hejaz railway 169, 171
Helga, HMS, gunboat 154–5
Heligoland 262, 333
Helldorf, Count Wolff-Heinrich von 379
Helmi, Mulazzim Awaal Effendi 52
Hemingway, Ernest, *A Farewell to
  Arms* 187
Henderson, Brig.-Gen. David, RFC 79
Henriques, Lt Basil 198
Herbert, A. P. 210
Hindenburg, FM Paul von 14, 54, 137
  appointment 190–2
  and armistice 373, 378, 380
  and conscription 224
  and Isonzo (Caporetto) 280
  and Mexico 206
  and resignation of Ludendorff 373–4
  and strategic withdrawal 235
  and submarine warfare 203, 212, 227
  war strategy 223
Hindenburg Line 235–6, 240, 288, 361
  allied attack on 365
  breached 367–8
Hipper, Adm. Franz von 35, 160, 374
  Jutland 161–3
Hoffmann, Gen. Max 308
Holbrook, Lt Norman, RN 46
Holtzendorff, Adm. Henning von 226,
  227, 228–9, 251
Hood, RAdm. Horace 162,
  163, 164
Hoppe, Kapitänleutnant Bruno 146
Horne, Maj.-Gen. Henry 98, 361
horses
  fodder for 239, 288
  Germany 225, 317–18

INDEX

Horthy, RAdm. Miklós 346–7
Hossack, Pte Anthony 69
Hötzendorf, Gen. Franz Conrad von 126
Housatonic, US grain ship 228
House, 'Colonel' Edward 219
Hudson, Lt-Col. Charles 344
'Hundred Days' (Aug.–Nov. 1918) 361
Hunter-Weston, Maj.-Gen. Aylmer 66
Hurcomb, Sgt Frederick 295
Hussein ibn Ali al-Hashimi, Grand
    Sharif of Mecca 170–1, 172, 174, 296
hydrophones 229

Ikaria, SS 49
Indefatigable, HMS 162
Indian Army 52
    Indian Cavalry Corps 22
    Indian Corps 22, 55, 96
    Lahore Division 71
    in Mesopotamia 31, 110, 111, 112–13
    Muslims in 110, 231
Inflexible, HMS 29, 30
Ingelnohl, Adm. Friedrich von
    35, 49
intelligence
    allied 318
    naval 48–9, 161, 165
    RFC 16–17
Invincible, HMS 29, 30, 164
Ireland, Easter Rising 147–56, **148**
Iris II, ferry 336, 337
Irish Citizen Army (ICA) 150
Irish Home Rule Bill (1912) 149
Irish Republican Brotherhood 150
Irish Volunteers 150, 151, 155
Isonzo river, Italian campaign 74–5,
    186–7, 250
    Tenth Battle of 250, 267
    Eleventh Battle of 267–8
    Twelfth Battle of (Caporetto) 269–70,
        271, 278–84
Italian army 261, 303
    2nd Army 268, 281–2, 283
    3rd Army 268, 282
    8th Division 352

Alpini 74–5
    at Asiago 344–5
    Battle of Vittorio Veneto 372
Bersaglieri 75, 344–5
    at Caporetto 279–84
    loss of morale 282–3
Italian Navy (*Regia Marina*) 345–7
Italy 45, 117
    and allied plans for Somme 177
    declaration of war on Austria-
        Hungary 74, 102, 104
    and papal peace note 271
    and surrender of Austria-Hungary
        375, 377
    war with Germany 190
Ivanov, Gen. Nikolai 19
Iveagh, Earl of 194–5

Jaffa 294
James, Lt B. T. 79
Japan, war with Germany 24
Jarvis, LCpl Charles, VC 13
Jeddah 171
Jellicoe, Adm. Sir John 10, 48–9, 159
    and convoys 145, 229, 250–1
    dismissal 336
    and Haig's 'Northern Offensive'
        262–3
    Jutland 162–3, 165
    and RAF 277
Jerusalem 220, 233
    surrender 293, 294–6
Jews, in German army 308
Jillings, Sgt-Maj. David 78–9
Joffre, Gen. Joseph, French C-in-C 12,
    16, 21–2
    and allied offensives 54–5, 72, 95–6,
        117
    Briand and 260
    and Sir John French 17–18, 22, 37–8,
        45
    as marshal of France 215
    optimism 34
    plans for Somme 135
    and strategy of offensives 260

INDEX

and Verdun 133–4, 183
view of Russia 125–6
at Ypres 34
Joynson-Hicks, William, MP 276
Jutland, Battle of 31, 115, 157–66, **158**

Kaiserschlacht (1918 offensive) **315**,
  316–22, 348–54, 356
  advances 325–6
  Operation Blücher–Yorck 338,
    349–50
  Operation Georgette 328–9, 330, 349
  Operation Gneisenau 342–3, 350
  Operation Michael 321, 328
  preparatory bombardment 321
Kamerun (Cameroon), German colony
  85–6
Karlsruhe, German cruiser 24, 30
Kavanagh, Lt-Gen. Charles 358, 359
Kemal Bey, Mustafa ('Atatürk') 65, 93
Kent, HMS 29, 30
Keyes, VAdm. Roger 336
Khan, Sepoy Khudadad, VC 23
Kiggell, Maj.-Gen. Launcelot 119
King Edward VII, HMS 115
King's Lynn, Zeppelin raid 77
Kipling, 2nd Lt John ('Jack') 95, 100–1
Kipling, Rudyard 95, 100–1, 114
Kitchener, FM Lord 34
  and ammunition shortages 57, 71–2
  and artillery 45
  and Dardanelles campaign 51, 67
  death 116, 214
  and Egypt 171
  and Sir John French 16–17, 45, 71–2
  on gas, use of 70–1
  and Haig 119
  and Mesopotamia 113
  and recruitment 44, 64
  as secretary of state for war 10
  and tanks 129–30
Kluck, Gen. Alexander von, German
  1st Army 12–13, 14
Königsberg, German cruiser 30, 87
Kosturino Pass, Battle of 106

Kressenstein, Col. Friedrich Kress von
  52, 232
Kriemhild Line 369–70
Kuhl, Generalleutnant Hermann 353
Kühlmann, Richard von 308
Kut al-Amara 111, 112–14, 173
  recaptured 232
  surrender at 113, 231
Kuwait, Sheikh of 169

Lake Naroch, Lithuania 186
Lansdowne, Marquess of, foreign
  secretary 207, 213, 219, 297
Lansing, Robert 50, 206
Lanzerac, Gen. Charles, French 5th
  Army 12, 13, 16
Latvia 308
Lawrence, T. E. 170, 171, 172
  and Feisal 173–4
Le Cateau 14
League of Nations 303
Ledwidge, LCpl Francis 265
Lee, CSM George 211
Leefe-Robinson, Lt William, VC 274
Leipzig, German cruiser 27, 30
Lenin, Vladimir Ilyich 250, 309
Lettow-Vorbeck, Col. Paul von 47,
  86–8, 381
Lewis, Lt D. S. 79
Lewis, Pte 'Stokey', VC 107
Libau, German freighter 151
Liddell Hart, Sir Basil 353
  on First Ypres 33
  on Gallipoli 94
  on Loos 99
Liebknecht, Karl 379
Liège, bombardment 12
Lithuania, Russian attack in 186
Lloyd George, David 67, 73
  as chancellor of the exchequer 44,
    109
  and convoys 145, 229
  and French army 248–9
  and Haig 209, 215, 241, 242–3
  as minister of munitions 57, 73–4, 123

Lloyd George (*cont.*)
  and Nivelle 242, 260–1
  and Palestine 230–1
  as prime minister 214
  and RAF 276–7
  and recruitment of 'New Armies'
    89–90
  relations with military leadership 306
  as secretary for war 182
  and strategic bombing 275
  at supreme war council at
    Abbeville 333
  and tanks 193
  and war cabinet 261–3
  war strategy 213, 216, 219–20
Loderer, collier 139
London
  blackout 274
  daylight raids 275–6
  Zeppelin raids on 77, 80, 273
Loos, Battle of 95–101
Lorraine, American army concentration in 305
Louis of Battenberg, Prince 28
Lowe, Brig.-Gen. William 153, 154, 155
Ludendorff, Gen. Erich 14, 108, 190
  and Bulgarian surrender 371, 373
  and Flanders attack (1918) 325–6
  Friedensturm (peace offensive)
    350–2, 356
  German Navy, view of 337
  and *Kaiserschlacht* (1918 offensive)
    304, **315**, 316–22, 348–54, 356
  in Macedonia 102
  Operation Blücher–Yorck 338, 349–50
  Operation Georgette 328–9, 330, 349
  Operation Gneisenau 342–3, 350
  Operation Michael 321, 328
  resignation 373–4
  and retreat from Amiens 360
  and strategic withdrawal 235, 237–8
  on trench warfare 285–6
  and war strategy 223–4, 225–6
  and Western Front (1918) 309, 314,
    316–19

  withdrawal from St-Mihiel salient
    363, 370
Lukin, Maj.-Gen. Henry 84
Lusitania, SS, sinking of 50, 143
Lyautey, Gen. Hubert 215
Lys, river 329, 331

MacArthur, Col. Douglas 311
McCudden, Maj. James, VC 351
Macdonogh, Brig.-Gen. George 119
Macedonia 102, 104, 216, 250, 316, 341
  defeat of Bulgaria 370
Mackenzie, Compton 91–2
MacMillan, Margaret 386
Madras 24
'Maginot Line' 136
Mahon, Maj.-Gen. Bryan 105
Mangin, Lt-Gen. Charles 217
Mannerheim, Gen. Carl Gustav 340
Mannock, Maj. 'Mick', VC 351
Manoury, Gen. Michel-Joseph 17
mapping, from aerial photographs 80
Maravic, Ritter Ernst von 360
March, Gen. Peyton C. 331, 335
Maritz, Lt-Col. Manie 84
Marix, AVM Reginald 79
Marne, river 17
  Anglo-French counter-attack 18, 21
Marne, Second Battle of the 352, 353,
  356
Marshall, Col. George C. 364, 366
Marshall, Lt-Gen. Sir William 371
Masefield, John 59, 62, 67
  on the Somme 175, 180
Masurian Lakes, Battle of the 14, 19, 52
Maubeuge, BEF at 12
Maude, Lt-Gen. Sir Frederick 94, 173,
  231–2, 233
Maximilian of Baden, Prince 373
  as chancellor 371, 378
  as regent 379
Maxwell, Lt-Gen. Sir John 155–6
Mediterranean Expeditionary Force
  (MEF), at Gallipoli 52, 63
Mediterranean Force (MF) 171, 172

INDEX

Meeke, Pte John 257–8
Megiddo, Battle of 371
Melun, BEF headquarters 17–18
merchant shipping
 convoy system 145, 229, 250–1, 335
 German submarine warfare against
  30–1, 49, 141, 143
 losses 144
Merville 330
Mesopotamia 31, 109–14
 and oil 231
Mesopotamian Expeditionary Force
 231–3
Messines 38, 329
Messines–Wytschaete Ridge, mining of
 249, 253–7
 German counter-attack 257
Mesudiye, frigate 46
Metropolitan Amalgamated Railway
 Carriage and Wagon Co., Birming-
 ham 193
Metz, allied advance towards 369
Meuse–Argonne 365, 369
Meux, Adm. Sir Hedworth 143
Mexico
 border operations 251
 Germany and 201, 205–6, 228
Micheler, Gen. Joseph 243, 246
Military Service Bill (1915) 120
Milne, Gen. Sir George 371
Mimi, HMS 87
mines, naval 18, 115, 334
 Mark 6 'antenna' 334–5
Minsk, German occupation 309
Moltke, Count Detlef von 377–8
Moltke, Col.-Gen. Helmuth Johann
 von ('younger Moltke') 18–19
Moltke, FM Helmuth, Graf von ('elder
 Moltke') 169
Moltke, German battle-cruiser 347
Monash, Gen. Sir John 65–6, 128
 Amiens 356–7
 on Western Front 252–3
Monastir, Serbia 203, 216
Monmouth, HMS 27, 28

Monro, Gen. Sir Charles 117
Mons, Battle of 13
 retreat from 13–14
Montagu, Edwin, minister of muni-
 tions 196–7
Montenegro 104
Montgomery of Alamein, FM Viscount
 on Brusilov 186
 on Falkenhayn 191
Montreuil-sur-Mer 361
Moreuil Wood 328
Morton, Maj. Sir Desmond 208–9
Mosul, oilfields 109, 231, 371
Motor Cycle Magazine 194
Möwe, German auxiliary cruiser 115
Mozambique 87
Murray, Lt-Gen. Sir Archibald 171–2,
 231, 232–3, 293
Mussolini, Benito 186–7

Nantucket lightship 204
Narva, Estonia 309, 340
National Security League (US) 202
Nelson, Sgt David, VC 16
Néry, BEF action at 16
Neuve Chapelle, battle of 34,
 54–8, 68
New Zealand 24
 see also 'Anzac' Corps
Newman, Pte Bert 70
newspapers 276, 297
 on shell shock 189
 see also The Times
Nicholas, Grand Duke of Russia 127
Nicholas II, Tsar of Russia 63, 127
 abdication 240
Nieuport, Belgium 23
Nigeria 86
Nivelle, Gen. Robert 220
 and Aisne offensive 218, 241–6
 on German withdrawal 236, 237
 and Verdun 134–5, 136, 137, 217
Nixon, Lt-Gen. Sir John 111–12, 231
Nolan, Brig.-Gen. Dennis 306
North Sea, mines 18

Northcliffe, Alfred Harmsworth, Viscount 131, 318
Northern Rhodesia (Zambia) 87
Nürnberg, German cruiser 28, 30
Nyasaland (Malawi) 87

Oberndorff, Count Alfred von 381
O'Brien, Constable James 152
oilfields 231
  Basra 31, 109–10
  Mosul 109, 371
O'Neill, Capt. Arthur 31
Operation Alberich 234–40
  scorched earth 237–9
Operation Blücher–Yorck 338, 349–50
Operation Fist Punch (against Russia) 308–9
Operation Georgette 328–9, 330, 349
Operation Gneisenau 342–3, 350
Operation Michael 321, 328
Oriole, SS 49
Orlando, Vittorio Emanuele, Italian prime minister 333
Ostend 261
  U-boat base 128, 144, 229, 249, 333
Otranto, HMS 27, 28
Otranto Barrage 346
Ottoman Empire
  and Arabs 170
  and Dardanelles 52–3
  and Egypt 167
  entry into war 24, 62
  and Indian Muslims 110, 231
  and Palestine 231–3
  surrender 371
  see also Turkish army
Ounsworth, Leonard 304
Owen, Lt Wilfred, MC 377, 383

Pacific Ocean, warfare in 24
Painlevé, Paul, French war minister 243, 244
Palestine 53, 171–2, **292**
  and 'national home' for the Jewish people 296

Paris, bombing of 327
Paris peace conference (1919) 385, 387
Parsons, Edward, US pilot 137
'Passchendaele' (Third Battle of Ypres) 74, 259–65
  preparatory bombardment 259
  tanks at 287
Passchendaele Ridge 329
Patton, Col. George S. 312, 363
peace negotiations
  Lansdowne's memorandum 297
  papal proposals 269–71, 303
  proposals for 202–3
  US and 218–19
  Woodrow Wilson's Fourteen Points for 301–3
  see also Armistice
Pearse, Patrick, and Gaelic League 150–1, 152, 156
Pershing, Gen. John J. 'Black Jack' 205–6, 251
  advance towards Sedan 364–6
  on AEF 338–9
  Field Order No. 9 363
  and Haig 298, 305–6
  on integration of AEF 312–13, 332
  and Patton 312
  and St-Mihiel salient 362–3
  on US Marines 350
  at Western Front 305–6
Pétain, Gen. Philippe 72, 96, 137, 247, 296
  and army morale 248–9
  and counter-attacks of 1918, 327, 328
  and German 1918 offensive 351
  and Verdun 132, 134–5, 136
Peter, King of Serbia 216
Piave, river 282
  Austrian offensive 342–5
Picot, François-Georges 170
Pless Castle, German GHQ conference 226–8
Ploegsteert 38

Plumer, Lt-Gen. Sir Herbert 71, 74, 249
  mining of Messines 253–7, 261
  and 'Passchendaele' 263
Plunkett, 'Captain' George 152
Pohlmann, Hartwig 321
Poland 19, 125
  Galicia 31, 137, 186
Port Stanley 29
Portuguese Corps 328
Portuguese Expeditionary Force 235
Pozières, battle for 208
Price, Pte George 383
Princess Mary Fund 38
Prinz Eugen, Austrian dreadnought 346
Prittwitz, Gen. Friedrich von 14
Putnik, Gen. Radomir, Serbian army
  20, 104, 106

Quast, Gen. Ferdinand von 329, 330
Queen Mary, HMS 162

'Race for the Sea' 19, 21, 23
Rafa, Egypt 172, 231
railways 11–12
  Germany 318, 378
  Ottoman Empire 169–71
Rapallo, allied emergency meeting 303
Rasputin, Grigori, murder of 216
rations
  Italian army 266–7
  military 225
Rawlinson, Lt-Gen. Sir Henry 90,
  177–8, 197, 198
  5th Army 324
  as deputy CIGS 310
  and offensive at Amiens 356–7, 358,
  361
  at Somme 208
Read, Sir Herbert 323
Redmond, John, and Irish Volunteers
  150
Redmond, Maj. Willie, MP 257–8
Rees, Hubert Conway 181
Reinke, Lt Miles 289
Reisbach, Baron von 228

Rennenkampf, Gen. Paul von, Russian
  1st Army 14
Repington, Col. Charles à Court, *Times*
  war correspondent 12, 248
  on air reconnaissance 78
  on ammunition shortage 73
  on French 118
  on Pétain 247
  resignation 318
  on spread of war 46
Richards, Frank, *Old Soldiers
  Never Die* 40
Richthofen, Manfred von 249
Ridley, Pte Arnold 197
River Plate, Battle of (1939) 30
Rizzo, Lt-Cdr Luigi 346
Robertson, Lt-Gen. Sir William 'Wully'
  171, 190, 242
  and AEF 306
  as CIGS 119, 219–20
  on Sir John French 120
  and Haig 262
  and RAF 277
  resignation 310
  and tanks 197
  and U-boat bases 249
  and war of attrition 230
Robinson, Lt Eric 51–2
Robinson, Harry Perry, *Times* war
  correspondent 318–19
Rogerson, Capt. Sidney 349–50
Röhl, John 386
Roman Catholic church
  distrust of 36–7
  see also Benedict XV
Romania 203
  capitulation 293, 341
  war with Austria-Hungary 137, 190
Rome, inter-allied conference (1917)
  242
Rommel, Lt Erwin 281
Roosevelt, Eleanor 387
Roosevelt, Franklin D., US president
  387
Roosevelt, Kermit 114

Roosevelt, Quentin 351
Roosevelt, Theodore, US president 114, 201–2
  and U-boats 205
Rose, Hans 204, 228
Rosenberg, Isaac 245, 323
Rothschild, Leopold de 118, 296
Royal Air Force (RAF) 81, 272–7
  at Amiens 358, 359
  losses 351, 372
Royal Aircraft Factory, Farnborough 78
Royal Flying Corps (RFC) 11, 16
  aerial combat 249–50
  aerial photography 56, 236
  bombing 264–5
  formation (1912) 78
  at Messines 255
  and Zeppelin raids 77
  see also Royal Air Force
Royal Naval Air Service 78, 273
Royal Navy 10, 45
  blockade of German Fleet 31, 35–6, 159, 382
  and control of the sea 157, 159
  conversion from coal to oil 109–10
  and convoy system 145, 229
  and Jutland 165–6
  Q-ships 143–4, 145–6
  reservists 22
  submarines 116, 141–2, 337
Ruhr, miners' strike 190
Rupprecht, Crown Prince of Bavaria 237, 329, 353
Russia 14
  and allied plans for Somme 177
  armistice with Germany 308
  call for attack on Constantinople 45–6
  civil war 291, 302
  and Eastern Front 125–7
  effect of Gallipoli campaign 94, 128
  offensive in Silesia 31
  and Ottoman Empire 169
  and papal peace note 271
  unrest 127–8, 216
  war in the Caucasus 24

Russian army 63, 224
  advance into East Prussia 14
  defeats 14, 19
  Eastern Front 125–7
  effect of revolution on 240, 250, 261
  in Lithuania 186
  in Poland 52, 137
  retreat (1917) 263
  and Western Front 128
Russian Revolution (1917) 226, 240
Rutherford, Sir Ernest 229

Šabac, Battle of 20
Salisbury, Marquess of 129, 193
Salonika 105–8, 216
Samsonov, Gen. Aleksandr, Russian 2nd Army 14
Sanders, Lt-Gen. Otto Liman von 64, 93
Sandes, Flora, in Serbian army 216–17
Sandford, Lt Richard, RN, VC 337
Sarajevo 46
Sargent, John Singer 86
Sarrail, Gen. Maurice 105, 106
Sassoon, Siegfried 182
  Memoirs of an Infantry Officer 179
Scapa Flow 10, 35, 159
  German minefield near 115
Scarborough, German navy raid 35, 48
Scharnhorst, German cruiser 27, 28, 29, 30
Scheer, Adm. Reinhard 160–1, 335
  Jutland 162–3, 165
  and U-boats 191, 203, 212
Schlieffen, Gen. Alfred von 7
Schlieffen Plan 7, 8–9, 10, 14, 15
Schmoller, Gustav von 226
Schneider, Kapitänleutnant Rudolf 49
Schulenburg, Maj.-Gen. Friedrich von der 378
Schweiger, Kapitänleutnant Walther 49, 50
Secret Service Bureau (later MI6) 165, 318
Sedan 365
Sedgewick, Sgt James 295
Seely, Brig.-Gen. J. E. B. 'Jack' 78, 239

INDEX

Senussi Arabs 167, 172
Serbia 203, 216, 341, 371
  Austria-Hungary and 20, 102
Sering, Max 226
Seydlitz, German battleship 162
Shatt al-Arab waterway 31, 110, 169
Shea, Maj.-Gen. John 295–6
shell shock 189
Sherriff, R. C., *Journey's End* 319
Shetland–Norway gap, anti-submarine
  mines 334
Shtiurmer, Boris Vladimirovich,
  Russian prime minister 216
Siebert, Pioneer Willi 70
siege warfare, on Western Front 252–6
Siegfriedstellung (Siegfried Fortress) 212,
  235, 243
Simpson, Pte Jack, Gallipoli 65–6
Sinai 167, **168**, 172
Sinn Féin 150
Skene, Lt Robert, RFC 11
Skopje, Macedonia 370
Skra-di-Legen, Battle of 341
Smith, Brig.-Gen. Clement, VC 172
Smith-Dorrien, Gen. Sir Horace 13
  1st Army at Second Ypres 71
  2nd Army at Neuve Chapelle 55
  dismissal 71
  Le Cateau 14
  on morale 37
Smuts, Lt-Gen. Jan 47
  and RAF 272–3, 276–7
  South African defence minister 24,
  86
Somme
  plans for allied offensive 117–18
  retreat to (1918) 327
Somme, Battle of the 175, 177–82,
  212–13
  Ancre attack 210
  attrition 207–13
  Beaumont Hamel 210–11
  casualties 182, 187–8, 207, 212
  Delville Wood 188, 197
  effect of Verdun on 177

end of offensive 210–11, 215
  first day **176**
  High Wood 188–9
  preparatory bombardment 179–80
  Schwaben Redoubt 209
Sorley, Capt. Charles 100
Souchon, Adm. Wilhelm 24
South Africa 24
  and campaign against German
    South-West Africa 82, 84–5
Southey, Pte James 358–9
Spa, Belgium 375, 377, 379
Spee, Heinrich von 29
Spee, Lt Otto von 30
Spee, VAdm. Maximilian Graf von 25,
  27–8, 29–30
Spencer, Stanley 107, 108
  in Macedonia 102
Spindler, Kapitänleutnant Karl 151
St-Mihiel salient 305, 310, 356, 362–3
St-Quentin, Battle of 321–4
St-Quentin Canal 289, 367
Stalin, Joseph 309
Stanley, Venetia 22
Stark, Freya, at Caporetto 278, 279,
  283, 284
Stead, W.T. 50
Steggles, Pte Harry 107–8
Still, Lt John 93
Stoddart, RAdm. Archibald 29
Stopford, Lt-Gen. Sir Frederick 90, 91–3
Strau enburg, Arthur Freiherr Arz von
  280, 342–4, 345
Sturdee, VAdm. Sir Doveton 28–9
submarine warfare 30–1, 139–46, 166
  counter-measures 333–5
  'cruiser rules' 49–50, 141–2, 201,
    226, 228
  depth charges 141, 229
  mine-laying 115
  Royal Navy 116
  unrestricted: pressure for resumption
    191, 203–4, 212–13, 218; resumed
    (1917) 143, 144, 145, 226–9; Tirpitz
    and 49, 160

415

submarines, German (U-boats) 30–1,
    35, 48–50, **140**, 141
  in American waters 204–5
  attacks on merchantmen 49, 141,
    160, 226
  attacks on neutrals 49–50
  and decoy ships 139, 141, 143–4,
    145–6
  new 226
submarines, Royal Navy 116, 141–2,
    337, 347
Sueter, Capt. Murray 273
Suez Canal 46, 48, 52, 167, **168**
Sukhomlinov, Gen. Vladimir 126–7
Sulzbach, Herbert 351, 352–3
Sussex, channel steamer 203
Suvla Bay, Gallipoli 89–94
Swinton, Ernest 194, 196
Sydney, HMAS 30
Sykes, Sir Mark 170, 173
Sykes–Picot agreement 170, 174
Szent István, Austrian dreadnought
    346, 347

Tanganyika, Lake 87
tanks 123, 128–30
  at Amiens 358
  British 'Whippet' 352, 358
  at Cambrai 286–9
  conditions 195–6
  crews 194
  French 246, 352
  increased production 290
  introduction 193–9
  'Mark 1' 195
  Mark V 'Star' 358
  at Messines 255–6
  in Middle East 232
  at 'Passchendaele' 263–4
  recruitment for 194–5
  in St-Mihiel salient 363
Tannenberg, Battle of 14, 19
Tanzania (Tanganyika) 47, 86–7
Taranaki, trawler 145
Tegetthoff, Austrian dreadnought 346–7

Thiepval 208
Thomas, Edward 244
The Times 310
  on RAF 274–5
Tirpitz, Grand Admiral Alfred von 49,
    50
  resignation 160
  and submarine warfare 142–3,
    159–60
Tisza, Count István, Hungarian prime
    minister 126
Tobin, Sgt-Maj. Robin 326
Togoland, German colony 85
Tokomaru, SS 49
Tomlinson, H. M., *All Our Yesterdays* 46,
    47
Toutou, HMS 87
Townshend, Maj.-Gen. Charles 111–14,
    173
transatlantic undersea cables 10, 200
trench warfare 38, 239, 304
  German trenches in Artois 57
  Somme 188
Trenchard, Maj.-Gen. Sir Hugh
  and RAF 272, 277
  and strategic bombing 372–3
Trevelyan, George Macaulay 283–4,
    344–5
Trieste 250, 278
Tritton, William 129
Trotsky, Leon 309
Troubridge, RAdm. Ernest 27
Truman, Capt. Harry S. 202, 382–3
Turkish army
  at Gallipoli 51–2, 63–4, 93
  in Mesopotamia 112–13
  in Palestine 293, 371
  reforms 167
Turkish Petroleum Company 109
Tuscania, SS, sinking of 311

U-boats *see* submarines, German
Ukraine
  German occupation 308–9
  peace treaty with Germany 307–8

INDEX

Ulster Volunteer Force 150
United States
  call for peace negotiations 218–19
  Council of National Defense 202
  declaration of war 228
  entry into war 114, 301–2
  and German U-boats 49–50, 227
  and Ireland 203
  National Defense Act (1916) 202
  Naval Act (1916) 202
  Selective Service Act (1917) 251
  U-boat sinkings of merchant ships
    204–5
  see also American Expeditionary
    Force; Wilson, Woodrow
US Marine Corps 350
US Navy 335

Valéry, Paul 132
Vann, Lt-Col. Bernard, VC 368
Vanselow, Capt. Ernst 381–2
Vaughan Williams, Ralph, in Macedo-
  nia 102, 107–8
Venizelos, Eleutherios, Greek prime
  minister 104
Verdun, battle for 131–8, 183, 208
  effect on plans for Somme 177
  Fort Douaumont 134, 136, 217
  French counter-attacks 190, 217
Versailles, supreme war council 303–4,
  309–10
Versailles, Treaty of 385–6
  terms of 387–8
Victoria Cross Warrant, rule 13 337
Victoria Crosses
  Canadian 70
  Gallipoli 66
  Indian 23, 33–4, 58
  Mons 13
  naval 46
  Neuve Chapelle 58
  Zeebrugge 337
Villa, Francisco 'Pancho' 205–6
Vimy Ridge 56, 72
  Nivelle offensive 244

Vindictive, HMS 336–7
Viribus Unitis, Austrian dreadnought
  346–7
Vittorio Veneto, Battle of 372
von Donop, Maj.-Gen. Sir Stanley, and
  ammunition shortages 56, 57
Vyborg, Russia 340

Waffenbund treaty 342
Waldkirch, Eduard von 381
war memorials 385
Warneford, Sub-Lt Rex 80
Warren, Sen. Francis E. 251
Warrender, VAdm. Sir George 35
Warrior, HMS 163
Watson, Brig.-Gen. Charles 295
Wavell, Brig.-Gen. Archibald 388
weather 18, 38–9
  and air warfare 79
  early 1918 304
  Macedonia 105
  'Passchendaele' 259, 264
  and use of gas 97–8
  Verdun 132–3
  winter (1917) 236
Wehler, Hans-Ulrich 386
Weissbach, Raimund 147
Wells, H. G. 385
  The War in the Air 76
Wemyss, Adm. Sir Rosslyn 336,
  381–2
West Africa 24
Western Front **376**
  air warfare 77–8
  deadlock on 43–5, 62, 128
  at end of 1917 291
  siege warfare on 252–3
  strategy of attrition 67, 120, 192,
    217–18, 260
  Ypres salient 69–70, 253, 261
  see also Arras–St-Quentin junction;
    Somme; Ypres
Westmann, Stefan 330
Wetzell, Lt-Col. Georg von 317–18, 326
Wheeler, Maj. George Massy, VC 111

INDEX

Wilhelm, Crown Prince 129, 136, 320–1, 352, 378
Wilhelm II, Kaiser 19, 38
    abdication 379
    and air campaign 76
    on Amiens 360
    appointment of Hindenburg 190–1
    call for peace 307, 308
    calls for abdication 377, 378
    Drang nach Osten strategy 169–70
    and 'dreadnought race' 142–3, 159
    and *Kaiserschlact* 316
    leaves for Spa 375, 377
    and Ludendorff 328
    orders to *Hochseeflotte* 35
    and submarine warfare 160, 203, 228
Wilhelmshaven, German fleet in 31, 35–6, 144, 159
Williams-Ellis, Clough 195
Williamson, Henry 234, 238
Wilson, Maj.-Gen. Alexander 53, 365
Wilson, Maj.-Gen. Henry 12, 21, 262
    as CIGS 310
    on ending of war 360–1
Wilson, Pipe-Maj. John 181
Wilson, Lt Walter, RN 129
Wilson, Woodrow, US president 49–50, 114
    call for peace negotiations 219, 223
    declaration of war 228
    'Fourteen Points' speech 270–1, 301–3, 360
    and German call for armistice 373

and German U-boats 228
    policy of neutrality 200–1
    re-election 206
Wimborne, Lord, lord lieutenant of Ireland 154
Windhoek, surrender of 85
Winnington-Ingram, Arthur, Bishop of London 276
Winterfeldt, Maj.-Gen. Detlef von 379–80, 381
Wittgenstein, Lt Ludwig 344
Wolff Telegraphic Bureau 379
Wright, Capt. Theodore, VC 13

Yanushkevich, Nikolai, chief of *Stavka* 126–7
York, Sgt Alvin 366
Ypres 22, 23
    First Battle of 31, 32–40
    Second Battle of 68–74
    Third Battle of ('Passchendaele') 74, 259–65
Ypres salient 69–70, 253, 261
Ypres–Comines Canal 256

Zeebrugge 226, 261
    U-boat base 128, 144, 229, 249, 333
Zeebrugge Raid 336–7
Zeppelins
    air defence against 274
    raids on London 76–7, 80, 273, 275
Zimmerman telegram 228